ALMOST AS AN AFTERTHOUGHT, EDWIN WILSON SUGGESTED ANOTHER MURDER, one that made even the tough-stomached "Little John" Randolph feel fleetingly ill. Wilson's former wife, Barbara, was suing him for her share of their property, and she wanted $7 million.

"I'm not going to give her seven million dollars," Wilson told Randolph. "I want her to go on a long, long trip."

The instructions described Mrs. Wilson: "54, 5-9, gray hair, thin, 120." Wilson added, "She cracked up when she was forty-eight. She shouldn't be any problem."

THEN, WILSON SAID OF HIS FORMER WIFE, "TAKE HER OFF SOMEWHERE AND BREAK HER NECK."

Randolph asked Wilson, "How can you justify Barbara's death to your sons?"

"That's just one of the things they're going to have to learn to face," Wilson replied. "It's to their good eventually."

With Barbara due to "disappear" forever, Wilson saw no reason for her diamond ring to go to waste. "It's my good-luck piece; I want it back," he told Randolph.

What would be the price for killing Barbara? "She's worth two hundred and fifty thousand," Wilson said.

THE DEATH MERCHANT

The Rise and Fall of Edwin P. Wilson

Joseph C. Goulden
&
Alexander W. Raffio

BANTAM BOOKS
TORONTO • NEW YORK • LONDON • SYDNEY • AUCKLAND

THE DEATH MERCHANT

*A Bantam Book / published by arrangement with
Simon & Schuster, Inc.*

PRINTING HISTORY
*Simon & Schuster edition published in 1984
Bantam edition / November 1985*

*Bantam Books are published by Bantam Books, Inc. Its trade-
mark, consisting of the words "Bantam Books" and the portrayal of a rooster, is Registered in U.S. Patent and Trademark
Office and in other countries. Marca Registrada. Bantam
Books, Inc., 666 Fifth Avenue, New York, New York 10103.*

PRINTED IN THE UNITED STATES OF AMERICA

H   0 9 8 7 6 5 4 3 2

Once again, for
Leslie Cantrell Smith,
wife and best friend

Contents

Part Three THE DEATH MERCHANT

Part Four THE QUARRY

Author's Note

Because this book mentions persons who were unwitting accomplices of a master criminal, and others with a covert role in American intelligence, I use pseudonyms in several instances. These persons include Brad Rockford, Charles X. Great, Charles Merton, Roger Homes, "Jungle Jim" or "JJ," Daphne and Charles Hills. Sources and methodology are in the Acknowledgments at the back of the book.

Preface

This book is the story of how a former American intelligence officer named Edwin Paul Wilson betrayed his country, friends, profession and, not least, his family. Wilson succeeded, mercifully briefly, by selling the clandestine skills he had learned as a twenty-one-year employee of the Central Intelligence Agency and, subsequently, a secret unit of the Office of Naval Intelligence.

Wilson's main client was Colonel Muamar Quaddafi of Libya, a sand-strip North African nation of 3 million persons. Quaddafi is rich (Libya sits on the world's fifth-largest pool of oil). He is also a Moslem fanatic whose avowed goal is to scourge the earth of "Western decadence" and create an "Islamic arc" stretching from Africa through the Middle East on into Asia. Quaddafi is the only chief of state publicly to proclaim assassination as an instrument of state policy; he has tried to overthrow, through murder or instigated revolution, more than twenty other governments in Africa and the Middle East. "A madman barking in his desert tent" is how he was described by the late President Anwar Sadat of Egypt, himself the target of several Quaddafi-supported murder teams.

Quaddafi's 40,000-man military boasts $16 billion worth of sophisticated Soviet equipment, but it is incapable of winning even a border war with such weak neighbors as Chad and the Sudan. And given his unpredictable fanaticism, Quaddafi is unable to effect lasting alliances with other Moslem states. (For a time his sole friend on the continent was Idi Amin of Uganda.) But in the arena in which Quaddafi plays, the Third World, a handgun or bomb in the hand of an assassin can be a more direct means of changing a government than diplomacy or the ballot box; a crate of rifles can be more valuable than an international loan. Hence Quaddafi's danger to the civilized world.

And hence Edwin P. Wilson's value to Quaddafi. Wilson supplied the hardware of terrorism Quaddafi spread around the world—the bombs, the handguns, the raw explosives—and at least one assassin. Fortunately, many of his plots and deals went awry; one of his collaborators joked that Wilson ran the proverbial "gang that couldn't shoot straight." Yet the success of this often charming, usually shrewd businessman was extraordinary.

Wilson operated behind two screens. His public pose was of honest merchant who peddled the Libyans such nonlethal items as military uniforms, foodstuffs, office supplies, oil-field equipment, even a powdered nonalcoholic wine for abstemious Moslems. On these "white" deals Wilson earned millions of dollars.

Wilson's second pose was as a covert American intelligence agent; he claimed that his sales of arms, his explosives shipments and other peculiar deals were part of an operation that would enable him to worm his way into the inner councils of the Libyan Government and steer Quaddafi back toward the West. Wilson used this story to deceive persons working for him who knew a bit about intelligence. The story had surface credibility. In his early months Wilson used as suppliers many companies and individuals who also did business with the CIA. Wilson gave the story further plausibility by continuing to fraternize, socially and professionally, with high CIA officials with whom he had served; two of these men, after retirement, became his business associates. Wilson skillfully created the illusion that he was "still in the business," and he was believed by many persons who should have known better.

That Wilson did fly the false flag of a deep-cover CIA agent caused much grief to an American intelligence community already under severe public attack for the supposed misdeeds of the past. Even after his arrest Wilson continued to proclaim his innocence because "I am working for American intelligence." One of his attorneys called him "the spy who was left out in the cold." Yet the evidence overwhelmingly disproves Wilson's claim. As Theodore Greenberg, one of the assistant U.S. attorneys for the prosecution, pointed out in his summation, Wilson was a "soldier of fortune . . . a merchant of death . . . who chose to suborn the national goals of the United States." That Wilson was caught, and imprisoned, "should be a message . . . that renegades like Edwin Wilson will not be permitted to erode the public's confidence in the intelligence community." Regrettably, much of Wilson's damage had been done by the time he was led away to prison.

In time, I think, Wilson came to believe his own lies, particularly about remaining with the CIA while in Libya. Wilson had been in "the business" so long that he considered any contact with his old organization as evidence that he was still "inside," as he longed to be. A retired CIA paramilitary officer told me a story about Wilson that he thought peculiar, and I did not understand it myself until many months later, after I had learned much more about Wilson. The paramilitary man needed to find a farm for an Asian general who had left his country in a hurry. By happenstance, he spoke with Edwin Wilson's wife, who sold real estate, and she showed him a farm. "The feedback I got later was that Wilson was talking about the farm in the context that he was helping the CIA run a resettlement program. That sort of stretched the truth beyond recognition." Which is what Wilson did much of his life.

Although I did not know of Wilson at the time, one insight into why he turned renegade was given me in the spring of 1978, when I was having lunch with an old friend who had spent twenty-five years with CIA as a covert agent. The intelligence community and its camp followers were still abuzz over the fact that Admiral Stansfield Turner, the Carter Administration's director of central intelligence, had cut the agency's covert Operations Directorate from 1,200 persons to fewer than 400 in the notorious "Halloween Massacre" of 1977. Many of the men suddenly thrust onto the street were in midlife; they had spent their adult careers either in the military or in intelligence. My friend had retired long before the massacre; his second career was well under way, for he had talents beyond spying. But I asked him: What happens when trained covert agents whose lives have been devoted to espionage, subversions, special weaponry and the like are cut adrift from their government—one they served with bravery and dignity—via a curt Xeroxed form letter? With the Vietnam War at an end, many former members of the Special Forces were in similar straits.

My friend obviously had thought about the same question. He swirled the ice around his glass for a minute or so, and then he looked at me with pained eyes. "Whatever they do," he said, "they are not going to be happy as a 'security officer' advising some grocery chain on how many strands of barbed wire it should put on the fence around its warehouses."

Edwin Wilson was an aberration of modern intelligence who turned against the society he had been trained—and trusted—to protect. He achieved great, if fleeting, financial success because he was willing, even eager, to betray and corrupt people who trusted him and thought him their friend. It was then also part of his makeup to blame others for his acts, and to seek revenge as the just due of his frustration. In this respect, one episode epitomizes the man. When finally captured and jailed, Wilson tried to hire hit men to kill his prosecutors and the witnesses against him—even his former wife, the mother of his two sons. When the woman had been killed, Wilson stressed, he wanted her corpse stripped of jewelry, for a ring she wore "is my good-luck piece; I want it back." Asked by a jailhouse crony what he would pay, Wilson responded, "She's worth two hundred and fifty thousand."

The Major Players

From the Intelligence Community:

EDWIN P. WILSON, contract employee of CIA and the Office of Naval Intelligence; after being fired, an international arms dealer and businessman.

THOMAS CLINES, CIA official who devoted much of his career to anti-Castro activities; friend of and borrower from Wilson.

RAFAEL "CHI CHI" QUINTERO, Bay of Pigs veteran; on-and-off CIA contract employee; soldier of fortune; Latin businessman; Wilson associate.

REAR ADMIRAL BOBBY RAY INMAN, intelligence careerist who directed naval intelligence (from which he fired Wilson) and held number two position in CIA.

FRANK TERPIL, low-level CIA technician fired for misconduct; arms merchant thereafter; short-time partner of Wilson.

KEVIN MULCAHY, one-time CIA analyst, electronics salesman, alcoholic; Wilson employee, briefly.

From the Wilson Organization:

DOUGLAS M. SCHLACHTER, JR., former service-station attendant become farm manager, then general factotum.

ALEX RAFFIO, electronics expert and man-about-the-Middle East.

ROBERTA J. BARNES, accountant, office manager and intimate of the boss.

PETER GOULDING, former army officer turned arms salesman.

REGINALD SLOCOMBE, devout Mormon, shipper and gun smuggler.

JOHN HEATH, military explosives expert who made bombs for Wilson and his Libyan clients.

BOB HITCHMAN, a pilot who would fly wherever the air would support his plane.

JOHN HENRY HARPER, a bomb man with shaky hands.

EUGENE TAFOYA, former Green Beret sergeant.

From the Arms and Electronics Worlds:

ARMAND "BIG CIGAR" DONNAY, French colonel who lost his toenails in Algiers and made an arms fortune in Belgium.

JOSEPH SANDS, who "can find anything electronic in the world."

JEROME S. BROWER, who sold Wilson explosives by the ton, for shipment to Libya.

From Libya:

SAYED QUADDAFADAM, cousin to Colonel Muamar Quaddafi and head of the Libyan purchasing mission in London; Wilson's first conduit to Libyan oil wealth.

ABDULLAH HIJAZZI, brooding, deep-eyed head of the Libyan intelligence, a man so suspicious that cynics said he did not even trust himself.

EZZEDINE MONSEUR, Libyan military purchasing official who gave Wilson more than $20 million in contracts.

"ZAK" ZACHARIAS, office factotum in Libya for Wilson; also a deep-cover agent for the Palestine Liberation Organization.

From the United States government:

RICHARD PEDERSON and RICK WADSWORTH, investigators from the Bureau of Alcohol, Tobacco and Firearms, who did the heavy digging on the Wilson case.

BILL HART, special agent of the FBI, who worked in conjunction with Pedersen and Wadsworth, often under circumstances that meant their respective superiors had to be kept in the dark.

E. LAWRENCE BARCELLA, a tenaciously dogged assistant U.S. attorney in Washington who became *de facto* overseer of the Wilson investigation and prosecution.

ERNEST KEISER, sometime contract employee of the CIA, who in his claimed role as public-spirited citizen talked Wilson out of sanctuary and into arrest.

From the Jail Cells:

WAYNE TRIMMER, DAVID RAY VOGEL, and JOHN RANDOLPH, multi-time losers who befriended Wilson, then betrayed him by revealing his death plots to authorities.

Part One

THE OPERATOR

1

Paying for the Calf

For many of us reared in the Depression years, the memory of hard times is not easily shaken; one grasps for security, and harbors dark-of-the-night fears of a return to penury.

The guidebooks describe the area around Nampa, Idaho, where Edwin Wilson was born, the second of three brothers, on May 13, 1928, as the "Treasure Valley," given over to cattle and dairy farming, with fruit orchards shielded from the harsh Canadian winter winds by mountains just to the north. Nampa is sixteen miles west of Boise, the state capital, and a few miles from the Oregon line. The area abounds with Basques, who find it similar in climate and terrain to their native region of Spain.

But the "Treasure Valley" was not pleasant for Wilson, who knew hard times from his birth. His father, of Irish Protestant ancestry—"an original foul-tempered black Irishman," Wilson would call him—had a small farm on the outskirts of town, and he bought and sold cattle; apparently he was not very good at either. By Wilson's statements, "there were some times when we didn't eat as well as we might have wished. In fact, the first time in my life when I really didn't worry about being hungry is when I went into the Marine Corps." The elder Wilson ran a tight household. He was quick to grab a strap or his belt when he felt his sons were slothful or disobedient. As it does everywhere in rural America, farm work began before dawn's first light, and the boys were

3

expected to hurry home from school to do whatever chores remained. As Wilson would tell one of his associates in Libya years later, "Jail doesn't scare me. But threaten me with fifty dairy cows to milk each morning when it's so cold your piss freezes before it hits the ground, and I'll roll over and do anything you want."

Wilson remembered his father as a demanding, undemonstrative man who treated his sons with the same impersonal detachment as he did the farm animals. The one time when the father did seem to reach out to Ed ended in bitter disappointment. By Wilson's account, his father entrusted him with the raising of a calf. "He gave me the calf at birth, and told me it was my responsibility, that how I raised it would show whether I was fit to take care of stock." Ed accepted the challenge. He was up a few minutes early each morning to care for "my calf"; he would hurry up the road from the school bus in the afternoon to ensure that the animal had the right food and water. For months Ed watched the calf thrive and grow, and he took great pride in what he was doing. That his father said nothing in praise was not considered out of the ordinary, for the elder Wilson was not given to kind words.

One afternoon Wilson came in from school and found his calf's pen empty. He looked around the farm. It was nowhere to be found. He approached his father. "Oh, that calf?" the father said. "I sold him this morning—he's at the size where he was ready to market." The father said nothing further, not a single word about Ed's diligence in rearing the animal. Nor did he offer the lad any share of the money.

Long-distance analysis is a risky business; the calf story was a passing childhood experience. Yet Wilson was to recount the episode many times in subsequent years, although with no attempt to draw any moral or conclusion from it. That he did talk about it repeatedly suggests that consciously or not, he learned a lesson from the experience: that to his father he was an inanimate object not unlike a water pump or a hay rake, something that could be expected to do a job without counting on reward or recognition. A child taught to think of himself in such terms—his parents were the only authority figures in Wilson's life at the time—is imbued with the concept that he is beholden to no one else. His only rewards are those which he can claim and hold on to for himself. Other persons are to be considered only to the extent that they are useful to one's own interests. They too are tools—to be used; to be distrusted or cheated; then, when their utility is exhausted, to be discarded. During Edwin Wilson's career, other persons were to "pay for the calf" time and again, often with true agony, and in several instances with their lives.

Wilson's father died of cancer in 1940. The immediate result was an end to the precarious life on the farm. Edwin, now 12 years old, moved with his mother and his older brother, Robert, to Eugene, Oregon. The sale of the Idaho property brought enough money to buy a modest house, and the widow held a succession of small jobs to keep her family together. With the nation still trying to shake off the Depression, she must have had a rough time, but Ed Wilson tended to glide over this period of his life with minimal commentary. He did not particularly care for his mother and the demands she put upon him; he referred to her, in nonaffectionate tones, as "a tough old broad." Three separate Wilson associates recalled the words. The first time I heard the phrase, I interpreted it as a backhanded compliment. Such was not the case, each of the three former associates stated. When Wilson's mother died, in 1976, he had the choice of attending either her funeral or a previously scheduled business meeting. He went to the business meeting.

Wilson's memory, conveniently pliant and sentimental when it suited his purposes, gave an entirely different picture of his relationship with his father in later years. In the 1970s, Wilson happened to learn that Colleen Goulding, wife of one of his arms purchasers, faced the sad task of putting a beloved but senile relative into a nursing home. Wilson told Mrs. Goulding and her husband, Peter, a long and touching story about his "last visit" to his own father before he too entered such a home. Wilson had been reluctant to let his impoverished father know he owned one of the largest cattle farms in Virginia; although he flew to Idaho, he took a bus to his hometown "so I wouldn't hurt the old man's feelings." There was a poignant scene as they drove past the town café, possibly for the last time together. "Son," Wilson quoted his father as saying, "let's stop for one last cup of coffee." Wilson's father had been dead for almost four decades at the time this moving episode supposedly occurred.

Lacking any family money, Wilson relied upon his brawn and wits to get to college. His last summer in high school Ed joined the wheat harvest, working for a labor contractor whose mammoth combines and crews roamed the Pacific Northwest. Wilson knew how to work—he had learned that on the farm—and he could spend twelve hours shoveling wheat from a tractor-drawn trailer, or steering a heavy combine across a seemingly endless field. Another summer, Ed and his brother Robert rented a combine on their own and found a few small farmers not covered by the larger crews. But they did not earn nearly so much money as expected; if Ed was to enter college, he must earn more.

The sea had appealed to Wilson from his first days in Oregon. He would go to the Portland harbor area and sit on a crate and watch the ocean freighters and their exotic markings, and dream of venturing out onto the Pacific himself. And that is what he did in 1947, as a freighter hand, lowest billet on a ship. What Wilson lacked in experience he made up for in strength: he had now grown to an adult 6 feet 4 inches in height, and muscles bunched on his strong frame. It was as a merchant seaman that Wilson first saw Asia, the continent he would visit frequently and come to love as Marine officer, intelligence agent and international businessman. Asia then intrigued a youth only several years distant from an Idaho farm. One searing memory was the Shanghai docks. The Nationalist government of Chiang Kai-shek was in its last frantic days of war with the Communists, and crowds of frenzied would-be refugees jammed the quay where Wilson's freighter docked. The Americans could do nothing to help them (though Wilson would later claim that he had helped smuggle a Chinese family to Hong Kong—a story, in the light of later events, implausible on its face).

Harking back to that first youthful voyage, Wilson would laugh about one experience in which he lost a fistfight, but proved a point.

"There was a crazy man aboard our ship, a real bruiser. For some reason, he took a dislike to another crew member, a smaller man named Joe who was a real boozer. He picked on this guy unmercifully.

"I got fed up with it. I said to the bully, 'I want to see you at the end of the dock when we go ashore.' Well, the crazy guy beat the living hell out of me. He hit me so hard the first punch broke my nose. We called it off in a hurry. Then we shook hands, and we became friends.

"We were having a drink in the bar later and this bruiser said to me, in all earnestness, 'Why did you bother to take up for old Joe? That poor bastard doesn't know what is happening to him.' "

Wilson's point was that he would take up for a weaker person, even at a risk. It was a favored way of joining people to his cause.

Wilson spent about a year at sea, long enough to obtain a membership card in the Seafarers International Union—an affiliation that would be of future professional value. He now had enough money for tuition at the University of Portland, a Catholic institution founded by the Holy Cross fathers which had aspirations of being "the Notre Dame of the Pacific Northwest." Such an ambition was never fulfilled, but the university did experience a post-Second World War boom that saw its enrollment soar from 1,600 to 4,000, chiefly because of veterans who used their G.I. Bill benefits for a low-cost education.

To Wilson, college was more work—hard work. He found a job in the university laundry, and while other students drank beer and socialized in the evenings, he put sheets into vats of boiling water and ran them through a huge steam presser. Wilson majored in psychology—he would tell his later associates, "I learned a lot of bullshit, but I also got some insight on how to deal with people." He left few traces on the Portland campus. Two pictures in the university yearbook, *The Log,* showing Wilson with a 1940s pompadour hairstyle and a sport jacket, appear without comment. In 1950, Wilson went out for football and played in the line for the junior varsity team, "The Babes." He made no lasting impression on his teammates. Twin brothers Doug and Dean Penner, who stood alongside Wilson in the team picture, thirty years later could not even remember the tall Idahoan. Doug Penner told me, "I saw a story in the paper about this guy Wilson who supposedly went to Portland the same year I did. I couldn't come up with him. I called my brother. He couldn't either." His brother, Dean, by coincidence spent his adult life as a career CIA employee. Dean Penner told me, "I've racked my brain. I don't remember this guy, either from college or from the Agency."

Wilson was graduated in 1953 as a bachelor of arts in psychology.

In the early summer of 1953 the Korean War was in its climactic months, with two years of erratic peace negotiations slowly leading toward an armistice. Wilson readily enlisted in a program that would put him into combat if the war continued: the Marine Corp's Officer Candidate School, at Quantico, Virginia, an hour south of Washington on the Potomac River. By the testimony of persons who have endured Marine OCS, no ritual on God's earth puts harsher demands upon human beings. The swamps, the sand hills, the heat, the drill instructors—Quantico seems structured to break the body and spirit of anyone who comes there. Ed Wilson, however, thrived in such a physical atmosphere. For a farm boy hardened in wheat harvests and on merchant freighters, whatever the Marines demanded of him was child's play.

Wilson made a longtime friend his first days at Quantico. Howard Wickham, a pleasant, open-mannered New Yorker, had just graduated from Syracuse University as a bachelor of fine arts (a major that brought him some undeserved derision from drill instructors; Wickham's innate toughness shut off the jibes). "The main thing we had in common," Wickham said, "is that we both were farm boys—me from the Finger Lakes region of New York State and Ed from Idaho. He was from what he called a poor family—a Depression-era farm family. We found it easy to get along."

To Wickham, Wilson was easily the most impressive member of the training class. "The first day," he said, "we were issued uniforms and ordered to double-time up and down a hill for what seemed like forever. Guys were falling down with the dry heaves. But not Ed. He had come to Quantico obviously in good shape, and was up front, leading. It seems he was barely breaking a sweat when everyone else felt like dying."

Nonetheless, Wilson took his share of abuse from training officers, and in good spirit. Wickham remembered an instructor putting a fire bucket over Wilson's head and banging it with a stick. "This is darned noisy, but it didn't seem to bother Ed. It was all part of the game."

One member of the training class was a man whom Wickham described as "a guy who must have gotten a waiver on the height requirement, he was so much shorter than anyone else. One night we took a long hike. When we came to a swamp, this man simply couldn't make it—the water was over his head. So Ed hoisted him up on his shoulders and carried him across."

The friendship of Wickham and Wilson deepened as the course continued. "Since our names started with 'W', we stood near each other in formations and sat close together in class. On marches we brought up the rear of the line. Given the accordion effect of a route march—where the people in front move out faster than the rest of the line—it seemed Ed and I were always running to catch up." On weekends Wilson and Wickham double-dated girls at William and Mary College, in nearby Williamsburg, Virginia. Wickham liked Wilson as a person, and he also recognized that his friend had acute powers of persuasion. "He was an absolutely charming guy; he could fix those big blue eyes on a person, and he was talking directly to him, and you got the idea he was interested."

The Quantico class was graduated a few days before the Korean War ended, in June 1953. Wickham was assigned to the Second Marine Air Wing, while Wilson went off to Korea. As is often true of service friendships, contact broke at this point for several years. But Howard Wickham was to have Ed Wilson weave into and out of his life for the next three decades, and not always happily.

To his later associates, Wilson would describe his years as a Marine in South Korea (briefly) and Japan as "the worst fucking period of my life." He had scut duties in a military force that had just fought an undeclared war to an unsatisfactory stalemate. He was an escort officer for prisoners. He held a succession of boring desk jobs. For one brief period his duties included responsibility for running a base laundry, which rekindled unhappy memories of his college job. Out of frustration, Wilson spent much of his time in Asia drinking and womanizing. For the first time in his life he had money for sensual indulgences.

In later years Wilson gave an entirely different—and fictitious—account of his years in Asia. A somewhat gullible former Army officer who worked briefly for Wilson asked him about the Korean War. Wilson responded with an emotional story about how "I lost so many men in combat that I still have nightmares. I hear those voices crying out to me in agony." As company commander, Wilson said, he felt "personal responsibility that these men died; I let them down. I wish I could get rid of these dreams." He asserted that his own body bore Korean War wounds.

The last shot of the Korean War was fired weeks before Edwin P. Wilson arrived in Korea. But Wilson's story impressed his associate. "I had been in Regular Army, and Ed sounded like a real fighter to me."

In September 1955, Howard Wickham received a surprise phone call from his old Quantico friend. Wilson was shortly to be discharged from the Marine Corps, but in the interim he had other exciting news: He was to be married on September 25. Could Wickham stand in as his best man? Barbara Hope Hagan, he said, was a medical technician he had met on the West Coast; they would be wed in her home town of Stanton, New Jersey.

Wickham had heard little of Wilson since they had left Quantico, and he thought it passingly odd that Wilson considered him close enough to be his best man. But he went to New Jersey—arriving late and "literally tying my tie as we started down the aisle"—and stood alongside Wilson during the ceremony. Barbara was a tall, austerely handsome woman, who obviously doted on her strapping husband. Her ring was a diamond of almost mammoth size. At the reception Wilson reached for her hand several times and rubbed the stone.

Wilson was discharged from the Marines on October 31 as a first lieutenant; the next day, November 1, he formally joined the Central Intelligence Agency.

2

Company Man

One of the great ironies of Edwin P. Wilson's life is that although he brought headline notoriety to the Central Intelligence Agency, he "was never really in the family," in the words of a former Agency official who came into contact with him from time to time. Wilson's role was that of "contract support agent," a free-lance job which required that his status be reviewed every two to three years. He never had career standing as an agent or officer. To an outsider the difference might seem piddling, but within CIA a "contract support agent" lacks the status, degree of clearances and opportunities that are afforded agents or officers. A person such as Wilson is hired because he possesses a particular skill. As long as the CIA has a need for the skill, he has a job; when the need ends, his job ends. The contract employee is not put through the Agency's intelligence equivalent of military basic training, the junior-officer training course at Camp Peary, the CIA's sprawling complex on the west bank of the James River a few miles distant from Williamsburg, Virginia. He is simply briefed on Agency security procedures, and told only what he needs to know to perform a specific mission.

Wilson joined CIA at a time of explosive growth for the Agency. Before Korea, it had been a mélange of old spooks from the Office of Strategic Services—the wartime intelligence agency—and a dumping ground for military misfits. Korea gave intelligence a new urgency, and CIA expanded to meet the need. In 1949, CIA's Office of Policy Coordination (OPC), then the cover name for covert activities, had total personnel of 302, a budget of $3.7 million and seven foreign stations. By 1952, OPC had grown to a strength of 2,812 direct employees plus an additional 3,142 "overseas contract personnel"—a catchall category that included both deep-cover agents and flunkies—with a budget of $82 million and forty-seven stations. Other branches of CIA grew proportionately.

Wilson's entry-level job, in the autumn of 1955, was as a "junior security officer," with the civil service rating of GS-7. His duty was to supervise uniformed guards at bases for the supersecret U-2 high-altitude spy plane. He earned a salary of between $70 and $80 weekly. Although Wilson later would boast to associates that he had been "right up there at the top of the U-2 program," his real role was something far less. One man described him as "a cut above a uniformed guard." Wilson served in Japan and Scandinavia and elsewhere. Years later, during liquor-sodden nights in Libya, Wilson would tell highly embellished stories about his role in the U-2 program. One favorite anecdote involved the alcoholic and sexually active wife of a U-2 pilot. "He'd fly off on one of his missions," Wilson said, "and I'd fly off to their quarters for my own mission." As is true of many of Wilson's anecdotes, the story is incapable of verification.

Wilson's next assignment put him deep into the world of clandestine operations and gave him a taste for covert activities that he would never lose. Recognizing Wilson's background as a merchant seaman and a member of Seafarers International Union (SIU), CIA gave him a contract under which he would pose as a union staff member and infiltrate left-learning labor unions in Western European ports.

Wilson's use of unions as a cover was possible because of the tight alliance between CIA and the American Federation of Labor–Congress of Industrial Organizations (AFL-CIO), the parent labor federation of which SIU was an affiliate. Here a bit of Cold War history is in order. In the 1940s the Soviets, directly and through fronts, tried to seize control of the West European labor movement. The AFL (the merger with the CIO came in 1954) fought back. President George Meany had a direct litmus test. If a country did not permit free trade unions, he would oppose its government, and he permitted the CIA to use his AFL to fight the Communists at street level.

One of the many unacknowledged CIA triumphs during the 1940s and '50s was in European labor. The AFL, with generous CIA funding, matched the soviet KGB dollar for dollar and man for man, and averted a Communist takeover of unions in such vital areas as steel, shipping and mining. The long-term Communist interest was in destabilizing Europe's industrial base and weakening the North Atlantic Treaty Organization; hence, CIA's countermoves had considerable strategic import.

And it was in this area of labor countersubversion that Edwin P. Wilson had perhaps his finest hours as an intelligence operative. For cover purposes, Wilson went onto the payroll of the Seafarers International Union. The SIU President, Paul Hall, was a rough-talking Alabamian who had gone to sea as a teenager and fought his way to the top of a rowdy union. Hall was close to George Meany personally and professionally, and he shared Meany's abhorrence of Communists and their tactics. Both men had fought Communist infiltration of American unions; they did not intend to see their European brethren fall victim to the same techniques. So Hall willingly gave Wilson credentials as an SIU staff member and put him on the payroll, first as a lobbyist in the Washington office, then as an international representative. The SIU signed Wilson's paychecks, but the actual money to cover them was funneled into the union from CIA via a covert conduit.

As a means of deepening Wilson's cover, the SIU arranged for him to study for a year at Cornell University's School of Industrial and Labor Relations, recognized as the premier training institution for labor unions' professional staff members. His credentials thus enhanced, Wilson went to Brussels as an "assistant port representative" for the SIU, for the ostensible purpose of assisting American seamen who encountered difficulties while away from their home ports. In actuality, Wilson had only tenuous contacts with the SIU. He posed as a leftist American seaman and sought out communist sympathizers in a variety of labor organizations. Even his detractors in CIA—and there are many—give Wilson high marks for his work in Brussels and other European ports. Although details remain murky, Wilson apparently carried out classic subversion. By his account, in at least two instances he charmed his way into the hierarchy of dissidents challenging union leadership and maneuvered them into can't-win situations. In each instance, according to Wilson, the Communists bore the onus for failure, and lost credibility.

Unwittingly or not, Barbara Wilson found herself drawn into her husband's covert activities. On one occasion, for reasons Wilson never made clear, Barbara was detained briefly by British authorities. The CIA station in London intervened to secure her release. A longtime family friend who heard Barbara talk about the detention later said, "Barbara could joke about it, but you could tell she was shaken." The episode also meant that Ed Wilson was now known to the British as an American intelligence operative—a minor breach of security, given the friendship between the American and British services. But in roundabout fashion, Wilson benefited. More than a decade later, when he used London as a base for some of his activities after leaving government work, British authorities remembered their first official encounter with him and regarded him mistakenly as still on the CIA payroll. The misinterpretation enhanced the image that Wilson sought to project at the time.

The Wilsons remained abroad for about two years, returning to the United States in 1961 and settling in Northern Virginia. Wilson's activities in the next several years once again become murky, with his claims unsupported by any direct evidence and contradicted by the statements of others. CIA's major undertaking in 1961 was the Bay of Pigs invasion—an operation in which Wilson asserted he had played "a major role." Persons involved in the planning and execution of the Bay of Pigs find Wilson's story strange, for they saw no trace of him at the time. Wilson gave varying accounts of his role: Drawing upon his Marine Corps experience, he helped train the anti-Castro guerrillas in their Nicaraguan camp; again, as a maritime specialist, he found the freighters used to transport the invasion force; yet again, he "ran agents in and out of Cuba" before the invasion.

But according to persons intimately involved in the Bay of Pigs, Edwin Wilson did none of these things, whatever he may have asserted later. The stronger disavowal came from a longtime Agency covert operative, Brad Rockford, who had been with CIA since 1952, first on detached duty from the Marine Corps and then as an agent. Rockford is the epitome of the career paramilitary. He served the Agency around the world as a fighter—in Korea, in Central America, in the Bay of Pigs invasion, in Laos, in the Congo. During the Bay of Pigs, Rockford was in charge of the Central American training bases, and thus was familiar with the Agency people involved in training the anti-Castro Cubans. Ed Wilson was not among them. Rockford also refutes Wilson's claim to have arranged shipping. "I would have known," he said, "because I was in charge of the Central American end of the thing. I know where the boats came from, and how. Ed Wilson was not involved." Wilson's role was minor, and fleeting—that of paymaster on one isolated phase of the operation. And even in that capacity he stirred controversy. "There was a question as to whether the money went where Wilson said it did," another contract agent told me.

Rockford also finds mystifying a further Wilson assertion that he was one of the masterminds of the post-1961 operation against the Castro regime, directed from the CIA station in Miami and code-named JM-WAVE. After the Bay of Pigs failure, the Kennedy Administration decided to try to do through sabotage and subversion what it had˙ not accomplished through military action. Literally hundreds of Bay of Pigs veterans, plus other anti-Castro Cubans who had managed to leave the island, jammed Miami and adjacent South Florida. For the next two years they ran an infinite variety of hit-and-run missions against Cuba, destroying petroleum facilities, bridges, docks, military installations and other targets of strategic value. Brad Rockford was one of the CIA paramilitaries running JM-WAVE. "Ed Wilson wasn't around," he said. "Had he had the role he claimed later, we would have crossed paths."

Despite Wilson's noninvolvement, two persons prominent in JM-WAVE were to be significant figures in his life. Thomas Clines, born August 18, 1928, had been with CIA since 1949. A gregarious backslapper, Clines was deputy chief of the Miami station during JM-WAVE. In 1961–62, Agency insiders regarded Clines as "a man to watch" in the Operations Directorate which ran CIA clandestine activities. Clines displayed a persuasive ability to lobby for his projects within the Agency bureaucracy and a notable talent for cajoling the persons doing the actual work. When a former associate called him a "consummate bureaucratic politician," he was not being unkind; as is true with any government department, CIA is riddled with administrative potholes that can knock the most noble of projects off course. Oddly, for all his work with Cubans, Clines carried a handicap: He could speak no Spanish beyond the kitchen variety. Late in his career, he decided he wished to be a station chief in one of the Latin American capitals. When Cline's lack of linguistic ability was pointed out, he agreed to take a crash course at the language school CIA runs in conjunction with the State Department. After a week, school authorities sent Clines back to CIA. Teaching this man Spanish, they said, was impossible. Clines never became a station chief; but he did attain high rank in clandestine services.

Rafael Quintero—"Chi Chi" to his friends in the Cuban community, "Omar" by his Agency cover name—was one of several anti-Castro guerrillas who became close to Clines during the JM-WAVE period, and later, through Clines, close to Ed Wilson. A stocky man with a receding hairline only slightly offset by an ill-fitted toupee, Chi Chi became known within the Agency as a man of limitless courage. In the months after the Bay of Pigs he personally led many forays against Castro Cuba; on one occasion he spent more than a month underground in Santiago de Cuba, in the island's eastern Oriente Province, directing sabotage activities. Several times he parachuted onto the island. "Absolutely fearless" was how one of Chi Chi's superiors characterized him. "If courage was measured in the size of a man's balls, Chi Chi would carry a couple of basketballs." Clines, as Quintero's superior, commanded his absolute fidelity—a loyalty later transferred, in large part, to Edwin Wilson.

The truth of Wilson's claims notwithstanding, Wilson in the middle 1960s did build a reputation within CIA as a master at a very specialized intelligence activity: creating and operating what is known in the intelligence world as a "proprietary company." Proprietaries are business enterprises covertly owned and operated by CIA. "Operating proprietaries" actually do business as private firms. They are incorporated where they do business, they file the applicable state and federal tax returns and they obtain the licenses necessary to the operation. They also often earn substantial profits.

A different type of enterprise is the "nonoperating proprietary," sometimes known as a "notional." Consisting merely of a letterhead, a mailing address and a phone number, it is essentially a mail-drop business based in the office of a friendly (although non-CIA) lawyer or business firm. The "notional" gives a covert agent a visible means of support; if he claims to work for Sunshine Enterprises, Ltd., in Washington, for instance, such a company can be found in the phone book, and someone will answer the telephone when it rings, and respond to mail.

The "operating proprietaries" are considerably more complex. During the Vietnam War, the thinly disguised Air American provided air support for CIA and military operations throughout Southeast Asia under the cover of being a private firm with government contracts. Another company, Intermountain Aviation, Inc., provided a variety of "non-attributable" air-support capabilities worldwide. (Both Air America and Intermountain are now out of Agency hands.) CIA ran a complex of insurance companies to pay annuities and other benefits to deep-cover agents who were not eligible for conventional U.S. government programs, and to provide self-insurance for risks involved in covert operations. Another chain of security companies performed, for CIA, such functions as document destruction, guard work, security-clearance investigations and security of office buildings; it did the same work for private businesses and other government agencies. All these enterprises—aviation, insurance and security—earned profits and paid taxes.

Wilson's new job with CIA called for him to set up a proprietary company to handle maritime traffic to Southeast Asia—cargoes that commercial shippers would not carry because of fear of getting enmeshed in the Vietnam War. To ensure maximum security, Wilson went totally outside the intelligence community to find the "public parties" who would be ostensible officers of the proprietary. Doing so necessitated that he lift, ever so briefly, his own cover. Understandably, Wilson turned to a person he could trust: Howard Wickham, his friend from Marine officer-training days, best man at his wedding and an occasional social acquaintance since.

Wickham by now ran his own graphic-design business in Washington, and over the past years, encountering Wilson here and there, Wickham had entertained a passing curiosity as to how his friend earned a living. Although Wilson claimed to be a "legislative representative" for the Seafarers' union, something in the story did not quite ring true. Wilson, however, had said nothing of CIA.

Then came a day in 1966 when Wilson told Wickham, "Buddy, I want to talk to you about something serious. I want to ask you to help me, and our government. And if you don't think you can do it, I want you to promise me not to say anything to anyone else—anyone at all."

Wickham nodded agreement. "Whatever you say, Ed," he replied. "If I can help you, I will. If I can't, mum's the word."

"I'm working for CIA," Wilson said. "I have been for years, ever since I left the Marine Corps. Europe, Cornell—that was all Agency business." Wickham was not overly surprised; he said nothing.

"Now I want you to do something for me, and more importantly, for the United States government." Wilson went

on to explain that he was setting up a company called
Maritime Consulting Associates, which would be a CIA proprietary that would provide cover for shipping operations
worldwide.

"I need someone who has no connection with intelligence to be the president," Wilson told Wickham. "I know
you were in Marine air intelligence, but that's okay—that's
too remote. There's no money in it for you, no dividends, no
glory. I want to put your name on the letterhead and the
corporate papers as president. I'll tell you enough about the
public operations of the company that you can carry on an
intelligent conversation. But the less you know, the better,
and therefore the less I'm going to tell you."

Wickham readily accepted. As he recounted later, "I was
proud to be asked, and I was proud to be able to serve my
country." Several days later Wilson presented him with incorporation papers for his signature.

MCA's visible function was to broker cargoes, chiefly
government, into South Vietnam for the Agency for International Development, the Navy and the Department of Agri-
culture. "Saigon harbor was mined, and ships were hard to
come by in those days," Wickham recalled. "That's where the
legitimate money was made. The rest I didn't know about, I
don't know about and I did not *want* to know about." Mone-
tarily, all Wickham received was a nominal fee for designing
MCA stationery.

Unbeknownst to Wickham, Maritime Consulting Associates did odd jobs for the Agency all around the world. Ships
and boats chartered through MCA—with no flags, registra-
tion numbers painted over and non-English-speaking crews—
surreptitiously delivered arms to Africa, the Middle East,
Latin America and the remote corners of Asia. All went to
client armies that the CIA could not support openly. By all
accounts, Wilson performed well. He knew the maritime
industry, he was a hard bargainer and he had a knack for
covert work. Although CIA had funded MCA with a minimum amount of money—$50,000 is the figure mentioned—
Wilson handled the non-CIA governmental contracts so tightly
that the proprietary operated close to a profit.

It was during this period that Brad Rockford, the CIA
man from the Bay of Pigs and JM-WAVE, first met Wilson in
the flesh. Rockford was visiting CIA headquarters in Langley

one morning in 1965 when Tom Clines, formerly the deputy chief of the Miami station, stopped him in the hall. "Come on to lunch with me," Clines said. "We can expense-account it. I have a contract agent to meet."

The contract agent was Edwin Wilson. Rockford looked him over. "He was a big, good-looking, swashbuckling man, very confident of himself," Rockford recalled years later. Over lunch Clines and Rockford talked about the war in the old Belgian Congo, where pro-Communist and pro-Western guerrilla forces were fighting for control of the country. "The Soviets were in this war up to their elbows," Rockford said. "They were using native fishing boats to ship arms across Lake Tanganyika to their flunkies. In a local war such as this, a few hundred automatic weapons can make a helluva difference."

Rockford saw as the answer the use of SWIFT boats, fast and highly armed—a 1960s version of the PT boats that had given the Japanese much trouble in the Second World War. Rockford's anti-Castro army had used the SWIFTs to good effect in raids on and about Cuba; surely the SWIFTs (and the Cubans) could also be put to good use in Africa. But the problem was getting the boats into the Congo, deep in the interior of Africa.

"How can we transport them into the country and clean up this mess? They're so big they won't fit into the guts of a C-130," Rockford lamented. He and Wilson began tossing ideas across the lunch table. "The best minds in the Agency have been muddling around this problem," Rockford said. Then he and Wilson had a brainstorm: "Cut the fucking things in half and put the boats back together when we get them up there."

The idea excited Wilson and Clines. "Goddamn! What an idea!" Wilson said in a near-shout. He reached across the table and punched Rockford on the arm.

As it turned out, the SWIFTs had to be cut into three sections, not two, to fit into the cargo bay of a C-130. The manufacturer supplied plugs and receptacles so that fuel and electrical lines could be easily rejoined. "It was a hell of an engineering challenge, but it worked," Rockford said. "They more or less ended the war so far as the lake was concerned."

This passing contact with Wilson suggested to Rockford that the man had imagination and ability. He was thus all the more surprised in the late 1970s when he heard that Wilson claimed to have been a key player in the Bay of Pigs. "You don't get away with a lie like that," Rockford told me. "You might fool the outsiders who listen to war stories, but then you get down to the core players who were there. Well, buddy, Ed Wilson wasn't."

But Edwin Wilson was active. As a contract employee he did not feel bound by the same strictures as did in-house CIA agents. He operated as a free-booter, a man who could divulge his CIA connection to a general or a senator or a defense contractor, and drop broad hints as to the extent of his influence. A ranking staff member of the Senate Foreign Relations Committee met Wilson at an embassy function in the late 1960s. "I can't remember his exact language, but he gave me the idea he was the number two man at the Agency, and that after some politics, he would be the top dog," the staff man said. Wilson inserted himself into the lobby network that the Pentagon and the intelligence community directs toward Congress. He did not have to account for expenses, so he could grab checks for luncheons and drinks. He joined the University Club, a mildly prestigious social group which occupies an elegant town house on 16th Street Northwest adjacent to the Soviet Embassy. The club has on its membership rolls a good number of active and retired spooks, and through their example Wilson put a patina on his outdoorsman's manners. Wilson always remembered the names of persons he met—a handy habit in a city of egotists—and he knew when to listen.

Two acquaintanceships that Wilson pushed with a single-minded determination were with CIA officials Theodore Shackley and Thomas Clines.

Wilson and Shackley had apparently met in the late 1960s, when Shackley was CIA station chief in Saigon. Shackley carried a mixed reputation among fellow CIA officials. Although he achieved considerable rank—eventually becoming deputy to the director of operations, making him the number two man in the Agency for clandestine activities—Shackley "was a desk man rather than a field operator," according to a former associate.

Shackley delighted in letting subordinates know that he was aware of intimate details of their personal lives. An agent who served under him briefly in Saigon remembered Shackley ending their get-acquainted interview with the casual remark "By the way, I know about you and _____," naming a woman with whom the man was romantically involved. "This was damned irrelevant, but I wondered how Shackley knew it," the man recollected later. Shackley impressed other persons as "a compulsive paper collector, someone who wanted a memo on every damned thing that happened."

Whatever his quirks, Shackley rose high in the clandestine arm of CIA; concurrently his longtime friend Tom Clines became director of training in the same branch—another key position. And it was on these two men that Wilson relied for his own ambitions within the Agency.

Wilson's claims to the member of the Senate Foreign Relations Committee might have been arrant nonsense, but apparently he did entertain the notion in the late '60s that he too could achieve high rank in CIA, possibly even the position of director. Given his career pattern, and his status as contract agent, such an ambition could be considered absurd at first glance, but Wilson intended to reach the top by an unconventional route. As he would tell an associate many years later, "I was building such a network of contacts and friends in Congress, mainly the Senate, and the Pentagon that I hoped to make myself an indispensable man. Given the right administration, I could call in some chips and ask for a favor." Wilson's idea, according to what he told the associate, was that the Agency had "been in the same hands since it was founded," and that "a hell of a lot of people in this town [Washington] thought that some fresh new blood was needed."

As Wilson's business expertise grew, the Agency entrusted him with an increasing number of proprietary companies. Wilson learned the tradecraft of clandestine operations: how to incorporate a company through front men so as to conceal its true ownership; how to use post-office boxes and mail drops; how to route money through a succession of domestic and foreign bank accounts so that neither origin nor destination could be traced. One corporation "given" to Wilson was Consultants International, Limited, which in addition to providing cover for covert CIA activities in the Middle East also acted as a registered representative for U.S. firms doing business in Libya. But one thing galled Wilson: "I was running two, three, even five million bucks a year through these Agency shells," he complained, "and I was being paid a piss-ant government salary. If I could have kept even half of what I made for the United States Government, I would have been a rich man."

But Wilson at the same time was in fact accumulating the start of a personal fortune, through real estate deals with his wife, Barbara. Their first investment, made soon after he was discharged from the Marine Corps in 1955, was the purchase of a service station just outside the gate of the Marine base at Quantico, Virginia. Although a manager ran the place, Wilson occasionally had to step in during an emergency. "I was the best damned gas-pump jockey on the Eastern Seaboard," he joked. After the Wilsons returned from Brussels, Barbara obtained a real estate broker's license and began buying and selling properties. Both she and Ed had a good eye for run-down houses that could be purchased, given cosmetic renovations and then resold at a profit. Wilson would laugh about a house "that I never saw in the daytime. We bought it at night, painted the inside of the place at night and then sold it by telephone."

Howard Wickham, when he renewed acquaintance with the Wilsons in the early 1960s, found them living in a "dumpy old fourteen-acre farm out on Route Seven" in Northern Virginia. Doing most of the work themselves, they made the house livable, if not a showcase, and they enjoyed entertaining friends. Two sons were born to them in the early 1960s: Karl Paul and Erik Scott. Wilson began to talk about a long-range ambition that would supplement his intelligence career. He wanted "the biggest damned farm in Virginia, a place where I can walk outside the house and not see any land that I don't own."

By happenstance, real estate values in the Washington metropolitan area started to skyrocket at just about the time the Wilsons began their investments. For persons with the foresight to invest, the profits were quick and often immense. The Wilsons sensed what was happening, and they trusted their judgment; whatever money they earned, either from CIA or from the sale of the property, they immediately put into other real estate.

Then, in either late 1970 or early 1971, Ed Wilson made a mistake. He had the opportunity to purchase a tract on which he felt he could make a substantial profit, but his own assets were not enough to support the loan required. So Wilson gambled: On his net-worth statement he listed himself as owner of a company that was in actuality an Agency proprietary. He had done the same thing once before, on a much smaller loan, and had not been caught. This time, however, someone at the lending institution decided to check into the value of the company. His inquiries hit trip wires within the Agency, and Wilson was called in and ordered to give an explanation. What he had done was in flagrant violation of Agency regulations—indeed, even federal criminal statutes. Wilson pleaded carelessness; he had been so used to thinking of the proprietaries as "his companies" that he had reflexively listed the company on the mortgage application.

The Agency inspector general found the explanation unconvincing. Wilson would not be prosecuted or formally disciplined, but when his contract expired in the spring of 1971, it would not be renewed.* The Agency would do nothing to hamper Wilson if he sought employment elsewhere in the United States government, and because he had worked outside the government pension system the past sixteen years, he would be given $25,000 as severance pay (a sum Wilson would later claim was a bonus for "special meritorious service").

Wilson took what was tantamount to dismissal in apparent good grace. He might be out of the Central Intelligence Agency, but by no means did he intend to be out of American intelligence. CIA had taught Wilson how to make money as an international trader. He was now to commence a brief but profitable transition from government agent to government entrepreneur.

---

*According to one source, Wilson had been called to task several times previously for imaginative expense accounts charged to Agency proprietaries. This person maintains that the loan application "was the proverbial straw that knocked down the camel."

3

Richard Nixon's Private Spook

When Wilson left the CIA in 1971 after fifteen years as a federal employee, the real estate investments he and his wife, Barbara, had made gave them a net worth of a shade more than $200,000. Although the Agency's termination of his contract had bitten Wilson to the quick, he later would put the best face possible on the circumstances. "I was getting too rich for the CIA's blood," he told one associate. "The CIA got to be a handicap for me; it was holding me back. I wanted to make money."

Wilson left the Central Intelligence Agency just as he had entered it as a contract employee, without fanfare. In fact, so quietly did he leave that many persons he had made privy to the secret that he worked for the CIA remained unaware that he no longer served the Agency. Which was just fine by Ed Wilson.

But cutting ties with the CIA did not mean that Wilson left the American intelligence community. Indeed, his time in the "private sector" lasted only a few days, until he signed on as a contract employee with an intelligence organization even more secret than the CIA: "Task Force 157," a special unit of the Office of Naval Intelligence.

Persons who worked in TF 157 say the origins of the numerical designation are lost to history; as one man put it, "This could have come from the 157th memo on the subject, or some admiral's office number." The direct parentage of TF 157, however, is traceable to an order by President John F. Kennedy, in 1962, that the Navy develop intelligence sources among Cuban citizens working on the American naval base in

Guantánamo, Cuba. The President's brother, Attorney General Robert F. Kennedy, who played a key role in investigating the intelligence community's performance in the Bay of Pigs invasion and the Cuban missile crisis, was said to have found that no systematic means existed of gleaning information from these Cuban employees, who could travel freely throughout Cuba even while working on the U.S. base.

The naval agent assigned the task was one Thomas Duval, a hulking officer of immense girth (at six feet four inches, he weighed upwards of three hundred pounds) whose absolutely bald head gives him a striking resemblance to Daddy Warbucks, the *Orphan Annie* comic-strip character. This similarity notwithstanding, there is nothing comic about "Smoke" Duval, so named because, according to a longtime associate, "When Duval got hot after some information, you either got it for him—or smoke came out of your ass." Duval normally did business with an unlit cigar clutched either between his lips or between his fingers. He had been with ONI since the Korean War—in the Far East, in Latin America and in Western Europe. And in the last-named, during the 1950s, he had had a mission parallel to that of CIA contract agent Edwin P. Wilson: the infiltration of European maritime unions and the exposure and neutralization of Communist agents.

Wilson and Duval became acquaintances; both liked covert activities, and they shared many an after-hours drink and war story. Their paths crossed again in the 1960s, when Duval began the TF 157 project aimed at the Guantánamo employees, and Wilson was helping support anti-Castro activities among Cubans in the Miami area and elsewhere.

Although details are scanty (and Duval is not talkative about his intelligence background), the Guantánamo project worked so well that in 1968 the Office of Naval Intelligence decided to develop a similar maritime spook operation that would cover ports and shipping lanes worldwide. A Department of the Navy order dated August 7, 1968, brought Task Force 157 into formal existence. About one hundred Navy personnel—thirty military officers, the remainder civilian—were assigned to the new organization.

TF 157 was intended as what one former member called "a low-buck, low-profile outfit," with cover for its operatives supplied through a series of proprietary companies incorporated in the Washington area. ONI civilian personnel signed employment contracts with the proprietaries, in effect leaving government employ as far as the paper record was concerned. These agents were assigned to port cities abroad—mainly in the Far East, Europe and the Middle East—where they in turn set up yet another series of local proprietaries which would employ local citizens. TF 157 was intended to give intelligence an "on-the-ground presence" that would supplement satellite and other coverage of shipping by Communist nations and their allies. However sophisticated the camera, a photograph taken from thousands of miles in the sky cannot determine the contents of a freighter's hold. By developing sources among dockworkers, seamen, shipping agents—even port whores, who hear a lot of bed talk—TF 157 hoped to develop a more definite analysis of Communist-bloc shipping.

According to two persons involved in the program at knowledgeable levels, TF 157's cost to the United States government was minuscule, a peak of around $8 million a year. Actual expenditures ran considerably higher. The difference was provided by the profits earned by the proprietary companies, which were run ostensibly as legitimate private businesses. (One rule of intelligence work is that a proprietary which purports to be an active business firm must churn out *some* work lest it become conspicuous.) The maritime trade is a tightly knit community. An American agent who opened an office in, say, Hong Kong and installed Telex machines and began frequenting the local shipping clubs would soon be asked, "Exactly what do you do?" CIA and other intelligence organizations learned early in their existence that the best means of creating the *illusion* of legitimacy was to provide the *reality* of legitimacy—that is, to run a straightforward business in one portion of the office, and do the secret work either in the back room or elsewhere.

In 1971—the year Wilson and the CIA parted company—TF 157's chiefs found they had a gaping hole in their coverage of the Middle East. Given the escalation of Arab-Israeli confrontation and unpredictable eruptions of warfare in the area, American shippers (save for the operators of the oil-tanker fleets) tried to avoid Middle Eastern waters. As a result, TF 157 agents had trouble maintaining credible cover. The flow of information virtually dried up from a region generally considered the tinderbox of the world.

Just where Ed Wilson got the idea is not known, but

soon after leaving CIA he approached naval intelligen̄
an offer. He wished to create, under TF 157 auspi̇c̄
company that would trade throughout the world, in alm̄ st
every conceivable commodity from soybeans to aircraft to
military equipment. By dealing in such a range of products,
Wilson would have access to virtually any major city in the
world. All that he wished from TF 157 was a nominal salary
and expenses. His major earnings, if any, would come from
whatever profits his company made. In return, he would set
up a net of intelligence operatives for TF 157 in the Far East
and wherever else required.

Wilson even had a tailor-made image to offer TF 157. He
would be the wheeler-dealer Washington businessman, friend of
congressmen and generals, a man with high-level access to both
the Defense Department and the Central Intelligence Agency.

Wilson had acquired impressive acquaintances over the
years, men whose names he sprinkled through his conversations. Brigadier General Robert C. Richardson, for instance,
had served as deputy chief of staff for science and technology
for the U.S. Air Force Systems command; he later was field
commander of the Defense Atomic Support Agency at the
supersecret Sandia Base, New Mexico. When Richardson
retired in 1967 he became a consultant in defense affairs; one
of his positions, which he was to take in 1973, was a vice-
presidency of Ed Wilson's Consultants International.

Another friendship Wilson cultivated over the years was
that of Major General Richard V. Secord, whom he apparently first met in 1975, when Secord, then a colonel, headed the
Air Force Military Advisory Group in Iran. Secord later came
to supervise the military sales program for the entire Air
Force, with responsibility for more than $60 billion in sales of
military equipment. (In 1981, Secord was to be named deputy assistant secretary of defense for the Near East, Africa and
South Asia, which involved setting defense policy toward
Saudi Arabia, Iran, Israel, Egypt, Lebanon and twenty-nine
other countries, making it one of the most sensitive posts in
the Pentagon. Secord was the first noncivilian to serve in this
position. But his linkage with Ed Wilson was to ruin his career.)

Yet another Wilson acquaintance of note was Brigadier
General J. J. Cappucci, who before retiring rose to the position of head of the Air Force Office of Special Investigations,
that service's top intelligence post.

Wilson also maintained his relationships with Ted Shackley and Tom Clines of CIA. Shackley's daughter boarded her horse at Wilson's Mount Airy Farm, and Mrs. Shackley and Mrs. Wilson frequently lunched together and went on shopping trips for antiques. Many mornings Wilson began his day by meeting Shackley for breakfast in a restaurant in suburban Virginia.

Later in the 1970s, when Wilson fell into disrepute, Shackley told CIA superiors that he had relied upon Wilson as an "outside source of information," who brought him intelligence not picked up by conventional Agency sources. Persons who heard Shackley's story thought it peculiar for several reasons. Such contacts are usually handled by another Agency unit, the Domestic Collection Office. Secondly, although Shackley was renowned within the Agency as a "paper-generator, a guy who wrote a memo practically every time he went to the john," only two "contact reports" could be found on his meetings with Wilson.

Wilson's relationship with Secord also extended beyond business hours. During a transfer the general faced a financial loss on the sale of a house; Wilson stepped into the breach and purchased the property. When Wilson's business expanded to the point where he purchased a private plane, on several occasions he permitted Secord to take it on personal flights. (Secord was to tell investigators later that "Wilson did me a courtesy; I needed the air time to remain proficient as a pilot, and he let me have the plane. Perfectly innocent.")

Through the adroit dropping of such names, Wilson contrived an aura of prominence that had infinite appeal to foreign officials imbued with the notion (not always a false one) that Washington is a city based not upon know-how but upon know-who. By telling these officials that he was a true insider in Washington power politics, Wilson could gather most any kind of valuable intelligence.

Wilson's proposition appealed to TF 157s then-commander, a Navy captain. In the spring of 1971, Wilson went on the TF 157 payroll at $35,000 a year, the equivalent of what he would have earned as a GS-13 employee of the United States Government. He incorporated a firm called "Consultants International, Inc." (close to the name of one of his CIA proprietaries) and set up offices at 1425 K Street, Northwest, on the eastern fringe of Washington's lawyer/lobbyist/trade-association territory.

Given the criminal laws, outright influence *peddling* in Washington is relatively rare; the actual handing over of a bribe, as the Abscam defendants in Congress sadly learned, is highly susceptible to recording on an FBI videotape machine. But no law has been written (and perhaps none can be written) that proscribes the even more pernicious system of influence *trading*. A newspaper reporter persuades an official to provide him with a dollop of information in exchange for the promise, stated or implied, that the official will receive flattering mention in the future. A Pentagon lobbyist* asks a congressman for a vote on a pet project in return for a promise to work diligently elsewhere to obtain approval for a deal dear to the solon's constituency. A "consultant" learns through a lunch-table conversation that an Air Force colonel is having trouble finding financing for a vacation cabin; he arranges for the colonel to meet a friendly bank loan officer—and a week later asks the Air Force officer if he would mind having a drink with a client, a defense manufacturer, who wants to discuss some business. . . . The variant chains are endless, and the rules are loose. Wilson had been stockpiling contacts for the day he would be an independent operator in Washington, and he now had the best of both worlds: a tie with naval intelligence that paid his overhead and continued his link with the intelligence community, and the appearance of being a private businessman not bound by the ethical codes restricting government employees.

Wilson's first step was to assemble an impressive list of retired admirals, generals, politicians and other influential personages on his Consultants International stationery. Some of these were listed for "show purposes" only and had no function in CI. (For instance, Robert Keith Gray, a prominent public relations executive who had been a confidant of President Nixon since the 1950s, discovered through another person years later, that he was on Wilson's letterhead. "I had met Wilson at some party or another, and shook his hand," Gray was to tell a reporter when Wilson's troubles became public. "Our offices happened to be in the same building. I had absolutely no business or professional contact with the man. Why he chose to use my name I can only guess.")

---

*By law, a federal agency is barred from lobbying Congress. Hence the agencies retain battalions of persons known as "congressional liaison officers"—semantical hypocrisy that permits them to evade the law.

For the retired officers, Wilson had an offer contrived to help avoid the letter of the federal statute prohibiting them from having any business contacts with the military for five years after leaving active duty. (The statute was aimed at putting a chock in the so-called "swinging door" through which brass regularly went from the Pentagon to defense contractors upon retirement, showing up at their old offices a week or so later to ask former subordinates to buy whatever weapon their new employer was selling.) As one of these retirees stated, "Wilson told me he knew I couldn't do any business with DOD [the Department of Defense] until the statutory period had passed. But he knew I had been assigned to Thailand twice, the last time high in the military advisory group. 'Go out there and find out what they're interested in buying, and let me handle it from there,' Wilson told me. He would either go to the manufacturer who made the item, or to the Pentagon and try to have it included in the next foreign-military-aid bill. What Wilson wanted was my entrée to the defense ministry in Thailand. As he laid it out to me, he would get his cut from the U.S. manufacturer, and he would 'take care of me.' " This particular officer declined because Wilson offered no guarantee of expense money. "He wanted me to spend five, maybe six thousand dollars to fly halfway around the world on a maybe deal. No, he would not go halves with me; no, he would not cover my expenses even if the deal worked out. I turned him down. Military retirement isn't all that great, and somehow I wasn't sure that I would get what would be coming to me even if the deal worked."

Other retired officers liked Wilson's proposition. Alexander Raffio, later to be one of Wilson's closest associates, recalls his surprise the first time he visited Consultants International's offices. "Half a dozen or so guys in their mid-fifties were sitting behind desks, with the nameplate saying they were Admiral So-and-So, U.S. Navy retired, or General So-and-So from the Army. Ed just kind of laughed when I asked about them. They were not on the payroll, but he gave them a desk, and some privacy, and a telephone, and they called around and put together whatever deals they could. They had to be careful to avoid any direct contact with the Pentagon or their old service; if they found anything, Ed took over. They got a share of whatever percentage Ed took.

"As Ed explained it to me, boredom is a big problem

among the retired military. They've had a hundred men at their beck and call one day; the next day they're sitting around the house, thinking that playing golf the rest of their life isn't all that appealing. Some are also in a financial bind; they're on wife three or four, and they're being killed by alimony. So for an operator like Wilson, who gives them an office and even the chance at some money, they jump."

So the retired brass would congregate at Wilson's office in the morning, make their phone calls and read their mail (and use the battery of Telex machines) and then stroll a few blocks to the Army-Navy Club on Farragut Square for a leisurely lunch. Wilson truly provided a refuge. All he asked in return was the possibility of exploiting the contacts these retired men had made during three decades of active military service. The sight was sometimes sad: "It was a scene from a Fellini movie, these old out-to-pasture generals and admirals calling around the country, trying to scratch up a deal on behalf of Ed Wilson."

But Wilson realized that his contacts for Washington contracts were of minimal value unless he could use them to help him obtain profitable business abroad. Energetic though he was (laziness was one defect never charged to Wilson), he needed deal-finders abroad, men already involved in the arms and defense industry who were willing to share their foreign contacts in return for whatever favors he could do for them. Such contacts would also be important to Wilson in fulfilling his mission for Task Force 157—the monitoring of Soviet-bloc maritime activities.

During his first year with Task Force 157, Wilson began to entertain the first stirrings of an even broader mission for the naval intelligence unit. He saw it as a successor group to the Central Intelligence Agency, with Edwin P. Wilson as director. The exact extent of Wilson's scheme, and the validity of the supposed insider information upon which he based it, are impossible to determine, but according to what he later was to tell such associates as Alex Raffio, his success depended upon the anticipated approval of President Richard Nixon. What Wilson told Raffio was a highly inaccurate version of TF 157's origin and mission, colored for his own purposes. The core of his story was that Nixon had ordered TF 157 created soon after taking office, for two reasons. (While the genesis of TF 157 was a directive from President Kennedy in 1962, the actual force came into formal existence in August 1968, five months before Nixon became president.)

Nixon, according to Wilson, felt that the CIA had waged a subterranean war against him both when he was Vice President and during the 1968 campaign, and that it was a creature of the detested "Eastern establishment" which he had fought his entire political life. Given the determination of Nixon and his national security adviser, Dr. Henry Kissinger, to shape and control their own foreign policy, they needed sources of intelligence separate from the formal State Department/CIA Defense Department apparatus. By Wilson's account, Nixon and Kissinger used TF 157 as the secure communications channel for the most delicate foreign-policy initiative of the first term: Kissinger's secret journey to the People's Republic of China to arrange the subsequent presidential visit in 1972. (The germ of truth in this Wilson story lies in the fact that the Navy historically has maintained the most secure communications system of any of the military services, for naval warfare depends upon maintaining secrecy of the whereabouts of fleets. That Nixon-Kissinger used the Navy for China messages would not be unlikely. But persons formerly associated with TF 157 say the force simply did not have such a capability.)

Wilson's long-term plan, as he confided it, was to build his part of TF 157 into such a formidable intelligence-gathering operation that he could become head of the entire organization. Then, he said, he intended to challenge the CIA for supremacy in the American intelligence community. He wanted TF 157 to be "operational"—that is, to run paramilitary missions—as well as collective. In due course, Wilson said, he would put together a supportive coalition—in Congress, in the military, even in the White House—that would enable him to carry out his dream.

Most persons who listened to various forms of Wilson's idea came away with mixed impressions. One man wrote it off as "nut talk, the 'I'll-get-even' rantings of a guy who didn't make it at CIA, and who now had the harebrained notion he could overthrow the whole damned organization. This overlooks much reality. This talk, remember, was coming from a GS-13 who wasn't even known outside ONI—and not very well known inside ONI itself, for that matter. To me it sounded like a priest in some rural Pennsylvania parish talking about overthrowing the Pope." Another former associate felt that "Ed talked that way to try to impress people with his importance. I'd hear this and I'd say, 'Uh-huh, that's fine, Ed. Now what about this contract for such-and-such?' and try to bring him back to reality. But he thought he was impressing people."

Whatever the reality of Wilson's plan, he seemed to have convinced himself of its feasibility. Success is an infectious condition, and Wilson's progress with Consultants International by mid-1975 gave him cause for pride. He and wife Barbara steadily added to their real estate holdings, piling property atop property. Wilson had the unique position of prestige in his chosen business world with no outside publicity—his name got into many important address books, but not into the newspapers. But then he found himself in a situation not unlike that of an executive of a conglomerate corporation: True satisfaction is achieved only through continuous growth. So the ever-restless Wilson always had his antennae at the ready, quick to reach out to a person who might be of commercial advantage.

4

Alex Meets Ed

In 1974, Alexander W. Raffio was a Middle Eastern sales executive for Fairchild Cameras, Inc., based in Teheran, Iran. Raffio had come a long way in his twenty-eight years. A native of Manhattan, where he was born January 31, 1946, Raffio had spent his childhood in the Westchester County suburb of Pelham, and had graduated from Fordham College with majors in history and political science. A stocky, aggressive man who vented some of his energies through competitive rowing, Raffio was strong-minded in support of his beliefs, even when unpopular. For instance, although Fordham was a Jesuit school with a strict tradition, as a big-city college it attracted a predominantly liberal student body. During the 1964 presidential campaign, Alex Raffio was one of the few students who had proudly worn a Barry Goldwater button, even though "guys I had known for years stopped speaking to me."

Upon graduation, with a pregnant wife and no money, Raffio had abandoned plans for law school and became contract officer for an engineering firm that did much work for the Federal Government. In this position—and in succeeding more responsible jobs—Raffio learned the realities of business bargaining, especially as pertains to government.

The term "government contract" connotes something far more concrete than actually exists. In theory, a contract obligates one party to perform a service for another party, for a stated fee. In reality, a government contract is but the starting point for ongoing bargaining. The specifications for the job to be done—"specs," in industry jargon—can be changed overnight; so too can be such things as delivery schedules and quantities. The system is imperfect but perhaps unavoidable: In defense work, technology grows by leaps and bounds, and what was vaguely feasible when a contract was signed may be outdated within a year. Hence in a defense company the contracts officer is a key figure. He knows how to wheedle, how to demand trade-offs, how to push his governmental adversary to the limit without alienating him.

Raffio learned these traits, and some natural abilities helped him along. He is a natural actor: he can feign rage; he can talk like a friendly priest one moment and an infuriated *mafioso* the next, shifting into commensurate facial expressions. Raffio is a mimic: on the telephone he can make a smooth transition from W. Courtney Mellenham III, visiting British lord, to Billy Al Randolph, an Alabama redneck in town to "check out the local pussy." And, finally, Raffio is an electronics natural, a man with an instant grasp of both the theory *and* the practicalities of communications.

A series of events in 1974 had landed Raffio in Teheran, then in the turbulent last days of the Shah's reign. Raffio was not particularly happy. Fairchild had transferred him from sybaritic Beirut, where he liked to lounge at a poolside café during lunch and inspect the latest bikini styles with the lush coastal Levant background shielded from the desert by mountains, lapped gently by the sparkling blue Mediterranean. Teheran, by contrast, was a hot, dusty and dreary inland city squeezed of any gaiety by political strife and the hypocrisy of Moslem rulers who imposed their religion on the masses with no diminution of their own sensual pleasures. The Shah's many relatives seemed to stand at the door of every office, corrupt hands outstretched for bribes. Recurring problems with higher-ups in Fairchild also plagued Raffio. And, as a final symptom of irritation, his marriage was rocky.

So it was a disgruntled Raffio who sat in an anteroom of the Iran General Supply Company on Soraya Avenue in February 1974, waiting for a meeting with Feydoun Bozorgmeir, Fairchild's Iranian agent. Suddenly he heard loud shouts from an inner office.

"You guys fucked this whole deal, you're fired, you're a bunch of worthless bastards." a voice screamed.

The door swung open and slammed into the wall. Raffio looked up to see an immense man, perhaps six feet four inches tall, "way over two hundred pounds, so big that his clothes actually hung off him."

Bozorgmeir ran out behind the big man, and Raffio put his hand over his mouth to stifle a laugh at the contrast. The Iranian, short and balding, had to look up to the American; he was fawning, obviously wishing to make peace. "Mister Ed, can't we make an accommodation on this thing? I am so sorry. . . ."

The American, nostrils flaring, continued cursing. "You dumb asshole, you . . ."

At this juncture the Iranian company's other partner, Victor Bakhitar, heard the commotion and stepped into the outer office. He raised a questioning hand. Suave, Western-educated, Bakhitar exuded authority. He nudged Bozorgmeir away, saying, "Mister Ed, surely we can talk this over during lunch at the French Club. Would you be so kind as to join me there in a few minutes as my guest?" The American nodded assent. Bakhitar continued, "Now, if you would be so kind as to permit me a few moments to chat with my partner . . ." He put his hand on Bozorgmeir's shoulder and steered him back into the inner office.

As Iranian shouts came from behind the closed door, Wilson sighed and settled himself into a chair alongside Raffio and said, "You know these creeps?"

"Yeah," Raffio said, "unfortunately. They're our Iranian agents, but not for long." Wilson stuck out his hand. "I'm Ed Wilson," He gave Raffio his Consultants International card. "Give me a ring at the Kings Hotel this evening; we'll have dinner." By this time the Iranians had reappeared, and

Wilson left with them, giving Raffio a wink over his shoulder as he departed.

That evening Wilson sounded out Raffio's background, and was obviously impressed with what he heard. "So about halfway through the dinner, he pitches me: 'Hey, look, we could use a guy like you, a guy with your natural ability. You could make a lot of money for yourself. All you have to do is a few things for us.'"

Raffio was bemused. "Ed was always a guy who wanted to minimize his costs, so I was a find to him, because here I am, based in Teheran, all my expenses paid. He figures that he can recruit me to do whatever he has to do for Consultants International and he doesn't have to pay flight fares and hotel bills and everything else." Despite the briefness of the exposure, "I recognized Wilson as an operator and a manipulator."

Raffio shook his head at Wilson, "Hey, how do I represent myself one day to SAVAK as Alex Raffio, Fairchild, and the next day as Alex Raffio, Consultants International? You just can't do that kind of thing. There's no way I can have two masters."

Wilson did not argue—that evening, at least—and the dinner progressed pleasantly. Wilson had a raconteur's delight in stories and gossip about the Iranian military and his connections with ranking officers. He seemed especially well connected with the navy, which had undergone three major shake-ups in two years. The last was precipitated when the Shah and his wife attended a reception at which an admiral's wife was sporting an enormous jewel. The Shah's wife had been shown the gem, and decided not to buy it because of the price. According to subsequent Teheran gossip, she told the Shah later that night, "Dear, did you see the big jewel on the admiral's wife? His hand must be in the till." There was an investigation, the admiral was found to have taken bribes and he was dismissed.

Wilson told Raffio that he had found ways of walking around such roadblocks as corruption investigations. He claimed to be in Teheran at the behest of Admiral Thomas H. Moorer, the Chief of Naval Operations (and thereby the ranking officer in the U.S. Navy) to sell the Iranians a research vessel. Wilson gave Raffio few details—baiting Raffio rather than briefing him. He did say that the Iranians really did not need the vessel, they had bought it solely to ingratiate themselves with the American Navy, and that Wilson made a substantial profit from the deal. "I had been around Teheran long enough to sense tall tales," Raffio said. "Based on my experience, Wilson had the place wired. He could make things happen. The Iranians obviously felt he had some sort of high-level connections."

As Wilson explained to Raffio, "I keep my home base in Washington, but to do business you've got to get out and stir the pot. I spend half my time running around the world— here, Lebanon, Egypt, all over the Middle East. I even get out to Asia a lot." The early and middle 1970s were especially lucrative years for defense salesmen in Iran, where the beleaguered Shah was trying to shore up his government with modern military technology.

Wilson contacted Raffio from time to time during subsequent visits to Teheran, each time repeating his offer that Raffio become his agent. To Raffio, the most impressive Wilson display was his familiarity with the so-called "black areas" of the U.S. Embassy.

As television viewers learned during the hostage crisis of 1979-80, the U.S. Embassy occupied a vast, walled compound. To the rear of the main office building, past the commissary, was a row of one-story stucco buildings surrounded by a chain-link fence and guarded by Marines wearing pistols. Raffio knew that this "black area" existed, and he had a good idea of its function: communications, radio intercepts, cryptoanalysis and some activities that might be summed up as "protective electronic measures." Given it's location, on the periphery of both the Soviet Union and the Arab states to the south, the "black room" of the Teheran embassy surely was one of the more secretive of all American intelligence installations.

Ed Wilson walked Raffio through the barriers with the aplomb of a tour guide showing someone the sights of Washington. "I'm Wilson, and he's with me," he would say, gesturing toward Raffio, who recalls: "We would walk right in, and he would introduce me all around. I knew many of the black-area officers from the officers' club and embassy functions; but there was *no way* that Alex Raffio was going to be permitted to go back there on his own. Wilson had phenomenal contacts."

Wilson further reinforced his position as an "in" person at

the U.S. Embassy by finding Raffio a secretary—the daughter of an American general who worked for Consultants International. Because of the sensitive nature of his work, Raffio needed a non-Iranian, and the woman—fluent in Farsi, as well as other languages—"was perfect."

On another occasion, Wilson took Raffio to dinner with a man whom he identified as "Tom, the head Navy spook." As Raffio was to learn, this man was a high official of Task Force 157.

That Ed Wilson had such ready access to intelligence facilities and personnel was impressive but did not seem particularly unusual to Raffio. In most foreign stations, the relationship between American industry and American intelligence is symbiotic. During his own work in defense sales, Raffio had worked closely with both CIA and the National Security Agency (NSA). Many of the items that Raffio sold required clearance by either or both of the agencies. During his trips back to the United States, he underwent routine debriefings both at CIA offices in Langley and Rosslyn, Virginia, and at NSA facilities at Fort Meade and elsewhere in Maryland. NSA's message, in brief, was "Look, we'll help you get your export license through and we'll give you this kind of aid." In return, NSA wished to know what Middle Eastern intelligence agencies were requesting. Such contacts saved both parties immense amounts of trouble. "For example, if I walked into Morocco cold, and I had a good buddy at NSA who could give me a good idea of what the signal density was like there, how many signals were on the air in VHF, what their threat was, this gave me a good overall picture of what I should offer. Knowing the problem is a large part of sales. NSA in effect was doing my legwork. So in turn, I told them what my clients were asking, and what I was peddling."

Knowing the electronic capabilities of foreign nations enabled NSA to intercept their communications with the same ease by which a private detective puts a tap on a domestic telephone line. "It was always one hand washing the other," said Raffio.

Subterfuge was also involved. For instance, in the last days of the Shah, Iran would not permit U.S. U-2 planes to operate from its air bases, thereby interrupting photoreconnaissance coverage of the U.S.S.R. But the Iranians were quite willing to do their own overflights of the Soviet Union, using photo systems supplied by Raffio's Fairchild Camera. As Raffio states:

"For the first couple of years, Fairchild technicians would be on the ground processing this data. It wouldn't have been hard for them to rip off some of the material they thought was interesting. And, of course, it's a lot better to have the Iranians overfly Russia and create an international incident than it would be for the United States to get caught."

CIA dangled interesting propositions before Raffio and other defense salesmen in the Middle East and elsewhere. If salesmen agreed to make regular reports to CIA, and to accept intelligence-gathering missions, the Agency would "pick up all the costs of that local marketing office. It has the advantage for the contractor [the defense company] that he gets a man in the Middle East for nothing. The salesman is still working at least fifty to sixty percent for the company. So they don't really lose. On top of that, he has all the contacts he needs."

Eventually, Raffio decided to pay closer heed to Wilson's oft-repeated suggestions that they become partners. One reason was Raffio's disillusionment with the contacts that his predecessors had developed in Teheran. To a man, they were worthless siphons who took money and delivered no deals. Raffio had come to loathe the Persian businessmen with their expressions such as *Ghorbanish shoman* (I dedicate myself to you) and *Chash, chash, mikonam* (Aye, aye, sir). "These Farsi phrases were cues to fear for your money or your life. You heard them, you asked, 'Where are the long knives?'"

And doing business in Teheran meant paying bribes to a bag man—the intermediary who would pocket money that *supposedly* went to the high official who could approve a contract. Many self-styled influence peddlers took the money and disappeared. And, obviously, salesmen such as Raffio had no recourse. A separate bag man—"they liked the professional term 'agent'"—was necessary for each deal—army, navy, internal security, "even for the goddamned grocer or laundry-man." When Raffio arrived in Teheran, an American Army major in the embassy predicted that within four months Raffio would be surviving only with the aid of Scotch whiskey. The major was right. "I was twenty-nine, my hair was receding, but my mind was holding, if not firm. Ed Wilson seemed like a breath of fresh air in a country that thrived on red tape, black markets and *baksheesh* (tips, by dictionary definition; bribery, by common usage). Wilson could deal with the top people—I mean the people who ran things, not just their assistants—on a moment's notice. We'd crawl a deal through in eight, ten months. Wilson's deals zipped through immediately. Most impressive."

Realizing that Wilson's contacts far surpassed those bequeathed to him by Fairchild, Raffio struck a deal: on any contracts that resulted from Wilson's introduction, Wilson would receive a percentage cut. In Raffio's view, both he and Fairchild would profit. When Wilson mentioned someone over dinner, it was in the context of his function or usefulness on future projects. Realizing he was playing with the devil, Raffio let his fellow American pick up the tab for lavish meals, all the while jotting the names and phone numbers of Wilson's contacts into his address book. "In my heart, I knew that someday Ed would call the chits," Raffio realized. "But someday seemed far away in comparison with the exigencies of the present."

Yet once Raffio struck his bargain, he could not carry through. The Fairchild hierarchy, half a world away in Syosset, New York, scoffed at his claims of new contacts. Stick with "our crowd," they said, meaning the agents they had used for years. Raffio protested in vain that he had been given *carte blanche* to exploit invaluable assets.

Raffio's next frustration—his terminal one, as far as Fairchild was concerned—began with a program devised by CIA's Operations Directorate to siphon dollars out of such oil-rich nations as Iran. Stated United States policy at the time was to curtail sales to Middle Eastern states hostile to Israel. But as was explained to Raffio by Frank Long, a former CIA operative then with Fairchild, CIA was running a project (by direction of the National Security Council) "to select certain contractors who had a high expertise in certain areas and help them sell high-dollar projects surreptitiously." The goal was to retrieve some $20 billion that the United States was spending for Middle Eastern oil. Some of the deals were to be made through CIA proprietary companies; others through such established (and trusted) defense contractors as Fairchild.

In June 1974, a high Fairchild executive came to Iran to sell the air force a sophisticated "real-time photoreconnaissance system." Any air force of note has photointelligence;

the key to its usefulness is fast development and dissemination. Fairchild offered to build a facility at the air base in Doushintabi that would develop and analyze the film within hours. As an extra feature, the pods containing the cameras were so configurated that they would fit onto the wings of a variety of aircraft (most other pods were designed for specific planes). The contract would net Fairchild about $100 million.

Raffio was told nothing about the contract proposal, nor the reason the Fairchild executive was visiting Teheran. His instructions were to contact Henry Precht, first secretary of the United States Embassy (and a luncheon friend) and ask him to arrange a meeting for the Fairchild executive with a General Toufanian, head of Iranian military procurement. Fairchild told Raffio the visit would be a "courtesy call." Since Fairchild, a major U.S. corporation, did considerable business in Iran, Precht was happy to comply. Raffio also knew Precht as the embassy contact with SAVAK, the Shah's secret police. "We weren't kissing buddies or anything like that," Raffio said, "but he knew that I was doing business with SAVAK, and obviously SAVAK told him, 'Yeah, this guy's got something we're interested in. So send us this Fairchild man.' "

Unbeknownst to Raffio, General Toufanian was being simultaneously advised by his bag man, one Hindu Ja, that an official of the U.S. Embassy would call upon him and ask him to approve a "proposal of great importance to the joint interest of Iran and the United States." Thus, when Precht telephoned, Toufanian interpreted his innocuous call as an official suggestion of the U.S. government that the project be favorably considered. Precht in fact never mentioned the project, an omission which Toufanian undoubtedly wrote off as diplomatic discretion. The Fairchild executive was not so restrained; he gave a strong sales pitch for the reconnaissance project, and seemingly convinced Toufanian.

Someone in Fairchild goofed, for a formal contract proposal was never submitted to the Iranians. In a classic left-hand/right-hand blunder, the Fairchild executive contacted Raffio and asked him once more to have Precht arrange a meeting for him with General Toufanian. Precht resisted. Such contacts, he told Raffio, could just as well be made through the military advisory group. But given their friendship, Precht finally agreed to make another phone call, although Raffio sensed that he "was being pushed, used."

Toufanian readily agreed to see the Fairchild executive again, but he asked Precht, "Why has not the Fairchild air-reconnaissance proposal been delivered? We have anxiously awaited it."

"What proposal?" Precht asked.

Toufanian replied, "The Fairchild proposal that the American government wished us to accept. You should know it— you arranged the meeting with the man from Fairchild."

Precht, livid, denied knowledge of the deal, and immediately went to Ambassador Richard Helms, the former director of Central Intelligence. The cable traffic between Washington and Teheran was busy, and biting. "The bottom line," Raffio says ruefully, "is that someone had to be the sacrificial lamb. Guess who?" Fairchild kept Raffio on salary through 1974 as a "consultant," but he never went near its offices.

Casting about for a new job, Raffio remembered Ed Wilson, and Wilson's constant solicitations: "Come with me; I'll make you rich." Raffio visited the National Security Agency near Washington for his final debriefing, then drove into downtown and told Wilson about the Fairchild snafu. Raffio did not plead; he simply said to Wilson, "I don't want to be a scapegoat and be blacklisted as a result of this thing. Can you help?" Wilson thought he could; he would talk "to my old friend Ted Shackley, out at CIA."

Whether Wilson or Shackley had any hand in Raffio's subsequently obtaining a job with the Standard Dredging Company, based in Baltimore, is impossible to establish. By Raffio's account, he answered a blind advertisement in *The Wall Street Journal*, as one of three hundred applicants, and was hired. The position was director of operations in the Middle East, where Standard Dredging had many projects under way. "I didn't know the first thing about dredging, but I did have contract and marketing experience. That's why I was hired," Raffio said. But Raffio's boss was a retired admiral, Edgar Keats, and Wilson, with a nudge and a smile, frequently told Raffio, "Hey, ol' fellow, we Navy people stick together, and I'm glad to have brought you aboard." Raffio preferred to think that he obtained the job on his own merits.

Raffio had been with Standard Dredging only a short time when Ed Wilson—just as Raffio had foreseen—decided to "call in a chit" for past favors. During a conversation one day in the Consultants International offices, Wilson said, "I want you to go to Iraq. You have a contract in Iraq. We've got some intelligence problems there, and I'm running an operation there now and I'd like to get you involved in the thing."

"Intelligence operation? What are you talking about? You keep telling me you are a 'consultant.' " Raffio said.

Wilson laughed and got up and closed the door to the outer office. He pulled a chair close to Raffio and leaned forward, as if ready to disclose a deep secret. "A lot of this stuff," he said "is cover for a naval intelligence operation— Task Force 157. I work for them; these other businesses bring in some good money, but they're mainly to provide cover."

Wilson then proceeded to give Raffio his highly colored background sketch of TF 157: that President Nixon had personally ordered its creation soon after taking office.

By Wilson's account, he ran the "Middle East desk" of Task Force 157, and persons such as Raffio could be most useful in helping him gather intelligence there. Wilson mentioned the mysterious "Tom" to whom he had introduced Raffio in the Middle East. " 'Tom' is my boss," Wilson told Raffio. "You'll be working directly under me, but Tom is over both of us."

Wilson winked and gave Raffio a soft punch on the knee. "Remember this too, old buddy: you make points when you do little errands like this. And in this business, points are convertible into deals, and deals mean money. Follow?"

Indeed Raffio did follow, although he was not sure how much, if any, of Wilson's story to believe. One part of Raffio wanted to accept Wilson's mission; a touch of the spook and soldier of fortune was in his spirit. Yet Raffio had practical reasons to say no. Yes, Standard Dredging did have some projects in progress in Iraq and its coastal waters, and yes, Raffio should visit there eventually. But he was still learning his job, and Standard Dredging had major operational problems in the offshore oil fields in the Gulf of Mexico. "I can't just pack up and leave Ed Keats by himself right now," he argued. "Besides, there's a hell of a lot of bad blood between Iran and Iraq. And if Iraq has any intelligence service at all—they do, by the way, Ed; you know that—they'll pick me up in an instant. Hell, my whole passport is crammed with Iranian visas." So he said, "Thanks, but no thanks."

Wilson grunted something to the effect that "you're

making a big mistake, because I'm giving you a helluva opportunity, my friend," and did not press the issue further.

To Raffio's surprise, several days later Admiral Keats walked into his office and said, "I want you to go to Iraq." Keats offered no explanation other than to say, "Check out what's going on there; make sure the dredges are doing what they should do." Raffio surmised two things: that Wilson had gone to Keats directly, and that Keats was either aware of TF 157, or connected with it.

Wilson, for his part, simply glossed over the matter the next time he spoke with Raffio. "I hear you're going out East," he said. "I don't want you to do anything in the way of intelligence on this trip. I want you to just get you water wings, feel your way around, find out what's going on. See how it is getting in and out, and know how to get out if you *have* to get out. But I'm not going to give you any specific targets at this point." It was a textbook briefing for an agent making a dry run on a mission.

Standard Dredging had two contracts in Iraq at the time, both through the Brown & Root Construction Company of Texas—with the Basrah Petroleum company and with Iraqi National Oil. Both companies were expanding their offshore terminals to accommodate supertankers, and Standard Dredging's job was to widen the channels so that four vessels, rather than two, could load simultaneously.

Although Raffio traveled ostensibly on Standard Dredging business, he thought it interesting that Wilson's Consultants International paid for his air ticket. Access to the dredging sites was by air to either Baghdad or Kuwait, where a Brown & Root car would meet passengers for a daily run to Basrah, on the coast near the oil facilities. Raffio visited the site three or four times during 1975, talking with supervisors and trying to learn something of his new profession. He realized on the first trip that his visits were useless insofar as Standard Dredging was concerned. "We had a qualified dredge superintendent who knew exactly what he was doing." With the survivor's instinct honed by years in the Middle East, Raffio did note that he was under surveillance—presumably by Iraqi intelligence—as he made his rounds. But although he traveled on the passport containing Iranian visas, he was not harassed.

Finally, in late 1975, Wilson again broached the subject

of intelligence, this time in terms of a specific mission for Raffio. Among his TF 157 duties, Wilson stated, was "tagging and tracking all Russian Navy vessels and any naval threat throughout the Middle East."

Raffio shook his head in wonder. Given the multiplicity of Wilson's other activities, how did he find time to play spook for the U.S. Navy? "Jesus Christ, Ed," Raffio said, "you've got to be bullshitting me."

"No, I'm not. I've been doing this since '72. Now I'm telling you what I want you to do for me—for the United States government. We've got some problems in Iraq, as I mentioned to you earlier. We are led to believe through some intelligence sources, which we find hard to credit, that the Russians are constructing a submarine base at the top of the Persian Gulf."

Raffio knew the gulf area intimately; he also found trouble with the report. "Way too shallow for submarines," he told Wilson. "We have to keep our dredges busy to get the oil tankers up there. There's no way the Soviets could run subs to the top of the Gulf."

Nonetheless, Wilson told Raffio, the National Security Council wanted the reassurance of a "positive negative"—that is, fact rather than surmise. Satellite pictures showed construction in the shore area, but the resolution was so poor that analysts could not decide what was being built. An overflight by a conventional aircraft was considered too risky, given the volatility of the area. Raffio agreed to scout it.

After some thought, Raffio came out with an approach to the mission. Standard Dredging had posted a standard performance bond at the outset of the dredging project. Some months before completion, however, the company had lost a small tugboat in the Gulf during a storm. The Iraqis had announced they intended to hold the bond so that they could pay off any damage claims. Unless Standard Dredging located the ship, and guaranteed that it was not a menace to shipping, the bond would not be returned.

So Raffio took a small launch with sonar equipment to the area where the tug had been lost and began a series of sweeps in ever-widening circles. The entire coastal area was perhaps fifty kilometers, and the Standard Dredging base was no more than fifteen kilometers from the supposed submarine base, which was near the Kuwaiti border. Iraqi patrol boats watched the Standard Dredging launch with obvious interest, and as it neared the suspect area they reacted swiftly.

Raffio heard the SMACK-SMACK-SMACK of naval cannon, and the swish of shells overhead. He dived for the deck as the warning barrage splashed into the water several hundred yards distant. The Iraqi boats came alongside, and an officer shouted, "Get back; you are in a restricted area. Get back."

"We're looking for a sunken goddamned boat, and we have your goddamned government's permission," an angry Raffio yelled back. The shouting to and fro went through several rounds; each time, Raffio's boat drifted closer to the shore. As he screamed at the Iraqis, his eyes searched the coastline. He could see construction, but nothing resembling a submarine base. His simulated rage apparently convinced the Iraqis of his legitimacy; they let him continue searching for the sunken boat. Over the next three days, Raffio got close enough to shore to convince himself that "nothing of merit was there," and that the Iraqis had been upset chiefly because his boat had come close to the disputed border with Kuwait.

Trying to confirm this finding, Raffio later tried to drive down the coastal highway to the site, but was turned away by border guards. He pretended to be lost, and the Iraqi soldiers politely gave him directions back to Basrah.

Another task on this trip was to try to identify any Soviet ships that Raffio saw in the Gulf. Wilson had given him a cram course in the configurations of various types of Russian vessels—how to distinguish, for instance, between an electronics intelligence ship and a communications vessel. Given Raffio's knowledge of electronics, and the differing antennae used for such functions, he easily committed the silhouettes to memory (he refused to take any ship-identification charts with him to Iraq, for fear they would be discovered at customs).

But other missions Raffio absolutely refused. Wilson asked him to try to recruit Iraqi nationals to work for American intelligence. Raffio felt such a task to be so risky as to be suicidal. If he lived in the country perhaps eighteen months, he could develop reliable sources, but as an in-and-out visitor, he was in no position to make trusted contacts. The one Iraqi he knew who openly expressed pro-American feelings was so outspoken that Raffio dismissed him as an intelli-

ones that eventually would result in war hero Paul Cyr's becoming a disgraced and convicted felon.

As Wilson explained the scenario to Raffio, he had "my good friend Paul Cyr, a Pentagon lobbyist," contact Senator Stennis, who by now was even more firmly entrenched in the Senate Armed Services Committee. What arrangements Wilson made with Cyr are not a matter of record, but Wilson was not reticent with Raffio. "You realize," Wilson said when the deal was still a possibility, "that this is going to cost you ten percent"—meaning that 10 percent of the gross proceeds would be due to Wilson as a "finder's fee." "Sure, no problem," Raffio said. "We get this contract, ten percent is yours." Both men realized that payment of such a fee to obtain a government contract is a felony, but Raffio and Wilson wanted business.

Raffio later was to encounter Paul Cyr in another situation in which the borders of morality were not quite so fuzzy. In late 1977—by now Raffio worked for Wilson full time, mostly in Washington—Raffio had four Middle Eastern nations interested in buying a "night driving scope" for tanks, trucks and jeeps. What Raffio wished to do was take the British night driving scope, the best on the market, and put in a smaller tube, cutting the three-foot length by about half and increasing the lens power. An official in the Chrysler Corporation's tank division told Raffio that yes, indeed, he would be interested in the improved night driving scope, and even offered to test it on M-60 and XM-1 tanks at the Aberdeen Proving Ground in Maryland—once Raffio had samples in hand.

Raffio's scheme involved the cutting and refitting of a U.S. Army scope and the grafting on of other features. Duplicating the basic U.S. Army scope would cost about £100,000, but if he had a sample scope to use in his workshop, Raffio could do his improved model for perhaps £25,000. Raffio casually mentioned his need to Wilson. "No problem," Wilson replied, "I'll get you one of those. I know how to get these things. You let me handle it."

Raffio's dinner that evening was interrupted by a phone call from Paul Cyr, who said he had a military friend who would "borrow" one of the desired scopes "from inventory" from an Army arsenal in Virginia.

Raffio up to this time had been involved in Wilson deals

that cut close to the quick of the law, but what Cyr proposed was a clear-cut crime. He told Cyr, "Hey, look, I have never violated U.S. law in my life, not intentionally. This is theft of government property. And since these things are worth more than five thousand dollars a shot, we're talking felony theft. Don't get me involved in this."

Wilson later joshed Raffio for being naive. Given Cyr's contacts, the disappearance of a single driving scope could have been attributed to a "computer error" in warehouse inventories. "Ed Wilson could laugh about jail. I didn't want to try it."

Wilson kept his contacts on constant display. One time Raffio mentioned to Wilson that a business friend was interested in bidding on electronics equipment desired by a particular Army command. Could Wilson be of help? Indeed he could. He arranged a luncheon meeting at the Crystal City Marriott in Arlington with Raffio and the contractor. As Wilson put it, he knew the Army colonel who within the next several weeks was to become Inspector General for the command in question. A military IG has extraordinarily broad powers to investigate the slightest hint of wrongdoing. This particular colonel, according to Wilson, proposed a sham. "He was going to feign an anonymous letter stating that he should look into the procurement. He would investigate his own letter. By doing so, he would be able to get the pricing information and then Wilson would feed it back to us. We could come in at a better price and obtain the contract." The contract was worth about $15 million. Wilson wanted 10 percent. The colonel's share would have been about $500,000. "Wilson said the colonel was willing to do this because he was, like, two years away from retirement and this was going to be his retirement fund."

The deal fell through because Raffio's contractor friend was unwilling to put up $10,000 to $15,000 in advance without any guaranteed results. Raffio would not fault either party. "In this sort of situation, you rely upon trust. And since the entire foundation of the deal is crooked, you have to protect yourself."

But the scope of the Wilson operation—Wilson's ability to find a cooperative "friend" in almost any agency of the U.S. government—dazzled Raffio, and reinforced his conviction that Wilson must have continuing ties with the intelligence community. "There was nobody, in terms of defense procurement, that Wilson couldn't get to," Raffio said. "I was truly amazed when I saw the extent to which he had a web woven throughout Washington."

5

Down on the Farm

The first months of their relationship, Raffio had no direct obligations to Wilson, other than their infrequent commercial deals together. Tired of living in the United States—Standard Dredging was being sold to a larger firm, and Raffio himself was in the last throes of a bitter divorce—the ambitious electronics specialist was attempting to put together his own deals in Europe and the Middle East. Because he did not yet work directly for Wilson, Raffio could deal with him at arm's length. And perhaps because Raffio had no direct connections with the intelligence community—save for his occasional odd jobs for Task Force 157—Wilson gave him glimpses into his personal life that were afforded no other associate.

The contacts began casually. Raffio, having business in Washington, would telephone Wilson at midday and ask him to dinner. Wilson would generally respond along the lines "I'm busy until early evening, but come on over to the office at 1425 K Street, use the phone, I'll pick you up and we'll grab a bite and spend the night at the farm." So Raffio would sit around Consultants International and probe the retired generals and admirals about their various deals, and then in early evening strike out across Northern Virginia en route to Wilson's Upperville estate.

Although Wilson earned a six-figure income, he cared little for fancy food or drink. "He was happy to stop at a taco place or a god-awful Chinese place in Middleburg," Raffio recalled. Putting food into Wilson's body was a function akin to buying gasoline for his car: As long as it kept the machinery functioning, he couldn't have cared less about the details. "A steak-and-potatoes man," Raffio described him.

Raffio and other visitors noted two things immediately about the Upperville estate, Mount Airy Farm. It was a comfortably luxurious place, with Persian carpets on the hardwood floors and four-poster beds in the many upstairs bedrooms. Winslow Turner paintings adorned the downstairs walls, and the silver and china were solid and heavy. Spur-of-the-moment guests did not have to worry about such things as toiletries: The bathroom cabinets contained fresh toothbrushes, razors, deodorant. If Wilson decided to take a guest hunting, or on a ride outside Mount Airy, he could even find a close-enough fit in outdoor clothing. But the genteel atmosphere was sullied by constant wrangling between Ed and Barbara Wilson. Visitors grew accustomed to hearing angry, loud arguments when Wilson would bring unexpected guests home for the evening. One shout heard more than once, from the upper floors of the mansion, was Barbara's raging question "When are you going to consider *me*?" Wilson would reply, in his own shout, "This is *my* house, goddamn it, and I'll bring home anyone I please."

In the actual presence of guests, Barbara and Ed Wilson treated each other with crisp hostility. One woman guest had the ill fortune to remark to Barbara, "I am sorry if our being here has put you out." A Southerner, the woman intended her comment as a means of patching over a tense social situation. To her discomfort, Barbara replied dourly, "That's all right—*everybody* puts me out."

Even such longtime personal friends as Howard Wickham and his wife felt distinct changes in both Wilson and his marriage during the 1970s. In Wilson's first years at Mount Airy, Wickham recalls, "Ed was the kind of guy who'd say, 'Hey, come on out to the farm this weekend; bring the kids. There's a pond to fish in, and horses to ride. . . .' You'd find yourself helping Ed set fence posts. He remained the same natural, outgoing friendly guy I'd known at Quantico." But Wickham realized that Wilson's natural gregariousness was putting strains on the marriage. "Barbara never knew how many people would show up for dinner on a given day. You'd go out there and twenty, maybe thirty people would be around, and she'd be in the kitchen cooking vast pots of spaghetti. These were two strong-willed people, so I suppose some clashes were inevitable." Eventually Wickham and his wife decided not to accept any more of Wilson's informal invitations, for they did not wish him or Barbara to think they were taking advantage of their hospitality.

What Wilson associates knew—even if Barbara did not at the time—was that her husband was enjoying steady sex outside his marital bed. Wilson worked with a handicap. A lingering low-grade venereal disease he had contracted in Asia was causing him constant prostate trouble (he had a standing order for medication from London during his later exile days in Libya), and he would complain, "For me, ejaculation is like having fire come out of my pecker." Nonetheless, Wilson had a voracious appetite for women. He found them in his own office, he found them in his travels; if all else failed, he would please himself with a prostitute. Wilson had several convenient locations in Washington for his philandering. To accommodate foreign business visitors, Wilson maintained an apartment in comfortable River House, just across the Potomac in Arlington, Virginia. Many afternoons, Wilson would drop into the downtown Consultants International, a woman with him, and then say, "I'm going across the river on this deal" —his signal that River House was not to be disturbed the next hours. Another trysting place was a town house he purchased with Consultants International funds on 22nd Street Northwest, near Pennsylvania Avenue, on the west fringe of downtown. Although set up as a business office, the town house became Wilson's personal retreat; at least one of his revolving paramours felt sufficiently at home there to keep a wardrobe in one of the bedrooms. Again, Wilson was not above telling Barbara on the phone, "I'm not coming out to the farm tonight; I'm staying late for some talks, and I'll stay at a hotel." When the meeting ended, Wilson would conspicuously leave in company with one of his secretaries, or perhaps another woman he did not even bother to introduce.

The growing rift between man and wife, and Wilson's tendency to immerse himself in business to the detriment of all other interests, inevitably affected the two Wilson sons. Karl, the elder, had recurring problems throughout his childhood. Raffio, who has two teenaged sons of his own, felt many of the problems were attributable to the iron hand with which Wilson proudly ran his household. Wilson's attitude, as he frequently stated at the breakfast table, was to the effect "When I was a kid, I worked eighty hours a week; you should be able to do the same, so stop whining." When Raffio first met Karl, he was in his mid-teens, a throw-out from several preparatory schools and living in tense coexistence with his parents at Mount Airy Farm.

"When Karl was kicked out of the last school," Raffio said, "Ed and Barbara said, 'Okay, buddy, that's it—you're going to school out here in Fauquier County with the local farmhands.'"

So each morning, young Karl would arise at five o'clock and walk sleepily into the kitchen. There Barbara would be cooking breakfast for Ed, herself and however many guests happened to be in the house. Son Karl, however, had to fend for himself; what he wished to eat he cooked, and there was no place for him at the table; he ate standing up. All his father and mother contributed to the start of Karl's day was biting comments about the advisability of his "shaping up." If Raffio or another guest had a kind word for Karl, Barbara responded with a tart remark or a dirty look.

One morning was particularly disturbing to Raffio, who had been raised in a family bubbling with Italo-American warmth. Karl overslept. Hurry though he did, he had no chance of sprinting the near-half-mile down the driveway to catch the school bus. Although the farm had more than a half-dozen vehicles, Wilson refused his son's plea for a ride. "You missed the bus, I didn't. Walk or hitchhike—it makes no difference to me."

After Karl left on foot, Raffio could contain his feelings no longer. "You treat your dogs better than you treat your oldest son," he told Wilson.

"I want to make him straighten up and fly right," Wilson said.

"Yeah," Raffio said—"fly right into drugs and an institution."

Which is what in fact happened in the late 1970s. The problems young Karl faced became too arduous for him, and he was committed to a mental-rehabilitation institution in a Maryland suburb of Washington. Wilson was by then living in exile a half-world distant, in Tripoli, Libya, and he told colleagues, with no show of concern, "Karl will never see daylight again."*

The Wilsons' younger son, Erik, was away at boarding school during the period when Raffio visited Mount Airy Farm regularly. But from what the youth was later to indicate to both Raffio and John Heath, another Wilson associate, Erik adored his father as "one of the top men in the world." Erik's adoration was to end disastrously—with his indictment on federal charges of trying to help his father hire killers to dispose of prosecutors and witnesses.

The deterioration of Wilson's marriage seemed to affect him only in the sense that he realized it meant the possible loss of his farm. The first years that he lived there he acted as something of a country squire, eager to show off his acreage to visitors, glib with his talk about the cattle he raised there and how much hay they consumed, comfortable in a pair of cowboy boots, blue jeans and work shirt. He was so proud of his John Deere tractor that at one time he even kept a picture of it on his office wall (where he did not bother to display photographs of Barbara or his two sons). And Wilson talked so enthusiastically about the black Angus cattle he raised at the farm that in later years his code name in the Wilson organization was "Angus."

As farm manager, Wilson hired Douglas M. Schlachter, a high school dropout he happened to meet casually at a service station in Bailey's Crossroads, Virginia, a Washington suburb. Schlachter did some minor mechanical work that impressed Wilson, and he invited him to take care of the farm's machinery. In due course, Schlachter left the service station, which was owned by his brother, and became a full-time employee of the farm. Associates such as Raffio and John Heath described Schlachter as "dumb but dog-loyal to Ed Wilson," which is apparently what Wilson wished; in short order Schlachter had made the rapid progression from gas-pump attendant to one of Wilson's key managers.

---

*Karl, however, fought vigorously against his demons. During Christmas Week 1982, a family friend was delighted to encounter the youth in downtown Washington; they paused for lunch. Karl explained that he had advanced to a program that permitted him to spend several days monthly outside the institution, working on his own. By coincidence or not, Karl's recovery began at about the time his father was convicted and sentenced to such a long term that no one expected to see him outside prison again.

Schlachter, however, was one of the few Wilson employees with the native intelligence to see what was offered, take it and leave in a hurry. For whatever reason, Schlachter could make Wilson pay him a share of deals, and he became a very rich man in relatively short order.

Schlachter did not believe in hiding his new wealth. His fingers sported garish jeweled rings; one man counted eleven on various digits. His wardrobe ranged from coordinated-color polyester to three-piece blue suits, with the tie a bit out of focus. Although married when he first met Wilson, Schlachter seemed compelled to seek younger, flashier women, and to impress them with his importance. One such girlfriend he inherited from Charles Wilson, a swinging Texas congressman who was a frequent guest at Edwin Wilson's Upperville farm. She took responsibility for decorating the 22nd Street townhouse/office complex, and spent an estimated $100,000 on furnishings. In the flush days of 1977–78, Wilson would not question such expenditures; he realized the value of lavish trappings. "Look prosperous," he would say, "and people you deal with know they aren't dealing with a ribbon clerk." But Schlachter emulated Wilson in a vain, almost comical fashion.

One time in May 1978, Alex Raffio was in New York, buying the ground-glass components for night-vision equipment. Schlachter called late one evening. "Ed called from Libya and told me to tell you to get your ass down here [to Washington]," Schlachter said. Raffio protested. His schedule was solid the rest of the week, on business that would make Wilson big money. Schlachter would not listen. "Be here," he said. "Ed says so."

The grousing Raffio drove to Washington the next day and arrived at the town-house office at about 1:30 P.M. No Schlachter. "He's out to lunch," the secretary explained. "He's been gone since about eleven thirty." Raffio cursed and sat and fretted another two hours until an expansive Schlachter returned from lunch. With an imperial wave of his hand—"Jesus, those rings would have dragged down a New Orleans whore," Raffio noted—he directed Raffio to his basement office. The girlfriend followed.

"Alex," Schlachter said, "explain to Tina exactly what we are doing in Libya. She's been working here only a few weeks, and I think she needs a full briefing."

Raffio came out of his chair in a rage. "You idiot," he shouted, "you take me away from serious business for *this*? You are a goddamned show-off. Tell her yourself." Raffio slammed the door when he left.

By late 1978, Schlachter had collected enough from Wilson to consider himself a wealthy man. Wilson thought so much of him that he even sold him a few acres on the corner of the Upperville estate, where Schlachter built himself an imposing house. (Barbara Wilson would gripe to her husband about this "*nouveau-riche*" person living so close to us. I find him despicable. He's a gas-station attendant!" Wilson, himself only a few years away from penury, could give Barbara no sympathy.)

The vastness of the Wilson farm—it is one of the dozen largest in Fauquier County—made it a veritable private hunting preserve, subject only to the occasional interference of an ambitious Virginia state game warden. Ed Wilson, in effect, wrote his own game laws, which permitted such stunts as hunting at night from a truck outfitted with a giant aircraft searchlight. Wilson's "season" was open anytime he cared to go in search of a deer. That this went beyond the pale of Virginia state game laws seemed to disturb few if any of his visitors—general, congressman or senator.

Wilson's favored mode of hunting was to go out in a truck late at night, the sharp-eyed Doug Schlachter at the wheel, and drive around for an hour or so in search of grazing deer. Alex Raffio rode on one of these hunts. (He vividly remembers Schlachter as "a guy with the damnedest night vision I've ever seen, and you must remember that night vision is my field of expertise. Schlachter could drive over these narrow dirt roads without any headlights, going across wooden bridges where one slip meant we were upside-down in a creek.") This particular night, Schlachter drove into the lee of a hill, braked suddenly and turned on the searchlight. The beam's harsh glare froze on a group of deer huddled some 700 yards away. "The light mesmerized them," Raffio said. "They stood and stared." (Such is the reason that "headlighting" is a forbidden mode of hunting throughout the United States— whether the property be public or private.) Schlachter grabbed up his rifle and aimed out the window. "I was sitting in the middle, between Schlachter and Wilson," Raffio said. "The blast of the rifle, confined in the cab, deafened me for hours. But when I looked up, Doug had knocked down a deer. We drove over. Right between the eyes, at better than seven hundred yards."

Both Wilson and Schlachter motioned Raffio back when he approached the fallen deer on foot. They laughed and told a story. A week or so earlier, they had made a similar shot while hunting with Senator Sam Nunn of Georgia. As Schlachter told the story, "The senator walked up to this 'dead deer' and he suddenly jumped up and started kicking. He chased the senator over that fence. Tore hell out of his pants."

Another night, a game warden did happen upon the Wilson hunting truck on a state road that runs near the farm. Schlachter, at the wheel, sped away; he knew that Virginia law permits a warden to confiscate any vehicles and guns used by illegal hunters, in addition to fine and imprisonment. Schlachter beat the warden over a hill, turned out the lights and skidded the truck off the road and through a tangle of brush abutting the stone wall surrounding the farm. The truck stopped six inches from the fence. One congressman sat petrified; Schlachter had to drag him from the cab and boost him over the fence onto the Wilson property. According to what Schlachter told Raffio, he hurried the congressman to the house and hiding. The warden poked around until he found the truck and came to the house; Wilson turned him away at the door, saying he knew of no such vehicle. Then he, Schlachter and the congressman enjoyed a drink and a laugh.

What Wilson did not realize was that such stunts were as repugnant to tradition-minded residents of the Hunt Country as if he had hunted deer with napalm dropped from jet planes. To Wilson the fact that he did not fit into Hunt Country society was irrelevant; the people he wished to impress were generals and senators and CIA officials out from Washington. But Barbara had other aspirations. Although not beautiful, she was considered attractive in an austere sort of way. A tall woman, she dressed in conservative clothes befitting the "Mellon matrons" who were her neighbors. Because she did share ownership of one of the country's largest farms, she would look down on the ladies of smaller houses.

A wife of a former CIA officer who lived a few ridges from the Wilson manse remembers the Sunday afternoon when the Wilsons dropped by for a visit. The former agent and his wife own a trim early-nineteenth-century farmhouse on a knoll high above a sparkling pond, a place of charm and taste. But by the wife's account, Barbara sized up the place by measuring square footage with her eye, rather than observing the Asian artifacts her hosts had accumulated during years in the Far East. "She sniffed, put her nose in the air and said she'd wait for Ed in the car," the woman said. Barbara Wilson thereafter was known in that household as "the Dragon Lady."

To the gentry of Fauquier County, money and family tree mean nothing unless they had been around, and accepted, for a century or so. Regardless of how much money Wilson accumulated through business, and how many acres Barbara Wilson acquired as a real estate broker, they could entertain no realistic hope of being part of what passed as the local "set." To an outsider unwise in the subtle code of the Hunt Country, the sprawling Wilson mansion and its neatly fenced acres denoted prestige. But caste is as keenly defined in the Hunt Country as it was, say, in nineteenth-century Victorian Britain. Barbara Wilson might dress right, and chat politely with the women she met at the quaint little inns and tearooms in Middleburg and Upperville. But to them, she would always be a farmer's daughter from New Jersey who had met her *nouveau-riche* husband while working as a hospital technician.

At times, Wilson would talk of leaving business altogether, "now that I am a rich man," and run for Congress from his Northern Virginia district. Politically Wilson professed to be a "mildly liberal Democrat," which at first seems a surprising declaration, given his military and intelligence background. But as a longtime friend points out, "You must remember that before the military and the CIA, Ed was a poor farm boy who had to work his way through college. Ed knew what it was like to be broke. In fact, I think the fear of being broke again was one thing that constantly drove him."

6

The Libyan Connection

Amazingly for a man who built his business empire through a combination of brashness and an ability to perceive which persons would be receptive to chicanery, Ed Wilson lost his connection with naval intelligence by trying to co-opt the very official who would probably have been the last man in Washington to make deals with a scoundrel.

In the early winter of 1976, Rear Admiral Bobby Ray Inman had been director of the Office of Naval Intelligence for two years. A native of Texas, Inman had spent his entire adult life in the Navy, mostly in intelligence assignments. Inman is blessed with a staggeringly brilliant mind in conceiving how technology can be used in intelligence. He knew the workings of the supersecret code-breaking machines used by the National Security Agency. He dealt with the Navy's portion of the satellite reconnaissance program. Under Inman's aegis, naval intelligence became heavily computerized. Given Inman's brains, he could easily have sold himself to civilian industry for high figures a year. Instead, he chose to serve his country, and he raised his family on an officer's pay—saving for his children's education, putting a few dollars aside for an occasional pleasure.*

One mandate Inman carried into ONI was to ascertain whether naval intelligence had committed abuses that might

---

*In 1981, at Senate confirmation hearings on his nomination to be deputy director of central intelligence, Inman listed a net worth of slightly more than $100,000—most of it representing equity in his family home in Arlington, Virginia. Wilson at the same time was circulating net-worth statements showing his holdings to be roughly 200 times that amount, or $20 million.

get it into deep public and congressional trouble. ONI's proprietary companies were one area of concern. "In February 1976, I had gone through about a year of trying to find out if we had put controls on the money that flows through those companies. I was satisfied that our auditors had done a good job, and that the civilians in the Navy Department and elsewhere had no cause for complaint. These questions, of course, were motivated by Watergate. We did find the flow of funds, but we didn't think to ask the other question of the people who ran the proprietaries: 'What are you doing part time when you are not working for the Navy?' "

One day in February of 1976, Inman went to the office of Senator John McClellan, the Arkansas Democrat who headed the Senate Appropriations Committee, to answer technical questions about the Navy's F-16 fighter program. Inman, with his intelligence background, was the most credible source on how the new plane would counter Soviet aircraft.

As the meeting ended, the Senator told Inman that someone from his office wanted to talk to Inman privately at lunch. The person was a McClellan aide whom Inman knew from past encounters, Charles X. Great. "He was a guy who liked to say he was 'up from hard times,' who had gone to law school at night and was out to get rich in a hurry. He had no scruples that I ever noticed. He had all the earmarks of being a bag man for the Senator."

An admiral who is lobbying a powerful senator for a project dear to his service is in no position to decline such a command luncheon. Inman's intuition told him that a friendly witness might be appropriate for the meeting, so he asked an old Navy friend, working for the committee in retirement, to come along with him. They walked a block or so to a small restaurant on Capitol Hill.

Inman and his friends were still studying their menus when, as Inman put it, "two characters slid into the booth. One was Great; the other was a big guy who took the seat next to me." The man introduced himself as Ed Wilson.

Great carried the first part of the conversation. He was concerned about the Navy's problem of selling the F-16 to Congress at a time when defense spending overall was in jeopardy. "Senator McClellan would like to be helpful. So would my friend and me"—gesturing toward Wilson. "I have a lot of information that could be of value to you." By now Inman's temper was rising a bit. He folded his menu and put it down on the table, then stared directly across at Great. He had a good idea what the next words would be.

"By the way," Great said, "we [again pointing to Wilson] are in the business of selling supplies. We have a lot of small companies that are terrific for getting anything the Navy might need for its offices. If some things would come our way, we are bound to be helpful to you."

Inman, a man who prides himself on having a restrained temper, was at the point of losing it as he listened to Charles Great make such a blatantly dishonest appeal. He was about to leave the restaurant—he and his Navy friend had already exchanged incredulous looks—when Ed Wilson turned to Inman and gave him one of his soft punches on the shoulder. "By the way," he said, "I work for you."

Inman sank back into his seat, "absolutely dumbfounded." He stared at Wilson. "What did you say?"

"I work for you," Wilson repeated. "I run a couple of cover companies for one of your task forces."

Inman thought back to the probe of proprietary companies that he had been conducting the past year. Son of a gun, he thought: so *this* is what these characters do in their spare time. He settled back into his café chair. An intelligence officer knows when it is time to listen. "Oh?" he said. "That's interesting. Tell me more."

As Wilson talked on about Task Force 157 and the wonderful things he was doing around the world, the realization came to Inman that this hulking stranger must know of his overall intention to begin phasing out the proprietaries. To Inman, the intelligence produced did not warrant the risks involved. The task forces might turn out massive volumes of reports, but much such information was little more than marketplace gossip or rumors overheard in waterfront bars. Throughout his career, Inman had been at the cutting edge of the confrontation in the intelligence community between the relative values of humans and machines. Although he appreciated the worth of a good agent, his prejudice was toward electronics and advanced surveillance techniques. And now he was hearing what was tantamount to a bribe offer from an employee of one of the task forces he wished to abolish.

"If you want a really good organization," Wilson said, starting in on his dream plan, "I am the guy you ought to take over to run it. I'm damned good at covert operations. I have sources all over the world. Flow the money to me, and I'll set up a string of cover companies the likes of which you've never seen."

As Inman recounted, "Then he started name-dropping like you never heard." Wilson mentioned "his good friend Ted Shackley out at CIA" and many congressmen and other politicians. He could be "very valuable" to Inman, and he had some ideas about how TF 157 could be restructured. Would Inman care to hear more?

Inman said that he certainly would. "The first thing I did when I got back to the office was ask, 'Who the hell *is* that guy?'" Inman learned that although known in TF 157 as a "troublemaker," Wilson had survived "because he has other people intimidated. He does so much dropping of big names that his superiors are frightened of the influence he claims to wield." Inman then found out about Wilson's problems at CIA, and that the Agency had been happy to strip him from its rolls.

Wilson arrived at Inman's office a week or so later under a full head of bravado. He repeated his claim to be a master of clandestine operations. He thought Inman should disband Task Force 157 and create a new organization, which Wilson would be proud to head. Wilson had an elaborate plan for a new system of covert companies that would shield his activities. Again and again he repeated that he had vast influence with Senator McClellan and other politicians "who can do good things for you and the Navy." At the end of his peroration, Wilson asked that Inman and his wife "come out to my place at Upperville this Sunday and meet the Senator and some other people." Inman declined, saying he had other plans.

The minute Wilson left, Inman ordered that all contracts with Wilson companies be terminated. At first he intended to cancel them outright, but when contracting officers told him they had only a few weeks to run, until the end of April, he simply let them expire. "Had it not been for that chance luncheon," Inman said, "the contracts would have been routinely renewed."

Wilson did not surrender quietly when he heard that Inman was kicking him and his companies out of naval intelligence. He had his good friends Senators Stennis, McClellan and Thurmond—all powers on the Senate Armed Services Committee—write letters to the Chief of Naval Operations and the Secretary of the Navy protesting Inman's action. Inman would not back down. On April 30, 1976, Wilson ceased to be a member of the American intelligence community.

In drunken soliloquies later in the Libyan capital, when he was a fugitive from his own land, Wilson would rage at Inman, calling him, among other things, "a chicken-shit little bastard who was about to pee all over himself, he wanted money so bad, but he was too cowardly to take it." By Wilson's deranged judgment, each problem that came down upon his head after April 1976 was directly attributable to Bobby Ray Inman. "Whatever happened to Edwin Wilson," Inman said, "Edwin Wilson brought upon himself. It wasn't a matter of 'Bob Inman not liking him.' Bob Inman just didn't like the way he was operating. I guess you could say we ain't the same breed of cat."

Edwin P. Wilson now stood alone. But his five years in Task Force 157 had been financially useful. His assets had increased tenfold in the five years since he had left CIA, to $2 million. But now Wilson's years of greatest gain—and loss—commenced as he embarked upon a new, independent career.

Wilson should have thanked Bobby Inman, not cursed him. His dismissal from naval intelligence freed Wilson from any accountability to higher authority. Moreover, for reasons the Navy still does not care to explain, when Wilson left Task Force 157 he kept control of the major proprietary company he had run as a cover—Consultants International, now known worldwide as a trading company. For anyone who was aware of it, and not many were, Wilson's firing meant that Consultants International no longer could be used as a proprietary, by naval intelligence or anyone else. But letting Wilson retain the shell of a former proprietary as his very own made it much easier for him to claim a continuing tie with intelligence.

Wilson's experience in CIA and naval intelligence suggested

where the vast fortunes of the future were to be made. For persons outside the mainstream of American business, Third World nations would be the major markets of the next years. And none of these nations appeared more lucrative than Libya. What Wilson did in Libya was nothing more than skillfully exploit several of the realities of twentieth-century geopolitics.

According to what is printed in civics textbooks, the disintegration of colonialism that began in 1945 brought freedom and self-determination to millions of persons. The world family of nations swelled to more than 150 sovereign states, many of them economically weak and politically unstable, but nonetheless "free" in some sense of the word. But reality is somewhat different from the textbooks. From the standpoint of practical world politics, the profusion of new states meant chaos. Many of these new states had old religious, ethnic and territorial quarrels to settle with their neighbors. Unable to field armies in the traditional sense, these mini-states adopted the tactics of the terrorist: the random bomb, the assassin, the guerrilla. A concurrent phenomenon was the rise of the extranational terrorist groups such as the Palestine Liberation Army, the Red Army of Japan, the Red Brigades of Italy.

To attain any significant power, many of these nations—and terrorist groups—relied heavily upon outside assistance. They needed both weapons and training in how to use them. Man has spent much of the past three decades devising exotic ways to destroy other people. The new technology of death is expensive. In terms of available cash, the nation best equipped to finance international adventurism was oil-rich Libya, the North African nation ruled by Muamar Quaddafi. And it was through Quaddafi that Edwin P. Wilson was to achieve his greatest wealth and notoriety.

Many Westerners can attempt to *explain* Quaddafi; few, if any, purport to *understand* Quaddafi. Fanatically nationalistic, eager to purge his country of any Western influences, Quaddafi used the likes of Ed Wilson to bring him sophisticated weaponry and electronics gear he could not obtain elsewhere. Devoutly Moslem, a puritan in his personal life, Quaddafi used murder as an instrument of statecraft. Quaddafi had a morbid fascination with the booby trap and the surreptitious bomb—the item he could give to a "friend" as a gift, only for it to explode with deadly force in that friend's keeping.

Ardently pan-Arab, Quaddafi sought union with neighboring states from the very moment he assumed power in Libya in 1969. Yet at one time or another he sought the assassination, directly or through surrogates, of more than a dozen leaders of countries with which he had sought "union." He ran what a Canadian diplomat once called "the world's one working model of a crazy state." Anwar Sadat, the last president of Egypt, spoke for many other Arab leaders when he called Quaddafi "a barking, frothing madman, someone who should be kept on a leash." Outspokenly anti-Communist during his first years of power, Quaddafi was to purchase an incredible *$12 billion* worth of arms from the Soviet Union in a single contract in 1976—for an army of fewer than 40,000 men.

An Italian protectorate at the end of the Second World War, Libya progressed to independence in 1952, under auspices of the United Nations, as a constitutional monarchy under the rule of King Idris al-Sanussi. To the West, Libya's only value at the time was strategic: It is on the flank of the Mediterranean sea lanes, and it hosted key American and British military installations, including the vast Wheelus Air Force Base, the Middle East headquarters for the U.S. Strategic Air Command. Economically, Libya was impoverished. Most of the population lived in a thin green strip along the coast, the desert interior dotted with a rare oasis and wandering Bedouin shepherds.

Life in Libya changed dramatically beginning in 1959, with major oil discoveries in the desert. Western companies swarmed over Libya in the next fifteen years, finding oil seemingly wherever they poked a hole in the desert crust; by 1969, Libya ranked as the world's fourth-largest oil producer, with royalty revenues to the state of $1.132 billion a year. But with the oil came corruption. By all accounts, the Western oil companies behaved abysmally, paying bribes to officials, conspiring with one another to keep prices low, grafting onto Moslem Libya the raucous morals of an oil-patch boomtown.

Muamar Quaddafi, born in 1941 to Bedouin shepherd parents, did not like the society in which he grew to maturity. He came to share Nasser's dream of a pan-Arabic state stretching through the crescent of the Middle East, with the detested Israelis driven from the land they had seized from helpless Palestinians with the help of Western powers. Like most Libyans he learned to scheme early, seeing his path to power through the army, the only Libyan institution with a national presence. Expelled from high school for protesting King Idris' lack of support for the Palestinians and Nasser, Quaddafi entered the Libyan military academy at Benghazi. Upon graduation, Lieutenant Quaddafi was detailed for advanced training to the British signal school at Beaconsfield, the United Kingdom, and there he learned the importance of modern communications in seizing and holding power—a nigh-obsession that was to continue when he dealt with Ed Wilson years later. Back in Libya in 1967, Quaddafi developed a revolutionary cabal that soon encompassed most officers in the army. The "overthrow" of the aged Idris in 1969, when he was at a health spa in Egypt, required not a single gunshot. Quaddafi emerged as the strongman of the Revolutionary Command Council, which supplanted the constitutional government.

The West treated Quaddafi with wary respect his first years. The United States accepted his expulsion of the American and British military as inevitable acts of a Third World Arab strongman. The oil companies, which were not unaccustomed to strange bedfellows, continued to do business with the new revolutionary government, even as they were shoved into an increasingly narrower corner. The Central Intelligence Agency, encouraged by Quaddafi's anti-Communist and anti-Soviet stance, warned him of several coup attempts by domestic foes. The United States' great fear was that Libya would cut the flow of its oil to Western Europe. Henry Kissinger, President Nixon's national security adviser, quoted in his memoir a governmental memorandum which summarized the administration's decision that the only choice was to "try to get along with Quaddafi." A few weeks after that memorandum was written, Quaddafi threw out the Western military.

Quaddafi's extranational ambitions did not permit accommodation with the United States—or any other power, for that matter, save the Soviet Union. Quaddafi hated Israel, and he gave lavish support to her enemies. But Quaddafi's hostility extended to other African and Middle Eastern chiefs of state as well. His gunmen tried to kill King Hassan of

Morocco at a beach resort. In 1971, Quaddafi broke a plot to assassinate President Gaafar Nimeiri of the Sudan—then two years later launched his own killers against Nimeiri, unsuccessfully. His public exchanges with President Anwar Sadat of Egypt were vitriolic even by the standards of Arab propaganda.

In 1973, as an aftermath of the Arab-Israeli war, Quaddafi was a strategic overseer of the disruption of the oil industry. Knowing the greed endemic among Western oilmen, he played one against another, using nationalization as his ultimate threat. Western Europe, fearful of losing a convenient oil supply, catered to him, and Quaddafi's oil revenues soared. In 1969, the year Quaddafi seized power, oil brought $1.132 billion to Libya; in 1976, the income was $6 billion; in 1980, an estimated $20 billion. He put most of this national wealth into an arms-buying spree unsurpassed in history.

By 1976, Quaddafi had made his peace with the Soviet Union. That year Premier Alexei Kosygin came to Tripoli to sign a contract for $12 billion in military aid and arms: 2,800 Soviet tanks of the first rank; 7,000 other armored vehicles; surface-to-air missiles; a mixture of sophisticated MIG fighter planes and long-range Tupolev bombers; navy vessels equipped with surface-to-surface and surface-to-air missiles, plus support equipment. Perhaps most significantly, Quaddafi opened his nation's doors to the Soviets and their friends. Soviet long-range bombers got landing rights at half a dozen air bases, including the former American Wheelus base. The East German security service sent more than 500 men to reorganize and direct Libyan intelligence.

The Western oil companies by 1976 had shadow holdings only. A consortium named Oasis Oil Company survived, chiefly to provide essential technical advice to the Libyans who were trying to operate a modern oil field, but Tripoli, the Libyan capital, had become a grim caricature of an Eastern European Stalinist state, with omnipresent revolutionary banners and portraits of a glowering Quaddafi.

Quaddafi wanted more than an open divorce from the United States and the West; he desired a public humiliation. Yet he also wanted two things from America. The Soviets were playing tight with their communications and electronics equipment; as did Quaddafi, they recognized the value of command-and-control in a military situation. The Soviets would give Quaddafi hardware, but not the means to control it. Hence Quaddafi desired Western electronics equipment.

With devilish cunning, Quaddafi also decided to seek Western armaments for his burgeoning terrorist activities. As one of the many Americans who later worked for Ed Wilson in Libya told me, "American-origin pistols seemed an obsession with the Libyans. Using a Colt pistol to shoot some guy—and knowing that the colt was traceable to the States—was a sort of ultimate ha-ha for the Libyans. Using a gun from Bulgaria or Poland would have been too easy; they wanted to rub us around. Also, the American pistol might make some European cop say to himself, 'Oho, we have a CIA plot at work here.'"

Hence, in 1976, a convergence of interests: Edwin P. Wilson, cashiered from American intelligence and looking for new business, found himself joined in interests with Muamar Quaddafi, comfortable with the Soviet military but looking for Western armaments. The alliance that ensued may not have been consummated in Hades, but it was accomplished at least close by.

In actuality, Wilson had directed wistful looks at the Libyan market months before Admiral Inman fired him from naval intelligence. Casting about among his contacts for someone who had entrée with the Libyans, Wilson hit upon Joseph Sands, an expatriate American in his early fifties who had been a quiet but important player in the international security trade for almost two decades.

Joe Sands tugged at his chin and thought. "I might have seen the bottom of many whiskey bottles—too many of them, according to friends—but he can be a charming tablemate for an evening of talk, business and fun. He has the knack of retrieving himself from seemingly drunken incoherency and matter-of-factly discussing a business proposal in intricate detail. Sands' chief asset, beyond his easy personality, is what one person called his "magic card file," which supposedly lists the address, private phone number and specialty of every significant electronics supplier in the world. It is said in the London electronics world, "If Joe Sands can't find it, and get delivery in a week's time, it doesn't exist."

In the early weeks of 1976, over glasses of Scotch in a London pub, Wilson mentioned to Sands that he wished to do business in Libya. "Do you know anybody who can get my foot in the door?" Wilson asked. "Tell you what I'll do: you find me the right partner, we'll go threes on a deal and make some good money for all of us."

Joe Sands tugged at his chin and thought. "I might have just the man for you," Sands said. "Now, you've got to know, up front, that CIA fired him a few years back because he is an all-around shady character. But he does know the Libs and how they spend their money."

"Good buddy," Wilson said, "lead me to him." And thus Wilson was to come into contact with a vicious, shaggy-haired freebooter named Frank Terpil.

Part Two

THE CORRUPTOR

7

Frank and Kevin

Terpil was 36 years of age the spring of 1976, a chunky man almost 6 feet in height. First-time acquaintances got the impression that he was 30 to 40 pounds overweight. But there was strength in Terpil's girth: he could pick up a 250-pound crate of rifle ammunition with the ease with which most men handle a bag of groceries. And Terpil was striking physically. He wore a dropping Fu Manchu mustache that always seemed a week or two overdue for a trim (as did his longish hair). Terpil exuded *machismo*. He liked men and their company, and he enjoyed good drink and a bawdy story and telling of his adventures around the world, both as a CIA operative and as an arms dealer. "Even when you discount the bullshit, of which Terpil had an ample supply, he was a fun guy to be around," recollected Alex Raffio.

Terpil had acquired his gift for gregarious banter in his native Brooklyn, where he was born November 2, 1939, at 223 East 8th Street. He made his first attempt at an arms deal at age 15, a time when most kids are content to chase baseballs and the neighborhood girls. Through the grapevine, Terpil had heard that a local policeman had acquired a machine gun and wished to sell it. Terpil promptly bought it, and found that another neighborhood youth would buy it from him at a higher price. The buyer, unfortunately, turned out to be a son of Terpil's high school science teacher. The father found the gun and called the cops, and Terpil was arrested and taken to the station house. Terpil's mother,

Viola, called in to account for her son, saw him sitting in an interrogation room and gave him some advice he was to heed the rest of his life: "Whatever your story is, stick to it."

Terpil learned some other things in Brooklyn: how to submerge his feelings and not let them interfere with whatever business was at hand, and how to ignore moral imperatives and devise one's own highly pragmatic code of right and wrong. From an early age, Terpil displayed a chilling ability to "blank out" his emotions. No one recalls him in a single moment of introspection. "Completely cold-blooded, not a caring bone in his body," said one man who had known him in the CIA. That Terpil had such traits at an early age is witnessed by his mother, Viola Terpil. Frank's father, a Second World War veteran who worked for the Western Electric Company, spray-painting telephones, died in 1951, when his only son was 12. The mother asked, "Frank, now that Daddy is gone, how do you feel?"

Terpil looked unblinkingly at Viola Terpil. "I would rather you not ask me, because I don't want to discuss it," he said. As Viola later stated, "We never discussed his father again."

The capacity for such emotional detachment stayed with Terpil in his later years, when he worked in the torture chambers of the despot Idi Amin in Uganda, and sold assassination equipment—bombs, poisons, guns—to anyone with the asking price.

Terpil did not like the prospect of spending his life in Brooklyn "with all those goddamned Archie Bunkers who think a night on the town is four beers at the corner slop chute." Terpil saw his older friends going to work in the factories of Brooklyn and marrying neighborhood girls and settling into humdrum lives. Not Frank Terpil. He "escaped from Brooklyn," as he put it, by joining the U.S. Army in 1958 at age 18. He spent four years in uniform, some of the time in the Far East. He married, had the first of three children and tried some hodgepodge jobs in electronics for a couple of years after his discharge. It was a life that did not leave Terpil happy. The military had given him exposure to weaponry, and sophisticated communications equipment, and the excitement of living abroad. So in 1965, Terpil decided to put some adventure back into his life. He joined the Central Intelligence Agency as a contract employee in the Technical Services Division, or TSD.

Because CIA has a policy of not talking about former

employees and what they did while in Agency service, the exact nature of Terpil's work is sketchy. Former and current Agency officials—men with no reason to fabricate—have stated that he was a low-level communications technician, "the equivalent of a guy who operates and maintains the switchboard." Terpil, in interminable bull sessions with other arms merchants, told varying stories after his discharge from CIA. He claimed to have been "deep undercover," assigned to spy on his own colleagues suspected of being Soviet moles. He claimed to have had a role in any number of "CIA-sanctioned killings" throughout the world. One especially bloody story that he was fond of relating involved the disembowelment of a prominent Thai leftist politician—while he was still alive. He claimed that Richard Helms, the director of Central Intelligence, once had him flown to Washington as the sole passenger in a 707 to receive an award for courageous service. "Terpil," he quoted Helms as saying, "You're the closest thing this Agency has to a James Bond, and I want to know that you'll always have a home here."

In none of these claims is there even the slightest germ of truth. But Terpil told his lies so often, and in such intimate detail and so convincing a manner, that in time he perhaps came to believe them himself.

What Terpil did not boast about was that early in his Agency career, he had earned a justified reputation as a cheat and a petty thief. Items of office equipment would disappear from stations where Terpil was assigned; once, when caught more or less red-handed in a theft, he tried unsuccessfully to blame a "local-hire" secretary. The station chief demanded that he be reassigned.

Terpil's first interest upon arrival in a new post was to check out the local black market in currency. In these years—the late 1960s—the American dollar was much sought after overseas, and could be traded for many times its official value. By his own account, Terpil made scores of thousands of dollars' profit on the black market. But he did not confine himself to currency. Because he traveled frequently, Terpil was a veritable peddler's wagon of contraband liquor, jewelry, watches and other items sought on the black market. One of the few men willing to discuss Terpil's CIA years stated flatly, "He was a disgrace—to himself and his family, to CIA, to the USG [United States Government]. Candidly, I think somebody should have taken the son of a bitch out in the woods and shot him. A bad actor, the very worst."

Terpil's wife, Marilyn, accompanied him on his overseas assignments, occasionally taking clerical jobs in the CIA station. (For security reasons, CIA likes to hire company wives as secretaries in its overseas stations.) What Marilyn Terpil knew of her husband's extra-CIA activities is unestablished; one person who knew them both stated, "If Marilyn couldn't control Frank, and she couldn't, no one could." Eventually, heavily caught up in her husband's illegitimate deals, Marilyn was herself investigated, though not prosecuted.

Terpil's CIA position did give him valuable entrée into the secretive world of arms merchants. A CIA station as a matter of course likes to know who is selling what weapons in its territory, and to whom, and at what price. Such information is routinely gathered in both formal and informal fashion. It can be as mundane a task as sitting around a hotel bar favored by arms dealers and exchanging trade gossip. Since such assignments would never be given to a low-grade technician such as Terpil, he sought out arms dealers on his own initiative, murmuring misleading hints as to his status in CIA, laying the groundwork for a possible post-CIA career. Terpil apparently realized early in his CIA tenure that he would never hold a position of any power within the Agency, for he lacked both education and unique skills. The circumstantial evidence is that Terpil spent much—and perhaps the majority—of his time building contracts and looking toward the future, one foot in the world of legitimate intelligence, the other in the world of illicit smuggling and currency deals.

Another part of Terpil's self-devised mystique was that he had spent his CIA career hobnobbing with high foreign officials. Of all these stories, the baldest was his claim that he had befriended Muamar Quaddafi in 1969 while a "CIA courier making regular runs form Malta to Libya." Quaddafi, then a young army colonel, was plotting the overthrow of King Idris, and Terpil told of spending many long evenings in his tent on the desert, listening to the Libyan tell of his plans for the future of the nation. Just why a dissident plotting a revolution would choose to confide in an American functionary is hard to conjure.

In 1970, Terpil was assigned to the CIA station in New Delhi, a crucial post with responsibility for gathering intelligence on the Asian subcontinent. Almost immediately he got into trouble with the station chief for smuggling illicit whiskey into the country and was warned that if he violated local Prohibition again, he would be sent home.. The warning did not dissuade Terpil from further crime, for New Delhi and the whole of India are a smuggler's paradise. Terpil was soon spending about as much time on black-market activities as he did on his CIA job.

Terpil later was to boast of this interlude as a prosperous conclusion to his CIA career. He told of living in a large house in the West End colony section of New Delhi, with thirteen to fifteen servants and a Cadillac limousine. Since his Agency salary did not support such amenities, Terpil had to supplement his income "a wee bit." As he told Antony Thomas, the British journalist:

"I would collect foreign currencies from various individuals, groups, take the foreign currencies to Afghanistan, which had a very large banking center there, reconvert the foreign currencies into Indian rupees, which had a very high exchange value, bring the Indian rupees back to New Delhi, reconvert them back to foreign currency... and it was a never-ending circle."

The unexpected outbreak of the Indian-Pakistan War in 1971 caught Terpil in Afghanistan; the frontiers were closed, and he could not get back to his duty station in New Delhi. That he would be absent without permission during a crisis meant *finis* to his career. He was shipped home in disgrace and fired.*

Terpil made a bumpless transition from intelligence func-

---

*Terpil would later claim that he had resigned under pressure. His story was that he had been posted to CIA headquarters in Virginia without either an office or an assignment, and had done nothing there but prowl the halls and drink coffee in the cafeteria. Terpil joshed that joining the "Walk the Halls Club" was the Agency's means of telling a person he was no longer wanted, and that he would resign. In fact, Terpil was given no such choice. He was discharged. As one Agency official joshed to me, "Had we kept him around the premises, he would have made a fortune stealing typewriters and mugging secretaries in the parking lot. We wanted to get rid of the shit as fast as possible."

Terpil told other persons an even more lurid reason for his dismissal: that he was fired because he was caught swimming the Ganges River with cork-blackened face, towing a sack of contraband whiskey. Given the deadly bacteria a swimmer would encounter in the Ganges, and the amount of liquor a swimmer can carry in a sack, Terpil's story sounds fanciful.

tionary to arms merchant. He made a whirlwind round of U.S. defense suppliers, touting his "high-level contacts" throughout the Arab world, claiming that he could get through doors closed to their regular salesmen. When asked about his status with the CIA, Terpil would reply with vague language to the effect "Well, one never totally leaves The Business," which the listener could interpret as he wished, often choosing to hear the broad suggestion that Frank Terpil still worked for the Agency.

Eventually Terpil cut some deals. The Arabs, smarting from yet another defeat by Israel, were eager to replenish their military arsenals. Leaving wife Marilyn and their two children at home in Virginia, Terpil flew to the Middle East with open-ended assignments from several electronics firms. He would receive no guaranteed salary, only partial expenses. But if he produced as promised, Terpil would earn commissions that would make him a very rich man in a hurry.

Even persons who disliked Frank Terpil—there are many— respected him as a salesman who could transform a casual contact into a friend eager to give him a contract. Terpil functioned best as a middle-man, as the "rainmaker" who would convince a country that it needed a certain quantity of rifles or grenade launchers, then steer the purchasing agent toward an arms dealer who had the desired merchandise. Terpil took a finder's fee. An intensely physical man who exuded vitality, Terpil moved at ease with another type of military supplier: soldiers of fortune of all nations who could recruit the equivalent of a private army for some individual or group seeking to keep control of a government, or to overthrow a government. Terpil within two years suddenly seemed omnipresent in both the Middle East and Central America. But to anyone who watched Terpil closely, a pattern soon emerged. As an initiator of deals, he was unsurpassed. As long as he acted as a middleman, with no responsibility for actually making deliveries, Terpil did his job well. But in instances where Terpil tried to act as both contracting officer and supplier, he seldom fulfilled a deal. He would coax as large a down payment as possible on the contract, disappear for several months, suddenly reappear with a blitz of Telex messages, claim that an unidentified third party was fouling up the deal, try to wheedle more money from the buyer and then vanish for good. Other persons brokering arms in the

Middle East came to know Terpil as a cheat and a corner-cutter, a man who would betray any apparent friend if he could make a dollar in the process.

In the early 1970s, to cite one case, he met an American electronics salesman in Beirut who had succeeded in obtaining a "demonstration export license" for a new piece of equipment. Under this particular license, the equipment could be shown to potential customers but not sold: within a given time, it must be returned to the United States; a conventional export license would be required for any purchases. Terpil and the salesman struck up a barroom friendship, and after some small talk Terpil asked if he could see the electronics gear.

"Hey," he said, "I think I know where I can sell some of this for you; I have some buyers in town. What say I run over to their hotel and let them have a look at it? There's money in it for both of us—you have the equipment, I have the contacts."

The salesman agreed, and Terpil went away with the equipment. Instead of going across town to another hotel, however, he went to Damascus and sold the equipment to Syrian intelligence. The hapless salesman had to explain to both his employer and the U.S. Government how he had lost the equipment. "He wasn't prosecuted," says Alex Raffio, "but his ass was in a sling for a long time. That's Frank Terpil for you."

Terpil and Wilson signed no formal agreement; the circumstantial evidence is that each recognized the other as a sharp dealer who could be expected to cheat and cut corners, with each other as well as with outsiders, so what would an agreement be worth?

Joe Sands' membership in a triad with Wilson and Terpil did not survive Sands' first trip to Tripoli. Somehow the man managed to smuggle several bottles of forbidden whiskey into the country, and he was staggering drunk when he appeared for his first meeting with Libyan intelligence officials. That a Westerner would behave so disgracefully in a Moslem country offended the Libyans deeply. There was even talk about "putting the drunken pig in jail where he belongs." In the end, the Libyans escorted Sands to the airport, put him on a plane to London and told Wilson that Sands would not be welcome in their country again. (As Sands was to say to a friend later, "In view of what happened to Cousin Ed, getting smashed in Tripoli and pissing off the Libs was the best thing that ever happened to me!")

Wilson and Terpil talked over their situation and decided to reorganize. Terpil would continue to do the contact work in Tripoli, for he had the necessary friendships with Libyan officers who did military purchasing. Wilson would work out of London, locating the required equipment—or the people who knew where it could be obtained. But since so much matériel came from the United States, Wilson desperately needed someone as an "anchor man" in a Washington office— essentially, an expediter who could sort out messages to and from suppliers, and coordinate shipments—while Wilson moved freely around the United States, Europe and North Africa. Wilson thought he knew just the man: a former CIA technician he had recently befriended by the name of Kevin Mulcahy.

In some respects, Kevin Patrick Mulcahy seemed the ideal person to run the Washington end of a combined military sales and intelligence operation. Mulcahy was second-generation CIA, the son, brother and nephew of men who had respected careers as CIA employees; when he spoke of being "in the family" he meant the Agency as well as flesh-and-blood kin. Because of the sensitive nature of their work, and their inability to talk casually except among trusted friends, CIA people tend to be clannish to a degree unknown in any other profession, even the military. Through the 1960s and early 1970s, even noncovert CIA employees would seldom divulge to an outsider where they worked, much less even the general area of their responsibility. So Kevin Mulcahy grew up in a household where the people who came over for Sunday picnics, or went fishing with father Donald, were Agency colleagues.

Born in 1943, Mulcahy spent most of his boyhood in the Northern Virginia suburbs of Washington (the area favored by CIA employees because of its proximity to the headquarters complex in Langley and other facilities in Arlington). Mulcahy called himself "the gung-ho all-American boy—Eagle Scout, altar boy, high school basketball player; if Norman Rockwell had still been around, I would have posed for him." Mulcahy spent 1950–63 in the Navy as an electronics technician and joined CIA almost immediately upon discharge, picking up on a career that seemed as natural a succession as a farmer's son following his father onto the soil. Mulcahy continued in communications, and he was good at it, friends from his Agency years attest. CIA and other intelligence agencies were going through a technological explosion during these years, increasing its capability to communicate worldwide, instantly and securely. Even from his technician's level, Mulcahy learned many of CIA's deepest secrets, the inner workings of equipment known only to a handful of persons.

Then things begin to slip for Kevin Mulcahy, all-American boy. First came the bottle, which he would later try to blame on the fact that "too many people knew me as 'Don Mulcahy's boy.' I was proud to be my father's son, but I also wanted to be somebody else." Drinking led to philandering; even though he and his wife by now had two small children, Mulcahy stated spending nights in a Warrenton, Virginia, motel with a woman who also worked for CIA. She was the most serious of many sexual involvements. Mulcahy's work deteriorated; finally, in 1968, he was asked to resign, "one step ahead of the headsman."

Mulcahy "went sober for a while" and found a job with a computer company that did considerable work for CIA. He began making a bit of money, $14,000 to $17,000 a year, and rebuilding his family life. Then booze intervened again. Two drinks at lunch turned into a bottle-a-day habit. Mulcahy would meet a business contact for lunch, drink until midafternoon, return to the office, then hit the bars again at five o'clock and continue drinking through the night. Mulcahy's first rationale, before blaming his father, was that he drank to help his career: computer sales depend upon contacts, and he was spending "too much damned time" in the restaurants and bars around Tysons Corners, Northern Virginia's mini-version of a Silicon Valley. Deep inside, Mulcahy knew better. He was turning into a hopeless drunk. One horrible morning he awoke in the front seat of his car, clothes covered with vomit, head splitting with a hangover, memory trying to decide whether the vision of running down a pedestrian was a dream or reality.

Mulcahy dried out, he drank again, he divorced, he lost his job. He made two attempts at suicide. One involved pills; the other was a jump off the Route 7 bridge into the Shenandoah

River. "I surprised myself. I floated. The water was warm, and I just let it carry me along for a while, until I asked, 'Just what am I doing here?'"

The next murky months Mulcahy managed to get off whiskey, through sheer determination and a boost from Alcoholics Anonymous. A "sense of guilt" about wrecking his marriage and bringing so much distress to his family led Mulcahy to change his entire life goal. He left the computer industry—admitting "I was such a mess that I wasn't any great loss to the industry"—and became involved in counseling for alcohol and drug abuse, particularly among young people. A good talker and self-promoter, Mulcahy found financial backers for his youth program among Northern Virginia businessmen and some money from his own large family. He applied for federal grants. And looking for a home for his programs, he rented a house in Northern Virginia offered by real estate agent Barbara Wilson.

The earnest young Irishman appealed to Mrs. Wilson, and she listened with sympathy as he told of his wrecked life. Eventually she asked him to come out to Mount Airy Farm for dinner with her husband. The circumstantial evidence is that Barbara Wilson told Ed of Mulcahy's CIA background, for when he arrived at the house Wilson "started talking about my work with the Agency, and how he admired what I was doing now, and did I ever think I'd like to go back into the business."

"I'm an old Agency hand myself," Wilson told Mulcahy. He reeled off a long list of "my good friends out there" and gave broad hints that "although I'm private sector now, I still give them a hand from time to time." To Mulcahy, listening to Wilson was like being back in "the family" once again. The names that Wilson dropped were in the Agency's highest echelon. "Ed was definitely out to impress me, and he did a good job of it. He came across as a top professional in the field, and it was most obvious that he was making money out of what he was doing."

The dinner was in early 1976, several weeks before Wilson involuntarily ended his association with Task Force 157. The next weeks, Mulcahy saw both the Wilsons from time to time (chiefly Barbara, who checked on the use he made of the house she had rented him). Wilson himself traveled frequently; once, when Mulcahy asked casually where he had been, Wilson replied, "A good long swing out in Asia. Korea, the Philippines, Bangkok. This had the blessings of the Agency. I like to check my contacts at the various embassies and see what is happening, what kind of business is going down." One person he mentioned meeting on this swing was Patry Loomis, a CIA contract employee Mulcahy had met in the past. Mulcahy knew that Loomis had long worked in Asia under commercial cover provided by an American aeronautical firm; that Wilson could have contact with such a deep-cover employee impressed Mulcahy as further proof of his continuing ties with the intelligence establishment. Finally, in the spring of 1976, Wilson asked Mulcahy to meet him downtown for lunch.

"You're a damned competent fellow," Wilson said. "I need somebody like you to stay here and mind the store while I travel." Wilson explained that "I'm getting more foreign contracts that I can shake a stick at, and I need somebody who knows where to find the stuff I'm selling, and how to arrange to ship it out." Mulcahy accepted Wilsons's offer of $1,000 a month to start, with the agreement that he could take whatever time was necessary to keep his youth program going.

What Mulcahy agreed to that day was to become his death warrant. But the headlines of getting back into the intelligence business, even on the fringes, with such a charismatic person as Ed Wilson caused Mulcahy to neglect to ask himself a rather basic question: As an arrested alcoholic, did he dare put himself back into the sort of world that had caused his ruin earlier?

The very first day on his job, Mulcahy learned that Consultants International was something other than an ordinary import-export business, the description Wilson had given it. As Mulcahy prepared to leave the office, Wilson called to him, "Hey, wait a minute, I want you to take a ride with me, there's this guy coming into the airport you gotta meet."

As Wilson drove along the George Washington Parkway toward Washington National Airport, he explained that they would be meeting another Wilson employee named Doug Schlachter, the former gas-station attendant who had gone to work for Consultants International.

"Look, now that you are working for me, I want to put you on notice that you're going to encounter some things that you might have trouble with, but I don't expect you to get involved in them," Wilson said.

"What are you talking about?" asked Mulcahy.

"A lot of times Consultants International supplies guns, ammunition, that sort of thing, to other nations. We pretty well run the spectrum of munitions," Wilson replied.

The statement surprised Mulcahy, for Wilson had given no previous indication that he dealt in arms. Mulcahy surmised that Wilson was promising not to involve him in such deals because Mulcahy had presented himself "as somewhat of a humanitarian who intended to devote the rest of my life trying to help fouled-up children."

The first days, Wilson did nothing to disturb Mulcahy's conscience. The assignments were mundane. "I'd get an order from overseas, or a possible contract, that a foreign government wanted to build a dayroom, a recreation room for the Libyan Navy or something like that. I would try and equip that dayroom and make them a proposal by Telex. I knew a number of vendors in the United States. I had a catalog of some ten thousand than I had used over the years in the computer business, and I knew a number of people that could help me find what I didn't know where to find myself, and I used those people."

But after watching Mulcahy perform for several weeks, Wilson apparently decided that his new recruit was fit for heavier matters. When Mulcahy arrived at the office one morning, Wilson told him, "Come on, let's take a walk. I want you to meet someone." He identified the person as Frank Terpil, "another old Agency hand. I do some business with him. He's a stand-up guy; you'll like him." Mulcahy did like Terpil, after a fashion, finding him a bluff hail-fellow-well-met with a high sense of himself and a natural gift for salesmanship. "This is a guy who literally could persuade an Eskimo to buy not one icebox but *two*, and maybe a block of ice to put on top of it. He was a natural. And to call him a name-dropper would be an insult. He didn't drop names—he *shoveled* names. He apparently knew everyone in Washington, and he spewed out Arabic names in the Middle East like he was reading a phone book. I have a pretty good built-in bullshit detector, and I tend to discount what sales types tell me, but this guy—even discounted he was heavy material."

But parts of the discussion disturbed Mulcahy. "I just didn't like the drift of the conversation . . . that I knew was flagrantly in violation of the law. They were talking about equipping M-16 rifles with silencers, and I knew that silencers are illegal." Remembering the conversation after the airport meeting with Doug Schlachter, Mulcahy had serious second thoughts about his new benefactor.

"When work was over that day, I went to a restaurant and I phoned the Federal Bureau of Investigation and told them what I had heard and gave them the names of the two gentlemen I was involved with and asked them to run a name check and see if what I was into was legitimate or not."

Whoever at the FBI took Mulcahy's call heard the word "firearms" and decided jurisdiction belonged to another federal agency—the Treasury Department's Bureau of Alcohol, Tobacco and Firearms, or BATF. This agency was created in 1920 as the Prohibition-enforcement arm of the Treasury Department, and over the years—as it shuttled from Treasury to Justice to Internal Revenue, before emerging in 1972 as a full-blown Treasury bureau—its responsibility expanded to include tobacco and then guns. BATF is what Pappy Yokum and other up-the-holler folks knew as "them infernal revenooer fellers." And in the 1970s, the time when Kevin Mulcahy asked a question about his employers, BATF was not a first-line intelligence/enforcement agency. Under loud and incessant pressures from Congress and the gun-control lobbies, BATF had built its statistics through arrests of easy-to-catch gun dealers who violated the hopelessly confused state firearms laws. BATF picked up carloads of Saturday-night specials, but was no match for big-time arms merchants and smugglers who supplied foreign mercenaries and terrorists.

Unsurprisingly, therefore, the BATF had nothing in its files on either Ed Wilson or Frank Terpil—nor did any agents stir themselves to pursue the investigative lead handed to them by Kevin Mulcahy. So two former CIA agents are talking about procuring M-16s with silencers? Two BATF agents came to interview Mulcahy and told him, in effect, ho-hum. They wrote a memorandum for their files and did nothing further.

Had Mulcahy been a bit sharper mentally—he was drinking again, now partly because of the strains of working with Ed Wilson—he might have recognized the FBI/BATF response as bureaucratic listlessness, one agency disclaiming jurisdiction because firearms were involved, the other agency pleading ignorance because it would not look beyond its own file cabinets. Mulcahy, however, took what he called the "clean bill of health" as evidence of something entirely else: "I felt whatever they [Wilson and Terpil] were doing, they were probably doing legitimately, and in light of . . . their past experience with CIA, I became fairly convinced . . . that what they were doing was probably undercover in the auspices of the Central Intelligence Agency."

For many weeks thereafter, Mulcahy watched Terpil in silent amazement, marveling at the sales ability of this "New York street thug who looked and talked like he should be mugging little old ladies and knocking off liquor stores." Terpil had the table manners of a high school sophomore; his grammar would embarrass a night-school dropout; whatever hotel room he occupied was strewn with dirty laundry, empty bottles and overturned ashtrays. Even the accepting Ed Wilson would yell, "Goddamn it, Terpil, you left the bathroom a mess." But Terpil's value to Wilson had nothing to do with social niceties. As Mulcahy would state years later: "This guy could sell. He sold those people [the Libyans] stuff they didn't even need, they could never use. Frank would tell them to buy something, and they would buy it. It was absolutely incredible.

"We even went to the point of trying to make them some powdered wine that had no alcohol in it because they like to drink, and Arabs can't drink on sacred soil. So we went to Wylers, the people who make lemonade and iced-tea mix, and worked out a deal where they would make powdered wine without alcohol in it for the Arabs. As I say, he literally could tell these people to buy anything."

While Ed Wilson acted as if he had the CIA behind him, partner Frank Terpil repeatedly demonstrated that he had friends at the highest level of the Libyan Government. In the early summer of 1976, Wilson directed Mulcahy to meet Terpil in a London hotel to discuss a computer contract then under negotiation. The site was a hotel called the Lowndes, in Belgravia. (Perhaps Terpil liked the Lowndes because the British author Frederick Forsyth used it as a gathering place for the mercenaries featured in his best-selling novel *The Dogs of War*.)

Terpil bubbled with excitement when Mulcahy joined him in his room. He tossed a sheaf of documents on the bed.

"These come from the competition," he said. "I got them directly from Musrati's office"—referring to the Libyan finance minister. "This Brit firm had the inside track, and the Libs are about to give them the contract. Can you beat these figures?"

Mulcahy spent several hours going through the competitor's documentation and pricing estimates. By shaving here and there and juggling parts, it could be done. "Sure," he told Terpil, "we can come in under the British." A grin split Terpil's face. "Good show, buddy," he said, "let's go downstairs and have one to celebrate." First, however, Terpil carefully shredded the other company's contract proposal and flushed the strips of paper down the toilet. "Can't afford to have that sort of thing go out in the trash," he joked.

"We won the contract," Mulcahy said. "I wrote a new contract proposal that was run in through some company that Ed and Terpil controlled in Teheran. Frank had that kind of power. He could pick and choose the contracts he wanted to supply, even if the contract was on the verge of being let to someone else."

But such cooperation from high Libyan officials cost Terpil dearly. The computer contract, according to Mulcahy, involved perfectly legitimate sales of equipment that had no military application; Wilson easily obtained an export license from the U.S. Government. But other Libyan demands were not so simple, or legal. As a *quid pro quo* for the standard contracts, the Libyans wanted to be supplied with the instruments of death repugnant to any civilized person: bombs and sabotage equipment.

8

A Good Man with the Boom-Boom

For deals with the West and non-Communist-bloc nations, Libyan oil money flowed into the world arms market

via a London conduit controlled by a man named Sayed
Quaddafadam. A cousin of Colonel Muamar Quaddafi's, and
his close friend since their childhood together in the desert,
Quaddafadam was a rarity among the Libyan leadership. For
reasons of propriety, he paid lip service to the Islamic slant of
the Libyan Revolution—he said his prayers the required six
times daily; he forswore any public yearning for pleasures of
the flesh. Yet in the privacy of his home, in the company of
good friends, Quaddafadam liked Western Scotch whiskey,
and his address book bulged with phone numbers of women
he courted on his visits to Europe. Quaddafadam would
listen to the fervent anti-Western rhetoric of the Islamic
firebrands and stifle a yawn. To his cousin, and to the ruling
Revolutionary Command Council (RCC), Quaddafadam would
argue a heretical and hypocritical double course. *Curse* the
West for public consumption, he said; *deal* with the West for
pragmatic reasons. Unless Libya put its hands on Western
technology, and pulled itself from feudalism into the twenti-
eth century, all of Libya's oil money would be as worthless as
the water in the sea. Erudite, outspoken, a skilled debater,
Quaddafadam could state his case well. Indeed, his charisma
at times seemed to overshadow that of Quaddafi himself.

Not surprisingly, Quaddafadam made important deadly
enemies—notably Abdullah Hijazzi, head of Libyan intelligence. Hijazzi, who also had direct access to Quaddafi's ear,
whispered frequently that eventually Quaddafadam's dissi-
dence would swell into open rebellion, and that he would
attempt to seize Libya for himself. A revolutionary policeman
by nature has trouble seeing colors other than black and
white. That Quaddafadam would question national policy,
even within the confines of the revolutionary council, was
proof enough for Hijazzi that he should not be left at large.
But Quaddafi knew better: Any arguments his cousin put
forth were intended to advance the best interests of Libya.

Nonetheless, in late 1976, Quaddafi felt it prudent to
remove Quaddafadam from the country for a while. Quaddafadam
was a visible and outspoken irritant to the Islamic militants
around Quaddafi, and although the Revolution had yet to
turn to assassination as state policy, his life could well be in
danger. So Quaddafi directed his cousin to proceed to the
Libyan Embassy in London, with the title of "military attaché,"
while giving him a far broader covert assignment. Using

Libya's unlimited oil revenues, he was to obtain the weapons systems and materials embargoed by the various Western powers, including the United States. Although a relative newcomer to world power politics, Quaddafi recognized the hypocrisies of the Western nations where profit was involved: the same government that denounced Quaddafi publicly as an outlaw was happy to trade with him privately. But for the sake of appearances, the contacts would be *sub rosa*. Hence the utility of Quaddafadam's covert "military purchasing mission."

Despite the Libyan regime's emphasis on personal austerity the country's diplomats in London lived in elegant comfort in a dignified building in the Princes Gate section of Knightsbridge. Quaddafadam was quick to shake the desert sand off his feet. With an unlimited expense account, and the aura of being the "number two man" to Quaddafi, Quaddafadam swept into London society, and he loved every waking minute of it. He did not hesitate to drink and party in public, and soon the darkly handsome Libyan became a familiar figure in West End and Mayfair clubs. Quaddafadam knew he was an obvious target of Israeli hit teams, but the prospect of being an assassination victim did not deter his prowlings. One concession he made to personal security was an omnipresent bodyguard. "Mustafa" was 6 feet 8 inches tall and weighed upwards of 300 pounds, most of it hard muscle. Savage scars crisscrossed his unshaven face. Mustafa wore traditional Arab dress, and no one doubted the story that he held a Black Belt in karate. Mustafa never left Quaddafadam's side. Any dish that was put before Quaddafadam, either at home or in a club or restaurant, Mustafa sampled (even if it meant shoving aside a protesting waiter). When Quaddafadam lured a willing young Englishwoman to his bedroom, Mustafa sat quietly in the corner, protective of his master even in the throes of coitus.

Finally, in what he must have intended as the ultimate defiant gesture to his Islamic detractors, Quaddafadam married an Englishwoman—a breach of religious faith that risked the Islamic equivalent of excommunication. Quaddafadam exchanged vows with the infidel with impunity: as far as he was concerned, he answered only to his cousin; the other Libyans were as so many sand fleas—irksome, but to be ignored.

To the arms merchants who clustered in London looking

for profitable deals, the young Libyan was almost too good to believe. He had ready money—millions upon millions of dollars—and an exhaustive shopping list: any weaponry, from handguns to heavy artillery pieces and jet fighter craft. He could make decisions himself, and rapidly, unlike other Arab buyers who had to submit proposals to ministries and layers of royal family. He enjoyed the convivial night life that makes hucksterism one of the world's more hedonistic avocations. Many a dawn would find Quaddafadam's limousine careening through the London streets, the stoic Mustafa sitting at his side, arms dealers and pretty girls giggling and pawing one another in the back seat, bound for a postnightcap party at his apartment. For anyone interested in making money, and having a jolly good time in the process, Sayed Quaddafadam was the man to know in London in early 1976.

When Quaddafadam and his aides began talking with Ed Wilson and Frank Terpil in the spring of 1976, they put direct demands upon the Americans. They wanted weapons of assassination.

Wilson and Terpil's first need was a plausible explanation to offer the retired American military men they would approach for the project: For two such experienced clandestine operators, the solution was simple: Write one version of the contract for the prospective recruits; another, true version for Libyan consumption. The language of this second, secret document reveals that Wilson and Terpil recognized they were embarking on a shameful and illegal project. The secret document was drafted and typed in final form by Terpil—not a good speller—and given to Libyans in London in March 1976. The pertinent paragraphs read as follows:

> Due to the sensitive and confidential nature of the "Project," absolute security must be firmly established and maintained. It is imparitive [sic] that a working "Cover Activity" be initiated. This "Cover" should parallel the actual operational activities wherever and whenever possible. Operational personnel must be able to function in both their "Cover Activity" and covert assignment with the same professional skill and expertise required by both.
>
> An ideal operational "Cover" would be a minefield clearing contract for one of the major oil com-

panies engaged in exploration and drilling. A team of Explosive and Ordnance Experts would obviously be employed in this capacity. These same experts would be simultaniously [sic] training selected students in covert sabatage [sic] operations, employing the latest techniques of clandestine explosive ordnance.

As the cover operation would be in the interest of Public Safety, all required material for the manufacture of special devices would be exported on the same license as the mine clearing material.

A suggested minimum contract, for minefield clearing services, of six months duration, utilizing five personnel, should be initiated immediately. After a six month program of intense training, the student would be completely capable and confident in the design, manufacture, implimentation [sic], and detonation of explosive devices effectively used in conjunction with Psycological/Espionage/Sabatage [sic] warefare [sic] activities.

The proposal next listed eight "additional courses of instruction that should be seriously considered": audio surveillance and countermeasure techniques; surreptitious-entry techniques; special weapons training; exfiltration and evasion tactics; disguise techniques; clandestine communications (including secret writing and agent communications); concealment devices ("dead drops") and photography (documents, night surveillance, etc.). But as the proposal stressed:

The main emphasis is placed on the design, manufacture, implimentation [sic] and detonation of explosive devices.

Physically, Wilson and Terpil required a classroom in a secured area ("perferably air-conditioned") of Tripoli to which only authorized personnel could gain access. They also wanted cast-off electrical transformers; at least two "non-reusable vehicles" which would be destroyed during training and an "abandoned building" which would be used first as a training lab, then as a target for a training exercise. The students, 15 to 18 of them, would be trained eight hours daily, six days a week, for sixty days. During the initial phase, the students "will be required to make, deploy and detonate explosive charges in a prescribed fashion." Once the student mastered "hands-on" skills, he would advance to more sophisticated techniques. As the contract stated:

SECONDARY PHASE: Will include some more advanced techniques in timing devices, delays, detonation (incendiary, chemical, mechanical) and special applications.

FINAL PHASE: Will emphasize Industrial Sabatage [sic] such as POL/petroleum, oil and lubricants/Refinaries [sic] and storage complexes; Dust initiate charges for cement plants, grain storage facilities, textile mills.

In addition to the training, Wilson and Terpil also offered to supply the Libyans with the explosive and accompanying devices that would enable the "students" to put their classroom learning into deadly application against Quaddafi's enemies.

Here some explosive technology is in order. For safety purposes, modern military and commercial explosives are manufactured so that, in themselves, they are inert. They can be burned, banged, dropped on the floor, transported in multi-ton quantities. Unless they are matched with the high-intensity impact of a detonator, they are as harmless as so many bags of cement, or drums of drilling mud. Wilson and Terpil offered both the explosives *and* the essential detonators, the latter in a style designed for terrorism.

All explosives can be detonated either openly or covertly. If a blaster has no reason to hide what he is doing, he puts his explosives into place, inserts a detonator or blasting cap and sets off the blast through either an electrical impulse or a fast-burning explosive cord called Prima cord. Such is the procedure for a miner, or a farmer who wishes to remove a stump from his field, or a construction worker who has come upon a balky rock. But the terrorist or clandestine bomber cannot work in the open. He needs a detonator that can be mated with the explosive charge and set to go off at a more or less certain time when he will be comfortably distant from the scene.

The basic clandestine detonator is known as the "timer,"

or "timer pencil." The timer is about the size of a ball-point pen, although perceptibly heavier. It consists of two parts. The "smart part" is a solid-state chip that can be programmed to emit an electrical impulse at any future time between thirty minutes and a year, to the minute. When this happens, the impulse sets off the high-intensity portion of the timer, which in turn detonates the main explosive charge. BOOM to all around.

To carry out his contract, Wilson needed two things: experts who could work with the Libyans under the guise of a "training program" or a "mine field clearing operation," and the explosives equipment itself. The first requirement Wilson satisfied quite readily. John Harper, and old Agency acquaintance from the Far East, had just retired from CIA after more than two decades of experience in dealing with explosives. (A man who worked with Harper in Libya remembers him saying, "I was the guy who rigged the U.S. Embassy in Saigon to explode after everybody got out." Given Harper's expertise, the story is unlikely, for the embassy building still stands.) When approached by Wilson in mid-1976, Harper was living in retirement in Virginia with his wife, Lou, and their son, John, also an explosives man. Harper's chief interest other than explosives was reflected by his Agency nickname, "I. W. Harper," for his favorite bourbon.

Terpil pitched the contract to Harper. "This is a clearing deal," he said. "The Libyans want to get rid of a lot of stuff left over from the Second World War and the 1967 war with the Jews." Here Terpil erred in history—the 1967 Israeli–Arab war did not involve Libyan territory—but the approach made sense to Harper, for he had read of the great tank wars waged in Libya between Generals Rommel and Montgomery. As he said, "A lot of stuff had to be out there in the desert."

Lou Harper was not as trusting as her husband. Before he went off to North Africa, she insisted that a full year's salary of $100,000 be deposited in a Swiss bank. She demanded also that she be hired by Consultants International to work in the Washington office, that she have the right of constant telephone contact with her husband and that she be kept fully aware of what he was doing, and where. That Wilson accepted such demands from the wife of a subordinate surprised Mulcahy. "Ed Wilson's idea of the perfect woman was that she be able to 'make love, make a drink and make herself scarce.' But he really wanted Harper. He griped about 'the shit that Lou throws out,' and that 'I.W. takes this crap without whacking her in the chops, which she deserves.'" Apparently under pressure to move the contract along, Wilson gave Lou Harper what she wished and hired her husband.

The next priority was to obtain the timing devices. Wilson chose the brazen approach. One of the CIA's longtime suppliers of timers was a company called American Electronic Laboratories, Inc., with offices and manufacturing facilities in both Falls Church, Virginia, a Washington suburb, and Colmar, Pennsylvania. "AEL did so much agency work that it was practically a subsidiary. I had been hearing of it for years," Mulcahy said.

Wilson walked into AEL as if he were on company business—and to reinforce his deceit he took along Patry Loomis, still on active duty as a CIA contract employee. Wilson spoke of buying vast quantities of timers and other electrical equipment. Terpil, he said, "has the Middle East locked up." Loomis "is the best man in the world to handle Southeast Asia." Wilson modestly claimed to be "the best man working in Europe today." He offered AEL a contract for upwards of 200,000 timers, at a price of $4 to $5 each. In return, he wanted the right to represent AEL in all international markets, on a commission basis. Wilson repeatedly stated that Loomis was "active-duty CIA." Although he never said so directly, his implication was that Loomis' presence meant that the timer contract had official sanction.

Surprisingly, Wilson's salesmanship failed. As an AEL officer stated later, "He came on a bit strong. He was also out of channels. Our other Agency work had come from a different route. Given our established relationship, we saw no reason for someone to come in the side door, as Wilson did. He also talked quantities that were absurd, given our past contracts. Two hundred thousand units. This approximates the number of timers used during the entire Vietnam War! We just didn't think so many Second World War land mines still littered the Libyan desert."

Rebuffed, Wilson turned to another Agency supplier, Scientific Communications, Inc. (SCI), of Dallas. Wilson was now under pressure, for as Mulcahy explained, "the Libyans wanted a demonstration of our capabilities very quickly before they would fund the contract and put the front money up." So Wilson contrived a meeting that would enhance his illusion of working on Agency business. At his suggestion, SCI sent engineer Ray May to Washington to talk over the contract. Wilson met May at the airport, got him a comfortable hotel room, then said, "Hey, let's do business tonight. We're joining an old Agency friend out in Virginia for drinks, dinner and maybe some talk. You must know Bill Weisenburger."

Indeed May did. Weisenburger was a CIA purchasing agent for explosives and electronics. If the CIA wanted timers, Weisenburger was the logical man with whom to discuss details. That the meeting was being held in a Virginia cocktail lounge, rather than an Agency office, May dismissed as one of the mysteries involved in dealing with the CIA.

Wilson made the introductions in lavish language. May was "one of industry's top men in his field." Weisenburger "knows more abut electronics than anybody in the Agency, probably in the whole damned government." John Harper "is the guy the Agency turns to when they need a job done well, and in a hurry." And, finally, "young Mulcahy here—you must know his dad, Don?—he's my right-hand man; what Kevin says, Ed Wilson says."

Mulcahy listened to these grandiose introductions with bemusement, then got himself a drink and tuned in on the technical talk between Harper, Weisenburger and May. Wilson's basic requirement, as Mulcahy understood the situation, was that the timers would "blow mines and do it remotely . . . they [the Libyans] wanted to be away from the thing that was going up, and they wanted a certain amount of time after the charge had been set . . . to be away from the source of the charge." Weisenburger said that what was needed was a timer that could be detonated at long range. Harper talked about technicalities, how the timer would interface with the actual explosives. May, who would be responsible for the actual manufacture of the timers, took notes and kept quiet. Finally he said that before committing SCI he would have to talk with other company officers. He too was suspicious about the quantities mentioned by Harper.

Mulcahy watched Wilson circulate in the room as he halfheartedly listened to the technical talk, backslapping his way around, pausing at a table here and there to sit for a drink, then move elsewhere to exchange a profane greeting with one person or another. Many of the hands that Wilson shook were familiar to Mulcahy: they were CIA employees with responsibility for areas where Wilson was doing business. "I'm no virgin," Mulcahy would state later. "I had a good idea about most of the people he was talking to. They treated Ed like he was still one of the boys. Weisenburger made no bones about the fact that he was still with the Agency, although he did say something about 'doing this on my own time.' I couldn't conceive of an Agency technician doing this kind of moonlighting unless he had approval."

What Weisenburger agreed to do that Friday evening was construct a dozen prototypes of the timers over the weekend, in his own home laboratory. He said nothing of the agreement to anyone else at the Agency, nor did be obtain approval from his superiors. Weisenburger delivered the timers to Wilson on Monday and received between $1,500 and $2,000 for his work.

Wilson now had the timers and his "expert." What he needed next was a sizable supply of explosives to be converted into bombs.

These explosives came from Jerome S. "Jerry" Brower, whose maimed hands bespoke his profession. An explosion had cleaved his left hand into the semblance of a half-moon, leaving just the nubs of his thumb and little finger. His right hand, his face, his neck all bore the faint but discernible scars of blasts that had gone awry. But such are the mishaps that one expects during four decades of working with explosives, both for the government and in private industry. People in the trade considered Jerry Brower "a good man with the boom-boom." He was one of the founders of the Society of Explosives Engineers, the elite 900-odd of the profession, and he had served as its president for three years. He had written an explosives manual for the U.S. Navy that is considered a classic, and his library of books on explosives is deemed the most comprehensive private collection extant; even researchers from the Du Pont Corporation would occasionally ask Brower to help them run down an odd fact or formula.

Brower had covered much ground during his time. He had directed a government explosives proving ground in Utah after the Korean War; he was a frequent consultant for the Treasury Department's Bureau of Alcohol, Tobacco and Firearms (which administers and enforces explosives laws); he had worked with a congressional committee that tried to write legislation requiring that each batch of explosives manufactured be marked with a distinctive "tracer" compound to permit close monitoring of shipments. (The "tracer" legislation was intended to keep explosives out of terrorists' hands. Once Brower's involvement with Edwin Wilson became known, his former friends at BATF smiled wryly when they remembered Brower's work in this area.)

In 1965, Brower retired from the government and went into business for himself. He bought an old government explosives and ammunition dump in Pomona, a few miles east of Los Angeles, whose chief asset was a Quonset hut covered with dirt. The site was in the center of Pomona, adjacent to the San Bernardino Freeway. The core business of his company (Jerome S. Brower & Associates) was the worldwide sale of explosives—to South America, the Far East, Europe. Much of this business was with oil and construction companies, but Brower also liked exotic sidelines. His company did some of the underwater explosions that were a special-effects sensation of the movie *The Deep*, based on the Peter Benchley novel. A subsidiary (Survival Systems, Inc.) prepared survival packs (signal lights, first-aid kits, food supplies) for boaters and campers. But Brower's forte was explosives. He had a reputation as a man who sold explosives abroad in bulk; he was respected by both the regulatory BATF and his competitors. What was not generally known about Jerry Brower was that he was a greedy man willing to violate the law to make an illegitimate dollar.

Ed Wilson and Brower first met in the spring of 1976, as Wilson was putting together a proposal for the Libyans to manufacture booby traps. The point of contact was an employee of a CIA proprietary company who knew both men. Wilson asked this man to "find me somebody who knows explosives, and who would like to make some good bucks the next years." The intermediary put Wilson in touch with Brower. Apparently only a few hours of Wilson salesmanship were required to persuade Brower to lend his good name to the scheme to disguise the Libyan operation as a "mine-clearing" contract. But the true thrust of the contract, as Brower later admitted, was to provide personnel and materials to make "clandestine devices... such as terrorists would use." He listed as examples "a lamp that would blow up when you pulled the chain; a fire extinguisher that would detonate when you took it off the wall and turned it over; briefcases that you would carry like salesmen's briefcases that could be left somewhere, a nondescript unit that would detonate with a timer on it."

In addition to trainers, Brower also provided Wilson with the technology of death: blasting caps, a thickener that transformed gasoline into napalm, miniature and subminiature detonators and a small quantity of explosives.

Brower warned Wilson that some of these materials could not be shipped by commercial airlines. Wilson shrugged aside the advice; legalities apparently no longer concerned him. "We'll get the aircraft," he said. The answer satisfied Brower. "If you get the aircraft," he told Wilson, "I can package it so that it [the explosives materials] will be nondescript." A few days later, Wilson introduced Brower to a man from a European airline, who in turn put Brower in contact with one of his firm's cargo officials at Los Angeles International Airport. When the shipments were ready, "we called him [the Los Angeles contact] and made the shipment."

That this entire operation was totally illegal was well known to Brower. "We knew what we were doing," he said. "We knew what we were being hired for, and if we were to be interrogated or questioned about it by anybody, we had to have a cover story to justify our presence." The cover story was what Wilson had concocted about "mine clearing."

Brower proved essential to Wilson and his Libyan contracts throughout 1976; indeed, had not Brower or his equivalent been found, Wilson might well have been shut out of the Quaddafi market. Brower made several mistakes (beyond his decision to violate the law). He remained visible in the United States, by acting as the hiring agent who recruited trainers for the demolition program, and later he appeared in Libya as the ostensible head of the program. Brower was a man with a physical identity—and a fixed business address in the United States. Throughout 1976 and 1977, he behaved as if he were either incredibly stupid or felt himself beyond the law. Whatever his reasoning, Brower was getting himself into what a lawyer would call "jailhouse trouble."

Within a matter of weeks, Wilson realized that John Harper had been a disastrous choice to head the sensitive Libyan mission. Harper had lost his stomach for dealing with explosives. As he told one colleague, "I basically don't like to touch the boom-boom." On one trip to Tripoli, Terpil arranged for Harper to travel through London's Heathrow airport on a Libyan diplomatic passport. "Harper was drunk and carrying two cans of binary explosives—enough to blow London off the map," Kevin Mulcahy recalled.

Upon his arrival in Tripoli, Harper's jangled nerves received another jolt. As he rode in from the airport with two Libyan intelligence officers, the car struck a pedestrian, killing him instantly. The officers looked at the battered, bloody corpse, shrugged and casually threw it into the trunk of the auto. "We'll take care of this later," one of the men told Harper, before they all drove on to the villa. "Harper was more than a little distraught at this lack of regard for human life," Mulcahy said.

Nor did Harper like the living conditions in Libya, which can charitably be called abysmal. No American I interviewed had anything nice to say about creature comforts in the country; as Alex Raffio put it, "Libya is a bicultural nation, incorporating both Arabia and Italy. Unfortunately, it picked up the worst traits of both." Omnipresent grit carried by a hot wind; filth in the streets, greasy, heavy food; packs of mangy stray dogs and snarling cats; a culture dominated by religious extremists—Libya was grubby even to persons who had endured Southeast Asia and other African countries. Harper would sit in his hotel room in Tripoli and moan, "*This* is retirement living? This is hell—this is worse than anything I saw, even in 'Nam."

Wilson gave Harper periodic pep talks abut his reputation as an expert. "You're the best in the business, old fellow, and I really need you," he told him. Privately, Wilson told other Americans he was wary of Harper. "That guy is good because he has a screw loose—he enjoys blowing things up. He gets a kick out of explosives the way normal people get a kick out of fucking. A real nut." And given that Harper was the operation's "only nut," Wilson had no choice but to try to cajole him along, even though the Libyans themselves were muttering about Harper's capabilities.

What finally pushed John Harper over the edge was his inability to have regular telephone communication with Lou. He became so agitated in Libya that he could not do his work. The other men on the demolitions team told Wilson, in effect, "Look, this crazy bastard is going to blow us all up; get him the hell out of here." Tired of the recurring problems with his wife, and aware from firsthand observation how difficult Harper was, Wilson told him late in the summer of 1976, "You are finished; get back to the States. We'll settle up your contract later."

Lou Harper waited until her husband was safely out of Libya; then she insisted that he report what he had been doing. Harper went first to the CIA, which in turn put him in contact with agents of both the FBI and the Bureau of Alcohol, Tobacco and Firearms. Agents interviewed both Harpers and their son, and took statements. But none of the three agencies—CIA, FBI or BATF—thought enough of the information to pursue it any further! By one investigator's reconstruction of the case, "Both FBI and BATF thought they had stumbled onto some kind of Agency operation, that Harper's old lady just didn't know what she was talking about. CIA—well, that's another story." Lou Harper's contact with the CIA was in August 1976. As shall be seen, she was the first of three sources to alert the CIA that year that something was amiss—criminally amiss—in Ed Wilson's overseas operations. But nothing was done; not for years.

9

"I Want Somebody Killed"

Concurrent with the explosives contract, Quaddafi escalated his demands upon Wilson and Terpil: he wanted them to recruit murderers to kill enemies of the Libyan regime. These demands were first voiced in the spring of 1976. Sporadically for the next five years, gunmen hired by Wilson and answerable to him—even if directed by Libyan intelligence intermediaries—were to become a *de facto* Murder,

Incorporated, for the Quaddafi regime. That many of the Wilson-originated assassination missions failed, the intended victim going either unharmed or only wounded, does not detract from the fact that Wilson was willing to participate in murder to earn his fortune. And in these schemes Wilson was to betray both longtime friends and the American intelligence community. Whatever his rationale, Wilson in 1976 became an outlaw in the most extreme sense of the word.

Muamar Quaddafi is one of the few chiefs of state in modern times not only to use murder as an instrument of national policy, but also to boast about it. Quaddafi intended to demonstrate that an enemy of his regime—especially an expatriate Libyan—dared not speak out against him. The most hated of these foes was Umar Abdullah Muhayshi, an early supporter of the revolution who by 1974 held cabinet rank as a minister of planning and heavy industry.

An economist, Muhayshi argued that Libya should devote its oil wealth to industrial and agricultural development, rather that to Soviet-arms purchases to support Quaddafi's meddling through Africa and the Middle East. But he could sway neither Quaddafi nor a majority of the members of the Revolutionary Command Council (RCC), the military clique that ran the country. Muhayshi continued to press his case, trying to enlist RCC colleagues to help him persuade Quaddafi to "correct his errors." In 1975, in one audacious gesture, he even urged Quaddafi to resign. Quaddafi refused, then proceeded to arrest several pro-Muhayshi members of the RCC for joining in what he called a "nefarious plot" to overthrow him. Muhayshi escaped over the border into Tunisia by auto. Although the anti-Quaddafi Egyptian press published reports that Muhayshi had tried a military coup, most serious analysts disagreed. John J. Damis, a State Department intelligence specialist at the time, felt that "Muhayshi wanted to convince Quaddafi to change his policies; there wasn't going to be a military coup." To Quaddafi's further embarrassment, his foreign minister, Abdal-Hun'in Al-Huni, defected later that year. Outraged, Quaddafi ordered that both men be killed.

The first attempt on Al-Huni's life came in March 1976, when he traveled to Rome for treatment of a chronic eye ailment. The day he was scheduled to return to Cairo, Italian security officers arrested three Libyans at Leonardo da Vinci Airport at Fiumicino, outside Rome, and charged them with plotting to hijack a flight to Tripoli. Unbeknownst to the Libyans, Al-Huni was not on the target aircraft; by either accident or design, he had changed his plans at the last moment and taken another flight.

The Rome attempt was on March 8. Two days later, the Egyptians announced the capture of a commando group of seven Libyans who had been ordered to "bring back Muhayshi dead or alive." On March 20, the Egyptians caught yet another group of Libyans, twenty this time, also on a kill-Muhayshi mission.

Muhayshi by now had been out of Libya for more than six months, without making any public statements about Quaddafi and his reasons for leaving his native land. But the assassination attempts shook him out of his silence. On March 12, he gave an interview to *Al-Ahram*, the Cairo newspaper. He denied having plotted against Quaddafi—all he and other officers had wished to do was "correct Quaddafi's errors" —but then attacked Quaddafi personally, calling him a "dangerous psychopath." He quoted a medical history compiled by British physicians in 1966, when Quaddafi was attending a military school in the United Kingdom, to the effect that a concussion suffered in a childhood accident had left him "mentally unstable."

What cut Quaddafi to the quick was detailed charges about the status of the Libyan military. Although Libya was spending about $2.4 billion annually on military purchases, the weaponry was far too great for Libya's use; soldiers were so ill prepared that they could not even do routine training exercises. Much of the costly equipment was rotting in warehouses and open fields.

In an extraordinary public reply, Quaddafi boasted that he had indeed sent Libyan agents in pursuit of Muhayshi, in both Tunisia and Egypt. Further, he was determined to continue to search for Muhayshi in Egypt "and to destroy him." For a chief of state to announce openly his intention to pursue his political enemies, regardless of where they might be, and to kill them was a staggering affront to international law and diplomacy. Quaddafi, however, was declaring his own rules: an enemy of Libya would be hunted down and killed, and the sovereignty of other nations be damned.

But Libya's performance could not keep pace with Quaddafi's threats. Three times his assassination/kidnap teams had tried to kill Al-Huni and Muhayshi; three times they had failed. So Quaddafi's intelligence services turned to Edwin Wilson and Frank Terpil. Exactly what was said is not a matter of record. Circumstances suggest that the Libyans told Wilson and Terpil that if they wished to do business with Tripoli, they must accept the occasional odd job as well— even if the odd job was murder.

To accomplish Quaddafi's mission, Wilson turned to anti-Castro Cubans, a group whom he had come to know during his years with CIA and naval intelligence. One of this group was Rafael "Chi Chi" Quintero, who had been introduced to Wilson in 1967 by his case officer, Thomas Clines. Quintero, a *habitué* of clandestine worlds most of his adult life, is reticent about the exact nature of his early dealings with Wilson, other than to say that Wilson was "helpful in some of the cover, business cover, for myself." And their relationship did include business as well as intelligence. As a CIA contract agent, Quintero used a variety of companies in Mexico and Central America as a front for anti-Castro activists. Frequently he had the opportunity to make an extra dollar for himself through these companies, and he would turn to Wilson for assistance. "We could get some business done, and I could get a commission out of it." Quintero left CIA about the same time as did Wilson, in 1971; over the next years he did occasional jobs on behalf of Task Force 157.

Although Wilson and Quintero were not social friends beyond an occasional shared dinner or drink, they were close enough that Wilson felt free to approach him for money in June, 1976. Saying he needed $10,000 to "get in a freight-forwarding business," Wilson asked Quintero if one of his Cuban banking friends now in Miami would consider such a loan. He sent along a balance sheet from Consultants International showing assets of $3 million. As it happened, Quintero had some cash available, so he lent Wilson the $10,000 himself.

Thus Quintero was not surprised when two months later, in August 1976, Wilson telephoned him in Miami and said, "Come on up here; I've got a deal to talk with you." The next day Quintero flew into Washington National Airport, where he was met by Wilson and Frank Terpil.

Wilson drove the car a mile or so from the airport and parked outside Hospitality House, a motel in the Crystal City section of Arlington. Terpil leaned into the back seat and handed Quintero a sheaf of photographs, some showing a man in Western garb, others in Arab robes.

"I want somebody killed," Terpil said. "This is a person who is sort of hated by several governments. This operation is going to bring about a million dollars." He paused. "Plus expenses. Are you willing to take it?"

Quintero thought over the proposal in silence for a few moments. He did not find it odd that the name of the victim had not been mentioned. "I had worked with the United States Government in certain capacities since 1961, and the way you are trained is that you don't ask questions; you follow instructions until you are told what to do." Because of the amount of money involved, and the Arab dress of the man in the photos, Quintero deduced that the intended target was Carlos Ramírez Sánchez, known as "The Jackal," the infamous terrorist linked to such atrocities as the Lod Airport massacre in Tel Aviv, the shooting of Israeli athletes at the Munich Olympics, the kidnapping of OPEC oil ministers and as recently as the preceding summer, 1975, the shooting of three policemen who tried to arrest him in a Paris apartment.

Quintero decided that ridding the world of The Jackal would be a humane act. "Yes," he told Wilson and Terpil, "I am willing to listen to it [the proposition]." He agreed to meet the men in Europe later to talk about details, then flew back to Miami the same day.

A few days later, Wilson telephoned Quintero and asked him to come back to Washington. The same day that Wilson made the phone call, August 30, Barbara Wilson went to Middleburg, Virginia, National Bank and withdrew $25,000 cash, in hundred-dollar bills, from a joint account she maintained with her husband. A bank officer put the bills into a canvas bag imprinted with the bank's name. Barbara Wilson cashed another check for $5,000, which she used to purchase a cashier's check for that amount. Both the check and the cash she gave to her husband at Mount Airy Farm that evening. (The prosecution stipulated during Wilson's 1982 trial on charges arising from this plot that Barbara Wilson did not know why her husband wanted the cash and check.)

Wilson handed the bag and check to Quintero when they met at the 1425 K Street Northwest, office. "This is for expenses," Wilson said. "Now I need something else as well. Could you get me a demolitions man?" Quintero thought for a moment. "I know a guy from the Bay of Pigs," he said. "He hasn't been in it for a long time, so I don't know how good he is right now, but I will find out."

The man's name, Quintero continued, was Rafael Villaverde. His brother, Raul Villaverde, had also been involved in anti-Castro activities, and he might be useful on the mission. "Fine," Wilson said; "bring them both along. I'll give you a call the next few days to set up a meet in Europe, probably in London."

Following Wilson's telephone instructions, Quintero and Rafael Villaverde flew to London in early September; Raul Villaverde was to follow. At the kiosk at Heathrow Airport, they noticed a new book on The Jackal. "His picture was on the cover, and we took it down and examined it," Quintero said.

After some more phone arrangements, Quintero and Rafael Villaverde met Wilson and Terpil in a suite at the Hôtel Méditerranéen in Geneva (the third Cuban was still en route). For the first time, Terpil identified the target: not Carlos Ramírez but Umar Muhayshi. "This is a Libyan politician who is living down in Cairo and shooting off his mouth about the Libyan government. He's a troublemaker and a revolutionary and the guy who runs Libya wants him shut up."

Quintero and Villaverde exchanged uneasy glances. Obviously there had been a lack of understanding. Neither man paid any particular attention to African politics, but each was unaware that the head of Libya, Quaddafi, was unfriendly toward the United States and himself supported such terrorists as The Jackal. Quintero gasped at the irony: They had been brought to Europe not to kill The Jackal, but to carry out an assassination on behalf of his benefactor.

Terpil apparently mistook their stunned silence for assent, for he continued talking. "We have to do it right away. Did you bring any assassination equipment with you?"

"What do you mean?" Quintero said. "We don't bring any assassination equipment." He arose and walked about the room, shaking his head in disbelief. Wilson remained silent.

Terpil got insistent. "You must go south right away," he said, meaning Egypt. Quintero argued back. "No," he said, "we agreed to come here to listen to Ed Wilson make a propostion—an assignment; not to go anywhere else."

Terpil grimaced in disgust. He kept pushing. "You got to go, and you got to go right now," he demanded.

"Well, we are not prepared to go anyplace," Quintero said. With that the meeting ended, and the Cubans withdrew to discuss their next move. Terpil and Wilson found them in the hotel bar that evening, and the discussion continued. Terpil, again the aggressor, told Quintero and Villaverde at one point, "Well, you *have* to go!" Quintero sensed a threat in Terpil's voice, but he had been in enough back alleys not to be cowed. "I am not going anywhere," he told Terpil in a tone that said he would not be shoved. Wilson played the peacemaker, trying to calm tempers. "Don't push this, take it easy," he repeatedly told Terpil.

Terpil shifted. "This is a very easy operation." he said. "The head of security for Muhayshi is on my payroll. He's in Egypt, and it would be an easy thing for you—no big problem at all."

"Well, if he's working for you, why don't you use *him* for the job?" Quintero asked. Terpil had no answer.

Raul Villaverde arrived the next morning, and after hearing the proposition agreed with his brother and Quintero that they should decline the offer and leave Switzerland as quickly as possible. They so informed Terpil and Wilson.

Realizing that the assassination plan was dead insofar as these Cubans were concerned, Terpil tried to salvage a portion of the proposal. He questioned Raul Villaverde about his technical expertise with explosives. (People who know the business say that Villaverde is very good at his trade; that his bombs have done much damage inside Castro Cuba to oil refineries, shipping installations and other facilities.)

Terpil offered Villaverde a salary of $75,000 to $100,000 a year, plus bonuses, if he would come to Libya and manufacture explosive devices. "I want ashtrays that can explode, clothes hangers that can explode, the whole ball of wax," Terpil said. Villaverde would not even need a weapon, for the Libyans would supply him with bodyguards. "Everything is very, very smooth, and all you got to do is your work. And you will be working with some people there that can pull some strings. There will be some Russians, Chinese, some of all kinds."

Terpil did not see the expressions of outrage that gnarled the faces of all three Cubans. "You mean I am going to have to be working with Russians?" Raul Villaverde asked in an even voice.

"Yes," Terpil replied. "There is no big problem. I have been invited to Russia. So you don't have no big problems with Russians."

Suddenly Terpil found himself facing three shouting, gesticulating Cubans. "You got to be crazy," Villaverde said, shaking his fist in Terpil's face, as if trying to decide whether to hit him. "I mean, you bastard, I've got a brother in jail by Castro. I would never go anyplace where the Communists or the Russians are. They would shoot my ass! Or I would get my ass shot trying to kill every goddamned one of them! I won't work with any son-of-a-bitch Communists. And I won't work with you either, because you are also a son of a bitch."

Terpil did not accept what the Cuban meant as an invitation to fight. Wilson tried to calm the situation. "Don't get into a big fight because of this. It's not as bad as Mr. Terpil is explaining. . . ." The Cubans left in what Quintero described as a "very unfriendly mood."

As the Cubans awaited the airport bus, Quintero sought out his friend Wilson for an explanation. "What is this?" Quintero demanded. "This is not a government operation. What we are getting into is crazy."

"No, this is not a government operation, this is not a CIA operation," Wilson admitted. "I'm really disappointed that you people don't want to be a part of it because [there] is a lot of money to be made in this." Wilson boasted that Terpil was "close to the second man in Libya"—referring to Quaddafadam.

"There are more things in the world than money, Ed," Quintero said.

On the plane trip back to Miami, the Cubans decided they must report the situation to the Central Intelligence Agency. Brad Rockford, the agent with whom Quintero had worked most closely, had since retired and was teaching school in Texas. Quintero thought of Rockford as a close personal friend as well as a superior. When telephoned, Rockford knew what should be done, and quickly. At his direction, Quintero telephoned Thomas Clines, who had been his overall superior in the Agency, and told him, in veiled language, what had happened. At Cline's direction, Quintero flew to Washington and gave him a full report. This was on September 19.

The next day, Ed Wilson called Quintero. "He said he was calling everything off, that he was quitting, getting off. Whatever we had talked before, he didn't want any part of it. All he wanted was for me to get him his money back." Quintero came to Washington again and returned somewhere between $12,000 and $14,000, deducting his expenses and the $10,000 he had lent Wilson earlier in the year.

Despite Quintero's disillusionment with the murder contract, he continued to do business with Wilson—but this time as a borrower rather than a lender. In 1977 or 1978, Wilson lent him $25,000 for some construction work. In 1980, through Kenneth Conklin, one of Wilson's many lawyers, he lent Quintero $100,000 for a business in Mexico. From time to time, Quintero also did odd jobs for Wilson—their nature remains undisclosed—for which he was paid.

Quintero never inquired as to what CIA did in response to his report that Wilson was involved in murder plots, for such was not his job. But one thing did strike Quintero as rather odd. Why, he asked himself, had not Wilson called him to say he was "quitting" the plot *before* Quintero had made his report to Tom Clines?

Thus the unbending opposition of the Cubans aborted Edwin Wilson's first venture into hired murder. But time and again in the coming years, he would accept such assignments for his Libyan clients.

10

"Dear Ed, I Quit"

By the summer of 1976 the pressures of working for Edwin Wilson had driven Kevin Mulcahy inescapably back to the bottle. What nagged at him was a growing uncertainty as to what Wilson was actually doing, and whether the CIA in fact sanctioned his operations abroad. In August, Wilson put Mulcahy a bit deeper into the picture. He ordered him to go to London to review a variety of projects that had been churned up by the peripatetic Frank Terpil. Being thrust into the lively band of spooks, mercenaries and arms dealers who use London as a base of operations was a heady experience for Mulcahy. In Washington, barroom talk tended to be about new computer developments and advances in satellite surveillance. The Middle Eastern and African wars serviced by the London spooks were conducted at a considerably more primitive level—the after-hours gossip was about market prices for rifle ammunition in 10-million-round lots, and whether the Belgians would turn loose a new assault gun for export. Alex Raffio, who was to mingle regularly with this group months later, says the atmosphere was reminiscent of a college fraternity. "Every Saturday morning at eleven o'clock," he said, "the group would gather at the Admiral Codrington Pub to exchange gossip and information—who was working what country, what the Saudis might be interested in buying, whether the Moroccans could get their act together on aviation equipment. Everybody was fishing for information, of course, and the flying bullshit sometimes was thicker than the smoke. But to be accepted at the Admiral Codrington on Saturday morning—this meant you were one of the boys." Mulcahy was accepted.

But the London visit brought Mulcahy into confrontation with his residual doubts about the legality of the Wilson operation. As he would reconstruct the story later, three separate episodes transformed his suspicions into the harsh fact that he had unwittingly signed on with a band of professional mercenaries and terrorists.

First was a message from Frank Terpil, then in Libya, directing Mulcahy to approach General Dynamics, the defense contractor, and inquire about purchasing one Redeye surface-to-air missile (or SAM, as the weapon is known militarily). Someone in the Libyan military had noticed a General Dynamics advertisement huckstering the Redeye in a defense-industry magazine. According to Terpil, the Libyans would pay $2.5 million cash for the Redeye. Terpil even specified how the money would be channeled through a European bank. Terpil hinted—but did not say directly—that Mulcahy would share a 10-percent commission on the deal.

Mulcahy had a vague awareness of the Redeye—that it was an antiaircraft weapon used widely in the Vietnam War. But a bit of checking brought out disturbing details. The Redeye is so small (a bit more than a yard long, weighing about 18 pounds) that it can easily be carried by someone on foot, and fired from the shoulder; in effect, the Redeye is as

portable as a rifle. Its guidance system homes on the heat
emitted by the target aircraft, and it is effective at a range of
more than 5 miles. Mulcahy realized that the only possible
use for the Redeye "in a quantity of one" would be to take a
plane out of the sky. And who was actively involved in
terrorist attacks against aircraft at that time? The Palestine
Liberation Organization. And Mulcahy knew that the PLO
received money and logistical support from Quaddafi.

Mulcahy's response to Terpil was, in effect, "I'll see what
I can find once I return to the States." His personal decision
was that "I'm not about to break my balls buying this weapon
until I know a hell of a lot more detail about where it's
going."

Terpil provided the answer when he appeared in London
several days later. He called Mulcahy to his hotel room
shortly after arrival, broke out drinks (both Terpil and Wilson
realized that a drunken Mulcahy asked fewer questions and
had less trouble with his conscience) and started waving a flag
around the room.

"What in the hell is that?" Mulcahy asked.

"An official PLO flag," Terpil said. "I got it at the PLO
headquarters in the Beach Hotel down in the sandbox [the
spook term for Libya]. They've got a whole floor of rooms
there, year-around, just above my suite. They gave it to me
as a souvenir."

Mulcahy asked himself, What have you gotten your poor
self into? That afternoon and evening, for the first time, he
drank even more than Terpil. "I was looking for something at
the bottom of a bottle of Scotch. I didn't find it then, but I
knew what I wanted. I wanted to get the hell out of this deal."

The next day, a Sunday, Terpil insisted that Mulcahy
come along on a barge outing hosted by an Austrian arms
dealer. The barge was lavishly stocked with whiskey, good
food and several girls who were amenable to going below
decks during the afternoon. Terpil brought along another
guest, a dark-complexioned man in his late twenties, whom
he did not introduce until the voyage was under way.

Terpil beckoned to Mulcahy, indicating he wished to
make the introduction. He put his arm around the shoulder
of the swarthy stranger. "Kevin," he said, "this is a guy you
really should know. You must've heard of him. Meet Carlos
Ramírez."

Mulcahy had reflexively taken the man's hand. Then the name registered. Holy shit! he thought, this is "Carlos the Jackal." Ramírez was at the height of his infamy as a terrorist. As Mulcahy was to relate later, "Every cop in Western Europe is looking for him, and here is Kevin Mulcahy, onetime altar boy, standing on the deck of a party barge on some quiet canal south of London, shaking hands with the bastard."

American intelligence officers who questioned Mulcahy later decided that they could not give what one man called "an honest evaluation" to the purported Carlos meeting. Mulcahy's information on other events that took place during this period was verified independently.

Mulcahy eventually passed out on one of the cabin bunks, in company with an unsatisfied party woman. As he was to admit, "Terpil had to help me get my goddamned pants back on and get me up the ladder. Bad day, all the way around."

Whatever the accuracy of Mulcahy's blurred memory, he broke away from the London crowd and flew back to Washington. He was "very scared." Moral decisions are seldom made spontaneously; they hover around the fringes of one's conscience until cumulative weight pushes the balance scale in one direction or the other. If Mulcahy continued with Wilson, he could make an enormous amount of money in a year's time—enough to pay off thousands of dollars of delinquent child support; enough to return to the halfway-house program that had brought him so much personal satisfaction. He also wondered how much of what he had seen and learned was actually known to Ed Wilson; Frank Terpil at the time seemed the activist, the man boasting of PLO contacts and urging Mulcahy into dirty work.

But the reverse decision carried risks. If Wilson and Terpil were in fact rogues working with terrorists, Mulcahy would endanger his own life by informing on them. Mulcahy had less than a thousand dollars cash;* Mulcahy knew that

---

*When Mulcahy arrived at Dulles International Airport, outside Washington, on his flight from London, he had about $5,000 cash that belonged to Ed Wilson. Somewhere between the airport and his motel in Northern Virginia, he met a prostitute; when he awoke the next morning, she had slipped away with about $4,000. Wilson was to assert later that Mulcahy had "stolen" this money from the Consultants International offices in Washington.

"the bottle problem still walked around with me; I drank two pints of cognac between Heathrow and Dulles." Mulcahy asked himself these questions countless times. He could not answer them. But sometime late the next day, Saturday of Labor Day weekend, Kevin Mulcahy made two decisions. The best information on Wilson and Terpil would come from their own files, and Mulcahy knew he could get to them over the weekend. To do so, however, Mulcahy would have to be cold sober. He had bought another bottle of cognac that Saturday afternoon. He poured it into the commode and went to sleep.

Mulcahy knew the general office routine in Terpil's suite at 1618 K Street Northwest. Because Wilson did business in many countries that take no notice of American weekends and holidays, someone was in the office for part of each day, seven days a week, even if only to deal with such mundane affairs as making hotel reservations. Mulcahy decided Sunday would be the best day. He waited until the lobby guard was away from his desk ("Everybody has to pee sometime during the day") and let himself into the building with his own key. He went up the stairwell to the Terpil offices. Four corporations were in the same suite: Adco, Intercontinental Technology, Stanford Technology and his own Intertechnology.

Mulcahy methodically went through Wilson's files for about four hours. "I had already anticipated what was going on; now I needed proof. I went through hundreds—hell, thousands—of pages of paper. I pulled stuff out and I ran it through the copy machine. I would read it later."

Tired, Mulcahy sneaked out of the building, again by passing the lobby guard, and had a sandwich. He then returned. "I wasn't satisfied that I had found everything there was to be found." On this return visit, he paid particular attention to Frank Terpil's desk. Nothing of import. Then he looked at the credenza behind Terpil's desk, and decided to check it out. One of the first documents he found was the secret contract with the Libyan government on the "mine-clearing" operation. Mulcahy read of how Terpil and Wilson intended that the true nature of their contract was to be shielded, and how the Libyans were to be trained for terrorist activities. Mulcahy's stomach churned, and he sat down in Terpil's chair and read through the document again. "I knew that I had been given a dummy contract, so to speak, to cover up the real purpose and intent of what these supplies . . . would actually be used for."

Mulcahy had expected the worst; now he had found it. "I thought about walking on up to the roof and seeing what it felt like to jump twelve stories down onto K Street. I thought about throwing the crap on the floor and writing a note saying, 'Dear Ed, I quit, sincerely, Kevin.' But mostly I just sat there and thought, 'Man, oh, man, are you in the shit.'"

Agency loyalty prevailed. Mulcahy dialed the CIA switchboard and asked for Theodore Shackley's home telephone number. There was intense discussion as to who Mulcahy was and why he needed the number. In interviews later, Mulcahy told conflicting stories. By his first account, he did obtain Shackley's number, and spoke with him briefly; he said Shackley had suggested he call the CIA Office of Security. By the second account, the operator refused to put him in touch with Shackley, but did contact the duty officer in the Office of Security.

Whatever the sequence, Mulcahy did receive the answer he sought. "I had to know whether this was an Agency operation or not. I found out that it was not. The Agency wanted nothing to do with it. They insisted that I contact the FBI right away. I did so." Simultaneously, the CIA passed the report to the FBI.

For the next several days, Mulcahy talked with the FBI and gave them copies of the documents he had pilfered. Because so much of the material pertained to firearms, the FBI in due course arranged for Mulcahy to talk also with the Bureau of Alcohol, Tobacco and Firearms. And, finally, someone from the CIA's Office of Security came around.

The interviews did not satisfy Mulcahy. "Lots of times, I got the distinct impression they thought I was some kind of drunken nut. One of the FBI agents asked me point-blank whether I had a history of drinking problems. I would tell them stuff, and they would nod and write it down, and look at me blankly, as if trying to decide what to make of me. I decided they were not taking me seriously. So I decided, What the hell, if they won't investigate Ed Wilson and Frank Terpil, I'll do it for them."

So Kevin Mulcahy disappeared. In the middle of September 1976, he took an assumed name and rented an unobtrusive house about an hour's drive outside Washington, in Northern Virginia. Kevin Mulcahy, onetime altar boy, onetime CIA technician, onetime unwitting accomplice of terrorists, had become Kevin Mulcahy, crusader.

That Mulcahy had defected was not known to Ed Wilson for several weeks. Mulcahy wisely used that time to try to glean as much information as he could from other Wilson associates. He spent his nights typing long memoranda on every aspect of the Wilson operation he could remember. Mulcahy felt that what Wilson and Terpil were doing was so audacious, so outrageous, that the federal investigators would share his rage and put them in jail.

But through the fall and early winter, Mulcahy realized that no one was listening to him. Federal investigators, he concluded, had written him off as a drunk and a nut. CIA was protecting Wilson not because he was on Agency business in Libya, but for fear of embarrassment should his activities be exposed. What he was witnessing, Mulcahy concluded, was a classic Washington cover-up. He made a vow: "I told myself that if I did nothing else in my fucked-up life, I was going to make the world pay attention to Ed Wilson."

Mulcahy's phone call to the Central Intelligence Agency marked the third time in the period of a month that someone had raised serious questions about the conduct of Edwin P. Wilson. Mulcahy was unaware that Quintero and Harper had spoken out before him, but his intuition that he himself was being dismissed as an unreliable drunk was exactly correct. Such was the thrust of what Theodore Shackley of the Operations Directorate told CIA internal investigators when they asked him about Mulcahy's allegations. Admiral Bobby Ray Inman, who reviewed the 1976 investigation five years later when he became deputy director of Central Intelligence, told me, "It's hard to dignify what happened with the word 'investigation.' The people running it seemed more interested in drawing the wagons in a tight circle around Ted Shackley and Tom Clines than in getting at the truth. I found it all most disquieting." For one thing, Inman noted, the probe relied almost entirely on personal interviews. "Little or no attempt was made to try to put together supporting documentary evidence."

That the CIA did not move more vigorously on such

serious allegations—made from three separate sources—is all the more remarkable because of the time frame in which they occurred. In late 1976, the CIA was just emerging from the most thorough public examination ever of an intelligence organization. Both the Rockefeller Commission and the Church Committee had spoken out strongly for stricter self-policing by the CIA. A strengthened mandate for the CIA inspector general, issued January 28, 1975, in the form of a "Headquarters Regulation," authorized the IG to:

> ...investigate the charges and reports and fraud, misuse of funds, conflicts of interest, and other matters involving misfeasance, malfeasance, nonfeasance, or violation of trust.
>
> In all cases involving possible violations of the U.S. criminal code, the investigation will be limited to developing sufficient facts to determine if a crime has been committed, and whether prosecution may compromise international relations, national security, or foreign intelligence sources and methods.
>
> The results of such investigations will be reported to the General Counsel of CIA for further reporting to the Department of Justice. *Reporting of the fact of a crime will not be delayed for an evaluation of whether prosecution will raise questions of national security, as outlined above*....[Emphasis added.]

The CIA's answers to critics of its handling of the Wilson case have followed two general lines, one sound, the other dubious on its face.* CIA's first defense is that in fact it did transmit the substance of the Quintero, Harper and Mulcahy charges to the Justice Department—specifically, to the Federal Bureau of Investigation. Wilson was no longer a CIA

---

*Even after Wilson's convictions, no one in the CIA would speak about him for attribution. Therefore, what I call "informal answers" came from officials who desired to state "CIA's side of the story," but who were also bound by the decision to say nothing publicly about Wilson. My own view, which I argued vigorously in the upper echelons of the CIA, is that the Agency could have shaken much undeserved mud from its boots by talking candidly about Wilson. I did not prevail. The persons who did talk with me, on a background basis, are of sufficient rank that I am confident they "spoke for the Agency," even if anonymously. Two of these three persons I had known before Edwin Wilson's name ever appeared in print. I do not think they lied to me, or tried to mislead me.

employee; he had done no work for the Agency since 1971. The CIA charter specifically prohibits any involvement in domestic criminal investigations. The referrals to the FBI satisfied the CIA's legal obligations. By the most narrow of definitions, CIA is right in this claim. But by realistic definition, CIA knew that the FBI would never be able to peel away internal-security barriers and do a definitive investigation of Wilson and his accomplices. Although the CIA and the FBI are agencies of the same government, they often treat each other in the manner of warring banana republics.

CIA's second "defense" was that it had no responsibility for Edwin Wilson. He had left the Agency's employ in 1971. As long as he did not violate contractual strictures against revealing intelligence data—that is, sources or methods he had learned while with the CIA—the Agency had no authority over him. If CIA got into "the Wilson case," it would run counter both to statutory law and to widely expressed congressional opposition to CIA's becoming "a supernational police force." In summary, CIA had no right or obligation to investigate the activities of a private citizen who no longer worked for the Agency.

Such an explanation ignores realities of the intelligence world. Once the Agency learned that Wilson was falsely claiming a continuing affiliation, it should have moved to alert its employees of his deception, and warn them against any involvement with him. The alert should have been disseminated throughout the intelligence and defense communities, so that anyone apt to come into contact with Wilson and his organization would not be deceived by him. Such was not to be done for many more months, with Wilson taking advantage of the Agency's lapse to continue his pose.

Finally, there are specific criminal statutes that cover anyone who passes himself off as a federal official. Proving that charge against Wilson might have been difficult, given the wink-and-nod methods by which he hinted that he was "still with the Company." But according to an FBI agent who worked on the case in later years, "Had this jerk gone around claiming to be an FBI agent, he'd have gotten a jolt that would have turned his hair green. CIA could have blown his scam. CIA didn't. CIA bought itself a lot of unnecessary trouble as a result."

So too did Wilson's old friend Thomas Clines of Operations Directorate—the man who had received Chi Chi Quintero's report of the Wilson-Terpil murder plan and nonetheless continued a close social and business relationship with Wilson.

11

An Assignment in the National Interest

At first, the defection of Kevin Mulcahy caused Edwin Wilson little more than passing annoyance. To those who asked about Mulcahy's sudden disappearance, Wilson would reply, "Oh, he fell into the bottle again. Once a drunk, always a drunk." When Wilson learned that Mulcahy was talking to agents of the FBI and the Bureau of Alcohol, Tobacco and Firearms, his answer was "that creep is peddling all kinds of crap about me. If you get any feedback about it, don't pay any attention—he's just a fucking nut."

The more pressing problem for Wilson was John Harper's failure to carry out the explosives training. The entire contract depended upon Wilson's supplying persons who could train the Libyans to fashion bombs. In his attempt to find a replacement for Harper, Wilson grew desperate. He canvassed his old friends in the CIA and naval intelligence; he talked with Cuban veterans of the Bay of Pigs and subsequent assaults on Fidel Castro's regime. He also asked his chief explosives supplier, Jerome S. Brower, to draw upon his own military and intelligence contacts to see if a good man could be found.

The search eventually got to John Heath, who in 1976 was ready to retire after two decades' service as a bomb-disposal expert in the U.S. Army. The men the army calls

"EODs" (for explosives-ordnance disposal) must have steady fingers and detached minds to survive their dangerous trade. When Heath entered the Army in 1956, the most demanding work in his first field post, Japan, had been disarming stray artillery shells and unexploded bombs left over from the Second World War. A decade later, schooled in outwitting the more devilish devices of modern techno-logical terrorists—nuclear and chemical bombs, as well as those charged with esoteric explosives—Heath was recog-nized by his peers as an expert (a title he plays down, pointing to a saying in the business that "the only experts we have are the dead ones"). Heath taught at advanced EOD schools both in the American military and in Latin America and Asia, and he was frequently detached to the Secret Service for presidential protection details. A slim man, a shade under 6 feet tall, with neatly brushed gray hair—his code name in the Wilson organization was "The Silver Fox"—Heath quietly looked for bombs in such di-verse places as Lyndon Johnson's White House swimming pool, Gerald Ford's desert house in Palm Springs and women's handbags at the 1968 Democratic National Con-vention in Chicago.

But by 1976, Heath had had enough of bombs. "I've had a couple of things go off on me; I've got some scars on my body. I just didn't want to have anything to do with explosives any longer. I felt like I'd been lucky. I had a number of friends who were either killed or maimed, and I felt I ought to leave it alone." He was 40 years old, and ready for a second career. Yet he found the post-military prospects bleak for someone of his specialized skills. A security executive for the Boeing Company had attended one of Heath's EOD classes and was so impressed that he said, "If you ever decide to get out of this crazy business, look me up. I have a job for you." Heath took him up on the offer. "I went to see him. It was $3.25 an hour and bring your own gun. I couldn't hack that." Other offers were of the same rent-a-cop variety.

In early September 1976, one of Heath's military superi-ors steered him toward what he thought would lead to "a good job and a hell of a salary and opportunities for the future." The superior also thought it would be "in my best interest and probably the best interests of the country, whatever that means." He gave Heath a phone number—"no name, no company, just the number."

Heath called the number, and spoke with a man who identified himself as Jerry Brower. Brower came right to the point. Heath had high recommendations; would he be interested in a job that paid $25,000 a year, with a $10,000 bonus at the end of the year?

Heath's military pay at the time was between $11,000 and $12,000. He said he would indeed be interested, and the next day he flew to California and met Brower at his office on North Towne Avenue in Pomona. The talk started on an unexpected tangent.

Brower motioned toward Heath's ring and asked him about it. Heath explained that it was a 32nd-degree Scottish Rite Masonic ring, which with its double-headed eagle and twin triangles is frequently mistaken by non-Masons for a military ring. Whereupon Brower began quizzing him, gently but deeply, about the Masonic order and its purposes. Finally Brower nodded, as if satisfied with the answers, and announced that he too was a Mason, and held high rank. Why, then, ask these questions? "I just wanted to see how you'd react under interrogation," Brower replied.

Then they got down to business. The job, Brower said, involved teaching basic demolition, and perhaps some advanced courses as well. Heath would be working abroad— Brower did not say where. He repeated the salary. "I thought that was great. I used to do that for $187 a month in the Army."

Brower handed Heath a silver coin about the size of a quarter, with Arabic inscriptions. "Every one of our operatives carries one of these," he said. "This is so that one of us that doesn't know another can immediately be identified, and you can establish trust and know you can talk to him freely. Always keep this with you. For God's sake, don't lose it."

Mystified by this mumbo jumbo, Heath flew back to Fort Lewis, Washington, his duty station, where the old boy network of master sergeants whisked through his discharge from the Army within hours. He then returned to Pomona, where Brower introduced him to three other members of the team who would be going abroad. Dennis J. Wilson and Robert E. Swallow both worked at the U.S. Navy's China

Lake Naval Weapons Center in the Mojave Desert in Southern California, which Heath knew to be a supersecret test base for military and CIA weaponry.* Douglas Smith, the third man, was identified as a Brower employee. Because Dennis Wilson already knew Swallow and Smith, and had worked with Brower previously, he was designated crew chief. Heath recalls: "Doug Smith and I were to be the explosives people and they [Swallow and Wilson] were the engineers. I wasn't quite sure what all that was about, but Jerry did a lot of talking. 'We're going to set up a cover company in the Middle East and sell explosives,'" he said. When Heath expressed curiosity as to exactly where they would be working, Brower mentioned only "North Africa."

A few days later, with a $4,000 advance and a plane ticket to Washington in hand, Heath received his final instructions from Brower. He was to meet a man named Douglas Schlachter at Dulles International Airport, and he should cut the labels out of any clothing he took with him.

The five men—Heath, Schlachter, Wilson, Swallow and Smith—met up at Dulles. They got into Schlachter's Cadillac and drove off into the Virginia countryside, Schlachter explaining, "We have some time before the plane to London, and I want to take you out to a friend's house."

Somewhere en route—Heath is uncertain as to the exact location—the group drove past a road sign that "said something about CIA or some damn thing. Schlachter turned around and leaned over the seat and said, 'That's headquarters.'" The facility most likely was the CIA's covert training and communications center at Flint Hill, Virginia, which lies along the cross-country route from Dulles Airport to Edwin Wilson's farm in Upperville. Flint Hill, however, had never displayed a sign identifying it as a CIA facility; its function is supposedly secret, although it is known to neighboring farmers and many other persons. In any case, while Heath does not purport to remember details, his recollection is strong

---

*Swallow made no secret of his destination. In an application for leave filed with China Lake superiors, he wrote, "I have an opportunity to assist in opening and managing an explosives sales and demolition consulting office in Libya for the J. S. Brower & Associates, Inc., of Pomona, Calif." Even though Libya was publicly known as a hotbed of terrorist training, the application received routine approval.

that the car went past something said to be a CIA facility, and that Schlachter called it "headquarters."*

This comment cemented, in Heath's mind, the notion that he was involved in an Agency operation, a notion supported by his having been referred to Brower by a military superior with the understanding that the assignment would be "in the national interest." Moreover, the two specialists supplied by Brower had come from a sensitive government intelligence facility, China Lake. Although Heath had not been *told* he was entering into secret government business, the circumstances convinced him this was indeed the case.

The "friend's house" proved to be Ed Wilson's Upperville estate. Schlachter introduced Wilson simply as "my friend." No mention was made of the fact that Jerome Brower was one of his contractors, and that Wilson in fact was responsible for the operation upon which Heath and the other men were embarking. But as Heath was later to learn, Wilson had asked Schlachter to "bring the new men out so that I can look them over before they go to Libya." Dissatisfied with the Harpers' performance, Wilson was determined to make no further mistakes.

Apparently Heath and friends passed inspection, for that evening they flew off to London. En route, Schlachter finally announced their destination: Tripoli, Libya. Heath recalls: "The only thing I knew about Tripoli was the Marine Hymn. I began to wish that I had time to open up the atlas."

Once in Tripoli, the party received red-carpet treatment and warm greetings from the two top Libyan intelligence officers, Captain Abdullah Hijazzi and Lieutenant Abdullah Sinusi. Then they were taken to King Idris' summer palace to view the "workshop" that had been used by the Harpers. Heath was not impressed, finding the facility "inept, not very creative." Although it stood on the palace grounds, the shop was clearly former servants' quarters, and its tools and equipment were few and outmoded. Even worse were the sample explosive devices left behind by the Harpers.

There was, for instance, a flower vase the Harpers had

---

*For Schlachter to have driven past the CIA's actual marked headquarters, off the George Washington Parkway closer in toward Washington, would have required an unlikely detour of some 30 miles.

filled with a common homemade explosive, a mixture of ammonium nitrate (lawn fertilizer) and diesel fuel. The mixture had been covered over with decorative rocks. The Harpers had left two bare wires sticking out the rear of the vase, one with a blasting cap attached. Very crude, Heath thought; you couldn't fool anyone with that. Nor was he impressed with some artificial incendiary rocks the Harpers had fashioned. "These are useful, say, if you wish to start a fire in a place where a rock would be unobtrusive. I've seen them made so that you really have to look to realize they aren't rocks. But the samples they had were so crude they wouldn't fool anybody—except maybe the Libyans." But the main significance of Heath's first view of the workshop was to make him realize finally that he and his associates "were going to be making homemade bombs" in addition to their stated mission of teaching classes on basic demolition.

"I don't know if I can describe how much that upset me. First of all, a bomb is a coward's weapon. That's one of the reasons I stayed in bomb disposal. I think everybody needs to feel useful in what they're doing, and I found a little bit of that in thinking that occasionally I saved a life or maybe some child being blinded by fireworks or whatever.

"The same thing with homemade bombs. Making them and taking them apart are two different things because you had two different motivations."

So Heath tossed and turned in his bed for several nights, wondering how he had gotten himself into such a situation— or, more important, how he could get out of it. The hints that he was on an assignment emanating from American intelligence dampened his moral doubts. "I kept thinking back to a number of things I'd been involved in—military, Secret Service, various agencies—where you would have one opinion just looking at the outside facts, and once you got inside to the higher echelons and found out the reasons for something, then it just becomes a 180-degree turn and you say, 'Oh, wow, if I'd known that . . . ' So I kept rationalizing myself by saying, 'Well, even if we start to make these things, there's most likely a higher purpose than I can see. The Agency's got something in mind. I don't know what it is. But they know more about it than I do.' And I decided to play along with it."

Since the workshop had neither the tools nor the explosives to make any workable bombs, the first order of business was to assemble a "shopping list" of necessary supplies, including tools and chemicals for homemade bombs and incendiaries ("iron shavings, magnesium, aluminum powder, potassium chlorate—that sort of thing"). Few of these items were available in Libya (Heath recalls shopping for two weeks, on and off, for a common claw hammer with which to make repairs around the palace), so they had to be ordered via Schlachter or Frank Terpil, both then in the United States.

Meanwhile, the four explosives men passed the time in the most mundane of activities: gardening. "We did this to keep from going nuts. In the beginning, we weren't allowed to go anywhere unescorted, even to eat."

The only project of substance those first weeks was an attempt, by Bob Swallow and Dennis Wilson, to manufacture silencers for pistols. Here the chief obstacle was unrealistic expectations by the Libyans, who had in mind the James Bond-ish exotica they had seen on video-cassettes of American movies. Dennis Wilson had made silencers at the China Lake facility, and what he produced in Libya would have been acceptable to his U.S. Government employers. But not to the Libyans. "They had the notion you could make a three-inch silencer that would completely muffle the sound of a gunshot. Well, that simply isn't true. I've fired more than one weapon with a silencer, and you certainly cut down the noise level a lot. But the silencer isn't three inches, and you can still hear it." By Heath's analysis—and the problem was to manifest itself many times over the next six years—the Libyans were at once crafty and childish. "Their mentality," Heath said, "is not something you can really explain; you have to see it. Because of the frustrations of their lifestyles, they tend to do a lot of what we used to call skylarking or grab-assing. You see grown men running around playing little practical jokes—and these are people in fairly high political positions. They are every bit as childish in what they expect of weapons. There's a streak of comic-book mentality even in the adults."

In any event, the Libyans looked at Dennis Wilson's silencers and shook their heads and said, "Oh, it's too big, it's too long, makes too much noise." The frustrated Wilson would return to his drawing board and work for days on a

new design. "He never did come up with anything that
satisfied them."

During these weeks, Edwin P. Wilson remained (to
Heath, at least) an invisible figure. Occasionally Doug Schlachter
mentioned his name, reinforcing the impression that they
were very close. But nothing was said to indicate that Wilson
was in overall command.

Heath made no attempt to break away from the project,
even though he often found it morally repugnant. His paychecks were being deposited regularly in a Swiss bank, with a
portion being sent on to his family in Washington State.

His moral rationalization was typical of persons working
for Ed Wilson: they didn't like the work and felt soiled by
association with such a state as Libya; yet the money was
good, and you took the soldier's attitude—"You can stomach
any kind of crap for a year; then you pocket your money and
go home."

Eventually, John Heath's role in the Wilson organization
was to expand far beyond explosives. Because of his administrative skills and his ability to satisfy Wilson, Heath became
his confidential assistant and *aide-de-camp*. He performed
the detail work on Wilson contracts, ranging from the sale of
sophisticated military equipment to complex intelligence-
gathering assignments. By reason of their joint isolation from
the rest of the world, their relationship took on a semblance
of friendship. (Heath questions this: "I don't think Ed Wilson
ever had a 'friend' in his life, in the truest sense of the term,
because he did not have the ability to either give or receive
trust."). And in interminable late-night conversations, usually
over drinks of "flash," a viciously potent home-distilled liquor, Heath perhaps more than any other person came to
understand the complex emotions that fueled Edwin Wilson's
ambitions, as well as the support of those he enlisted in his
operation.

"In a word," John Heath said: "*greed.*"

The explosives-training team finally got down to serious
work in early 1977. After several false starts, Ed Wilson had
procured the necessary equipment. John Heath's doubts
about his participation were at least partly absolved during a
brief Christmas visit home, to Washington State, when he
came to realize that his long-shaky marriage was in jeopardy.

If he fulfilled his contract with Wilson, he would have the money to make the down payment on a house and to pay for the college education of his children—steps that might draw him and his wife back together.

Wilson was insistent that the training proceed. "You've got to get moving," he told Heath; "otherwise the Libyans are going to put our asses in the slammer. They're mad." Heath, however, would not be hurried. "You start taking shortcuts with bombs," he told Wilson, "and you take a shortcut to the graveyard." He insisted that before the Libyans were taught how to make bombs, they must learn the essentials of basic chemistry, electricity and demolitions: Unless a student understood why explosives work as they do, he was apt to blow up both himself and anyone else who happened to be in the area.

Teaching the Libyans was a laborious task, even though the first eight students assigned to the course were said to be the cream of military intelligence. Since many of the students came from the desert, they had only a passing acquaintance with such things as electricity and plumbing. None spoke any English, so all instruction was through an interpreter. But using American military manuals provided by Brower, Heath and his associates managed to put together a training course. When a "bomb" made by a Libyan student exploded, he saw the sharp light of a photographic flashbulb, rather than hearing the boom of an explosive. To stress the dangers of blasting caps, Heath went to a butcher shop and purchased a chunk of meat with bones in it. "I would fill a boot or a rubber glove with the meat and bones, and set off a blasting cap beneath it. This made quite a mess, and I would tell them, 'This is what happens to your hand or your foot if you do not do what Mister John tells you.' Nonetheless, even these demonstrations had no lasting effect, for the desert Arabs have the attitude 'If I am to die, it is Allah's will.'"

Heath insisted that the Libyans have an ambulance and medics present during any demonstration demolitions. Here, again, many frustrations: One day the instructor and trainees drove ninety minutes into the desert, to a tank training base where the temperature sometimes got above 130 degrees. The promised ambulance did not appear. The Libyans promised to do better the next day. They did not. They sent along an "ambulance" which was nothing more than a truck with a red crescent painted on the side. It contained neither medics nor medical supplies. "I can look back on these things now and laugh," states Heath, "but at the time, they weren't very funny."

The normal class "day" was six hours or less, and on many days instruction had to be cut even shorter because of student inattention. Even the better students, Heath recalls, "weren't motivated by much more than their boss's desire for them to succeed and a fear of discipline. Of all the classes I've taught all over the world, this was probably the slowest and most dangerous from the instructor's point of view."

Schlachter and Wilson, catering to Libyan whims, did not help matters by bringing in a constant supply of exotic but basically worthless equipment that Heath and the others were supposed to incorporate into bombs. One such item which excited the Libyans was remote-radio-control devices. Even at 1,000 meters, the devices worked only one of perhaps a dozen times. "That's line-of-sight, mind you, with no interference or anything around, no antennas, radio stations or transmitters or anything like that. Schlachter, Terpil and Wilson cut so many corners trying to make their windfall killing on profits that they just bought a lot of odds and ends and junk. Of course, *we* were told this was good equipment, and then *we* were the ones who were embarrassed in front of the Libyans when it didn't work."

During the late spring of 1977, several things became obvious to Heath. Wilson was around so often, and gave orders so authoritatively, that Heath finally came to realize that he was the man in charge of the mission. Schlachter deferred to him, the Libyans treated him with respect and all the while Wilson walked around with the aura of a commander. The few times he and Heath spoke personally, the former sergeant was impressed. "Ed comes across very strongly as a can-do guy, and he seemed to like dealing with someone who had a professional record, such as I did. I liked him."

One reason Wilson began to appear so frequently was that the Libyans were becoming irked at the lack of progress in the training program. Further, a subordinate, Dennis Wilson of China Lake, was making an obvious attempt to take over the contract and run the project on his own. An easygoing man when he had first come to Libya, Dennis Wilson had grown increasingly irritable as the weeks passed and promised equipment never arrived or, when it did, proved worthless. At one meeting with the Libyans, Dennis Wilson and Robert Swallow happened to see Ed Wilson's invoices for one batch of timers which were mostly junk. The price was several times the cost of manufacture. According to Heath, "They [Dennis Wilson and Swallow] blew up and told the Libyans that Ed Wilson and Doug Schlachter were cheating them, and if they wanted something decent, they should give them the equipment and the proper materials and they'd make something a hell of a lot better and a hell of a lot less expensive."

Ed Wilson was away at the time of this small revolt, and when he heard of it he hurried back to Libya and managed to discredit Dennis Wilson and Swallow. It was also during this return that Heath heard something which reinforced once again his impression that Wilson worked for the Central Intelligence Agency.

Early in their stay in Libya, Heath and the other Americans had met a local fixer named Morrie. A merchant of Italian extraction, Morrie boasted of having gotten his commercial start in life by pimping nonexistent whores to American soldiers in Rome during the Second World War. (Morrie would take the soldier's money, tell him to relax "while the girl finishes her shower," then vanish.) In Tripoli, he was pleasant and raucous company—the man to see for scarce tools or an occasional bottle of good Scotch whiskey. His devout capitalism notwithstanding, Morrie also could deal with the cumbersome and hypersuspicious Libyan bureaucracy. But his *sotto voce* comments told of his disdain for the Quaddafi regime.

One day Morrie came to Dennis Wilson with an astounding proposition. He said he represented a group of businessmen who wished to overthrow Quaddafi. These persons, he said, "knew" that Edwin Wilson worked for the CIA. They did not need any support for their coup, which they felt certain would succeed, but what they did wish was an assurance from the CIA through Ed Wilson that when they succeeded, the U.S. Government would support their new regime.

Morrie wished to raise the question directly to Ed Wilson. When he arrived back, a meeting was arranged; it involved Morrie, both Dennis and Ed Wilson, Doug Schlachter and John Heath. By Heath's account, all parties got so drunk that the meeting soon collapsed into chaos. Morrie did manage to get Ed Wilson and Schlachter alone for a few private minutes. They gave him no encouragement whatever on his supposed coup plot. After Ed Wilson and Schlachter left, the others tried to figure out why. Perhaps, with Morrie so drunk, it had been hard to tell whether he was babbling nonsense or discussing a serious proposition. Also, Morrie was unknown; perhaps Wilson had figured he was acting as an *agent provocateur* to test the Americans. Or, finally, was Wilson hesitant to help topple a regime from which he stood to earn millions of dollars? (Whatever the reason for his rejection of Morrie, Wilson did not report the scheme to Libyan intelligence, for Morrie remained active in his business.)

The rejection infuriated Morrie. Later that evening, he and Dennis Wilson—both men were most drunk by now, it must be remembered—fell into vitriolic discussion of Wilson and Schlachter. According to Heath, the following dialogue took place:

MORRIE: They didn't want to talk to me. I'll tell you one thing, I'm not worried about that little guy [Schlachter], but the big guy [Wilson] is a very dangerous man.

DENNIS WILSON: Yeah, he's a dangerous son of a bitch. I'd like to kill the both of them.

MORRIE: Really? Hey, my cousin runs the Libyan mafia. You want them killed tonight?

DENNIS WILSON: Yeah, if you can do it.

MORRIE: Well, I'll tell you what. We'll go kill them ourselves.

To Heath's horror, Morrie drew a 9-millimeter pistol, checked the magazine to ensure that it was loaded with ammunition and jacked a round into the chamber. "I'm saying, Oh, shit, what am I doing here? How did I get myself into this one? What am I going to do to get out of it?" Morrie decided he was too drunk to shoot Wilson himself. "Dennis says, 'That's all right. You give me the gun and I'll do it.'" There was more drunken talk (the terrified Heath by this time was refusing any further drinks) and someone suggested that if Wilson was in fact a CIA agent, his friend Schlachter might also be armed. So Morrie went into the next room and found a .25-caliber automatic for Heath.

During the drive to Ed Wilson's hotel, Heath managed to slip the 9-millimeter pistol from Dennis Wilson's pocket. Dennis Wilson pounded on Ed's door and barged into the room shouting drunkenly. He accused Ed Wilson of not keeping his promises on commissions and of being a general double-dealer. Ed Wilson, nostrils flaring and neck swelling with rage, leaped from his chair and pointed to Dennis Wilson and yelled, "You sit down. You shut up!"

To Heath, the display was sheer physical intimidation. Dennis Wilson, who had come to the hotel to shoot Ed Wilson, sank into a chair shaking with fear. Wilson proceeded to repeat what he had told the demolitions team: If they brought in any business, they would get commissions. But the work wasn't going well, and he (Ed Wilson) was damned tired of having "to take all the heat and the gruff from the Libyans because you bastards aren't doing your jobs." Then he switched to a conciliatory tone. He put his arm over Dennis Wilson's shoulder. He told him what a good man he was. "Yes, Dennis, we'll all make money, old buddy; you just ride it out with me. I understand why you are upset, Dennis. Now why don't you just go home and sleep a bit and we'll talk later, hey, old buddy?"

Within the space of several minutes, Dennis Wilson had been transformed from potential murderer to old buddy. As he left, Ed Wilson muttered to Doug Schlachter, "Get that asshole out of the country as fast as you can; I don't want him around anymore." Two days later, Dennis Wilson left Libya.

By the spring of 1977 the Wilson crews had been in Libya for a full year without producing a single workable bomb. Wilson continually made excuses; finally, a short-lived border war between the Libyans and the Egyptians forced his hand. The incident began with classic international intrigue. In early 1976, General Hacka Hofi, head of Mossad, the Israeli intelligence service, learned of detailed Libyan plans to assassinate President Anwar Sadat of Egypt. The information apparently came from a Mossad mole in the Palestine Liberation Organization. At the direct order of Prime Minister Menachem Begin, Hofi met in Rabat, Morocco, with Kamal Ali, the head of Egyptian intelligence, to pass along the information. The Mossad dossier contained the names and Cairo addresses of the PLO plotters, who were seized in predawn raids a few days later. They confessed, and turned over arms caches and documents proving they were working on Quaddafi's order. "It is time," Sadat said, "to give this madman Quaddafi a sting." He ordered punitive raids across the Libyan border—strong enough to put Quaddafi on warning that his country could easily be overrun by the superior Egyptian military.*

Although the fighting lasted only four days, one observer said it cost the Libyans a "major bloodletting." Other Arab heads of state finally intervened and persuaded Sadat to declare a cease-fire.

The episode humiliated Quaddafi. It showed that despite having spent billions of dollars on military equipment, he could not defend his own borders. To judge from reactions from Libyan intelligence officers, much of Quaddafi's rage was directed against Wilson and his bomb "experts." You have been here for months, the Americans were told, and not a single Egyptian or Israeli has been killed by one of your so-called bombs. Our patience is at an end. You are going this very day to Tobruk, on the Egyptian border, and your students are to go with you. We want many, many sabotage devices and booby traps that can be planted around the Egyptian border towns. We paid you for your so-called expertise and for Mister Ed's bombs. We want them now, and no further excuses or arguments.

The Wilson team in Libya had three American explosives trainers at the time—George Kness, Andrew Brill and George Dorrity—all with long service in either the military or intelligence. Dorrity, a bantam of a man at 5 feet 7 inches, had what one associate called "a little man's complex, a chip on his shoulder." With the most tenure in Libya after John Heath, the normal commander, who was in the United States on business, Dorrity took charge of the contingent in Tobruk. Within a matter of days, the Americans produced bombs

---

*Israel's sharing of this intelligence information was the first break in the logjam that had marked its relations with Egypt. After the raids into Libya, Sadat told the Israelis he had always harbored hopes of a nonbelligerency pact between the two nations. This led to his historic visit to Tel Aviv and, eventually, the Camp David accords that formally ended three decades of hostility.

hidden in a peddler's-bag variety of household items: clocks, cameras, portable radios, calculators, lamps, telephones.

In one of his early lectures, John Heath had remarked that even under ideal circumstances about 10 percent of ordnance was duds, and that "the more safeties you have, the bigger chance you have of something being a dud." The Libyans, bloodied by the Egyptians and eager to retaliate, remembered this comment; hence the Tobruk bombs would be built without safety devices. The American trainers felt they were not in a position to object: The Libyans held their passports, and they were told, in no uncertain terms, that unless they produced bombs they would never see the United States again. Given the war atmosphere in Libya, these threats seemed plausible.

Rigging such commonplace items to explode is a calculated business. A citizen who finds a portable radio in the street reflexively turns it on to see if it works. The saboteur has left the radio dialed to either end of the band, so that no station is received until the finder does some tuning. The explosive is set to detonate when he reaches a popular local frequency— say, Radio Cairo. A booby-trapped clock may work well for eighteen hours—until the hour hand makes two complete circuits and then touches the timing device. Because such devices are so innocuous in appearance, no amount of warnings can dissuade a civilian populace from picking them up from the street.

Through pure, dumb luck, the Americans and their Libyan trainees managed to assemble literally scores of these booby traps without serious incident. The last afternoon, the Americans sat on a curb outside the workshop and watched the Libyans load their deadly products onto a three-quarter-ton truck. The day was hot; someone suggested, "Hey, let's go inside and see if we can find something cold to drink." (For reasons unclear to the Americans, the intelligence compound in Tobruk was the only place in Libya—outside Western oil camps—where liquor was readily available.)

One of the Americans was nervous about the cavalier manner in which the Libyan youths handled the explosives. One would stand in the workshop and toss each bomb to another youth at a window, who in turn dropped it to a man on the back of the truck. "Hey, hey, take it easy," the American called, then stepped around the corner.

A few seconds later came a horrendous explosion. It shook much of Tobruk, tore the front from the workshop building and obliterated the three Libyan youths who had been loading the truck; only scattered bits of body were found in the wreckage. One of the victims was a nephew of Abdullah Sinusi, the assistant chief of Libyan intelligence.

The only American to suffer serious injury was George Kness, who sustained third-degree burns across the lower part of his back. Dorrity received a concussion and a scalp laceration. But as Dorrity commented later, "If we had not developed a thirst for Johnnie Walker when we did, BLOOEY —all of us, up in smoke with the Libs."

The Tobruk accident, rather than deterring the Libyans from their seeming obsession with booby traps, caused them to envision even more grandiose bombs. John Heath, by coincidence, had arrived back in Tripoli the day of the accident. Grim-faced Libyan intelligence officials put him on a plane to Tobruk, with armed escort, and there he received a firm dressing-down. You Americans, a Libyan officer told Heath, are incompetent. We have tried you on the smaller bombs, and you failed, you failed miserably, and you cost the lives of three of our valiant soldiers. Now we intend to try something different, something bigger, and you will do this for us, do you understand, Mister John?

Heath understood. His string of excuses for not producing bombs had run out. He knew, from the tone of the Libyan command, that if he stalled now he was dead. No matter how he attempted to rationalize the path that had brought him to this remote Libyan city, Heath now must make booby traps to kill people.

For the next Libyan scheme, Heath was shown a military water tanker, a truck capable of carrying more than 10,000 gallons. Mister John must create "a monster bomb that we can leave in an Egyptian city and kill many, many Egyptians, hundreds of them, thousands of them." The Libyan saying this seemed to smack his lips in anticipatory delight, as if envisioning shreds of Egyptian flesh flying through the air.

Heath gave the truck a careful inspection. He knew that the Tripoli warehouse in fact contained liquid explosives that could transform the water truck into a lethal vehicle of death. The explosives involved were a so-called binary compound.

In essence, two liquid components—by themselves harmless, and shipped in separate containers—once mixed became a compound with a deadly explosive force. Heath's own envisioning saw the truck parked in the center of an Egyptian town, one whose citizens had the chronic desert thirst for fresh water. A young woman accompanied by three small children held her bucket up to the tap, and someone turned it, and...

Heath shuddered. "What we could put into that truck could blow away half of Egypt, figuratively." So he argued with the Libyans, fighting a verbal holding action. He asked a practical question. Just how did the Libyans intend to sneak the truck across miles of watched desert road and leave it in an Egyptian town? The Libyans didn't worry about such details. "We kill many Egyptians," they repeated. Heath persisted with another point. "Okay, how are you going to get that many Egyptians around this thing, anyway?"

"No, no, that's not your problem, that's our problem. You just make the bomb."

Heath lied. With the rudimentary tools at hand, he could have "rigged it up some way or another" with 75-percent certainty. But Heath gave the Libyans double-talk about solenoid switches and lathes and pressure valves; eventually the ranking officer said, "Okay, Mister John, maybe you are right. So now we must look for something else."

The Libyan substitute was six small camper trailers. "They wanted them rigged so that when the door opened, the explosives went off," Heath said. Again he pointed out several drawbacks. Campers are seldom seen in the Middle East; the appearance of one on the street would be sure to excite curiosity, and examination. "People are going to be suspicious; nobody in their right mind is just going to go up and open the door, especially with all the trouble you people are having on the border," Heath told the Libyans. There was much arguing about how the explosives should be disguised. The Libyans finally decided to board over the windows with plywood. "Ridiculous!" said Heath. "That makes it ten times as conspicuous." But he did not argue too loudly, realizing by now that the project was almost bound to fail even if carried out.

Eventually, as Heath relates, "I did the wiring on all of it, and the lovely, sophisticated devices that we had to work with were switches made out of clothespins." The Libyans dragged in old washing machines and refrigerators, and the Americans stripped off pressure switches and other electrical gear for use in the bombs. Here again, Heath claims to have done subtle sabotage. A switch taken off a refrigerator that operates at 220 volts A.C. is not compatible with an explosive device energized by a 9-volt D.C. battery. "There's just too much resistance in the circuit and it's not going to function. Yet you put a galvanometer on there to test the circuit, it shows a complete circuit and they're happy."

Six of the campers were made into bombs and driven off over the desert at night toward Egypt. Heath later heard that Libyan agents had managed to detonate only one of them. He did not hear whether the bomb had killed any Egyptians. He did not really want to know.

Years later, when the Central Intelligence Agency conducted a long-overdue investigation of the Wilson organization, it ran into an anomaly. Despite Wilson's widely publicized portrayal as a master of bomb-makers, no credible evidence could be found that his workshops ever produced a single device that harmed an enemy of Libya. The sole fatalities found were the three Libyan students who had died because of their own horseplay with explosives. The credit, however, must go to John Heath rather than Ed Wilson. Through his failure to satisfy Wilson's contract, Heath deterred the Libyans from finding more willing instructors.*

Somehow, Wilson's reputation with the Libyans as a bomb-maker did not suffer. Yes, his instructors might have dallied and been overcautious. Yes, Libyan intelligence was miffed that Heath and colleagues did not give the bomb project the demanded urgency, did not deliver all sorts of hellish devices. But even in failure Ed Wilson succeeded. His ability to obtain explosives of Western manufacture impressed the Libyans. Soon after the sting of the Egyptian border war, Quaddafi's intelligence officers gave Wilson an

---

*After several weeks of interviews I asked Heath, "Had you really wanted to, could you have given the Libyans what they asked for?" Heath fell silent a few moments. "Given the materials we eventually received, we could have made the Libyans enough stuff to blow up all of North Africa. No, I didn't think of myself as a 'deterrent.' But I wasn't busting my ass to make stuff I didn't want to make."

open-ended order. His earlier shipments had included an explosive known as C-4, a variety of *plastique*. C-4 is the superbang of explosives. A chunk of C-4 the size of a can of beer can shatter a six-room wooden house. Chemically, it consists of the active ingredient cyclotrimethylene trinitramine, mixed with isomethylene, a chemical powder, and motor oil, all blended together to form a substance with the physical characteristics of putty or soft plastic. C-4 is a high-impact explosive tailor-made for a terrorist who must work with a concealable bomb. And it was for international terrorists that Libya wanted the C-4—the Palestine Liberation Organization, the Irish Republican Army, the old Baader-Meinhof gang of West Germany, Italy's Red Brigades and lesser known groups throughout Africa, the Middle East and Europe. Quaddafi was out to become the *de facto* explosives quartermaster for any terrorists whose ideology he found attractive.

12

"The Bird Has Flown the Coop"

In the late spring of 1977, Wilson called Jerry Brower, the California explosives merchant. "Get into Washington as soon as you can," Wilson told Brower. "I have some good business for you."

Brower obliged. In Wilson's office he met a Libyan whom he recognized as a procurement official with boundless authority. "I want some C-4 for these people," Wilson said without ceremony—"as much as I can get. What can you do for me?"

Brower told Wilson, "I don't know how much I can get, but as soon as I find out, I'll let you know."

Wilson suggested that Brower and the Libyans "take a

break. . . . I need to talk to some people on the phone about this." Brower took the visitors downstairs to a strip joint on the ground floor of Wilson's office building. They watched the dancers for fifteen to twenty minutes, and the Libyans enjoyed stuffing dollar bills into the girls' panties. There was no talk about business. (Pressed on this point later by Wilson's lawyer, Brower sounded defensively indignant: "Haven't you ever stood and watched a girl with your mouth open? I am getting to be an old man. I enjoy stuff like that.")

Back upstairs, Brower got final approval from Wilson: Buy what you can find, and get back to me with the quantity and price.

Brower began on the telephones. As a licensed explosives dealer, he did not have to explain to suppliers *why* he wanted C-4, only whether it was available. By midsummer, he telephoned Wilson and reported, "I can get around forty thousand pounds at a price of $13.75 a pound."

"Get it," Wilson said. "You run the paperwork."

Brower did as Wilson directed, but via a route intended to keep him a safe step away from the transaction, which he knew was illegal. He chose to use an aging lawyer named Edward Bloom.

Bloom was 70 years old in August 1977 when Brower called him to his offices to draft the initial contracts for the explosives deal. Bloom is a quiet small-town lawyer who did his professional work with pride and skill, although without a great deal of remuneration. He passed the bar in Idaho in 1928 after graduation from Gonzaga University, a Catholic school in Spokane. He studied mining and engineering at the University of Washington, then did graduate work at the Woodrow Wilson School of Public and International Affairs at Princeton. During the Second World War, he spent thirty-nine months abroad as an Air Corps officer. As Bloom proudly told friends, four generations of his family occupied graves at Arlington National Cemetery.

Bloom had met Jerry Brower in 1969 in a civil suit in which they were on opposing sides. With this action settled, they had become business and social friends. In 1971, Brower had retained Bloom for $100 per month to do routine legal work for his explosives business. Bloom knew federal and state laws governing explosives, for he had served as general counsel of the Society of Explosives Engineers (the trade group which Brower had founded and which he served as president). Bloom had attended Brower's daughter's wedding, and the Browers' fortieth-wedding-anniversary fete. He felt the relationship was "extremely friendly, but not intimate."

By Bloom's account—one difficult to accept, given other evidence—he was an unwitting participant in the C-4 smuggling scheme from the very outset. As Bloom recounted the first meeting on the subject, "He [Brower] said he was going to sell some chemicals and he would like to have me draw a *pro forma* contract." Bloom saw nothing unusual in the request, for he knew Brower's business. "His catalogues show him to be an extensive dealer in chemicals as well as explosives."

The seller of the 42,300 pounds of "chemicals" was to be Explosives Engineering International Contractors, Inc., a corporation based in Liechtenstein. Bloom knew the company: on Brower's instructions, he had scouted the minute European country for an inactive corporation, and bought a charter from some Italian lawyers. Brower used EEIC for many deals outside the United States, rather than his own Jerome S. Brower & Associates. The buyer of the "chemicals" was to be MEPROCO, the Libyan purchasing mission in London. The billing was to be to Consultants International, 14 Avenue Industriale, Geneva—the Swiss office of Wilson's company. The price would be $13.75 per pound, for 42,300 pounds, payable in advance to Brower's Swiss account. Bloom drafted a rough contract on a legal pad and handed it to Brower, telling him to have it typed on his stationery.

Such is Bloom's story. Unfortunately for his future well-being, over the next weeks he immersed himself in the C-4 sale to such an extent that he cannot be considered a totally innocent intermediary. Bloom witnessed enough oddities, and at enough intervals, that he could have gotten out of the transaction. He did not. (In 1983, Bloom was convicted of conspiracy to violate federal laws on export of explosives.)

At Brower's direction, Bloom flew to Geneva in late August and went to the Union Bank. Wilson a few days earlier had deposited $588,000 there to Brower's credit. Bloom presented three sealed envelopes to a bank officer that contained instructions to send checks to the three explosives suppliers from whom Brower was to buy the C-4. Still following

Brower's instruction, Bloom next flew to Montreal, where he met with an official of Canadian Industries, Ltd., a subsidiary of Imperial Chemicals, Ltd. Here, Bloom says, he learned for the first time that the "chemicals" deal on which he had been working actually involved C-4. He was not surprised. "Mr. Brower operated on the military theory of having to know, and I was not privy to what was going on inside the business. I had no idea what the company was doing. For a hundred [dollars] a month, you don't stay in a guy's office and run the business."

Bloom began assembling the C-4. He had the Canadian firm ship about 10,000 pounds of C-4 to Brower's bunker in Pomona. To avoid the red tape of taking the explosives through American customs, the firm drew the C-4 from one of its warehouses in upstate New York.

The remainder of the explosives came from Technical Explosives, of New Orleans, and Goex, of Cleburne, Texas. Brower bought the C-4 openly, using his Bureau of Alcohol, Tobacco and Firearms License; the firms that sold it to him did so in full compliance with the law. Even so, getting the explosives to California proved ticklish. Louisiana law, for instance, required that the C-4 be shipped with a police escort. So the truck went deep into the Louisiana bayou country at night, where workmen removed the C-4 from a remote bunker and carefully loaded it. The truck traveled in a convoy of police cars until it reached the Texas border; several hours later, it stopped at the Cleburne firm for the remainder of the purchase, then proceeded to Brower's bunkers in California. In all, Brower bought some 54,000 pounds of C-4, at a total cost of $250,353. The excess over the 42,300 pounds desired by Wilson he put into storage. Hence Brower's cost for the Wilson portion was $198,000, give or take a few hundred dollars. Since Wilson had paid $588,000, Brower had $390,000 left to cover expenses—and provide a profit.

Now came the difficult part of the deal. C-4, as a prohibited munition, could not be shipped to Libya without U.S. Government permission. And as a Class A explosive, it could not be shipped *anywhere* on a passenger or cargo aircraft. Yet the immediacy of the Libyans' demand meant that Brower must ship by air, which required that he deceive both an air charter company and U.S. Customs.

Wilson's instructions were that Brower work through his

shipping expert, Reginald Slocombe, but without any documented involvement for either Slocombe or his company, Aroundworld Shipping and Chartering. Slocombe should help Brower arrange the shipping, but through a third party. As Wilson told Slocombe, "If something goes wrong... we don't want to take Aroundworld down with it." Any telephone discussions Slocombe had with his Houston office manager were in code to avoid revealing either the nature or the destination of the C-4 shipment. Slocombe and Brower discussed several airports as shipping points; Brower decided upon Houston International Airport because "it had the least security." During a stroll through Aroundworld's warehouse, Brower discovered the ruse he would use. Among other cargo being held for shipment were numerous drums of oil-field drilling mud, a compound used to cool drilling bits. Drilling mud has the consistency its name would suggest. Brower took labels off several of the drums and told Slocombe, "I've got the solution."

The C-4 arrived at Brower's warehouse packed in plastic bags inside fiberboard cartons. Brower's workmen put the C-4 into empty five-gallon cans and compressed it tightly. "We put a drilling-mud overlay over the explosives to mask the explosive. Then we sealed it." Next, Brower's workmen put black-and-white stick-on labels on the cans—some 856 of them—identifying the contents as "drilling mud additive," with the manufacturer listed as a Houston firm that Brower concocted from whole cloth.

Lawyer Bloom happened to see the shipping labels a few days before the drums left California for Houston and noticed that the labels said nothing about C-4. He argued to Brower that the cans must be properly labeled. Besides, he said, if Brower intended to export explosives to Libya, he needed a permit from the State Department. "I'll be happy to go to Washington to get it for you," Bloom volunteered. Brower replied that Consultants International or someone else in the shipping chain would arrange the necessary permits. Bloom was given to understand that the shipment had been cleared "by some agency of the government."

As frequently happened in Wilson deals, a last-minute snag threatened the shipment. Slocombe telephoned Brower to say that he did not have the required cash for the charter airplane, and could not locate Wilson to raise it. The obliging

Brower went to the Pomona Bank of America branch and borrowed $82,000, which he carried away in hundred-dollar bills. He gave the money to Bloom and told him to go to Houston and straighten out matters. He could then ride the charter to Lisbon, an intermediate refueling point, but Brower forbade him to go on to Libya. Brower himself intended to fly by commercial airliner to Lisbon, then get on the charter for the final leg. He did not wish to board the charter in Houston because "I didn't want to leave any tracks."

As a parting gesture Brower handed Bloom a silver medallion weighing perhaps an ounce. One side bore the words "God, Man, and Country"; the other showed an engraving of the Liberty Bell. "This is a National Security Council identification piece," Brower told Bloom. "If anybody tries to interfere with the movement of that aircraft after you have secured the charter, show this to them and they will go away." Bloom claimed to accept what Brower said at face value. "I thought there was a national-security motive in getting this shipment to Colonel Quaddafi."* Flashing the spurious "NSC medallion" was a repetition of the same stunt with which Ed Wilson had temporarily deceived John Heath in 1976. Like Heath, Bloom did not grasp the essential absurdity of Brower's claim that the medallion gave free passage to its carrier.

And so, the coin in his pocket, Bloom flew off in quest of the charter, first to Houston, then to Miami, where he paid $63,815 cash to officers of Aviation Technical Services, the leasing firm (and an unwitting participant in the smuggling scheme). The customs declaration filed in Houston showed the contents of the containers to be "drilling mud additive," and the consignee "Sociedad Comercial, Lisboa"—a nonexistent company. The plane, a DC-8 ordinarily used to fly beef cattle from South America to the United States, left Houston late the afternoon of October 3, and Slocombe went to a phone and called Wilson in Tripoli. "The bird has flown the coop," he reported.

Aboard the charter, Bloom sat on one of the pails of C-4

---

*Even after his indictment for his role in the C-4 shipment, Bloom insisted that the medallion was a legitimate NSC identification disk. He did not mention it even to the federal agents who questioned him about the C-4. Just before his trial, he sent it to U.S. District Court Judge Ross Sterling with an explanatory letter. Sterling told Bloom, through his lawyers, that he had been hoodwinked.

directly behind the pilot's cabin. He was not comfortable. The drum had no back rest, and the stench of cattle manure was an odious reminder of the craft's usual cargo. By his later account, Bloom noticed that the clipboard the pilot had given customs in Houston was hanging on the back of the cabin door. Bored, Bloom reached for it, and read that customs had been told the shipment was going to Lisbon—not to Libya; further, it was described as drilling mud, with not a word said about explosives. What goes on here? Bloom asked himself. Such, at any rate, is Bloom's story.

Brower climbed aboard the DC-8 when it landed in Lisbon, and Bloom confronted him. "Forget it," Brower replied.

"I don't like it, national-security operation or not," Bloom said. "There was no reason for false documents."

Bloom persuaded Brower to let him fly on to Libya, and there one final insult awaited the elderly lawyer. As he prepared to get off the plane in Tripoli, he tripped over the pilot's map case and fell through the cargo door onto the runway, badly scraping his hands. That evening, at a communal dining table in a Tripoli hotel, a large man sitting across from him extended his hand for a shake. "Hello," the man said. "I'm Ed Wilson."

This casual meeting was Bloom's only direct contact with Wilson. Three or four months later, Brower gave Bloom $10,000 "in appreciation of your ten years' service." Bloom's only other pay was his $100 monthly retainer and expenses.

The Libyans confiscated Brower's passport immediately upon arrival and said it would be held until they verified that the drums indeed contained C-4. And so the Californian spent several days with Wilson in his hotel room. By Brower's account, much of the time was devoted to conmanship and *braggadoccio* of one kind or another. "How much do you stand to make on this deal?" Wilson asked Brower. "Oh, about seventy-five grand," Brower replied. (Actually, his profit was much higher, but he was not about to share any trade secrets with such a shrewd operator as Wilson.) Wilson boasted that he was doing fine for himself as well. "I've made about six or seven million dollars up to now from these people in various deals," he said. He laughed that he had convinced the Libyans the C-4 was stolen from U.S. Government arsenals and magazines. "Puff it up a little bit," Wilson said, "and you can get deeper into their pockets."

Wilson read through the invoices; he saw a chance to milk some additional dollars from the deal. "I told the Libs there are sixty pounds of C-4 in each can," he told Brower, "and you've got fifty pounds listed here. What say you rewrite them to read sixty? Leave it at the same [per-pound] price." Brower did as asked. Adding 10 pounds to each of 856 cans meant Wilson could charge for about 8,560 nonexistent pounds of explosives, increasing his profit by $172,000. Brower shook his head in silent admiration at the casual manner in which Wilson overbilled his clients. Clearly, he was in the presence of a true business buccaneer.

Muamar Quaddafi, through the good offices of Edwin P. Wilson, now had 20 tons of deadly C-4 for distribution to his own terrorists and others around the world. John Heath, who was to learn of the C-4 purchase only after the shipment arrived in Tripoli, was to say later, "For years, every time I read about a terrorist bomb explosion anywhere in Europe or the Middle East, I thought about Ed Wilson's C-4."

13

An Old Man Who Liked Young Women

While explosives were high on Quaddafi's want list, of equal importance was intelligence on the many enemies he had provoked through Africa and the Middle East. Given the free flow of persons across the unmanned borders of North Africa, Libyan intelligence had little problem infiltrating agents into Egypt and Chad, Quaddafi's prime enemies in 1977.

Under ideal circumstances, these agents should have had little difficulty in finding such essential elements of information as troop locations, troop strengths, dispositions and movements. Libyan intelligence, however, put little trust in these spies. As one American intelligence source with expertise in the area stated, "Going behind enemy lines might sound like a glamorous assignment. But in reality, one really hesitates to muck around in situations where you might get your neck stretched at your own personal hanging. The Libyans sent out a lot of people, an awful lot of people. But the Egyptians had their own nets at work in Tripoli, and many of these poor souls were blown long before they got to Cairo. Anyone in the Lib intel setup knew this for a fact, so the cream of the crop wasn't being dispatched across the border. You had the expendables, and the Libs got, in return, just about what you would expect: a big fat zero."

In 1977, Libyan intelligence officers demanded that Ed Wilson help fill their information gap. He had spoken of his "high connections" in American intelligence, and of the sources he could exploit because of his long experience. Mister Ed, they said, please convert your boasts into facts for us.

Wilson knew just where to go for the desired information. He went through a card file he had assiduously compiled over the years and found the name of an intelligence analyst he had met long ago on the Washington party circuit: Waldo H. Dubberstein, of the Defense Intelligence Agency.

In 1977, Waldo Dubberstein ("Doobie" to friends and colleagues) was 70 years old, a trim academician and spook/ *roué* with a pencil mustache and a charming cocktail-party manner. A native of small-town Kansas, Dubberstein at one time had wished to be a Lutheran minister, and he had earned the necessary degree from Concordia Seminary in St. Louis. But seminary studies had exposed him to the fascination of ancient Assyria, and instead of entering the ministry he had studied ancient civilizations at the University of Chicago's Oriental Institute, earning his doctorate in 1934. After several minor teaching and research jobs, he had come to Washington in 1942 as an analyst for the Office of Strategic Services (OSS) and spent most of the next four decades in the intelligence community. When the OSS evolved into the CIA, Dubberstein had joined the new agency as an analyst, still in Middle East affairs. A former associate called him "sound, methodical, damned good at the bureaucratic fighting that decides what goes into an estimate." Dubberstein had retired from the CIA in 1970 and spent the next five years in a hodgepodge of jobs, all on the periphery of intelligence. He taught at the National War College; he did a study for the American Enterprise Institute, the conservative think tank; he advised the Justice Department on narcotics intelligence. And in 1975—an old spy who couldn't stay out in the cold—Dubberstein returned to the formal community as an analyst for the Defense Intelligence Agency, the Defense Department's in-house intelligence arm.

Specifically, Dubberstein worked for DIA's Directorate for Foreign Intelligence with the mission of providing "all-source finished basic military intelligence and technical intelligence" for the Pentagon hierachy, as well as coordinating Defense Department contributions to national intelligence estimates. Dubberstein's areas of responsibility were the Middle East, South Asia and North Africa; he worked closely with CIA national intelligence officers in evaluating and analyzing information.

A key word in Dubberstein's job description was that he dealt with "*all-source*" intelligence. He was not a file clerk or a paper-pusher. Dubberstein had access to satellite information; he had access to reports from live in-place agents; he had access to any piece of information on his areas gathered by the entire American intelligence community. His job was one that the Defense Department called a "critical sensitive position," further defined in Pentagonese as a position "the occupant of which could bring about, by virtue of the nature of the position, a material adverse effect on the national security." A person in such a position, in addition to undergoing a thorough background investigation, had other obligations: he must report any foreign travel, even to non-Communist countries; he must report any off-duty jobs and he must report "any connections with foreigners." Dubberstein signed a statement acknowledging his awareness of these regulations on February 20, 1975, soon after he joined DIA.

When Ed Wilson renewed acquaintance with Dubberstein in 1977, the old spook was going through a late-life crisis. The fact that he had been married for more than thirty years had not diminished his interest in other women—particularly much younger women. "Doobie saw young girls as his own personal 'fountain of youth,'" said one longtime colleague. "To charm a woman forty years his junior was a reaffirmation of his virility." During one period, Dubberstein was on the periphery of the group-sex orgy scene in Washington (as "Wally Davidson," to protect his identity). But open-door sex apparently proved too strong for his fastidious character, and after several parties at a Northern Virginia high-rise apartment building, "Wally Davidson" was seen no more.

Years of casual philandering took a more serious turn for Dubberstein in 1977. At a cocktail party, he met a vivacious German-born woman, a political scientist who worked as a research assistant in the press-and-information section of the Iranian Embassy. The woman had been raised in the United States and received a political science degree from the University of California at Berkeley, then did a year of Middle Eastern research at the Johns Hopkins University School of Advanced International Studies in Washington. She left without a master's degree, telling friends she felt the Iranian job (which paid only $600 a month) was a stopgap. But it did give her an area of common interest with Dubberstein. And when Dubberstein met a woman who not only was young and pretty but shared his area speciality, he was "entranced," according to the associate. The casual encounter escalated into a love affair, and Dubberstein left his wife, Marie, and moved into an apartment with the younger woman. As might have been expected, he paid a high price. "The wife wouldn't give him a divorce, and he didn't have the heart to go after one himself," a friend related. "But she pretty well cleaned out his pocketbook, and he had to keep paying her bills. On top of that, he was more or less supporting the other woman as well." (The youngr woman lost her job after the Shah's government fell, which made her even more dependent financially upon Dubberstein.)

During one of his many trips to the United States in 1977, Wilson talked with Dubberstein about supplying intelligence on Middle East troop dispositions, particularly those of Chad. According to what Dubberstein later told his lawyer, Howard Bushman, Wilson asked him to help in an "Agency operation." Dubberstein had met Wilson both socially and on intelligence matters, and they had worked together on interagency forces, even on operations that paralleled the Libyan request. "Given Wilson's background and the nature of the request and the mission, Walso didn't even think of checking on it," Bushman related.

Dubberstein's claim is absurd on its face. Although the varied agencies of the U.S. Government that work in the field are known collectively as the "intelligence community," the term is misleading. Each agency jealously protects its sources and the information they produce; to provide intelligence of value to a competitor without exacting something in return is simply not done. Given bureaucratic realities, Dubberstein's response to a request for back-channel help from a casual CIA acquaintance should have been abrupt, and negative. According to a Pentagon counterintelligence officer, "Even if Waldo had wanted to go along with Wilson, he knew the procedure. He could go through his own channels. Or if he really wanted to be secretive and help Wilson, he knew the right phone number in Langley to confirm his *bona fides*. One phone call and he could have established whether Wilson was on Agency business. To put it bluntly, Waldo was a pussy-crazed old geezer who saw the cash money that gave him a way out of his troubles, and who was willing to risk his entire career. Part of Waldo might have believed Wilson's story. But that part of Waldo was self-deception."

According to what federal investigators were to establish later, Dubberstein first gave information to Wilson on or about December 23, 1977, through Douglas Schlachter. The item was a paper titled, "The Middle East Situation," and the circumstances suggest that its passing was a trial run intended to convince the Libyans that Dubberstein could provide useful information. The Libyans apparently were satisfied, for they authorized Wilson to invite Dubberstein to Tripoli. Dubberstein met Wilson and his secretary in the Washington Hilton Hotel in the spring of 1978 to discuss the trip; a day or so later, the secretary gave him $1,000 cash for travel expenses.

Using an assumed name, Dubberstein flew to Tripoli, where John Heath met him and escorted him on a busy round of meetings with Libyan intelligence officers. "I didn't know who he was, only that Ed had arranged for him to see all the proper officers," Heath related. At these meetings with the Libyans, four or five sessions over a period of a week, Dubberstein drew upon his classified knowledge for briefings on Middle Eastern military forces. When he finished, Douglas Schlachter gave him $6,000 in cash, and

Dubberstein returned to the United States. Later, on another
trip to Europe, Ed Wilson gave him another $25,000, again
in cash, and an ongoing assignment: Dubberstein was to send
the Libyans regular written reports, drawn from U.S. intelligence data, about their Middle Eastern rivals.

Over the next months Dubberstein cribbed material
from the highly classified DIA and CIA reports that came
across his desk and incorporated it into estimates specially
written for the Libyans. The exact number of documents that
Dubberstein slipped to the Libyans—via Schlachter, for the
most part—was never firmly established. But John Heath
remembers seeing documents that "were obviously of United
States Government origin" in Wilson's Tripoli office. They
bore no designations or classification stamps, but Heath had
seen enough similar material during his military career to
realize they were intelligence estimates.

Dubberstein's young German-born paramour typed some
of these documents. And as investigators were to determine,
the breach of security was serious. For instance, on October
1, 1978, Dubberstein gave Schlachter a document on Middle
Eastern military affairs drawn from two in-house DIA papers,
a "Defense Intelligence Agency Monthly Estimated Inventory of Selected Armaments and Forces in the Middle East,"
the issues of August 7 and September 15, 1978, classified
Secret, and another study, "Middle Eastern Military Capabilities Study, DDI-2680-46-78," which in turn was incorporated
into a National Intelligence Estimate, "The Arab–Israeli Military Balance," classified Secret. On November 11, 1978,
Dubberstein used a Top Secret DIA Intelligence Notice as
the basis for another report to the Libyans. In each instance,
Dubberstein lifted entire sections from the U.S. reports
verbatim.

What appalled American counterintelligence agents once
the Dubberstein affair came to official notice was the strong
probability that he had compromised sensitive intelligence
sources throughout the Middle East. That the Libyans pass
information to the KGB is accepted as a matter of course by
the U.S. intelligence community. As one person put it, "By
studying the material Dubberstein supplied, any good intelligence analyst could answer some important questions. How
accurate is American intelligence reporting in the Middle
East? What are the likely sources of information? The fact

that the Syrians had X number of surface-to-air missiles certainly would not be a secret to the Soviets, who supplied them. But what the Soviets *would* like to know—and what Ed Wilson helped them find out—was how well DIA could count the missiles. And that is the tragedy of the Dubberstein affair."

14

The Trail: I

On the afternoon of April 4, 1977, two young assistant United States Attorneys sat in a fourth-floor office of the Federal Court House in Washington discussing strategy in their investigation of the brutal murders of Chilean dissident Orlando Letelier and his research assistant, Ronnie Moffitt. On the morning of September 21, 1976, Letelier and Ms. Moffitt had been riding down Massachusetts Avenue—Embassy Row—en route to their offices at the Institute for Policy Studies. Ms. Moffitt's husband, Michael, sat in the back seat. A few yards past the Chilean Embassy, a bomb concealed under the car exploded into a huge fireball. Letelier died instantly, his lower torso blown away; Ms. Moffitt survived only a few minutes.

By the next spring, prosecutors Eugene Propper and E. Lawrence Barcella had reached what proved to be the right conclusion in the case. Letelier, ambassador to the United States under slain President Salvador Allende, was killed because of his strident opposition to the successor rightist regime of General Augusto Pinochet. Ms. Moffitt's murder was incidental. Whoever did the actual bombing was in the hire of the Chilean intelligence service, DINA.

Establishing the killers' identity occupied Barcella and Propper, an odd but harmonious couple. Around the U.S.

Attorney's Office, Propper was known as an eccentric but productive prosecutor. (A recalcitrant informant once laughed at the toy basketball goal Propper had over his wastebasket. Propper challenged him: "I get more baskets out of ten shots than you do, you testify; you win, you walk without going to the grand jury." Propper won, dropping nine wadded balls of paper through the goal to the other man's six. The informant testified.) Propper won guilty verdicts in a string of more than fifty felony trials. He was a lawyer whose record justified his arrogance.

Barcella took a softer route. He was 33 years old that spring, a native Washingtonian who had done his undergraduate work at Dartmouth, then joined the U.S. Attorney's staff immediately after graduation from Vanderbilt law school in 1970. Behind Barcella's lank, benign facade is a mind akin to a human computer. Whatever fact Barcella hears or reads, however seemingly innocuous it may be, he remembers, and in detail. In the hopelessly complex Wilson case, such a knack was invaluable. Barcella also knows how to scheme his way around roadblocks. (As a Vanderbilt student Barcella noticed a pretty girl on campus. He tried several times to strike up a conversation, but failed. So he sold a pint of blood and bought a bottle of Rebel Yell bourbon, which he presented to the lady. As it turned out, she did not drink whiskey, but one thing led to another and she is now, besides being an economist, Mrs. Larry Barcella and mother of a child.)

In April 1977, neither Propper nor Barcella had ever heard the name of Edwin P. Wilson.

Their conference on April 4 was interrupted by a telephone call from Bob Woodward, the *Washington Post* reporter who had, with Carl Bernstein, broken and then pursued the Watergate story. Propper answered the phone, covered the receiver with his hand and said, "It's Bob Woodward." Barcella twirled his finger in the air in mock admiration. "Whoopee!" he said *sotto voce*.

Woodward told Propper he was working on a "hot story" about the Letelier killing. He had information that a former CIA man named Edwin P. Wilson was a key figure in the investigation; indeed, the prime suspect. Wilson supposedly had conspired with three Cuban explosives experts who had come to Washington on September 19, only two days before the bomb blast killed Letelier.

"That's news to me," Propper told Woodward.

Woodward seemed convinced his source was accurate. Persons elsewhere in the Justice Department had been "investigating Wilson for a long time." They considered his role in the Letelier murder "so sensitive that they are intentionally keeping the whole thing from you."

Propper could not believe Woodward's scenario, exclaiming, "That's impossible." But Woodward persisted. Wilson was "the prime target in the case," he said.

Propper knew Woodward only by reputation, but the reporter's confidence in the validity of his information shook him. He could not accept that anyone in the Justice Department would conceal such information from him. Yet Woodward, almost tauntingly, repeated, "I think it's clear that there are things going on that you don't know about." He claimed his sources "are pretty high up."

Propper told Woodward that he would check to see if in fact Wilson was a target in the Letelier probe. If he found this to be true, he would make a public statement "that'll probably get me fired." He and Woodward exchanged home telephone numbers. Woodward would not promise to hold the story, but he would listen to what Propper had to say.

In a half-hour's time Propper and Barcella established that Woodward's "information" was bogus. Propper so informed Woodward. But Woodward preferred to believe his sources. On April 12 the front page of *The Washington Post* was dominated by an eight-column headline:

EX CIA AIDE, 3 CUBAN EXILES FOCUS OF LETELIER INQUIRY

Woodward's story did not support the headline. He had vague details, but no names, about the Wilson-Terpil attempt to recruit three Cubans (Quintero and the Villaverde brothers) to assassinate the anti-Quaddafi dissident in Cairo. Had Woodward stopped there, he would have had a legitimate news story. But he chose to try to tie the Quintero-Villaverde plot to the Letelier murder. His lead paragraph read:

A former CIA explosives expert and three Cuban exiles will soon be sought by federal authorities for questioning of last year's Embassy Row bomb-murder of former Chilean Ambassador Orlando Letelier, according to informed sources.

"Woodward told me later, 'That was the worst story I ever wrote,'" Propper said.* "I agree. But it did have one good side effect. We got a call the same day the story ran. William Bittman, Wilson's lawyer, wanted to bring Wilson in to talk to us. Wilson had nothing to do with Letelier, and he wanted to set the record straight."

Larry Barcella did not do much talking the day Wilson came to the U.S. Attorney's Office. Wilson was in a laughing mood (as well he should have been: not only did he have no connection with the Letelier murder, but if the Justice Department was running down this false trail only now, months after the Mulcahy defection and the complaints given CIA by the Harpers and Chi Chi Quintero, he figured he was home free). Buried deep in the Woodward article was significant information—that Wilson had tried to buy thousands of explosives timers for shipment to Libya—although Barcella and Propper did not know it at the time. Lacking any knowledge of the timers, Barcella and Propper were not prepared to question Wilson with any authority, so in effect he laughed at them. "Timers? I don't know a timer from a teapot," he said.

When Wilson and lawyer Bittman left, Propper turned to Barcella and asked, "What do you think?"

"He's not involved in Letelier," Barcella said, "but he's lying to us. About what, I don't know. He's bold, he's confident—and he's also a goddamned liar. Let's put a little star by his name and watch him."

Inaccurate though it was, the Woodward story did catch the attention of Admiral Stansfield Turner, who only a few months earlier had become director of Central Intelligence. A classmate at Annapolis of President Carter's, Turner came

---

*The *Post* never acknowledged that the headline did not match the story—that is, that the *Post* had run an inaccurate eight-column banner headline accusing a person of complicity in the city's most notorious murder case of the decade. All the *Post* did was run a statement, on an inside page, that Wilson's lawyer "took exception" to the headline, and that he denied that Wilson was a "target" in the investigation. The Woodward article is one instance in which Wilson clearly had reason to object about unfair press treatment.

into CIA suspicious—"with a chip on his shoulder," according to one official there at the time. The press and politicians were in their sixth year of pillorying CIA for supposed past abuses, many of them dating well back into the 1960s and 1950s, others committed at Presidential direction during Watergate and its congeries of related scandals. One of Carter's mandates to Turner was "Find out what kind of mess they have out there, and clean it up."

Turner shared Carter's disdain for much of what CIA did. With his naval background, he accepted the supposed supremacy of electronics and signals intelligence over so-called "humint," or human intelligence—information gathered by live agents on the scene or through networks. According to what he confided to staff members who went with him to CIA, Turner's notion was that a housecleaning of the Agency's clandestine services was a necessary first step toward "reform."

The Wilson-Terpil indiscretions gave Turner an opening to go after the Operations Directorate. First, he summoned in Patry Loomis and William Weisenburger, established through questions that they had in fact helped Wilson on the timers and summarily fired them. He "promoted" Theodore Shackley to a more or less meaningless job on the CIA's Policy and Coordination Staff (PCS), which meant thereafter that he spent his days reading papers and talking with other agencies with which CIA did business. He was told to expect no further promotions. William Wells, head of Operations Directorate and Shackley's immediate superior, was also stripped of any authority. When Wells protested that he had had no dealings with Wilson, Turner is said to have replied, "Well, you should have known."

Turner did perform two positive acts. He sent a message to all CIA stations abroad directing that they have no contact with Edwin P. Wilson. The message stressed that Wilson had no connection with CIA, and warned that he had apparently been using his past association for business purposes. Secondly, Turner updated existing CIA guidelines on permissible activities for agents once they retired, and circulated them throughout the Agency, establishing thereby a new Code of Conduct (see Appendix B).

But Turner did not stop there. Over the next months he subjected the Operations Directorate to a searching study of its past performance and current practices. Undoubtedly the division had acquired some fat over the years, and the end of the Vietnam War meant that many officers had been left with nothing but make-work duties. Turner was singularly unsympathetic to arguments that much of the overstaffing was an unavoidable result of the end of the war, and that attrition in time would reduce the clandestine agents to a workable force. On Halloween weekend 1977, Turner abruptly fired some 800 career agents, many via a curt sentence circulated on a Xeroxed note.

Included were many officers in their late thirties and mid-forties, men and women who had devoted their professional lives to the CIA, often in the dark and dangerous back alleys of the world. Initially they were given no guidance as to how to go about finding other jobs in the intelligence community or elsewhere in the government; Turner's order asserted only that they were terminated, and that they should turn in their identification badges and get off the premises by a certain date.

In time the mass firing came to be known within the Agency as "Turner's Halloween Massacre." In the words of one embittered clandestine careerist (a man not touched by Turner; he retired voluntarily three years later), "The Admiral did more damage to CIA in one afternoon than the Church Committee, the press and the KGB did since its founding. Halloween 'Massacre,' hell—call it the 'Halloween Pearl Harbor.'"

Given his mind-set, Turner in all probability would have purged the Operations Directorate even if an Edwin P. Wilson had not given a pretext. Wilson's significance was that he attracted the Admiral's attention to the clandestine services in a fashion that justified—to Turner, at least—any action he decided upon. CIA was gutted as a result.

Even before the Wilson scandal touched them, Ted Shackley and Tom Clines had talked about joint business ventures once they left the CIA. According to what the men told friends, the plan was for Clines (who had been with the government longer) to retire first, and to set up a business which Shackley would join a year or so later. In fact, however, Clines began his private business activities while still with the CIA. In 1978, a few months before he retired, Clines formed API Distributors, to supply oil-drilling equipment to

Petróleos Mexicanos, the state oil company in Mexico. Wilson had his lawyers help Clines with the paperwork, and Wilson gave API office space in Houston in the same rooms occupied by one of his own companies, Aroundworld Shipping, Inc. Legal work was done by the Washington firm of Dickstein, Shapiro & Morin, which represented Wilson at the time.

Some familiar CIA names were on API's registry. Rafael "Chi Chi" Quintero was secretary. Ricardo Chávez, another Bay of Pigs veteran and a longtime friend of Quintero and Clines, served as treasurer. Ted Shackley was listed as a consultant.

API was created in June 1978. Five months later, soon after his formal retirement from the CIA, Clines, with Wilson's assistance, set up two more companies: Systems Services International (SSI), to sell security and military equipment, and International Research and Trade, Ltd., a Bermuda firm which dealt, according to its incorporation papers, in "logistics systems." Shackley served as a consultant to both firms.

When Shackley retired in September 1979, he went to work formally for all three Clines companies. But, as he complained to a long-time CIA friend, "Clines screwed me, in effect. The deal was that these were going to be joint ventures, a kind of partnership. Clines's attitude changed. He had formed the companies, so he intended to be top dog. I would be just an employee." The turnaround embittered Shackley, and he gradually withdrew from the Clines complex and began forming his own consulting and sales companies in the Washington area.

Clines, however, continued to expand his private business interests, now with Wilson as an indirect partner. His boldest venture was born with the 1979 Camp David accords between Egypt and Israel, which President Jimmy Carter brokered in hopes of bringing peace to the Middle East. The accords included an American agreement to lend financially strapped Egypt $1.5 billion to buy and transport such military equipment as M-60 tanks, F-16 fighter planes, antiaircraft missiles and radar units. The loan required that the equipment be transported in U.S.-flag vessels or aircraft, which mandated involvement of an American shipper.

As purchasing agent in the United States, Egypt designated a newly formed firm called "Egyptian-American Transport and Service Company," or EATSCO, which had offices in suburban Falls Church, Virginia. The EATSCO president, Dr. Hussein K. E. I. Salem, had served in Egyptian intelligence before coming to the United States just prior to creation of EATSCO. And one of his closest American friends was Edwin P. Wilson, whom he had met early in the 1970s, and with whom he had brokered some small deals for communications and electronics equipment. According to incorporation papers, Salem owned 51 percent of the stock of EATSCO; the remaining 49 percent was owned by Clines.

In fact, however, Wilson was a silent partner with Clines. He lent his former CIA friend half a million dollars with which to start EATSCO. The arrangement was that the $500,000 be repaid from EATSCO earnings, and that Wilson thereafter would share in the profits. Several other Americans also held hidden shares; Salem and Clines, however, would serve as front men. The mechanics of the investment were hammered out between Wilson, Clines and the other Americans in meetings in Europe in early 1979. According to Roberta J. Barnes, Wilson's aide, "Little if anything was put on paper; the whole idea was to keep the other people besides Clines and the Egyptian as invisible as possible."

Salem apparently convinced Pentagon arms-sales officials that he spoke with the authority of President Anwar Sadat. When he stipulated that EATSCO be permitted to choose the American-flag shippers that would transport the equipment to Egypt, high Pentagon officials acquiesced.

For the actual shipping, EATSCO contracted with a Baltimore firm, R. G. Hobelmann & Company, and its wholly owned subsidiary Air Freight International (AFI). Rolf Graage served as president of both the Baltimore companies. On the surface, EATSCO was the linchpin of a complex but legitimate enterprise. In reality, however, it was the cover for a fraud intended to cheat the U.S. Government out of millions of dollars in inflated shipping fees. And former CIA official Tom Clines and his friend Edwin Wilson stood at the core of the conspiracy.

But for the moment, Wilson was so confident of his ability to outwit the Justice Department that the fear of prosecution gave him no pause whatever. Clines had made the transition from the CIA to the private sector without a hitch; having Clines as an unacknowledged but visible "associate" gave further credence to Wilson's continuing claim that he still worked for American intelligence.

15

"Hi Diddle Diddle, Right down the Middle"

Edwin P. Wilson made a serious misjudgment after his first encounter with the Justice Department. As he told one associate later, "These little bastards are bureaucrats, flunkies; they couldn't make a dime in the real world. I tied them in knots." What Wilson did not realize was that the U.S. Government, once stirred into action, can be an investigative juggernaut, a legal doomsday machine with the money and manpower to overwhelm an adversary. During their first interview with Wilson, prosecutors Larry Barcella and Gene Propper knew the man's name and little else. In due course they came to know a great deal more about Wilson.

Meanwhile Wilson set out to enjoy his most prosperous years. Although his actual performance had been uneven, Wilson convinced the Libyan military and intelligence establishments that he was a valuable ally. His ties were so strong that (aside from the oil companies) he became the West's leading trader in Libya. Within the next two-year period, 1977–78, Wilson's contracts would bring him multimillion-dollar annual profits—in arms, in aviation, in military trainers, in electronics, in assassins, in relatively mundane fields such as clothing and foodstuffs.

Wilson's deals followed no chronological pattern. He would pursue half a dozen contracts at a time, from as many Libyan purchasing agencies. Some came to fruition almost immediately; others he nursed along for months; others failed outright. In later years, the U.S. Government put its best financial sleuths onto Wilson's trail, and as often as not they lost themselves in a maze of false documentation, shadow corporations, Swiss bank accounts, obscure post-office boxes and other convenience addresses. Even the usually meticulous Internal Revenue Service capitulated, after a fashion. In a tax-deficiency judgment filed in 1982, the IRS admitted it could not determine in which of two years Wilson had earned more than $8 million on a certain contract; hence it demanded taxes on the contract for both years.

But during the early months of 1977 such troubles could not be foreseen by the cocky Wilson. In less than a year's time he had transformed his old Task Force 157 *apparat* into a flourishing private business. And no longer did he share profits with Frank Terpil. Sometime in early 1977, for reasons that neither man ever discussed fully, even with trusted associates, Terpil and Wilson ended their association.

Wilson's cryptic explanation was that "Frank was too crazy; he was leading me down some paths I didn't want to follow"—an apparent reference to assassination plots. But persons who came to know Wilson well, such as Alex Raffio, dismiss this reason as "pious excuse-making." As Wilson repeatedly demonstrated over the next years, he had no aversion to murder contracts. Terpil's reasoning was both cynical and realistic: Wilson was a cheat and a crook; given his superior business acumen, he would inevitably end up the winner in any joint business deal. Terpil chose not to play the underdog's game. "Ed Wilson was the sort of prick who would steal money out of his own pocket just for the experience," Terpil joked to a London acquaintance later. "I'm a crook, but I'm up-front about it. Ed played the businessman. Bullshit."

Another factor in Terpil's leaving was that the Libyans discovered that his performance did not always live up to his boasts. According to Alex Raffio, Sayed Quaddafadam of the London purchasing mission became so angered with Terpil that he said, "My friend, you come to Libya again and I shall see to it that you are shot." Terpil laughed when he repeated the story; nonetheless, he did not test Quaddafadam's sincerity.

The paths of Wilson and Terpil were to cross occasionally in coming years, but their original association in 1976 was to mean a tenacious linking of the two names, in the press and elsewhere, for years to come, even after Terpil found a new patron in the odious Idi Amin of Uganda.

Terpil's chief value to Wilson was that he gained him an entrée into Libya that was convertible into a series of multimillion-dollar contracts in virtually every area of the military. Much of this business involved perfectly legitimate deals that violated neither U.S. law nor U.S. policy. Alex Raffio mourned years later, in the sad words of a man who felt himself denied the chance to become a millionaire, "Had Ed stayed legitimate, we could *all* have walked away from Libya rich. The money was there, and the Libs were willing to spend it. But Ed had to cheat on everything, even the legitimate deals."

Wilson spent much of 1977 tightening his organization. His behavior suggests that the encounter with the Justice Department, harmless though it was, prodded him to begin shifting his operations out of the United States. Nonetheless, Consultants International remained his home organization, with its offices at 1425 K Street Northwest in Washington. For operational and personal reasons, in the early 1970s Wilson had purchased a town house on 22nd Street Northwest, just off Pennsylvania Avenue, and furnished it lavishly. It served as an office, a trysting place for Wilson's many affairs (Wilson's marriage by now was more myth than reality; the few occasions he visited Mount Airy Farm he came away raging about "that goddamn Barbara") and sleeping quarters for employees temporarily in Washington.

In London, Wilson took offices under the corporate name "OSI" (he used variations of the meaningless name in half a dozen other countries, through lawyers, post-office boxes and convenience addresses). Wilson liked London. The city abounded in arms merchants, mercenaries and extranational deal-makers. The British, with their long history of overseas political involvement, tended to wink at arms deals, as long as they did not adversely affect Commonwealth countries. The United Kingdom also offered geographic proximity to the Continent. Finally, Wilson liked English prostitutes—"the best bang for a buck in the world," he liked to boast.

Wilson chose to keep most of his money in Switzerland. He did his banking in Geneva, where he used the services of an international lawyer and money-handler named Edward J. Coughlin, an expatriate American who in collegiate days had been sports editor of the *Harvard Crimson*. Coughlin kept in almost daily contact with Wilson by telephone and Telex, receiving and paying out money on his behalf; many of Wilson's contracts listed Coughlin's post-office box as the mailing address. Persons in the Wilson group described Coughlin as "basically a mechanic, a guy who performed business services without involving himself directly in the business." Coughlin did seem to delight in handling large sums of cash. As one former special-forces officer remembered, "Eddie could riffle a stack of hundred-dollar bills and count you out ten grand like he was dealing cards." In addition to using Coughlin's offices, Wilson also maintained a lavish *pied-à-terre* apartment in Geneva.

In Tripoli, the Libyan capital, the government permitted Wilson to rent a succession of villas that served as both offices and housing. Each villa had a similar layout. The ground floor contained offices, Telex machines and file space. The upper floors had a kitchen and three bedrooms. When Wilson attained notoriety, he was said to live in a "luxurious seaside villa." Such was not exactly the case. The final "villa" in which he lived, beginning in 1980, was a stucco-faced detached house with a small weed-infested yard. In the United States it woult have been considered middle-class housing at best. The Mediterranean did lie only a few hundred feet distant, but the separating beach was littered with garbage, clots of oil, human and animal feces and other filth. Alex Raffio once tried to use the beach. "I lasted about fifteen feet; I came back determined to leave rotten Libya." But Wilson was one of the few Westerners allotted a private dwelling in Libya; other businessmen had to make do in hotels.

Wilson shuffled his employees between the United States and abroad with no discernible pattern. Reginald Slocombe, his shipping expert, spent perhaps half his time traveling (even though his office was in Washington, and his home in rural Virginia). Douglas Schlachter was on more or less permanent detail to Libya (although his wife and three small children remained in Virginia, on a farm on the fringes of Mount Airy) as general factotum. Alex Raffio remained in his own flat in London, pursuing deals for Wilson and himself throughout the Middle East and Africa. Wilson did not hesitate to shift other employees swiftly, seemingly arbitrarily, to meet a current demand.

One such movable person was Peter Goulding, a taciturn, meticulous New Englander who had spent four years as an Army officer, worked in parachute schools and studied for an advanced business degree. Wilson's people first approached him as a supplier of what Goulding called "high-tech parachute equipment." Goulding furnished some of the required items, fell into an argument with his superior and left the parachute business. He had returned to school when Wilson's people sought him out again and offered a handsome profit if he could supply $1 million worth of parachute gear. When Goulding hesitated, Wilson's man opened his briefcase and counted out $85,000 in hundred-dollar bills. "Here's the money, and here's a list of what we want," he said. "Holy smoke," Goulding replied; "What a way to go into business!"

Goulding came to Washington—this was in the summer of 1978—and met an array of Wilson associates, including Patry Loomis, with whom he stayed for several weeks. Loomis talked volubly of his CIA employment, so much so that Goulding concluded that Wilson's entire business was an Agency operation. He and his wife, Colleen, moved to Washington, and Goulding was immediately immersed in a world of seeming glamour and intrigue. A former first lieutenant, he was awed at the admirals and generals clustered around Wilson. He did not question Wilson's "intelligence connection." "As a twenty-seven-year-old former first lieutenant, you don't ask a two- or three-star general whether he is real," Goulding said. Goulding and his wife had incorporated their business as Material Designs, Unlimited, in Massachusetts. Wilson reincorporated MDU in Delaware taking 50 percent of the stock. Goulding did not care. He was on a big-bucks track.

In three months in Washington, Goulding fulfilled the $1-million contract—"everything from sleeping bags and shovels to weapons." His performance impressed Wilson. Although other employees considered Goulding stiff and somewhat naive, he had delivered. Goulding had made money, for himself and for Wilson. Thus when Wilson suggested that Goulding move to Geneva and handle arms purchase throughout Europe, he readily accepted the offer. "I saw it as a chance to go see the cuckoo clocks and eat chocolate," Goulding said. Within seventy-two hours the Gouldings vacated their Northern Virginia house and were off to Switzerland. Goulding carried a promise of $18,000 to $20,000 a year in salary, plus commissions on any sales he made for Wilson.

The immediacy of an association with a person such as Ed Wilson, Peter Goulding reasoned, far outstripped the value of a graduate degree in business. Goulding plunged into arms-brokering with puppy-dog enthusiasm. "It was hi diddle diddle, right down the middle," he told me. In fact Goulding plunged ahead so fast, so enthusiastically, that not for months did he realize that Wilson was not even paying his full salary, much less the promised commissions.

But in terms of ongoing importance, the central figure in the business side of the Wilson operation came to be Roberta Jean "Bobbi" Barnes, who had the dual role of Wilson mistress and London office manager. Not everyone in the Wilson organization liked Bobbi Barnes. In Telexes Wilson called her by the code name "Wonder Woman." Some other employees referred to her as "Super Bitch." But no one doubted Barnes's importance to Wilson, both professionally and personally. When Barnes joined Wilson in 1977, as an accountant in the Washington office of Consultants International, she was in her late twenties, divorced and with a young son. Barnes was (and still is) a strikingly handsome woman with luxuriant swirls of reddish-blond hair, the sort of woman who attracts admiring male glances when she walks through a restaurant. The daughter of a career Air Force officer, she says, "I never had a home as a kid. I grew up everywhere—Germany, Turkey, any place that had an air base." Divorced in 1977, and living in Washington, Bobbi answered a classified ad for a bookkeeper and found herself working for Wilson and Consultants International.

Bobbi took an immediate liking to the tall, gregarious Westerner; she told one friend, "I got the flutters the first time I met him, just talking with him." Or as Bobbi put it later, "Ed Wilson is a charmer, and he certainly charmed me. Ed was fun to be around. He was a good talker, and he knew how to make you feel good. With Ed Wilson, you felt that you were important." Wilson's relationship with his wife appeared to be at an end by the time they met, and in January 1978, although he was legally still married, Wilson and Bobbi became open lovers. They traveled together with no pretense at concealment; when Wilson was in Washington, they stayed together, either at the town house or at Wilson's hotel. Other persons in the Wilson organization accepted them as "a couple."

Although Barbara Wilson had no hope (or desire) to rekindle the marriage, she did not take kindly to her husband's new love. "She couldn't even bear to say Bobbi's name," one acquaintance said. "To Barbara she was always 'Ed's red-haired slut.'" Barbara remarked to another person, "Let them have their fun—I'll have my fun, spelled m-o-n-e-y, at divorce court."

Early in 1979, Wilson phased out his Washington office and shifted his major base to London. Bobbi Barnes went along, first as bookkeeper, then as office manager, then as *de facto* second-ranking person in the organization.

Bobbi settled into a comfortable town house in a small, out-of-the-way mews off Hyde Park ("the best place in the world for an early-morning jog"). For a few happy months, Wilson was a surrogate father to Bobbi's preteen son, Mark. A snapshot taken soon after Bobbi's arrival in London shows the lad snuggled closely into Wilson's arms as they sit on a couch.

By Bobbi's account, Wilson was candid with her only to a point. The first months she was in London, she was unaware of the exact scope and nature of Wilson's operations. Wilson regularly used coded references in Telex messages; she would write checks without knowing exactly for what the money was being paid. In time, however, she came to be intimately trusted.

But then, paradoxically, Wilson put Barnes directly into the arms business, much to her surprise. "Ed told me—*me*, who knows not the first thing about guns—to go to the Continent and negotiate for him. I was the only person he had around he trusted. So I would go into meetings with men who had sold guns all their lives. They would look at me, and laugh, and say, 'What are you doing here? Go away; send a man—we must talk with a man.'"

Barnes stood tough. She was there as the representative of "Angus"—Wilson had assumed this as his code name, even when dealing with people who knew his identity—and she was talking per-unit price for weapons, not their rate-of-fire or muzzle velocity. As far as she was concerned, buying 5,000 rifles was little different from doing the Saturday grocery marketing. "Here I was, trying to buy five thousand M-16s, and I'd never even seen one of the damned things."

Barnes dealt with men who could charitably be called rough-and-tumble. A key Wilson source in arms deals was a swarthy Frenchman named Armand Donnay, a former colonel in the Foreign Legion who had done mean duty in both the Second World War and the Algerian revolution. An intelligence officer, Donnay was much hated by the Algerian insurgents. How much so? John Heath once asked Donnay that question. Without a word, Donnay stripped off his shoes and stockings and showed Heath his feet, which were horribly mutilated. "The Algerians, they pulled out my toenails, and they laughed at me as they did so," he said. "I did not give them the satisfaction of a scream." The Legion rescued Donnay before he was executed; he left the military and became a licensed arms broker, based in the Belgian city of Liège.

Although a licensed and legitimate dealer, Donnay did have an occasional problem with the law. Indeed, Bobbi's first meeting with him came under most awkward circumstances. Wilson drove her to Liège to introduce her to Donnay and explain that she would be acting as his representative. They pulled up in front of Donnay's stone house to find the driveway filled with police cars. Wilson tried to drive away, but the police stopped him, and escorted him and Bobbi inside.

Donnay, it seemed, had attracted official attention because of a shipment of machine guns which either did or did not qualify as a legal transaction; the police were at his house to sort through the matter. And since his warehouse was close by the house, the subject machine guns had been brought into the family living room for inspection. As the detectives talked with her husband, Mrs. Donnay walked about the room in her bathrobe, hair in curlers, stepping over machine guns as she politely served coffee to the policemen. Wilson managed a perfunctory introduction. "Perhaps it would be more convenient if we talked at a later time?" Donnay suggested. Wilson and Bobbi left hurriedly.

According to Alex Raffio, Wilson deliberately cut Barnes out of knowledge of many of his criminal deeds because he was "too smart to let Bobbi in on things. There's nothing more vicious than a girlfriend or a wife who has been spurned. Since Ed played around, he realized he'd eventually get Bobbi mad at him. Why give her information she could use to hang him with the cops?" (Raffio underestimated Barnes's emotional dependence on Wilson. She remained loyal to him through many hard times, including her own arrest in late 1981.)

Because she handled the books and signed the checks for a man who disliked paying salaries, commissions and other bills that he owed, Bobbi constantly found herself in an unpopular position, with a reputation for nastiness she claimed was undeserved. Wilson, she maintains, used her as the conduit for bad news because he disliked unpleasant personal confrontations. "Ed used me as the 'heavy' so he wouldn't have to do the nasty stuff himself." When she refused to pay bills, she did so, she asserts, on Wilson's orders, not her own initiative. Alex Raffio, who worked closely with Barnes, scoffs at this claim. "Not true," he exclaimed. "She would confide in me that Angus said to pay someone, and she would decline. Why? God only knows. Maybe she thought of the money as her own. But she was tight as hell with it."

But the money did roll into Wilson's coffers. As a born salesman, he did not wait for business; he went out and looked for it. In a chance conversation, he heard that the Libyan national petroleum agency, which had taken over most of the formerly Western oil properties in the country, needed housing for workers in remote areas. Wilson remembered a similar demand several years earlier from a German company that had a contract to build a water project in a remote area of Guatemala. The industriousness of the German workers was directly dependent upon their off-hours comfort. But building conventional short-term housing in a Central American wilderness was considered too expensive to be practical. Wilson had persuaded the German company to let him supply elaborate house trailers, which were airlifted to the construction site by large helicopters. Reginald Slocombe, who had a share of this housing deal, called it "Ed Wilson at his best: he found somebody who needed something, and he supplied it at a good price." But, Slocombe added, "Of course, lots of people down along the line, including yours truly, didn't get their due." For the Libyan oil-field workers Wilson worked out a similar arrangement, buying house trailers in Western Europe, transporting them to Tripoli by ship and then airlifting them to the remote oil fields. Wilson's role was that of intermediary: finding someone who had what the Libyans wanted, and arranging the purchase.

16

Training a Cross-Eyed Army

Although Colonel Muamar Quaddafi invested much of Libya's wealth in Soviet and Soviet-bloc weaponry, he refused to put his military in the hands of Russian advisers. The occasional odd-job Soviet expert did appear in Libya, but on the whole Quaddafi refused offers that would have put Soviet officers in the heart of his military establishment.

Yet the abortive border war with Egypt in early 1977 demonstrated to Quaddafi that hardware alone does not make an army. The entire Libyan command, from Quaddafi through field commanders, was sharply disappointed with the army's poor showing. Quaddafi ordered a restructuring of the entire Libyan military-intelligence apparatus, with the intent of correcting defects fatally obvious during the skirmish with Egypt.

Specifically, Quaddafi wanted better Libyan capabilities in the fields of small-unit tactics, transport aircraft, electronics and intelligence gathering. Quaddafi would continue to rely upon the Soviet bloc for such big-buck items as tanks, artillery and fighter planes. But for military activities involving contact with his troops, he preferred to use American and other Western advisers.

Politically, it was a shrewd decision for Quaddafi. It meant the Soviets would supply his army but not control it.

He recognized that the Soviets would be tightfisted in their supply of advanced equipment such as night-vision devices (to this date the Soviets withhold many military items from even such allies as the Bulgarians and East Germans). So Quaddafi would go to the West for advanced military and electronic technology.

Edwin P. Wilson happened to be the American in the proverbial right place at the right time. By undertaking the "dirty-work" contracts of supplying explosives and timers, Wilson had proved his trustworthiness. Although some Libyan officers thought poorly of Wilson because of his performance on the booby-trap project, he nonetheless obtained key contracts in training, in weaponry and in electronics. Cumulatively, these contracts were valued at $18 million. Given Wilson's profit margin of at least 50 percent, he stood to make $9 million in short order.

Craftily Wilson drew each of the contracts so that they could be legal in terms of U.S. law while illegal in reality. Such a bifurcation worked to Wilson's distinct advantage in several ways. The "legal" programs provided a natural cover for work that Wilson and the Libyans wished to keep secret. They provided a recruiting mechanism for Wilson. He could hire a man—a former Green Beret explosives expert, say—for aboveboard work, then entice him into *sub-rosa* activities. And, finally, they gave Wilson an opportunity to deceive himself into the illusion that he was actually working on behalf of his own country, as an insider in the Libyan national-security hierarchy who could provide valuable intelligence to the United States... if anyone ever asked for it.

The military training program, in essence, was designed to help the Libyans develop cadre (the military term for field instructors) who would transform a ragtag of Bedouin into the semblance of a modern army. Quaddafi would no longer depend upon revolutionary zealots for his military. In 1977, he decreed that every male between the ages of 17 and 35 must go into the military—an edict that his lieutenants enforced with draconian efficiency. According to an American living in Tripoli at the time, "Stores literally closed because the owner and his brothers and their sons were suddenly in the army. Virtually overnight, you just didn't see males of that age-range in the streets." Press-gangs went into the desert to dragoon eligible men into uniform. A former American Special Forces sergeant working for Wilson remembered one particularly pitiable "recruit" who was brought into the training base at Benghazi. "This fellow apparently ran away several times before they got him to camp. They had chained him to a pole. He was moaning and groaning; he had no shelter or water, although it was 130 degrees in the shade. I asked why. 'He keeps running away,' one of the Libyans said. I really couldn't blame him. The Libyan Army was grabbing people off the streets. Men who had never even seen a motor vehicle, who were living out in the desert, they were put on buses and trucks and sent to training camps. The Libyans were cabbaging up everyone they could find."

Wilson's contract—at $1.2 million annually—was to provide former American military officers and noncommissioned officers to conduct the equivalent of an advanced basic-infantry-training school at the base at Benghazi, on the coast several hundred miles east of Tripoli. This time, the Americans did not deal with raw recruits. The Libyans they trained had a semblance of military skills. The Americans' task was to give them intensive schooling in small-unit tactics, radio procedures, concealment, demolitions and such mundane but essential skills as how to live in the field. The Libyans, in turn, were to become instructors themselves and pass along their supposedly superior knowledge.

In dealing with a people with no military tradition, foreign "advisers" have two choices. They can follow the British colonial example, imposing their own people at the command levels and keeping the "natives" in the rank-and-file. Or, alternatively, the foreigners can attempt to train indigenous officers and noncoms who eventually run the military. Given Quaddafi's strong bias against outside influences in his country, his military opted for the second route, one that Wilson's people vigorously tried to follow—at least for the first months.

The program was doomed from the start. Seldom did Wilson have more than ten Americans in-country at the same time. For such a handful of men to modernize an army of upwards of 40,000 troops was a logistical impossibility, even if the conscripts had been amenable to instruction. The Libyans definitely were not amenable, and no volume of Quaddafi rhetoric could make them happy in the army. Language was a formidable barrier. None of the Americans knew more than a few rudimentary phrases of Arabic. So their instruction was through interpreters—a laborious process which doubled and trebled the time spent on each lesson. Military training in the army, even that of an advanced nation, is based on the lowest-common-denominator principle—that is, the pace of instruction never exceeds the capability of the slowest learner in the class. The Libyan recruits were not stupid—their instincts had been honed by generations of survival as nomads in a harsh desert climate—but few, if any, had an interest in serving in an organized army, regardless of their allegiance to Quaddafi. A citizen's enthusiasm for shouting revolutionary pro-Islam slogans at a mass rally does not imply a willingness to submit to military discipline and march around with a rifle on a morning when more entertaining diversions can be found.

To the dismay of the American trainers, the Libyans immediately overreached. No sooner had the basic-training program commenced than key officers demanded that the Americans teach selected recruits such advanced skills as precision and high-altitude parachuting. "Ed Wilson never said no to the Libs," Alex Raffio said. "If they had asked him to build them a rocket to the moon, he would have taken the contract. Provided, of course, he got enough money up front."

The man Wilson hired to run the Libyan parachute-training program was a legend among his fellow Green Berets. Known by the cover name of "Jungle Jim," or "JJ," the former officer specialized in parachute technology—specifically, equipment that enabled men to drop to earth more quietly, and from greater distances, than anyone would have thought possible. For years, JJ was chairman of "the HALO Committee" at the Special Warfare School at Fort Bragg—that is, *H*igh *A*ltitude/*L*ow *O*pening parachute drops. The very description of HALO causes an instinctive tightening of lower orifices for someone trained in conventional parachuting. HALO is a guerrilla infiltration technique whereby men are dropped from an altitude of 25,000 to 30,000 feet, free-fall to about 2,500 feet and then glide in on the target. It is not a technique for the faint-of-heart. One goes out in a plane with an oxygen tube clamped firmly in mouth, and bundled against sub-zero temperatures; despite the protection, any parachutist with HALO experience eventually acquires the burned cheeklines of frostbite. HALO works because no enemy expects the Special Forces to do anything so audacious as to jump from 32,000 feet (JJ's personal record) and fall 6 miles to earth. For purposes of perspective, transcontinental aircraft cruise at between 30,000 and 35,000 feet.

As was true of many Wilson recruits, JJ found his retirement pay insufficient to carry him in civilian life. He had two college-age children and held a variety of jobs, none that really interested him. So he was most receptive when a former Special Forces sergeant whom he knew by reputation asked if he would like to earn $50,000 a year teaching Libyans how to jump from planes. "Send me a plane ticket," JJ said.

En route to Libya, JJ met Wilson in London, and was favorably impressed with the man's hearty handshake and outgoing personality. JJ would have two weeks' home leave after his first six months, then a full month, all at Wilson's expense. More tantalizing was Wilson's offer that although JJ's primary mission would be training, he could also do military sales. "Ed talked a lot of percentages on the contracts, but the gist was that I could easily make five or ten thousand dollars extra." JJ went away feeling he had met "a real operator, and a guy who was a good host and a good fellow." Wilson boasted that he had "made millions already" in his dealings with the Libyans, and he strongly implied that JJ could do the same. Wilson did *not* make any claims to JJ that he was working for the CIA in Libya, although he had been insinuating such a connection to other former Special Forces veterans who joined him during the same period. As JJ later explained, "Those guys were sergeants; I had been a lieutenant colonel who knew CIA people at a fairly high level. I could have cross-checked such a story in a minute. The sergeants couldn't have done so. I figure that Wilson didn't want to lay a phony story on me because he wasn't sure that I wouldn't call him on it."

When he arrived at Benghazi, JJ discovered that the Libyans' expectations went far beyond the bounds of reality. The parachute equipment, all of it provided by Wilson, was of mixed quality. The Libyans had a quantity of T-10 parachutes—the basic chute used by the American military, and more or less foolproof. But Wilson had also purchased dozens of chutes from a West German firm that were now worthless. "Some of these chutes were so old that you could pull them apart with your fingers. They had not been dried or aired. The Libyans had left them sitting in wooden crates out in the weather for months. A chute must be popped every ninety days or so if it is to remain in workable condition." The Libyans were eager to start training for the HALO jumps, for Wilson had described JJ as "the world's leading specialist" in high-altitude jumps. Fine, JJ said; where are the oxygen bottles? The Libyans looked at him blankly. Oxygen bottles? Why? JJ patiently explained: "If you come out of a plane above fourteen thousand feet, and you don't have oxygen, you ruin your brain and maybe kill yourself; that's why you need oxygen bottles." Oh, the Libyans said.

The Libyan army had assigned a captain to the school, ostensibly as commander, but he proved to have no influence with anyone else in the military. JJ put the recruits to work doing pre-jump drills from the 34-foot practice towers, so that they could learn the basics of controlling their chutes. But as the weeks passed, the Libyan captain could not provide an aircraft for actual training jumps. "All we could do was repetitive drill with the trainees. This got pretty boring for all hands concerned. Jumping requires some psychological preparation, for first-timers. The longer you think about it, the harder it becomes."

The training craft finally appeared, although on irregular schedules, and JJ put the Libyans through their first jumps. Superior officers immediately began talking to JJ about forming a competitive jump team to participate in Pan-Arabic Games scheduled for several weeks hence. JJ explained, again with strained patience, that the trainees were "lucky to hit the pit in the drop zone"; by no means would they be able to come close to the 3-inch disk that is the target in parachute competition. In diplomatic language, he persuaded the Libyans to avoid the embarrassment of a poor performance before an audience of their neighbors.

In 1979, the American trainers at Benghazi began to hear vague stories about Libyan troops' being in trouble in Uganda. Suddenly "heavy-drop" parachuting became a training priority. "We had unclassified U.S. military manuals on the subject that someone had brought in earlier," JJ said. "The Libyans were particularly interested in dropping 106-millimeter recoilless rifles, ammo and water." For an experienced parachutist such as JJ, heavy drops were routine; in Vietnam, he had supervised the dropping of light tanks and artillery pieces into jungle terrain. In Libya, unfortunately, he had to rely upon the equipment furnished him. One of the first early-drop tests went spectacularly awry. The parachute, in a cargo drop, is opened by an explosive timer set to detonate at a given time after being shoved from the aircraft. As a test, JJ dropped a jeep from a C-130 cargo plane, with the Libyan-provided timer supposedly set to go off after three seconds. "The jeep fell out, and I began counting, and after I passed five seconds, I said to myself, 'Oh, Lord, what are you doing to me?'" The timer went off at twelve seconds—an instant before the jeep crashed into the desert. "It was the mother of all fuckers," JJ said. "The jeep was smashed to bits. The Libyans didn't like this; never again did we drop another 'live' vehicle. Instead, we used crates filled with sand and rocks, to simulate ammo, and water drops."

Ultimately, JJ decided that Wilson was running the equivalent of a scam with the Libyans, intentionally or not. "He had offered these people a capability he could not deliver. Once he had a contract, he did nothing to ensure that it was executed," JJ concluded. "I made a good-faith effort at Benghazi. But there's no way in the world that anyone could have made parachutists out of the Libyans who came to me for training. My gripe with Ed Wilson, I suppose, is that he took deals that were impossible, and then left the trainers— me, for instance—out in the open when they didn't work."

To a spit-and-polish soldier such as JJ, the lassitude of the Libyan military was frustrating. On days when no planes were available for practice jumps, "the Libyans took the whole damned day off; they lolled around the barracks and slept." Eventually the American trainers did the same thing. "This might be easy duty, but we sure as hell weren't getting the job done," JJ recollected. The Americans lived in the Omar Khayyám Hotel in Benghazi. "This was the best in town, but that isn't saying much." Although each man had a private room and bath, "I wouldn't stay in such a place in the States. Electricity was kind of on and off, as was the hot water." The Americans had a sedan and a military driver at their disposal, although the monotonous local scenery paled after a day or two of sight-seeing. Liquor was absolutely forbidden, and the diet was steak, rice and pasta. "I was bored out of my skull, and realizing I wasn't doing a damned thing worthwhile," JJ said.

In JJ's view, Wilson's main interest was the profits he could make on deals that derived from the training missions. Some of the items seemed petty. For instance, regulation U.S. military jump boots could be obtained at the Fort Bragg post exchange in 1978 for $40 a pair. Wilson sold them to the Libyans for $160. "The Libyans are like kids looking for toys," JJ said. "If the special forces had it, they wanted it." Wilson persuaded the Libyans to purchase a heavy, German-made overhead crane for one of their Benghazi warehouses. According to JJ, the crane "pulled down the roof by about six inches the first time anyone tried to use it. The Libyans didn't blame Wilson—they blamed the West Germans. For a time, the Libyans refused to buy anything else from Germany. They still did not realize that Ed Wilson was the phony."

JJ left Wilson after eighteen months; by his computation, Wilson still owes him thousands of dollars in back salary and expenses. His months with Wilson were traumatic, a period he wishes to forget. As a professional soldier, how would he evaluate the training he gave the Libyans under Ed Wilson? "Let me answer this way," JJ says: "I wouldn't like to be in the boonies, under attack and look around me and realize that the only thing between me and deep shit was the Libyan Army. They are good people, but as soldiers they are cross-eyed; in effect, they couldn't shoot straight. Part of the tragedy of Wilson is that he halfway convinced the Libyan power structure that they had a first-class army."

17

An Aircraft Bonanza

Among Colonel Quaddafi's most nagging frustrations in the late 1970s was his inability to force the United States to deliver eight Lockheed C-130 cargo planes which the old Idris regime had purchased just before the 1969 revolution. After seizing power, Quaddafi paid the balance due on the planes, but then the Nixon Administration, through the State Department, forbade their export on the ground that the Libyans would use them against other African states or in support of international terrorism. The U.S. export ban also applied to spare parts for the C-130s.

Denial of the planes put Quaddafi in a difficult position. Pride was one matter, for the United States would not accept his promise that the C-130s would not be used for military purposes.* The refusal of Lockheed to return his money also smarted. (The manufacturer took the position that the planes had been built as ordered and that Libya's inability to obtain delivery was none of its problem; meanwhile, the planes sat at an airport in Georgia.) Finally, the nondelivery left Libya without some sorely needed aircraft.

So the Libyans worked vigorously to keep their existing C-130s in operating condition. But they faced a major problem in finding a supply of the banned spare parts.

Devising ways to avoid the export ban became Peter Goulding's first assignment from Wilson when he arrived in Geneva in 1978. This procurement Goulding called "totally black"—that is to say, illegal. (Goulding still had the misconception that Wilson was acting on behalf of the CIA.) As a conduit for the purchases, Goulding found a Belgian couple who had the European dealership for a respected American aviation firm (one not involved in the C-130 parts deals). With a computer-network link to the United States, the couple could track down and purchase C-130 parts with relative ease.

Goulding then used a variety of guises to divert the parts to Libya. Perhaps half of the parts sought were common to the C-130 and the L-1011, a smaller cargo plane. So parts were ordered as if needed for the L-1011. Another ploy was to buy overhauled parts, rather than new ones, which Goulding

---

*Libyan promises had the substance of a rope of sand. In late 1978 and early 1979, the Carter Administration got written assurances from Quaddafi that two 727s and three 707s he was obtaining from the United States would not be put to military use. Within a month newsmen saw the planes in Uganda, transporting Libyan soldiers to the defense of the besieged dictator Idi Amin and ferrying wounded troops back to Tripoli.

found were "less sensitive" to customs officials. According to Goulding, the parts "came in bits and pieces from all over the world. They were amassed in Belgium, repalletized and the labels changed, then shipped on to Libya." The money involved in these contracts ran up into the millions of dollars.

The profits Wilson earned on the C-130 parts convinced him that aviation was lucrative business, and he cast around for an even larger share of the Libyan market. That the Libyans were satisfied with the existing contractors did not deter Wilson. If Goulding could find parts for the C-130s, Wilson reasoned, nothing should stop his organization from obtaining contracts for servicing and maintaining the planes within Libya. He saw a similar market for the CH-47 Chinook helicopter, an American-made craft which the Libyans had in relative abundance (although sales were embargoed much of the 1970s). Wilson felt he could supply "trainers" for the Libyan Air Force who would fly combat and supply missions in support of Quaddafi's many foreign adventures in Africa.

In 1977, the time when Wilson began looking for aviation business, Agusta Bell, an Italian firm, was dominant in Libya. Agusta was European licensee for Bell Helicopter and Lockheed Aircraft. Dislodging a contractor is a tricky business: the fact that a company is doing business in such a byzantine country as Libya means that it has powerful connections. Wilson went about the chore as if he were planning an intelligence mission.

He soon found a vulnerable chink in Agusta. The Italian company paid its pilots well: $50,000 per year. But Wilson discovered that Agusta Bell was charging the Libyans $100,000 per pilot under its contract—a markup of 100 percent. There was a similar spread in salaries for mechanics and other technicians. (Actually, such a markup is not uncommon in such a contract. The margin covers administrative overhead and recruiting expenses—plus, of course, profit.) Wilson invited the Agusta contingent to his Tripoli villa for an evening of partying, which turned into a marathon gripe session against the Italian firm. Wilson began by casually asking the men how they liked Libya. Predictably, they were happy with neither their working nor their living conditions: their housing was substandard, their food inedible, the Libyans intolerable persons with whom to work. When Wilson oh-so-casually remarked that given Agusta's tremendous markup, the men deserved better treatment, the meeting turned into an open revolt. Within the space of a few hours (and a dozen jugs of Scotch whiskey), Wilson converted Agusta's own employees into ardent lobbyists for the proposition that his organization take over the aircraft contracts.

As it happened, Wilson knew that the Libyans were unhappy with Agusta—not because of the company's performance, which was superb, even with unhappy employees, but because they did not like dealing with a mandatory sole-source contractor. Given Agusta's exclusive concession, the Libyans dealt with the Italian firm or with no one. Or so Agusta thought, at any rate. The Libyans told Wilson, in effect, "Give us an offer, and perhaps we can do business." Wilson did, and the Libyans accepted it, and told Bell Helicopter and Lockheed that entrée to their country's market thereafter would be through Wilson. The aircraft company was not inclined to protest.

Given Wilson's total ignorance of aircraft contracting, he wisely decided to use an experienced Englishman, Tom Sharp, as front man in his negotiations with the Libyans. Sharp was a gregarious fellow who had worked in Libya as a draftsman for a subsidiary of the Oasis Oil Company. He eventually joined Wilson as a broker and salesman, handling such items as trucks and tractors. Sharp had bargaining skills, and Wilson used him to work up the aircraft contracts, under terms that would prove highly profitable. "He talked up the Arabs; he did good legwork," Alex Raffio says. "This was Tom Sharp's deal."

Unfortunately for Sharp, his own contract with Wilson had a number of loopholes which were quickly exploited. Given Wilson's power base in the Libyan military, he quite easily, within a matter of months, squeezed Sharp out of the picture. Even persons then friendly to Wilson felt a twinge of sympathy for the Englishman, nudged out of the very deal he had helped create. How much money was due Sharp? In pub conversations in London, Sharp accused Wilson of bilking him of "millions of dollars." No accounting exists of those first aircraft deals. But in the tight world of arms brokers, the word began to circulate: "Do business with Ed Wilson at your own risk. He cheats, he steals."

*   *   *

The essence of Wilson's contracts was that he charged the Libyan Government about twice what he paid the pilots and maintenance technicians, and paid his expenses and took his profit out of the difference. His contracting company was Services Commerciaux et Financiers du Moyen Orient, which had as an address the Union Bank of Switzerland. The Libyans insisted on secrecy, a condition with which Wilson happily complied. Wilson agreed that Services Commerciaux would "deal with this contract as top secret and commit itself not to leak any information related to it through publication, conversation or whatever." He gave the Libyans the right to reject any employee "who is not acceptable."

Figures from Wilson's own ledger books show the huge size of the profits he made from the aircraft contracts—once he got through a poor first year of mismanagement. Consider a C-130 pilot. The Libyans agreed to pay Services Commerciaux £36,000 sterling a year for each pilot. (The British pound sterling was worth about U.S. $2.40 during the period.) Wilson's expenses averaged £21,866 (£16,200 for salary was the main component; the remainder went for food, housing, air fare, office overhead, use of an auto and a year-end bonus). Wilson's margins were of a similar nature for other personnel. According to Wilson's account books, he was clearing an average of $35,136 per man on the C-130 contracts in 1980–81, and $22,982 per man on the CH-47 contracts. Applied to the entire contracts, this came to a net profit of $474,149 for the C-130 deal, $344,730 for the helicopters, for a total of $818,879. These figures are contained in a section of ledger sheets that Wilson's accountant in Tripoli labeled "Real World." Wilson kept a second, spurious set of books for the benefit of the Libyans—to conceal the amount of his profit, and to bargain for higher fees when the contracts were renegotiated.

Other profits did not appear in the books. The Libyans frequently asked Wilson to have his pilots and crews go beyond their stated mission of "training" and to fly actual combat sorties. The exact amounts Wilson received from the Libyans for these secret missions were never revealed to anyone who worked for him in Tripoli. A portion, of course, would go to the pilot and crew members who flew the mission. But as one person familiar with Wilson's books said, "If Ed Wilson ever saw a man drowning in a shallow river, his mind would click out a profit-and-loss statement before he'd make a single move to save him." In terms of realized profit, the aircraft contracts were a substantial contributor to Wilson's income.

For the Chinook helicopter program, Wilson decided that he would deal exclusively with Americans—pilots, mechanics, flight technicians. The Chinook was an American-made craft whose utility had been proved during the Vietnam War. Wilson recognized that he knew nothing about helicopters and how they worked, and he did not have the time or inclination to learn. So in staffing the Chinook program, Wilson delved into the storehouse of mercenary soldiers left jobless when the Vietnam War ended. The man he selected to head the Chinook project (after an earlier choice did not perform as expected) has been described by former colleagues in both glowing and biting words. But even his detractors agree with admirers from the CIA and the Green Berets that Robert W. Hitchman was "the hottest goddamn helicopter pilot you can imagine" and "a son of a bitch who could look death in the face and reach out and chuck it under the chin; absolute ice water." A bulky Californian whose personality was touched with not the slightest taint of self-doubt, Hitchman had received his first combat experience in Marine fighter planes during the Korean War. Just what he did immediately thereafter is not known, for "China Blue" Hitchman was not the sort of man who talked much about his personal life, even during free-drinking off-duty periods. But in 1961 he had gone to work for Air America, the proprietary company that was the equivalent of the CIA's private airline in Asia during the Vietnam period. And during these years China Blue had learned to fly helicopters.

"Man, oh, man, could he fly helicopters," said an Army pilot who was to work with Hitchman in Libya. "When you're kicking around the boonies in Laos and North Vietnam, with an A-team of Green Berets aboard, you get in as fast as cat-shit and you get out even faster, which means flying low and hard. Hitchman was a guy who could put it down on the deck, just a tick off the treetops, and follow the contours of the hills like he was taking a Sunday drive down the Santa Monica Freeway." Another acquaintance, a former Air America pilot, tells of the time Hitchman flew into Laos to attempt to rescue a downed fighter pilot. A Viet Cong patrol fired on his chopper as he approached, wounding the gunner. "Hitchman put an automatic rifle out the window and made matchsticks out of that particular piece of jungle. When the VC decided they'd had enough of him, he got over the pilot, dropped the winch sling, hoisted him up and flew back to base."

Hitchman apparently spent the years 1975–79 adding to what had become sizable real estate holdings around San Bernardino, California. (Because of their hazardous assignments and nongovernmental standing, Air America pilots earned upwards of $60,000 annually, with minimal living expenses. Many of the pilots banked the bulk of their salaries.) Hitchman confided to one colleague in Libya that "I'm worth a million easy, no matter how you count it."

Despite their parallel backgrounds in intelligence, there are conflicting stories as to when and where Ed Wilson and China Blue first met. Hitchman told at least two colleagues in Libya that "Ed came to me out of the blue; never heard of the guy before." Yet Alex Raffio's recollection is that Wilson said he had first encountered Hitchman during one of his Vietnam tours. Whatever the connection, Wilson hired Hitchman in late 1979.

There are also conflicting accounts as to how Wilson and Hitchman viewed each other. One observer saw the relationship as instant friendship. "They were big men, loud talkers, sure of themselves," a former Air America pilot said. "Sometimes men so similar physically tend to rooster-shove each other, to see who's the big man. But Wilson respected Hitchman as a professional; they hit it off like brothers." But Alex Raffio, who because of his standing with Wilson had an insider's vantage point, says that Hitchman was "an ass-kisser, a guy who said, 'Yes, sir,' and 'Mister' and the whole crap. Most fawning towards Ed Wilson. He was always trying to make points." The relationship was further complicated by the fact that Wilson and Hitchman slept with the same woman in Tripoli, a British citizen who worked for a Western oil company. Just who bedded the woman first was a subject of frequent conjecture. The woman was said to be "head over heels in love with Ed." But when Wilson was not in the country, she cheerily made do with Hitchman. Physically, Hitchman was the better choice. A physical-fitness fanatic, he performed a daily exercise regimen that would exhaust a

professional football player. Wilson, conversely, still suffered
the lingering venereal infection that made him (according to
the testimony of two women) less than an ideal sexual partner.

Hitchman's original recruitment was as a training officer
and maintenance supervisor, for the Libyans felt that their
own pilots—discreetly supplemented by Soviets, Pakistanis
and Palestinians—could fly the necessary missions. But after
several weeks in-country, Hitchman came to Wilson and
shook his head. "These rug-heads have twenty Chinooks
now," he said. "The rate they're going, they'll be out of
aircraft in a month. They can't fix 'em, they can't fly 'em—
hell, this is some kind of Camel Air Force." On one mission,
a Libyan helicopter pilot froze at the controls at a critical
moment. Hitchman, sitting in the copilot's seat, had to take
over and steer the craft out of danger. Eventually, according
to John Heath, Hitchman said he would stay in Libya only on
his own conditions: "that the Libyans keep the hell out of my
way; they can come out and stand around the planes and do
whatever they want to do, just so long as the keep their
hands off the goddamned aircraft."

Wilson passed this message to his contacts in the Libyan
Air Force, presumably in more diplomatic language. The
Libyans protested. Their pilots, they told Mister Ed, were
skilled fliers; all they needed was training. If the Americans
were as good as Mister Ed claimed, they would be proficient
within a few months' time.

"When Hitchman heard this," a colleague stated, "he
said, 'Well, time to pack the suitcase. I don't need this kind of
jerk-off operation.' Wilson told him to sit tight, that he'd work
on the Libs and get something going."

John Heath, himself not enraptured with the Libyans,
felt that Hitchman was overly harsh, that the pilots were
trainable, although "it just took triple or quadruple the time."
Heath also felt that there was no real motivation for the
American trainers to make the program a success. "There are
some people who say, 'Hey, I'm getting paid fifty grand a year
whether these guys ever learn to fly or not.' Some people
took this job as a lark, or in between things, or to get that big
down payment on the house, or whatever."

Ed Wilson somehow managed to bring about a truce
between Hitchman and the Libyans, for in the late spring of
1980 the Libyans expanded Wilson's contract to bring in not

only more American trainers, but also pilots. The decision
marked a significant escalation of Wilson's involvement with
the Libyan military. Henceforth, American pilots would replace the Libyan pilots currently flying combat and supply
missions in the undeclared war with Chad. In sum, Wilson
set out to recruit combat helicopter fliers, not trainers.

18

The Golden Squeeze

Wilson's first recruits were drawn from the pool of pilots
and mechanics who had worked for the Italian company,
Agusta, both in Iran and in Libya under the old contract. But
these recruits, by and large, did not satisfy China Blue
Hitchman. As one American stated, "Many of these guys had
been kicking around the Middle East for years. You had
drunks, you had incompetents, you had 'master pilots' you
wouldn't let drive a jeep. They might have fooled the Libyans
and the Iranians, but Bob Hitchman was a different story."
Alex Raffio remembers that many of the Agusta veterans
made the unfortunate discovery that the Soviet-built MiG
fighter planes sold to the Libyans were cooled with pure
alcohol. "At the Breida air base, out beyond Benghazi," Raffio
said, "the Wilson people and the Russians shared the same
flight line. The Russians shared the alcohol with our boys,
and wow, oh, wow, what drunks they would put on."

So at Hitchman's urging, Wilson started recruiting in the
United States, with a quota of a dozen pilots. As his hiring
agent he chose Kenneth G. Beck, a retired Army sergeant
and helicopter pilot with Vietnam experience. Beck knew just
where to look. Retired Green Berets tend to congregate
around their training station, Fort Bragg, North Carolina.
Similarly, retired helicopter people settle around Dothan,

Alabama, site of the Fort Rucker Army Aviation Center, chief helicopter training center for the U.S. Army. More than a dozen helicopter service companies are in the Dothan area, employing hundreds of persons. Given normal human restlessness, on any given day a sizable number of these people are thinking of greener pastures.

Beck flew to Alabama and ran a small display advertisement in *The Dothan Eagle,* the local newspaper, which must have excited fantasies throughout northern Alabama one July morning in 1980. A "London-based company"—unnamed—"urgently" needed people who knew about helicopters, including mechanics, electricians and other support personnel. "Starting salaries" were $4,000 to $5,000 a month—astronomical by local standards. Interested people were told to contact Beck at the Holiday Inn in Ozark, Alabama, a few miles outside Dothan.

Roger "Squirrel" Homes was one of the men who called the motel and was told, "Come on over." Homes remembered the evening vividly. "I was going through wife trouble, and the idea of gettin' out of 'Bama and making sixty thousand dollars a year made me so happy I drove mighty fast gettin' over there. I had to laugh when I drove my truck into the motel parking lot. It looked like the Rucker commissary lot on a Saturday: 115 percent of the cars had the Rucker bumper sticker—and the lot was full. Everybody and his second cousin had come over to talk to this man. . . ."

Homes's disillusionment came when he heard where the money was to be earned: Libya. "I ain't smart, but I knew enough to know I didn't want any of that sand-Ayrab money. I told the fella thanks-but-no-thanks and finished the beer he had handed me and left."

Some other persons had the same reaction. Bobby Motes, of Ozark, a few years later told *New York Times* reporter Edward T. Pound that Beck's pitch was direct: "money." Motes at the time was earning $15,000 as an electrician for Northrop, one of the local helicopter companies. Beck told him that Libya "wasn't an exciting place, no whiskey, no women, but that I could earn a lot of money." Motes thought a moment and declined because it would be "unpatriotic" to work for a country unfriendly to the United States.

The proposition that turned off Homes, Motes and many others did not prevent Beck from finding his appointed dozen recruits. They signed contracts with "Western Recruitment, Inc," a Wilson company which had as its address a post-office box in Geneva. The contract described Western Recruitment, Inc. (WRI) as a "Swiss-based Liberian Corporation whose purpose is to provide technical and management personnel to Third World Nations." The employees agreed to pay their own air fare to Libya (although some persuaded WRI recruiters to finance their travel, either by loan or directly; Wilson's recruiters had broad leeway in this phase of the negotiation). The terms were tilted sharply in WRI's favor. The first ninety days of employment were considered a probationary period, during which time the men were paid only 70 percent of their salary. If at the end of this period "the Company decides that the new Employee has met all the criteria for the position," he would draw full salary. But the 30 percent withheld during the first three months would not be paid until they completed the full year's contract. If the "Company" was not satisfied with the employee's performance, he could be terminated, or else face a renegotiation of his contract. WRI's control was obvious: a technician working half a world from home essentially had no bargaining power.

The WRI contracts acknowledged Libyan sensitivities. The employee had to agree to "totally abstain from drink nor be in possession of alcoholic beverages or drugs of any kind, except those prescribed by a licensed medical practitioner for a diagnosed ailment." He would be fired if he "willfully neglects the interest of, or publically [sic] depreciates the Company or the Company's customer." In other words, Wilson did not want any WRI pilots bad-mouthing either his organization or Libya.

Withholding of a portion of a mercenary's first months of pay is an accepted practice. Tom Sharp, who ran the Wilson aviation program its first few months, once said, "If they come out a few months and bank ten or fifteen thousand dollars, Libya suddenly becomes unbearable, and they head for home. Keeping back part of the money is an incentive to stay the full course." But so desolate was Libya, and so confused the working conditions, that even the prospect of full pay kept few of the men in-country the full period.

Once the pilots and mechanics got into the pipeline for Libya, much of their logistical support (and salaries) came through yet another company, Brilhurst, Ltd., based in London.

Persons working for Wilson considered Brilhurst a "Wilson outfit," but Diana Byrne, listed in corporate papers as the principal figure in Brilhurst, denies that this was so. She calls Brilhurst "my company" and describes it as a "corporate-service company created to do routine logistical and administrative things for companies operating in the United Kingdom." For the Chinook group, these services included the acquisition of Libyan visas and airline tickets to Tripoli.

The Alabama group tells disparate stories of their experiences in Libya. Despite urging by Wilson and Hitchman, the Libyans at first flatly refused to permit the Americans to fly combat missions into Chad. They could ferry choppers as far south as Sebra, the Libyan military post closest to the Chadian border, but no farther. According to Alex Raffio, who heard the issue argued at several meetings, "the question wasn't one of national pride, but because Ed Wilson, as always, wanted to charge them too damned much money." Thus for some of the mercenary pilots, the assignment was as promised: maintenance, instruction and in-country flights, with no exposure to danger. For at least two of the men, however, the Libyan mission proved a brief but traumatic reenactment of their service in the Vietnam War.

Charles Menton, a former Army helicopter pilot from the Tulsa area, flew a supposedly routine resupply mission to Sebra in early 1981. "A Lib pilot was supposed to take over and proceed on into Chad. I was carrying one hell of a lot of ammo, and apparently there was some urgency. The way the story came to me, the Lib pilot really screwed it his last time around. He drew some ground fire when he got close to the base, and soon as he got back he packed up and went home. *No way* he was going back. What happened to him I don't know, but there were some radio calls back up the line—to Hitchman, I guess, and the Libyan brass—and I got a 'suggestion': five hundred bucks extra for me if I would tool on down into Chad."

Menton agreed, one reason being that the "suggestion" was put to him in such a fashion that he really had no choice. "The name of the place I flew to I don't know—it was a matter of go south on an X-degree heading for X miles, then look for a river, and follow it for X minutes more until I saw some landing panels on a hill to the left or the right. We went in armed. I had a Lib gunner at the machine guns. I got the river, I went in fast and low and I picked up the landing panels about the same time I picked up ground fire. I'd been briefed that the uglies [the enemy soldiers] had some of these fire pockets all around the base. I decided, Hell, I know where *these* bozos are, so let's get a little exit cleared out right now."

Menton turned and gestured to his gunner that he intended to make an attack run. "Bastard. He was star gazing out the door. I finally picked up a Coke can and hit him alongside the head with it. I pointed down towards the little clump of brush where these jaspers were shooting from, and I held out my hands and shook them like I was shooting off his gun. He grinned and nodded his head Yes-yes-yes, and I snuck over behind a little hill on the opposite side of the river, then turned around and came at 'em, at an angle to the uglies' right. Basic Rucker stuff—give the gunnie a clear shot from the left door. The Lib cut loose, and he was on target; we were on it and off it in just a few seconds, and I think we shot some sense into their heads."

Menton landed at the base without further incident, cut his motor and smoked a cigarette and drank a couple of bottles of bootleg beer while Libyans hustled the boxes of rifle ammunition off the chopper. He tried to fire the craft's engine again. "Dead as Uncle Albert's left asshole," he said. "No spark. No generator. Dead dead dead." Mentor sighed and dug out his tool kit and worked past dark. He did not sleep that night. At dawn he got the chopper moving, and cautiously retraced his route of the previous day. "All the time I thought I'd hit the same fire pocket, that they'd have guns there again. Nothing. We zip past it, go up river and zip back to Libya. Whew. I said, then and now, Never more."

Another former Army pilot was less detailed in his recitation of a combat mission: "Because of some foul-up or another, I flew down into Chad with some replacement troops. They apparently had an operation going in which they had lost some people. We got there, and the Lib in charge said he wanted transport a bit farther on. Gave it to him— you don't argue with a man who has a gun and says he wants a ride. We got to the other place, and there was some shooting going on. So I flew past, and put down on the other side, and the Libs tried some half-ass sort of pincer move-ment. How it came out, I don't know; once the Libs stepped off, I did a pedal-to-the-metal and got back where I thought I belonged." When he landed in Libya, the pilot looked over his chopper. There were twenty-nine bullet holes in the fuselage. "Long after I came back to the States, I read stories in the papers that this thing was run by some dude named Ed Wilson. News to me. I also read that I was some sort of 'ruthless mercenary.' What shit. I'm a guy who flies people where they want to go; what they do once they step on the ground is *their* business."*

Although the chopper pilots and the transport planes often operated from the same Libyan airfields, Wilson kept the two programs separate. Security was one reason. His involvement in direct military actions increased steadily, and in classic intelligence fashion Wilson passed information only to those persons with a "need to know." Another reason for the separation was the wide professional gap between the predominantly American helicopter crews and the transport pilots.

The persons working on the C-130 program—British, for the most part—seemed drawn from a grab bag of drunks, incompetents, overage military veterans and other screw-ups. Some even showed up with bogus credentials—forged certificates affirming them qualified as pilots, for instance. John Heath blamed sloppy recruiting. Had the system worked properly, the misfits would have been weeded out in London. As Wilson's system functioned, however, almost anyone who could stand upright and board a plane was shipped off to Tripoli. "We got some really crazy guys, even though they'd sort of been sifted through the filter," Heath said. One problem drinker, a Britisher, set fire to the Wilson villa his first days in Libya. He was forgiven and told, "Okay, just don't do it again." He did not. His next stunt was even more bizarre. At a mixed party one evening, the man left the room

---

*Upon hearing the name Goulden—which is pronounced "Golden"—at the start of the telephone interview, this pilot said, "I don't talk with no Eastern Jews." Upon being told that he was a bigoted son of a bitch, and that his interviewer was actually an East Texan of Methodist origins, the pilot agreed to an interview. Bob Hitchman, when telephoned by Philip Taubman of *The New York Times* in November 1981, responded, "You Jewish [expletive] are trying to destroy the CIA." My own feeling, after eleven interviews, is that the helicopter mercenaries had the same sampling of anti-Semites that one would find in any group, and that their service to Quaddafi was motivated by the promise of money rather than by ideology or racial hatred.

briefly and returned naked and stood on his head in a corner. Someone took a Polaroid snapshot that got wide circulation among Wilson employees. The man left Libya after several weeks and told the attentive British press that he "had conscience problems." According to Heath, "he had *performance* problems. He was drunk all the time, he couldn't fly an airplane; we sent him home."

In conversations with some of the C-130 pilots, Heath discovered that they had been told that combat missions were not in their contract. Once in Libya, however, they learned otherwise. Wilson subjected them to a combination of persuasion and coercion. The mercenary aviators were in a poor position to resist. At the border, they surrendered their passports, which would be returned only by Libyan sufferance. Since they had traveled without visas, no one knew—or could prove—where they were. Wilson and his aides also suggested strongly that the Swiss bank accounts could cause tax and other problems should their existence be made known to American authorities.

Mostly, however, Wilson relied upon persuasion. Many times, John Heath heard Wilson subject a man to what he called the "golden squeeze." The typical spiel, both to aviators and to other mercenaries, went roughly as follows: "Hey, buddy, I'm paying you fifty grand a year. The Libyans are paying me. I make a little profit. I don't make much. But tell you what, buddy. We're both going to end up in a Libyan jail, and I don't know what a Libyan jail is like, but I've talked to some people who've been in them, and . . ."

If the person did not respond favorably, Wilson would change moods abruptly, violently. "You're not going home unless you fly this goddamned mission. Hey, buddy, I really want to help you out. There's nothing I can do. I'm in the same spot you are. You got to help me out."

Wilson's ultimate hold on the pilots and technicians was the confiscation of their passports when they entered the country; without Wilson's permission, they could not leave Libya. Wilson also kept them slightly behind in salary payments. A monthly stipend would be several hundred dollars short; if confronted, Wilson would complain, with feigned earnestness, "The goddamned Libs are slow paying this month, but don't worry, I'll make it up to you." He seldom did. Indeed, most of the aircraft personnel left with Wilson owing them money. Wilson or a subordinate such as Bobbi Barnes in London would say, "The bank accounts are low, and your money will be sent along in a couple of days." Few of the men ever saw all the money due them.

Actually, the aviation program did suffer from chaotic bookkeeping the first months. Wilson decided to try to instill some order into the system in June 1980, when he asked Gloria Streeter to take over as manager of his Tripoli office. Gloria's husband, Steve Streeter, was a former Army explosives expert and longtime friend of John Heath's who had come to Libya earlier to work for Wilson, first on the bomb program, then in military training and procurement. Wilson so prized Streeter's work that he permitted him to bring his wife and young daughter to Tripoli to live—a privilege accorded no other employee. Gloria Streeter, who had an accounting background and experience in retail management, found that few bookkeeping or cash-flow controls existed at the office. No bound records were kept of payments to pilots and technicians. Such persons as "Zak" Zacharias, a Palestinian expatriate who worked as Wilson's general fixer in Tripoli, had more or less open-ended drawing rights on the office petty funds. Wilson seemed unconcerned. "You mean *everyone* here is trustworthy?" she asked. Go ahead, do what you need to do, Wilson told her. Her first reconstruction of the Wilson accounts showed almost $900,000 missing in a single year. "Everyone was stealing from the office, drawing funds they didn't account for," Gloria recalls.

In trying to institute some sort of control system, Gloria asked Bobbi Barnes to begin keeping a ledger of general expenditures made in the London office; payment of much of the aircraft expenses was done from there, and she needed systematic figures if the books were to balance. "Bobbi ignored me," Gloria said.

In fact, Bobbi Barnes ignored the other woman at almost every opportunity. When Bobbi sent a Telex message to Tripoli, she would begin by tapping out the query, "Who is in the office?" If Gloria responded, Bobbi would direct that someone else be brought to the machine to take the message. As Alex Raffio saw the situation, "Bobbi saw Gloria as a woman who was smarter than she was; hence she was a competitor. Bobbi didn't like the idea of another woman doing anything in what had been her own little playpen."

But Wilson was far more careful in another phase of the aircraft contracts: that of getting his quarterly payments from the Libyans. A contract signed between Wilson (Services Commerciaux, technically) and the Libyans on September 20, 1979, had a total value of £1.123 million. Services Commerciaux under the contract was to submit documentation of expenditures each quarter and receive £280,750. But the contract required that all submitted documents be stamped by officials of the Libyan military procurement—a bureaucratic task that could take as long as the Libyans desired. According to Steve Streeter, Wilson had such close ties in the Libyan Air Force that he could walk the paperwork through in an afternoon. "Ed regularly paid off the key officer in the air force, who would get him fast payment," Streeter said. (Such, anyway, is what Wilson told Streeter, along with the name of the Libyan officer who took the bribe. Given the demonstrated excesses of the Quaddafi government, his name is not cited.)

Although Wilson earned more than $800,000 profit the first year of the aircraft contracts (on an income of slightly more than $2 million), he was not satisfied. In the summer of 1980, he instructed Gloria Streeter to prepare what was tantamount to a "second set" of books for the aircraft accounts; what he wanted, he said, was "some good solid losses." As Gloria explained, "Ed told me he wanted some figures that would justify him getting a twenty-one- to twenty-five-percent increase in the C-130 and CH-47 contracts." Some weird bookkeeping was required; Gloria ultimately gave Wilson the desired figures, and in the next year of the aircraft contracts Wilson earned a profit of a shade over $2 million.

Although he would snarl and curse at men in the aviation program, and ultimately cheat many of them out of part of their promised money, Edwin Wilson did have a knack for coaxing extraordinary performances from difficult persons. John Heath attributes this to a combination of salesmanship and *machismo*. "Ed always gave the impression that he was as tough as the next guy, that he had been in tight dangerous spots himself, that he could relate to what his people were doing. Well, the fact of the matter is that Ed Wilson never risked anything more dangerous than an elevator ride; but he could pick the right story." Whatever his knack, Wilson's persuasive abilities brought him the services of a man who proved immensely valuable in his Chad operations.

Bill Norris, a onetime Navy aviator, had left the military because, as one associate put it, "He's one of the most cantankerous people in the Western world." Heath (who liked Norris, and considered him a friend) described him as looking "like a lemon you'd squeezed and then left out of the fridge for about four days—little, skinny, puckered-up, sour." Someone decided that Norris looked like a nineteenth-century prospector who should have been in the California hills with his mule, panning gold. Hence his organization name, "Sourdough." But Norris had much more than an abrasive personality. He was a unique mechanical genius who could repair a computer, a printing press, a washing machine or astronavigational gear with equal ease. Coupled with his devotion to flying, these talents made him an invaluable man to Wilson.

Wilson first hired Norris to help him maintain what was called informally "Air Wilson"—a Convair, a Piper Cherokee and a Beechcraft Baron. Norris also did some of the detail work in forming a Panamanian company, Wendy Airlines, which held actual title to at least one of the planes (and had the secondary purpose of being a tax shelter for Ed Wilson).

Wilson had bought the Convair, a transport plane, with the idea of using it rather than commercial or chartered craft to ferry arms to Libya. But it proved ill equipped for such missions. The Convair had no cargo door, and therefore automated equipment such as forklifts could not be used for loading; everything had to be passed in by hand. Wilson toyed briefly with the idea of starting a sort of "fruit express" by which he would fly oranges, dates and the like from Libya to Malta to Europe, then fill the plane with arms for the return trip. Then he saw the cost figures, and thought better of the scheme.

But Wilson had other things in mind for Norris than flying fruit. Although Wilson later was tight-mouthed about specifics, even when talking with such trusted associates as Heath, he said the Libyans pressured him into using his C-130 pilots to fly supply missions to Libyan-supported guerrillas in Chad. Bill Norris by now had a more or less permanent copilot, "Johnny" Johnson, a white-haired man in his middle fifties who was almost totally deaf. Perhaps because Johnson could not hear Norris' steady flow of billingsgate, the two men got along famously. Promised bonuses, Norris and Johnson took the Chad assignment.

Flying supplies to the guerrillas pushed a pilot's skills—and nerve—to the limit. For the Chad missions, the general procedure was to navigate to a recognizable geographical feature—say, a mountain, a bend in a river or an outlying farm—and then fly in a general direction until, it was hoped, the guerrilla band sent out a radio transmission the pilot could home on. Unsurprisingly, such a system contained ample opportunities for error: the guerrillas might lose the generator that supplied the power for the radio; the radio might break; someone might forget to turn it on; the Chadian Army might overrun the guerrilla position. Each of these things happened at least once.

On one of their missions to Chad, Norris and Johnson flew to their turning point without incident, then began listening for the expected guerrilla transmissions. Nothing. They flew about the area a few minutes; they tried their own transmission on a frequency the guerrillas supposedly monitored. Nothing. By now they had exhausted so much fuel they could not return to Libya.

Norris said something nasty about Africa and the wisdom of people who fly planes and fight wars there, and began looking for a place to land. All they could see, for the moment, was the hills, rocks and scrub brush of northern Chad, surely some of the most unattractive terrain in all the world. Just as the engine began its first sputters, Norris spotted a small strip of relatively clear land—it looked as if someone had had the idea of building a road, then changed his mind in mid-course.

"Hang on to your balls, partner, we're going in," Norris said to Johnson.

Amazingly, Norris managed to get the plane down and rolling in a straight line. Then came a lurch and a swerve as the craft went up and over a steep rise in the ground. The Convair skidded through a clump of trees, sheared off a wing and ground to a halt, its undercarriage ripped away.

Flames immediately engulfed the fuselage. Norris and Johnson managed to slip from their seat belts and squeeze through the cockpit door and jump to the ground. They sprinted away from the burning plane.

Johnson stopped. "Oh, shit," he exclaimed, and turned and started running back toward the craft. Norris grabbed his arm and spun him around. "Where the hell are you going? Are you trying to kill yourself?"

Johnson gestured toward his ear. "My hearing aid," he said. "I lost it in the crash. I can't get along without it. I've got to go find it." Norris bodily dragged him several hundred yards away and shoved him to the ground behind a copse of trees. At that moment, the munitions in the plane exploded, sending flaming bits of wreckage skyward.

A patrol of Chadian militia picked up the two Americans before dark. Since neither side could find a semblance of a common language, even rudimentary phrases, Norris tried to talk with American dollars. All he learned was that a double handful of local fruits and vegetables cost him $100, and that haggling was not encouraged. Prodded by rifles, Norris and Johnson began a march through the brush with their captors.

The next several days, Norris and Johnson were passed to another band of militia which seemed to outrank the original captors. They spent much time walking, and Norris doled out his money $100 at a time when he and Johnson got hungry. Both men realized that if they were turned over to the Chadian Government, they faced a public show trial and perhaps even execution. "That sort of thought sort of puckers one's arsehole," Norris was to comment later. So he looked about for a way out of captivity.

At night, the Chads' idea of security was rather loose. Norris and Johnson would be put in a hut by themselves, and by gestures be told they should stay there until called. A soldier or two would take up positions at the doorway, and eventually fall asleep. Since the Americans were uncountable miles from anyone they could call a friend, the concept of escape apparently never occurred to the Chads.

The third night, as he was shoved into the hut, Norris glanced across the militia encampment and saw a bicycle. A rusty bicycle to be sure, and one whose rear tire had seen better days. Still, given even this crude advantage, he and Johnson could try to dart north to sanctuary in Libya. He tried to whisper his plan to Johnson, but without his hearing aid Johnson could not understand a word. Norris decided to wait until the guards went to sleep, which they did in short order. He tried Johnson again.

Pulling the old man close, he said into the better of his ears, "Tonight, we escape." He pointed through the gathering darkness toward the bicycle.

"Huh? What did you say?" Johnson replied, his voice many decibels higher than Norris thought necessary. Norris got even closer, and spoke louder.

"Escape. Tonight. Soon," he said.

"ESCAPE? TONIGHT? YOU THINK WE SHOULD ESCAPE FROM HERE?"

Though the guards did not understand what Johnson was saying, his voice had brought them wide awake. Norris and Johnson spent the rest of the night with their arms and legs bound. Norris cursed beneath his breath until dawn.

In Tripoli, the first reports reaching Libyan military officers said that both Americans were dead. "Ed and I took this pretty hard," John Heath said, "because we really liked both those guys." But Wilson told Heath to say nothing of the matter for the time being. "I surmised he was trying to think up some story to tell their families," Heath said.

Some three weeks later, Heath was astonished when Abdullah Hijazzi called him and Wilson to his office and announced, "We found them. They're alive, and they will be back in maybe two or three days." Hijazzi would give no details.

Nor would Norris when he and Johnson appeared several days later, emaciated and sick. Obviously, the Libyans had done some hard bargaining to buy their release from the Chadian military, and part of the deal seemed (to Heath) to have been that no details would be divulged. All that the taciturn Norris would say was "Well, one day these people appeared and there was a big powpow in Arabic and so on, and we went off with the good guys."

Both men were so physically depleted that Heath had to arrange for them to be flown to London for medical treatment. Johnson was the worse; he was so thin that Heath barely recognized him at the Tripoli airport, and he suffered mental confusion as well.

As a final blow to Johnson's psyche, the Libyans searched the airport customs office almost an hour for his passport (which he had surrendered when entering the country). The flight was delayed while Johnson "stood around looking like an encrypted mummy you expected to see collapse into a pile of dust," as Heath put it. The upset Libyans rummaged through desk drawers and file cabinets, and finally someone said, "Oh" and pointed to the floor. Johnson's passport was being used to prop up an uneven desk leg.

Norris was to return to Libya two, perhaps three times more, before he finally broke with Wilson. Unsurprisingly, he was owed money. He had put up some of the cash for the airplane. But he was never repaid, nor did he receive his promised salary.

Months later, Norris talked about his experiences in Libya with another pilot he had known during his mercenary days in Vietnam. "That prick Ed Wilson," Norris said: "what I'd really like to do is fly him down into Chad, land on a road and suggest that he jump out and check the air pressure in the tires. I'd gun it and leave that miserable bastard standing in the road, and I'd laugh all the way home thinking about what would happen to him when the local blacks picked him up. Bad news."

19

Electronic Successes—and Scams

The Soviet Union, which was to sell Colonel Quaddafi an estimated $8 billion worth of military equipment, was at once generous and close-fisted. Certain "second-generation" items Quaddafi could purchase in unrestricted quantities: decade-old designs of jet fighter planes, tanks, armored personnel carriers and artillery pieces. But not even Quaddafi's oil billions could persuade the Soviets to turn loose their more advanced military gear. Perhaps the tightest restrictions were imposed in the sale of electronic gadgetry—advanced communications equipment, radar and sensory devices.

And here again Wilson could fulfill a Libyan need. The Egyptians were making Quaddafi nervous. Their lightning success in the early-1977 border skirmishes had convinced Quaddafi they could sting him at will. But geography was somewhat on Quaddafi's side. Despite the fact that the Egyptian–Libyan border stretched for hundreds of miles, only a handful of routes were feasible for an invasion. What Quaddafi needed was night-vision (NV) equipment so that his patrols could detect Egyptian troops and tank columns should they attempt to sneak across the desert and through mountain passes under cover of darkness.

Out of his experience in Task Force 157, Wilson had a smattering of knowledge about NV equipment, though by no means enough to fashion the sort of deal the Libyans wanted. However, given the high prices—and low manufacturing costs—of NV equipment, Wilson could afford to bring in a partner. So he turned to Alex Raffio, who had been working with electronics for more than a decade. Wilson was at his most persuasive when he approached Raffio in London.

"You griped before because Frank Terpil was involved with me," Wilson said. "Well, he's gone now; out. Joe Sands can't work with the Libyans—they can't stand him. I need somebody who knows the sources of supply for night-vision gear, and who can get the stuff without going to the States and stirring up a lot of mud and broadcasting to the world what you're after. I don't have anybody who knows shit about night vision. How about getting in with me? We'll make some money—a lot of money."

At the time—the summer of 1977—Raffio had seen several of his own deals go belly-up in Syria and elsewhere. If he was to continue living in Europe, he must get more out of Wilson than the occasional small odd job. Raffio realized that Wilson was probably getting close to illegality with the contracts, what with his emphasis on the necessity for covertness, but he agreed to help on the contracts.

Raffio already controlled a company called Moore Industries, Limited, based in London, which he had been using in Syria. In August 1977, he and Wilson set up another corporation, Moore Industries Liberia, to obtain contracts in Libya and throughout the Middle East. The actual incorporation was done in Geneva by Wilson's lawyer and money handler, Edward J. Coughlin. The initial agreement was that Wilson would pay Raffio $1,500 monthly and expenses, with profits split 50–50. Raffio's contribution would be his expertise in electronics.

Raffio had a sample night-vision device in hand from an earlier sales effort. (The device, put simply, is a telescope and lens that exaggerates existing light, however dim, and permits the viewer to see objects at a range of several hundred yards that otherwise would be invisible. Depending on its size and configuration, the device can be mounted on a rifle or an artillery piece, or it can be hand-held.) Wilson introduced Raffio to Patry Loomis, the CIA contract employee who was concurrently on the Consultants International payroll, and instructed both of them to fly to Geneva to meet the potential Libyan buyers. Although Raffio did not know it at the time, Loomis was in the process of being fired from CIA because of his involvement with Wilson; his wife, Joanne, worked for Wilson as "girl Friday" in his Washington office.

Raffio stuffed the sample night-vision device into his suitcase under spare shirts and underwear, and got it through Swiss customs without detection. In Geneva, he and Loomis met with Ezzedine Monseur, a powerful figure in Libyan intelligence. Ezzedine liked the device. "He turned out the lights and poked it out the hotel window and looked up and down the street. He got real excited."

Before soliciting a formal contract, however, Wilson wanted a more elaborate presentation package. He sent Raffio to Washington to meet with his old friend Howard Wickham, now a commercial designer and printer, who had agreed to produce multicolor brochures on the equipment. Raffio spent more than a month with Wickham, going over the artwork and the descriptive specifications. The resultant brochures, although impressive in appearance, were also "bloody expensive" —they cost more than $10,000. Back in London at the end of 1977, Raffio picked up several more samples of night-vision gear, buying them openly, and legally, from British manufacturers. Each time a former Green Beret came through London en route to Tripoli, Raffio would give him one of the devices, saying, "Here, bury this real deep in your bag, and someone will pick it up from you in Libya."

Raffio, a consummate tinkerer, was not satisfied with the

readily available equipment, so he set out to design, for the Libyans, what he called "advanced-state-of-the-art gear." Two general types were then being manufactured. The so-called "first-generation" NV device had good range and magnification; it was also fairly free of noise interference. But then U.S Army engineers at Fort Belvoir, Virginia, came up with what they called a "second-generation" NV device. Its significant advantage was that the user could aim it into direct light without adverse consequence, whereas the first-generation devices would "ripple and tear"—that is, yield a distorted image. But the second-generation NV devices were also highly vulnerable to noise interference.

Raffio decided that he could meld the separate devices into an NV device superior to anything manufactured by either the British or the Americans. Working with a computer and two experts at a British optical company, Raffio tried variations of his concepts for days. By grafting new optical lenses onto standard NV sights used by the British and the American military, Raffio came up with a scope that increased range and visibility by 25 to 50 percent, depending on the type of unit involved. "I made a better widget," Raffio said. With the first-generation American unit, "you can see maximum five hundred, six hundred yards. But with our device, we're getting eight hundred, nine hundred yards. You can't hit a man and kill him, but you can certainly see him, which is what night vision is all about. You can make him out. You can follow him until he gets within range of your weapon and then hit him, whereas with the U.S. sight, you probably couldn't hit him at less than three hundred or four hundred yards."

Only a handful of manufacturers—half a dozen in the United States, France, the United Kingdom and Germany—produced the sort of intensified optical tubes needed for the NV device Raffio had designed. Fortunately, he had a close relationship with a director of one of the companies. The director told Raffio, "We'll make you a deal. You agree to buy our tubes exclusively and we'll give you a good price, and we'll give you engineering support." The company even gave Raffio free tubes to use in his experiments, also the use of its research-laboratory facilities in the south of England. With the company's help, Raffio designed and ground an improved lens to replace an optic that had been developed a decade earlier.

The sample scopes in hand, Raffio flew into Tripoli the night of January 27, 1978—his first visit ever to Libya. He was greeted by chilling winds and human confusion. Before starting on the trip, Raffio had asked Wilson about a visa, only to be told, "Don't worry, it's all greased." The lack of the paper did worry Raffio, for he knew the importance that Third World bureaucrats put on the minutiae of formality. Hence he was not surprised when a scowling black customs official hectored him on the lack of a visa, and ordered that he sit on the floor "while I decide what to do." Raffio was just beginning to reconcile himself to going to a Libyan jail when John Heath appeared, introduced himself and walked him through the immigration area. To Raffio's horror, the Libyan official dropped his American passport into a drawer and said, "You can go now, Mister Alex."

"But my passport," Raffio said. "Won't I need it?"

The official, angered, arose with a glare. Heath grabbed Raffio's arm. "Routine," he said, "they give it back to you when you leave."

"Yeah," Raffio said, "but that means I leave on their terms, not mine. I don't like this at all. I'm playing hardball in a hard place."

"Not to worry, not to worry," Heath said.

Raffio's first glimpse of Libya bothered him even more. The airport parking lot was dirt, with deep ruts and a few lights that did little to pierce the evening gloom. Taxi hawkers grabbed at his arm, offering their services in shrill Arabic, with a few Italian phrases mixed in when they realized that he was Caucasian. "From Mussolini to Quaddafi: a strange progression," Raffio thought. They got into a battered BMW sedan. Raffio was pleased to finally see a familiar face, that of Douglas Schlachter, whom he had met in the United States and in London. The car bounced over the potholes of a dirt road for perhaps half an hour. Even in the darkness, Raffio could tell that he was in an extraordinarily dirty city. The few autos had flapping fenders and burned-out headlights; swirls of gritty dust danced up from the roadway. In almost every block, one or more smoldering heaps of garbage sent up acrid smoke.

In the darkness, Raffio saw a drab four-story stucco building with crumbling walls—Wilson's "villa." There were no outside lights, but Raffio could see—and smell—a pile of rotting garbage on the sidewalk. He put his hand over his nose and got out of the car. The garbage suddenly seemed alive, and Raffio realized that literally dozens of gaunt cats were pawing through the pile.

"Silver Fox, have you got the sling?" Schlachter solemnly asked Heath.

"Right here, sir," Heath said with military formality.

"Give it to me, quick," Schlachter demanded. Heath handed over a large slingshot and two stainless steel ball bearings.

Schlacter took careful aim at a large black-and-white cat and snapped off a shot. But the cat jumped away in time, and the yowling pack disappeared into the night.

Raffio shook his head and stumbled up the unlit stairwell behind Heath and Schlachter. "Goddamn," Heath complained— "if we only had our BB gun back."

Heath picked up a 5-gallon metal can in the entryway and disappeared down a flight of stairs off the hallway. "The only water we have comes out of a hydrant in the basement," Schlachter explained. "So we bring up a load every time someone comes upstairs."

The apartment, on the fourth floor, proved to be a living room, a bedroom and a crude kitchen. A thin red veil hung from the ceiling. ("The 'decor,' if one could call it that, was sort of a caricature of what a Class-B-movie producer might have thought of Arabia," Raffio said.) A pile of cheap inflatable beach mattresses occupied one corner.

A paramilitary trainer who introduced himself only as "Bob" greeted Raffio. Schlachter noted Raffio's shocked reaction to the quarters, and he laughed. "Last week we slept eighteen men here," he said. "Tonight we're lucky—only four."

Bob complained that he was hungry, and that it was Schlachter's turn to cook. "There's plenty to eat; just wait," Schlachter said. He rummaged in a cupboard and found a box of crackers. Raffio took one and started to put it into his mouth. Something moved under his fingers, and he looked at the cracker. It teemed with weevils. He dropped it to the floor.

Heath came up with the water and announced he would make a salad. He pulled some wilted greens from the refrigerator, and some overripe tomatoes. Raffio got out of the way. Once the "meal" was over, Raffio lay down on one of the mattresses. Schlachter and Heath had talked during dinner about some mysterious plans for the evening that relied upon the absence of someone they called "Benny." After they left, Raffio slept fitfully, until Schlachter and Heath returned at 3 A.M., howling drunk. They shook Raffio awake and told him of a riotous evening with two women who worked for the Oasis Oil Company. One of the women was married to the aforementioned "Benny," and he indeed had been out of town, so his wife had been available. They went to sleep chuckling about having cuckolded the man.

Raffio stayed awake, pulling the blanket over his head and indulging second thoughts about Wilson's "covert operations." Wilson had firmly warned him about the Libyan ban on liquor; yet here two of his top men were obviously drunk. Further, they had courted unnecessary trouble with their sexual adventures. Contrary to James Bond novels, no thinking intelligence operative would risk enraging a husband who, with a single complaint to a puritanical government, could cause the agent's expulsion from the country, or worse. What a fucked-up operation, Raffio said to himself as he finally went to sleep.*

The next day, Raffio began a dreary series of rounds to Libyan intelligence offices, trying to persuade officers to buy his night-vision equipment. Schlachter, his escort, seemed to have little rapport with the Libyans. Wilson had told Raffio,

---

*The other Americans sensed Raffio's discomfort in the villa. Schlachter began referring to Heath as "a dangerous killer, one of the most deadly men in the world," and he implied to Raffio that Heath was offended that Raffio was using so much water. Through an elaborate ruse, Heath lured Raffio into the dark basement on the pretext of getting water, stepped close behind him and for several horrifying seconds convinced Raffio he was about to cut his throat "just for the sport of it." Heath succeeded in momentarily frightening the wits out of Raffio. During a later trip, Raffio complained of a sore shoulder and asked Heath for a massage to relieve the pain. Heath did as requested, but with a carrot thrust through the front of his trousers. Raffio, a much smaller man, screamed at what he thought was the onset of sodomy. Heath, who has an unusual sense of humor, told me, "Raffio was the kind of man who would monopolize the only bathroom for an hour in the morning, what with his hair-restoration lotions and the like. I like to rattle him on occasion just to keep him off-balance." The men eventually became friends, more or less, bound by a shared hatred of Ed Wilson.

"Doug talks for me. What he says, I am saying." The Libyans, however, correctly saw Schlachter as a not-too-bright functionary. So on their calls, Raffio and Schlachter would get into the offices of military and intelligence officials with the understanding that they were being received solely as a courtesy to Hijazzi, the intelligence chief. After polite openers, the Libyans would ask, "Where is Mister Ed? When does Mister Ed come to Libya?"

From Schlachter, Raffio learned that the Libyans were justifiably suspicious of anyone purporting to offer night-vision equipment. A year or so earlier, two Frenchmen claiming to have modern night-vision gear had cheated the Libyans out of several million dollars. Schlachter sought constant reassurances from Raffio that his equipment indeed was new. "You better be right," Schlacter said, "or we'll all be arrested." Raffio was seized with the vision of some functionary deciding he was on a scam and favoring him with a few years in jail, or a firing squad. And then, even more disturbing, the Libyans did not seem to appreciate the capabilities of his night-vision gear, even when demonstrated to them.

On the return flight to London, Raffio sat in a blue funk, thinking his presentation had been a "dismal failure" and that he had wasted six months of his time on the project. He was enraged that Wilson should be represented in Tripoli by Doug Schlachter, "a damned grease monkey who didn't know the first thing about serious business." He wondered, again, how he had become involved with Wilson: "a shlock operation." He wanted nothing more to do with Libya—or with Ed Wilson.

"How'd things go?" Wilson asked Raffio. Raffio gave a negative report, stressing Schlachter's incompetence. Wilson brushed off the complaints. "Oh, you just don't know what the hell's going on," Wilson said. "You don't know what you're talking about." What a fool, Raffio thought.

In late February, to Raffio's utter astonishment, Schlachter returned from Libya with a firm contract for 200 units of night-vision equipment—100 for hand-held mini-scopes, 100 for rifle and artillery mounts. The entire contract covered several pages; the night-vision scopes were just two of dozens of items that the Libyans wished to buy through Wilson.

Wilson could not resist a gibe. "Deliver these on time, you little motherfucker," he told Raffio, "and we'll sell them three thousand more. Now don't give me any more shit about how you know more about my business than I do."

The Libyans insisted on ordering the weapons scopes as if they were a similar U.S. Army device, the AN/PVS-2B (their contract used this designation). This requirement Raffio felt to be both amusing and irrelevant. "If they had asked us to call the damned thing the 'Cracker Jacks Two,' we would have obliged them," he said. "Dumb Libyans. They wanted everything U.S. So we gave them what they thought was U.S."

Raffio told Wilson where in the United States they could buy the external housings for the NV devices (no law forbade the export of the housings, which by themselves were of no value). "These weren't stamped 'United States Army,' but they were identical to American military. Or close enough, anyway, to fool the Libyans. The housing was what would be different. The Libyans thought they were 'buying American,' because otherwise they weren't a-buying. We gave them a unit that was entirely designed and assembled by Moore Industries Liberia."

Their next concern was to put together the 200 devices and get them to Libya without violating any export or customs law. "My great worry was, where the hell were we going to put the stuff together?" Raffio says. "We needed a central point to which the components could be shipped from a number of locations—the housings from the United States, the internal lenses from England, the camera lenses for the mini-scopes from Japan—and where we could assemble the stuff in bond so that we didn't have to pay taxes, and *then* ship them out." If the host country decided the assembly was illegal, parts valued at more than $700,000 could be confiscated. "You're not going to play games with that kind of stuff because it's all going into a foreign nation on a bonded basis. If your information is not correct, or if you can't trust the guy who's bonding it for you, all these goods could be seized and you could be screwed. So it was a sizable investment and it had to be well thought-out and planned very carefully."

For several weeks, various Wilson functionaries scouted Europe for a suitable site. Reginald Slocombe, the shipping man, finally found the right location: an immense warehouse in Rotterdam built to house oil equipment for the North Sea fields. A German-born shipper named Wolfgang Steiniger owned the 50,000-square-foot warehouse. Raffio flew to Rotterdam to inspect the building—he would be directing the assembly of the night-vision devices—and he liked it. "Give us some heat, and you've got a deal," he told Steiniger. "You're on," Steiniger replied.

In November 1978—more than a year after Raffio and Wilson forged their night-vision deal—the components began arriving in Rotterdam. "For a period of about five or six days, we put together two hundred weapons sights under the watchful eyes of Dutch customs people, who were looking on as we're assembling these quite lethal-looking black things." But the Dutch had no concern as to what was being assembled; their sole interest was that every part that came into the warehouse go out again, under bond. Ownership of the components was vested in a specially created company, Moore Industries BV, a Dutch corporation. (Moore Industries BV was the third version of Raffio's original company, Moore Industries. Incorporating similarly named companies in separate countries helped Raffio, Wilson and associates create a paper trail to confuse investigators.) This move guaranteed continued title to the goods. "If we had a falling-out with Steiniger or with the Dutch officials, we theoretically had control of our materials." Raffio was nervous because if the components were seized, "it was my profit going down the drain."

Because the Libyans refused to pay any money for the night-vision equipment until it was physically delivered in Tripoli and accepted, and since the equipment suppliers, once the parts left the United Kingdom, wanted cash immediately, Wilson was forced to come up with slightly more than $400,000 to pay for the parts. "Ed howled. 'What if this deal doesn't go through? I'm out on my ass.' Ed had to scrounge around to find the money. At one point, I thought he would walk away from the deal altogether."

Once the assembly was finished, Steiniger chartered a small jet transport at the Rotterdam airport, and the night vision devices, packed in khaki-green canvas bags, were transported there and put on board, again under constant customs scrutiny. There was brief snag when a suspicious airport official thought the bags contained weapons; he opened several and satisfied himself that they did not, and the plane left.

Raffio sat in the cargo area, on a box of equipment labeled "Malta," their final destination on the flight plan filed in Rotterdam. Once airborne, he talked back and forth with the pilot. "Good weather ahead," the pilot said. "We should be landing in Nice in a couple of hours."

Raffio arose with a scream. "Nice! Nice? Why the hell are you going to Nice? Don't you know where Nice is?"

The pilot looked back in puzzlement. "*Oui*. Nice is in France, on the coast. Why do you ask?"

"You dumb fuck," Raffio shouted. He told the pilot of how, only a year earlier, two Frenchmen had been arrested for trying to sneak NV devices out of the country; *Time* magazine had devoted two columns to their case, to point up the value of NV gear in the Middle East. "France seized the last goddamned aircraft on this thing," Raffio told the pilot. "I don't want to go anywhere near French soil. Go to Italy, go to Sardinia, follow a flight plan anywhere but Nice."

"It's too late," the pilot replied. "Our altitude and climbing speed are set just so that we can reach Nice, and I can't file a flight plan for anyplace else. We've got to refuel in Nice."

"Well, God help us on the ground if they look at this aircraft," Raffio said. For the rest of the way to Nice, Raffio sat "shitting bricks" and wondering how he would survive in a French jail.

No one in Nice showed the slightest interest in either the plane or its cargo. Raffio crouched behind a bulkhead in the cargo area, expecting a *gendarme* to appear at any minute, and did not relax until the plane was in the air again. A few minutes after takeoff, the pilot amended his flight plan by radio to announce a new destination of Tripoli.

This evasion of customs controls was the first of many such experiences for Raffio, who became something of an expert on the subject while a Wilson associate. As he related:

"The Dutch are businessmen, pure and simple. Wolfgang Steiniger once said to me, 'You could assemble an atom bomb in a bonded area. The Dutch don't give a damn. As far as they're concerned, whatever goes on in bond is not going on on Dutch soil.'

"Holland was one of the few countries [in Europe] that

would allow you to ship in, let's say, ten boxes of equipment, and make it all into one box. The Dutch relied on strict accountability. For example, they made us put all the empty shipping boxes into a separate pile, and they carted these empty boxes away themselves so that we couldn't slip out parts later as units of another assembly. They wanted nothing to come into Holland and stay there without the duty being paid. The customs agent watched us like a hawk the week or so we worked.

"When you are going to export or smuggle arms, you always want to do it via airplane. An airplane is easy because you can amend your flight plan while in the air. Other than shooting you down, what the hell are they going to do about it? If you are in a ship, they can chase you down.

"In this deal, the Dutch had no reason to know the pilot wasn't going to fly to Malta, as his flight plan said. Who was going to check up on him? There are hundreds of flights around Europe every day. If there is an investigation, of course, somebody might be found out. But the chances of that happening are slim."

Excited Libyan military and intelligence officers clustered at the Tripoli airport to greet the long-sought equipment. Raffio was told, "We wish a field demonstration this very evening." Some sample scopes were put into a military truck, and Raffio was driven by car to the demonstration site, in the desert near the coast. Several former Green Berets were on hand to attach the scopes to howitzers, machine guns and rifles. Raffio handed mini-scopes around to the Libyan officers.

As targets, the Libyans sat some old buses out in the desert, perhaps a thousand meters from the artillery, turned head-on so that they had the rough configuration of approaching tanks. A former American sergeant sighted the 106-millimeter howitzer, using the scopes, and scored three successive hits. The Libyans murmured approval. Colonel Kalifa, the ranking officer present, tried his hand; he hit a bus with his first shot. We're in, Raffio thought; they absolutely love this stuff.

Meanwhile, other American trainers led a simulated attack on the machine guns fitted with the night-vision devices. Still other trainers picked them up on the scopes and fired live ammunition over their heads. Raffio stood amidst all the noise, fingers stoppering his ears, trying to avoid the scorching backfire of the artillery. One American marksman hit a target 16 of 20 shots.

The demonstration lasted past midnight, and when it ended Raffio was treated like a hero. The Libyan officers lined up to shake his hand and congratulate him on the equipment. "I should think," Colonel Kalifa said, "that we shall be ordering two thousands of these items from you." Raffio joined the Libyans for a five-course dinner—"mostly macaroni, but they tried"—and went to sleep that night with visions of multimillion-dollar contracts.

Such was not to be, for reasons that had much to do with internal Libyan politics. Colonel Abdullah Hijazzi, the third-most-powerful man in Libya, was conducting one of his periodic crackdowns on corruption in government. Despite the professed "greater morality" of Quaddafi's Moslem Revolution, many government underlings were conducting business as usual, insisting that they be paid bribes of up to 10 percent of the value of any contract they approved. Wilson (and the people under him) paid these bribes from time to time as an accepted expense of doing business in Africa. Yet many Libyan procurement officials were wary of Wilson. They were uncertain as to the closeness of his ties with Hijazzi; if they solicited a bribe and he reported it, they could be imprisoned, or even shot. Or, worse, the fact that they were doing business with a free booter like Wilson might lead Hijazzi and his hatchet men to assume they were taking payoffs.

Given such qualms, the Libyans often took the safe middle course and refused to do business with Wilson. They seldom rejected him outright, but would simply make impossible contract demands, and stall the negotiating process until the deal evaporated. One frequent ploy was to refuse payment until all the equipment covered by a contract had been shipped into Libya. "This was ridiculous," Raffio said. "Once you ship something into Libya, you ain't about to get it out again, under any circumstances. If they decide to refuse to pay you on some pretext, you're out your entire investment, and they get to keep the stuff anyway."

It was a lesson Raffio learned the hard way. When he confidently began trying to obtain a firm contract for the

2,000 night-vision devices mentioned by Kalifa, he was rebuffed at every turn. Colonel Henesh, the head of military procurement, hated and feared Hijazzi; since Wilson was presumably Hijazzi's friend, he hated Wilson as well. The Libyans stalled Raffio with crude bluntness: for three solid months he could not even get an appointment at the procurement office, despite daily visits. Raffio was to sell no more night-vision equipment, and Wilson gave him only a small percentage of the amount due him on what they had delivered.

Nonetheless, Raffio was to continue working for Wilson, driven always by the prospect of making a fortune. He spent almost a year designing a so-called "clean room"—a dust-free chamber with controlled temperatures—where explosive timers and other delicate instruments could be manufactured. "The experience was a nightmare," Raffio related. "Wilson was cheating me and the contractors, the Libyans were cheating Wilson and the contractors were cheating one another." To exact his own revenge at being bilked, Raffio deliberately made engineering errors that destroyed any value the clean room might have had. "The Libs spent millions," Raffio boasted. "All they got was an elaborate air-conditioned room."

To Raffio, Wilson's venture into electronics "consisted of one lost, bungled opportunity piled atop another." Aside from the initial sale of 200 night-vision devices, few of Wilson's electronics deals came to fruition.

20

An Arms Bonanza

One index of Edwin P. Wilson's sales ability was his adeptness in staying on the crest of constantly shifting Libyan politics. The Libyan military was fraught with internal feuds and professional jealousies. Keeping himself above the petty bickering of his subordinates, Quaddafi apparently took the attitude that as long as his intelligence and military officers fought among themselves, they were less likely to unite against him. Wilson made an earnest attempt to avoid an alliance with any of the several factions, and he ordered his associates to do the same. "We're out here to sell; we don't want any role in palace politics," he told one man.

Wilson even shunned identification with Quaddafi—a man he never met personally, although he spent six years in Libya, on and off, and had contacts at the highest levels of government. "If the Libyans get the idea I'm going over their heads to the top man," Wilson explained, "they'd cut me down in a minute." Wilson followed hard-and-fast rules. He avoided criticizing any Libyan official in the presence of another, even if he knew that the men involved were rivals. He paid lip service to Moslem strictures on drinking; when Libyan officers came to social events at his villa, no liquor was served until they had left. (The sudden, unexpected appearance of Libyan officials frequently sent Wilson and John Heath dashing to the bathroom to gargle mouthwash.) Wilson paid bribes, to be sure, but always through an intermediary, and the fact that he was paying for contracts, or for expeditious service, was never mentioned to the ultimate recipient of his money. In this sense Wilson had a keen respect for Libyan hypocrisy: If the officials with whom he dealt wished to pose as revolutionary purists, taking his money all the while, he would do nothing to disturb their impression.

It was an abrupt turn of Libyan politics that brought Wilson his largest single contract. Wilson's original entrée into the Libyan market, in 1976, had come through Sayed Quaddafadam, Quaddafi's cousin and head of the Libyan purchasing mission in London. But in early 1978, Quaddafadam came under suspicion by British police for trying to arrange the murder of two Libyan dissidents in the United Kingdom. According to British press accounts, a London gunman told authorities that Quaddafadam had tried to hire him for the killings. Since Quaddafadam's position did not afford him diplomatic immunity from arrest, he hurriedly left the country.

Quaddafadam thrived back in Tripoli. He took responsibility for internal counterintelligence, seeking out enemies of

Quaddafi and suppressing them with brutal efficiency. But Quaddafadam's taste for Western comforts, acquired through his self-indulgent years in London, precluded his acceptance of Tripoli's Moslem austerity. He outfitted for himself the most opulent office in Libya (Quaddafi, by way of contrast, liked to do his business from a tent he would pitch somewhere in the outskirts of Tripoli). Quaddafadam continued to drink fine Western spirits (which his counterintelligence agents could smuggle into the country), and he enhanced an already notorious reputation as a womanizer.

The Wilson people liked Quaddafadam—and not only because he had readily given them contracts in London. Alex Raffio thought that "he'd be much better at running Libya than his dumb cousin. He was a pragmatist, Western-oriented. He was the exact opposite of Hijazzi, Sayed Rasheed and Ezzedine. I could understand why they hated him. You could spend all evening with him and have a fascinating time—he could talk in concepts about the future of Libya, and how it could be developed. Hijazzi, by contrast, would say three words to you all evening. He had beady eyes in deep sockets, and when he fixed that gaze on you, you felt a shudder. Even Ed couldn't handle him. He'd come back from a meeting and shake his head and say, 'Hijazzi really ate my lunch.'"

Inevitably, Tripoli proved too small for two such strong-willed men as Hijazzi and Quaddafadam. Hijazzi felt that Quaddafadam encroached in intelligence matters that were none of his business. Although the Libyans were tight-lipped about their internal politics, especially to Western outsiders, the Americans got the idea that Quaddafi had come to recognize Quaddafadam as a problem. In Raffio's view, Quaddafi "didn't like to have Hijazzi's people bring up the fact that Quaddafadam was out drinking the night before. If this sort of thing continued, cousins or no cousins, Quaddafi would have to shoot him."

Quaddafi solved the problem by giving Quaddafadam a new military command in Serte, a coastal city on the gulf of the same name, a comfortable 300 miles from Tripoli. Quaddafadam received a mandate for creating what was tantamount to a second Libyan Army, with a strength of 3,000 to 5,000 men. The group was built as a strike force for Quaddafi's foreign interventions—a well-armed, highly mobile contingent that would operate beyond Libya's borders.

This would be the Libyan arm. Another group to be trained at Serte was Quaddafi's so-called "Islamic Legion," composed of mercenaries recruited from other African and Middle Eastern nations. For the "legion" Quaddafi sought foreign dissidents who could be trained and armed and sent back to fight in Libyan-inspired "wars of national liberation" in their homelands. These men were paid the equivalent of $250 monthly, a princely stipend by African-mercenary standards. The first months the Serte base was in operation, Quaddafi brought in an estimated 3,000 recruits from Chad, the country whose conquest he had long sought.

Quaddafadam spent weeks talking with Ed Wilson about his needs for the Serte facility, and in 1979 they signed what came to be known as the "Serte contract," a multipage document calling for dozens of varieties of military equipment, from M-16 rifles to grenade launchers, land mines, small arms and clothing. The total price Wilson was to receive was $11.6 million, which he realized would be but the first installment; once Wilson established himself as a reliable supplier of arms, he knew that supplemental contracts would come his way. John Heath remembered Wilson's elation the day after the Libyans signed the agreement. "This contract gives us a way to get around those procurement bastards in Tripoli," he said. "We're going to be able to write our own ticket." Given Wilson's policy of charging the Libyans exactly double what he paid for an item, plus an "overhead" charge of 18 to 25 percent, he stood to earn a profit of more than $6 million the first year of the Serte contract.

Wilson directed Heath to move to Liège, Belgium, where he could work more closely with Armand Donnay, whom Wilson intended to use as a major supplier of the arms specified in the contract. If Heath could buy the weapons legally, he should do so; otherwise, he and Donnay should use their combined guile to find a way around the law. Wherever possible, the contract specified, the weapons supplied should be of U.S. or Western origin. Since the weapons would be used in Quaddafi's foreign adventures, he did not want his troops to be caught with arms from the Soviet bloc.

Of the fourteen to sixteen categories of items on the "shopping list"—Heath cannot remember the exact number—Wilson managed to deliver all save the M-16 rifles and 7.62-millimeter rifles with scopes. The Libyan military wanted

100 of the latter; given the requirement for scopes, the rifles were intended for snipers. In this instance, someone unwittingly made an error in writing the contract specification which precluded delivery of the rifles. The contract specified Remington Model 700s, in 7.62-mm. caliber. Similar rifles are readily available in other calibers, both larger and smaller. But the 7.62 is a specific military weapon, and cannot be exported from Belgium unless sold to a military purchaser. And since it was on the embargo list for Libya, the deal never materialized.

Guided by Donnay, Heath had much better luck in obtaining the other arms. The rifle grenades, for example, were manufactured by a Belgian firm. "Cigar [Donnay's code name] knew all these people and he was friendly with them," Heath related. "When we shopped for the first shipment, he took me to the factory. I met the sales manager; they gave me the grand tour, let me test-fire grenades." They sold them with the same detachment as if delivering truck tires. As Heath observed, "Once again, people that are in that kind of business, as long as it's legal, no moral questions are involved. They figure, 'Somebody's going to sell them [the Libyans] that sort of thing, and we're in business to make money.'"

Although the weapons ostensibly were for the Libyan Army, sizable numbers were diverted to Quaddafi's international friends—revolutionary regimes and terrorist organizations that could not do their own shopping in the world's arms bazaars. Several times, Heath saw an Iranian 747 transport plane sitting on the runway at the Serte air base. Weapons Wilson imported from Eruope would immediately be transshipped to Iran, where the post-Shah government of Ayatollah Khomeini was preparing for war with Iran's archenemy Iraq.

Heath learned of some of these cross-deals by accident, such as the day when a fellow mercenary, a hulking ex-Marine named John Dutcher, remarked that he was attempting to buy 175-millimeter artillery pieces.

"Jesus Christ, that's ludicrous," Heath said. "The Libyans won't be able to maintain them."

Dutcher chuckled. "Don't worry," he assured Heath, "they're not for the Libyans—they're going to Iran." (Dutcher never obtained the supersized cannon, but on behalf of

Wilson he did find the Iranians shells for the 175s they already had in their arsenal.)

In the aftermath of the Vietnam War, enormous quantities of U.S. arms were available to Europe, and at a fraction of their manufacturing cost. Even today, legitimate international dealers such as the famed Samuel Cummings can outfit an entire army from warehouse stocks. So the arms-export policies of nations such as Belgium and France were notably unrealistic, even allowing for the general rule that a nation will not permit the sale of weaponry that may be used against a former colony (unless, of course, the incumbent ruler is unfriendly to the former colonial power). And of course policies can change overnight. An arms dealer can put together a consignment of weapons legally, only to learn that exports to Country X are forbidden.

Given such uncertainties, arms dealers go over and around the law in two ways: the use of phony "end-use certificates," and outright smuggling. The "end-use certificate," or EUC, is a document that, in essence, specifies the ultimate recipient of any arms shipment. For example, if a manufacturer of light machine guns receives an order for 1,000 units, he requires that the purchaser supply an EUC from the government of the purchasing nation. The EUC must be approved by the manufacturer's own government, and a diplomatic officer supposedly confirms that the arms in fact arrive at the stated destination. In the United States, the EUC process is directed by the State Department's Office of Munitions Controls; European nations have a similar office.

In his dealings with European arms manufacturers, many of whom produced U.S.-designed weapons under license agreements, Ed Wilson had a direct solution to the EUC problem. He had printers counterfeit EUCs from several African countries to which arms sales were routinely permitted. These bogus EUCs were sufficient to satisfy the manufacturers involved in the sale. Wilson gave them the required piece of paper, then relied upon diplomatic inefficiency to ensure that no one would confirm, in the alleged purchasing country, that the arms had actually arrived. As Raffio puts it, "What military attaché is going to run all over town to confirm that two dozen grenade launchers actually got to the local army?" With the false EUCs, Wilson would obtain the weapons, do some shipping sleight-of-hand once they left the country of manufacture and deliver them in Serte for use by the Libyan army.

For larger shipments, where confirmation would be more likely to be attempted, Wilson resorted to outright bribery. He found that defense officials in small African nations would readily sell EUCs that he could use as he wished, and swear that the weapons had been received should anyone inquire. "Wilson had a pretty high source in the defense ministry of Nigeria," said one former employee. "He once said to me, 'If all else fails, use our man in Nigeria. He'll swear to anything I tell him to. Hell, he should—I paid him enough.'"

The largest arms item in the Serte contract called for Wilson to deliver 3,000 M-16 rifles, the basic infantry weapon of the U.S. Army. The M-16s represented about half the value of the contract. And, at the outset, acquiring and delivering the rifles seemed like a simple matter. The rifles, as standard military issue, are manufactured by the thousands annually, both in the United States and by licensees abroad. For an arms dealer of any standing, buying 3,000 M-16s should be about as challenging as delivering a crate of air rifles. But Wilson "overcomplicated the deal," in John Heath's phrase, spent scores of thousands of dollars trying to save a few hundreds of dollars and ultimately defaulted on the M-16 portion of the contract. It was one of his larger losses, with a touch of comic opera about it.

Wilson's first approach, the logical one, was to Sam Cummings, the American-born president of Interarmco, and perhaps the world's largest private arms broker. Through an intermediary, Wilson asked Cummings about buying 3,000 M-16s. The intermediary was frank about the rifles' destination. At the time, the United States did not bar such shipments to Libya, so the sale would have been legal. According to Heath, the Cummings company said, in effect, "No problem; we've got them. The only requirement is that you have the correct paperwork."

But Ed Wilson did not like the price. He thought he could shave a few dollars by buying elsewhere. No sooner had he rejected Interarmco's deal than the United States suddenly imposed a ban on all military sales to Libya, to protest Quaddafi's support of international terrorists. By Heath's account—and he did much of the legwork on Wilson's behalf—

"Ed had shopped the M-16s so hard, in so many places, that every arms dealer in the world knew he had a contract with Libya for the rifles. How can you lie in such a situation? Even with a phony end-user certificate, you're screwed. You go in to a dealer and ask for three thousand M-16s for Lower Slobbovia, and the guy looks at you and smiles and says, 'Oh, you're shopping for Ed Wilson's M-16s for Libya.'" The deal was too small, relatively, for a dealer to risk prosecution by fulfilling it. As Heath said, 3,000 M-16s "are a rattle in the barracks for dealers." Arms dealers, by the nature of their trade, are watched closely. "Ed might as well have advertised for M-16s in the *International Herald Tribune*," Heath said. "It was an open secret across Europe." (What Heath eventually did was "dangle the carrot" by telling the dealers the 3,000 rifles were an initial order; that if they were delivered and were satisfactory, he would order 20,000 to 25,000 more. At least one dealer still has a document signed by Heath committing Wilson to the purchase of 25,000 M-16s. "I don't think he'll be suing—or collecting, at any rate," Heath says.)

The Libyans, through their own intelligence network, apparently learned that Wilson was having trouble acquiring the rifles. Given the high priority for the item—the M-16 was to be the basic weapon for the men in Quaddafadam's command—the Libyans tightened the pressure on Wilson, to see if he could fulfill the contract. They told Wilson, Since you are under agreement to supply us 3,000 M-16s, we would like very much to have a sample rifle as soon as possible. Wilson heard the implication. Unless he produced a sample M-16 soon, he could lose the Serte contract.

Evidently the demand put Wilson into something of a panic. Associates who had been searching for 3,000 rifles were told suddenly to find just *one* rifle. Peter Goulding, working then in Wilson's Geneva office, spent the spring of 1979 "trying desperately to get this one-each sample." Despite his contacts, "I just was unable to do it." When Goulding reported failure, Wilson replied, "That's all right. I can get one in the United States."

Once again, Wilson turned to his friend Paul Cyr, who now was a lobbyist for the Federal Energy Commission. Wilson telephoned Cyr at his home in Fairfax Station, Virgin-

ia, outside Washington, at about seven o'clock one morning
in May 1979. He wanted, rather urgently, a sample M-16,
and he would pay as much as $10,000.

Cyr sensed easy money. "I told him I would try to get
one." Cyr, a hunter and sometime gun collector, knew that he
could not "just go out to a firearms store and buy an M-16";
possession of an automatic weapon was in itself illegal without
a difficult-to-obtain federal permit. But Cyr knew exactly
where to find an M-16; he had one on the wall of his den.

Cyr had obtained the weapon in casual fashion. In the
late 1960s, when he worked as a Pentagon lobbyist, the
army's M-16 acquisition program had been headed by Major
General Roland B. Anderson. Cyr had gotten to know both
Anderson and his staff, and he remembered a young lieutenant coming into his office one day and asking, "Do you want
an M-16?"

"I said no. He said, 'You better take a good look at it.' He
pointed out that the weapon had a plaque on the trigger
guard . . . to the effect that it was . . . Anderson's weapon," Cyr
said. Cyr recognized the M-16 as a "wall-hanger"—the Pentagon term for the souvenirs that arms contractors frequently
give to friends in the military and the Congress. Anderson
was leaving the Pentagon, and he had no use for the M-16.
Cyr took it because "I thought the gun would be very
valuable to a gun collector, because it was an oddity, just like
a stamp or a coin that was misprinted." The M-16 bore no
serial number.

Smelling his $10,000 profit, Cyr took the rifle off his wall
and telephoned Reginald Slocombe, as Wilson had instructed. They met during the noon hour at 12th Street and
Pennsylvania Avenue Northwest (Cyr's office was nearby),
and the exchange was made. Cyr told Slocombe he wanted
the rifle back, eventually, and that he wished to keep the
presentation plaque. So they went to Slocombe's downtown
office to remove the plaque. "We didn't have the tools, so I
used letter openers and pencils, and finally was able to get
the plaque off." In return, Slocombe gave Cyr a handful of
bills. (Slocombe told him he was giving him $2,000, and that
the $8,000 balance would be along shortly. When Cyr got
around to counting the money the next day, he found that
Slocombe had given him only $1,000. But Slocombe eventu-
ally gave him the remaining $9,000 in the parking lot of the

Hechinger Company lumber store at Routes 50 and I-66 in suburban Fairfax County, Virginia.)

Slocombe, an experienced smuggler, put the M-16 into a tool chest and took it to Rotterdam. He called Goulding in advance and told him to have a chartered aircraft ready for a flight to Libya. Goulding, short of cash, borrowed $25,000 from Raffio for the charter. Slocombe brought the chest through customs without incident and handed it to Goulding, who put it aboard the charter.

Goulding and Slocombe had an anxious few hours' wait in Rotterdam. If customs officials found the M-16 when the charter landed in the south of France for refueling, it could be traced back to them. Thus Goulding was much relieved when Wilson telephoned him from Tripoli.

Wilson roared with laughter. "You fuckers!" he said. "We just bought the most expensive M-16 in history. This thing cost me thirty-five to forty thousand dollars, counting the charter plane. But it was worth every damned dime. Soon as we got it here, Quaddafadam loaded it up and gave it a full function test out the window. He burned off a full magazine of thirty rounds. He loved it."*

Wilson's delight proved short-lived. His quest for the 3,000 rifles was to continue for many more months and end in failure. John Heath spent a lonely Christmas week in Taiwan in 1979 trying to persuade the Nationalist Chinese to sell Wilson the rifles. The Chinese refused; they did not trust Wilson. (Wilson ignored Heath's cabled requests for expense money; Heath had to hock his gold wristwatch to pay his hotel bill.) Wilson and Bobbi Barnes came to Taiwan early in 1980 to try to renew the deal. For a while it seemed firm; then it fell apart. "The reason seemed silly," Barnes said. "The contract called for a certain kind of shoulder strap, and the Chinese price for this one little thing was so much that it put the whole deal out of kilter. Poor Ed. He never found the M-16s." In the end, Wilson had to forfeit a performance bond of more than half a million dollars.

---

*At Wilson's trial for arms smuggling in U.S. District Court in Alexandria, Virginia, in 1982, Cyr insisted that the "wall-hanger" M-16 had been permanently altered in such a way that it could not be fired. Cyr said that there was "no way" Quaddafadam could have fired a test burst out the window. Wilson's lawyers did not produce any testimony to support Cyr's assertion that the weapon had been disarmed. The jury convicted Wilson. One government expert told me the M-16 "could be made operable in about thirty seconds."

But even as Wilson and his people scoured the globe for M-16s, the Libyans put a new military demand upon his organization: direct operations in support of Quaddafi's undeclared war against the neighboring state of Chad.

21

A Dogs-of-War Raid

In the spring and early summer of 1978, the Libyan-supported insurgency in Chad was intensifying, with Quaddafi's "advisers" assuming a dominant, if unacknowledged, role in the war against President Félix Malloum. French-educated, and supported strongly by Paris and French intelligence, Malloum had won his post in bloody tribal warfare that erupted after Chad gained its independence from France in 1960. It is said that he personally cut off the head of his chief rival—Ibrahim Abatcha, founder of the Front de Libération Nationale du Tchad, or "Frolinat"—and carried it through rebel villages in the northern part of the country as a symbol of victory and a warning to future dissidents. But Malloum ruled tenuously, with northern Chad never under his government's control.

Malloum's survival depended in large part upon a force of French Foreign Legionnaires based at a post outside N'Djamena, the Chadian capital. These government-hired mercenaries, and the ragtag Chad army they assisted, were supported by perhaps half a dozen Jaguar fighter-bomber planes based at N'Djamena. The Jaguar is built for support of ground operations; it is fast and durable, and a match for any fighter craft in Quaddafi's air force. As long as Malloum could employ the Jaguars against the Quaddafi-supported rebels, they had scant chance of winning.

Attacking the Jaguars with his own air force posed diplomatic problems for Quaddafi. Despite the fact that he and the French were fighting an undeclared war in Chad (and also in Mauritania, in the western Sahara), Quaddafi still entertained hopes of improving his relations with other Western European nations. So Libya's intelligence chiefs decided upon a highly secret operation that would attempt to shield responsibility for an attack on the Jaguars and the French Legion mercenaries. The person entrusted with devising and overseeing the attack was Ed Wilson. The Libyans told him, in so many words, that they wanted him to hit the N'Djamena base, and hit it hard—but covertly.

The assignment gave Wilson the opportunity to draw upon the varied resources he had developed during his years in the Middle East and Africa. In terms of audacity, the N'Djamena assignment far surpassed the gunrunning deals and the several assassination attempts in which he had been involved.

Wilson's first requirement was reliable intelligence. Although the Libyans purportedly had many agents working in Chad, not even their own control officers trusted them, or the information they produced. African distances are vast, and African communications are problematic. By the time reports filtered back to Libya, they were often distorted or hopelessly outdated. So Wilson turned to one of his more trusted paramilitary soldiers, James Clinton ("Jimmy Blue Eyes") Dean, a former Green Beret with an illustrious combat record and a reputation among his peers for utter ruthlessness. Dean had special status with the Green Berets: He was a former president of the Decade Association, whose membership is restricted to veterans with at least ten years' service in the Special Forces. Although the Decade Association has never involved itself in mercenary or terrorist activities, persons seeking special talents have been known to visit the association's clubhouse near Fayetteville, North Carolina, just outside Fort Bragg, and "talk with whatever boys happen to be around the bar."

On Wilson's orders, Dean left Libya, got a clean passport and a visa for Chad, and flew to N'Djamena in the guise of a tourist. He dressed for the role in a florid sport shirt, with several cameras draped around his neck. Chad is many light-years from being the French Riviera, or even East Africa, which does attract the occasional legitimate tourist.

Somehow Dean managed to pass himself off as a man truly interested in the flora and fauna of Chad, and during a stay of several days he measured the military base with his practiced soldier's eye and snapped photographs of the Jaguar aircraft and the Legion barracks. In the safety of his hotel room, Dean sketched maps showing runway lengths, security fences, the exact location of the separate barracks housing the French mercenaries and the Chadian soldiers, and the location of guard posts. Dean noted that security was lax, particularly after the late evening—understandable, because the guerrilla armies were several hundred miles to the north. (Dean told one colleague when he returned to Tripoli that he had actually gotten into the N'Djamena base and had several beers with French legionnaires in the noncommissioned officers' club.)

Back in Libya, Dean told Wilson—and then the Libyans— what he had in mind for "taking out the base, the Frenchmen and their planes." The legionnaires numbered from 100 to 150 men; as fighters, they could not be discounted, so the key elements of a successful raid would be speed, darkness and deception. If the Chad rebels went against the base in a head-on fight, they would be wiped out. Dean's plan was dazzlingly simple.

A cargo plane—a DC-3 or DC-4—would fly into Chadian airspace at night with an announced destination elsewhere in East Africa. The pilot would radio the tower at N'Djamena and claim mechanical problems and request permission for an emergency landing. Since the African skies are littered with odd aircraft, many held together with the proverbial baling wire and flown by men who belong on alcoholic wards, the request would not be out of the ordinary.

After landing at N'Djamena, the plane would taxi to the end of the runway, then slowly retrace its path, as if headed for the hangar area. In the gloom at the end of the runway, some 40 guerrillas would jump from the side doors onto the grass. Half would race to the parked Jaguar aircraft and plant timed charges of C-4 explosives. The others would deploy against the barracks housing the legionnaires and the Chadian soldiers, and unleash a barrage of fire from light machine guns, M-79 grenade launchers and automatic rifles. This brief spasm of intense firepower would be intended to kill as many of the enemy as possible, and to prevent them from going to the defense of the aircraft.

Meanwhile, the transport plane would do a U-turn and taxi slowly back up the runway. The raiders would break away from the skirmish line and reboard the plane via short ladders thrust out the side cargo doors. Another U-turn, and the plane would vanish into the African night—a dogs-of-war assault lasting a mere three to five minutes, and leaving the Chadian military, ground and air, reeling from a lethal blow.

Such was the plan developed by Dean and presented to Hijazzi and Sinusi of Libyan intelligence by Edwin Wilson. The Libyans liked it. John Heath, who sat in on the planning sessions as a silent observer, recollects that Wilson told the Libyans, "Yeah, I can provide an aircraft, crew and somebody to train your people." The Libyans would provide the weapons and ammunition—and, of course, the commando force. Since Jimmy Dean had designed the mission, he was the logical choice to train the guerrillas.

Dean began with the raiding party in a remote guerrilla stronghold near the hamlet of Zouar, in the mountains of north Chad. The "base" was little more than an accumulation of crude huts and lean-tos strewn over the steep side of a mountain, concealed from air scrutiny by brush. A dirt landing strip had been hacked across the undulating top of the mountain.

As the Libyans made plain to Wilson, the key element had to be secrecy. Quaddafi did not want to be publicly identified with an attack on the French military. "Mister Ed" must design the mission so that Libyan involvement would be shielded. Wilson's solution, a most devious one, was to use Frenchmen as the key figures in the attack.

An unwritten, if often breached, rule of mercenary warfare is that one does not fire upon one's own countrymen, regardless of the price. France's capitulation in the Algerian war of liberation in the early 1960s had left a residue of deep bitterness among many military men who felt betrayed by their government. Disaffection had degenerated into treason, with rightist officers forming the Secret Army Organization (OAS, by its French initials) and attempting to assassinate President Charles de Gaulle. The plot had failed, and the OAS veterans had scattered, many of them to wars elsewhere

in the world. The OAS contingent, in a sense, is the generic
equivalent of the Bay of Pigs veterans who felt betrayed by
the Kennedy Administration.

Through a French intermediary, Wilson hired three veteran OAS mercenaries for the mission. The leader, one
Roland Raucoles, born of French expatriate parents in Algeria,
had been a pilot in the French Air Force. A key figure in the
OAS code-named "Sebastopol," he had since taken a variety
of mercenary jobs. He had flown planes for President Anastasio
Somoza of Nicaragua; he had been the personal pilot for
President Omar Bongo of Gabon; he had been a combat pilot
for the Biafran rebels in the Nigerian civil war. In the
mercenary community, Raucoles was known as a right-winger
who nonetheless would work for anyone who could pay his
fee. Raucoles' best friend was another OAS veteran, Michael
Winter, who had fought up and down the African continent
for more than a decade.

According to what French intelligence agents later put
together in June 1978, Raucoles asked a friend in the aviation
business, Pierre Tesseydre, to find him a suitable DC-3 for "a
little job I have to do down in Africa." Raucoles gave no
details, but he promised that "an enormous amount of money
is involved, and all of us will share in it." Tesseydre found a
venerable DC-3 owned by General Air Service, of Nice, and
Raucoles decided it would do just fine. He chartered the
craft, telling General Air he intended to "fly some cargo over
to the Far East, to Thailand and Hong Kong." Tesseydre, his
suspicions aroused by the sudden change of destination from
Africa to Asia, decided he wanted out. So Raucoles hired yet
a third pilot, a young man named Philippe Toutut, who
worked for a small charter company named Uni Air.

With Winter along as flight engineer, Raucoles and Toutut
flew out of Toulouse on July 27, 1978, listing as their destination Palermo, Sicily. There they picked up two Libyan intelligence officers, had extra gas tanks installed the next day at
another airport in Catania, Sicily, then flew away under a
flight plan that listed Brindisi, Italy, as their next destination.

In fact, the DC-3 broke contact with air-traffic control
soon after takeoff and vanished from official view. Instead of
flying to Italy, it proceeded to the guerrilla base at Zouar, in
north Chad. Aviation authorities listed the DC-3 as missing.
At Zouar, the ragtag irregulars had been undergoing basic

combat training under the tutelage of Jimmy Dean. On July
29, the band went through several dry runs of the planned
N'Djamena raid. With the yelping enthusiasm of youngsters
playing war games, the guerrillas dived through the cargo
doors of the DC-3 as the Frenchmen landed and taxied up
and down the runway, racing around the base and firing their
automatic weapons into the air, placing C-4 charges on trees
which represented the French Jaguars to be destroyed. According to reports that later reached the American contingent
in Tripoli, the Chadians, even though running around "like a
bunch of wild Indians," at least seemed "to understand the
fundamentals of what they were to do."

The next evening, July 30, the guerrillas, some 30 of
them, boarded the DC-3 and flew south toward N'Djamena.
The night was stormy, and the plane pitched and bucked
through the sky; within minutes, many of the guerrillas were
sprawled on the floor, retching with air sickness. (As one
sympathetic American noted later, "Some of these poor guys
had never even ridden in a truck.") As the storm increased in
intensity, the power system failed in N'Djamena, blacking out
both the city and the air base. Lacking any formal guidance
system, the French pilots had no chance of finding the target
in the dark African night. After a few sweeps over the general
area, they returned to Zouar and landed on a runway lit with
torches. By this time, few of the guerrillas could even stand
up. The Libyan liaison officer with the Chadians chided
Raucoles for not finding N'Djamena. "Fuck you, sir," Raucoles
said. "We are lucky we did *not* find the base, for if we had,
your soldiers were too sick to get off the plane, and we all
would have died."

The Libyans and the Chadian officers insisted that the
mission be rescheduled for the next day. After some talk
among themselves, the Frenchmen refused. Raucoles and
Winter, both trained soldiers with long experience in guerrilla warfare, said the plan had too many uncontrollable varia-
bles; even if they managed to find N'Djamena, the green
soldiers could not be expected to outfight the legionnaires
and destroy the French aircraft. The argument raged throughout the day, with the Chadians and Libyans demanding that
the Frenchmen "fulfill your contract." Neither side would
yield.

On August 1, Hijazzi summoned John Heath to his office

and, with some displeasure, told him of the situation. The Frenchmen, he said, "have been paid money, and the guerrillas have made plans for all of this, and now they will not fly." With Wilson out of the country, Hijazzi said Heath was responsible for getting the mission into motion again. "It's very simple," Hijazzi said in a tone that told Heath he would not broach argument. "You are getting on the airplane this afternoon to fly to Sebha. And from there, you will be flown to Chad. You must then convince the Frenchmen to do as they agreed."

With an unsmiling Libyan intelligence officer as escort, Heath flew to Zouar, where he found the Frenchmen under guard in a crude, partially underground hut built of limestone blocks. Raucoles explained the impasse. The guerrillas had no reliable weather forecasts; no one knew whether the power had been restored in N'Djamena. "I am no coward," he told Heath. "I am willing to fly the mission. But we are taking a risk, and we're not going to increase the risk by these other factors."

What Raucoles wished to do was fly on to Asia, as if fulfilling the original charter he had listed when leaving France, and then return to Chad several weeks later; he did not wish to sit around Zouar for an unpredictable period. "We've got wives and families, and our flight plans are a matter of record," he said. "If we don't get back, then everybody's going to be very suspicious and there will be reports going in."

The request sounded reasonable to Heath, and he explained it, through a translator, to the head of the Chadian guerrillas. "This guy—a general—replied through a translator words to the effect 'No fucking way.' He was not about to let these Frenchmen out of the country. Nor me either, for that matter, until they flew the mission. We had reached an impasse."

Heath talked with the Frenchmen all afternoon. A cold rain began falling as they huddled in the hut and ate some tinned meat and drank bottled water. In desperation, Heath suggested that they fly to N'Djamena, land and let the guerrillas disembark from the aircraft. "But when you taxi down the runway, don't turn around—keep on going and take off and fly like hell for home." Heath would go along with them—as a false guarantee that the mission was being attempted—and cover himself later as best he could.

Heath knew that such a betrayal would doom the guerrillas to certain death. "There's no way that little planeload could have done in the garrisons there, especially the legionnaires." But to Heath, morality is situational. He was certain that if the French refused to fly the mission, they would be killed, and that in all probability *he* would be killed to cover up the fact of their murders. "In that sort of situation, you tend to think about your own survival."

The Chadians made the point moot at dusk when several soldiers appeared and ordered Heath and the Frenchmen to get into a truck. The Libyan officer who had flown down with Heath said, "I have good news. We've been talking with the general, and you are all leaving." The truck drove up the winding mountainside to the airstrip and stopped near the DC-3, which was sitting amidst several small aircraft.

The guerrillas motioned for the Frenchmen to walk several hundred yards away, behind a clump of trees. Then one of the Chadian officers motioned to Heath, and indicated through a combination of hand signals and grunts that he wanted him "down."

As Heath recalled what followed: "I thought he was saying, 'It's going to be a while before the pilot gets here. Sit down and take it easy.' That was my first interpretation. I sat down and he said, 'Up!' very sharply. I looked at his face and his eyes, and it was just twilight then, starting to get very dark, and I thought, Oh, shit.

"So I started to get up, and then they demonstrated for me. They wanted me to kneel on the runway. That's when I began to—well, to put it mildly, to get suspicious."

The officer made Heath put his hands behind his head; since he could not see his watch, "each second seemed a minute, and each minute an hour." The soldiers stood in a loose circle around Heath, their automatic weapons pointed at him. There were no more attempts to speak English with "Mister John." The rocks bit into his knees, and sharp pains coursed through his legs and back. Heath asked himself, Why the hell did I ever get mixed up with Ed Wilson? He remembered the close calls with death he had survived as a demolitions specialist. *To have life end here, on the top of a mountain in Chad that I couldn't even find on a map* . . .

The ordeal lasted for perhaps half an hour, with Heath wondering whether he would be allowed to stand before being shot dead, or whether there would be an unceremonious crack of a single rifle shot. Then the Libyan officer reappeared from the darkness and held out his arm and helped Heath struggle to his feet.

"Okay, Mister John, you can get up now," he said. "I'm sorry. I'm very sorry. Big mistake." Heath rubbed his legs to restore circulation, and the officer continued talking. When the Libyan had learned that the guerrillas intended to shoot Heath, he had radioed Hijazzi in Libya. Hijazzi had responded with rage. He had had the lieutenant put the Chadian leader on the radio, and he had told him, "You shoot Mister John, you can forget about weapons, arms or money from Libya. He is our friend. You let him go."

The Libyan officer led Heath over to the plane which they had used on the flight from Libya earlier that day. Heath saw the Frenchmen standing in a nervous circle in the brush. He listened to them talking with the Libyan and the Chadian officers. They were agreeing to fly the mission that very evening, as soon as the raiding team could be assembled and put aboard their DC-3. Heath shook hands with them and said, *"Bonne chance."* Within minutes, he was airborne for Sebha. The next day, back in Tripoli, he visited Hijazzi to report on what had happened. He thanked Hijazzi for intervening.

"It's not necessary to thank me," Hijazzi said.

"Well, I think I was in a very bad situation," Heath said, "and your friend told me that you helped me."

"I didn't help you," Hijazzi said. "I gave you your life."

"What about the Frenchmen?" Heath said.

Hijazzi waved his hand in a gesture of dismissal. "Oh, they're dead. They shot them right after you took off. They never even got to their aircraft."

Heath could not remember another word of his talk with Hijazzi that day. But one vivid recollection of what one of the Frenchmen had told him did come to mind later. This man had mentioned his sweetheart, and how he wished to get back to her in France. He had wept a bit, most quietly, as he talked. "Four hours later, he's dead in the dirt on some godforsaken mountainside," Heath said.

When Wilson returned, Hijazzi called him in with Heath and repeated the story of what had happened to the Frenchmen, and how he had saved Heath from the same fate. "This was one of the few times I saw Ed physically react to a situation," Heath said. "He turned a little white."

Wilson forbade Heath to tell anyone of the Frenchmen's fate. "There's going to be problems about this, because their families are going to make inquiries," Wilson said. He thought a minute. "Our cover story is this. I arranged to charter an aircraft. The goddamned thing never got there. I don't know what happened to it. It must have crashed somewhere over the Mediterranean, and I'm damned pissed off about it. I want my money back." Wilson gave Heath a small bonus and several days of holiday.

Some weeks later, Heath was in the Wilson office in Geneva when a British businessman who had been involved in the charter called to inquire as to the whereabouts of the plane. Heath told the cover story directed by Wilson. And even later, the wife of one of the Frenchmen called the office. She feared—but did not know for certain—that her husband was dead. She became hysterical. She screamed to the Wilson employee who took the call, "You killed him, you son of a bitch." But as Heath said, "She never knew."

Heath had his own second thoughts. "Why couldn't Ed have told the families? At least they wouldn't fret the rest of their lives." But Wilson did not; he continued to press for the return of the money he had paid for the charter; he cared nothing about the French widows.

What did give him concern, however, was a revived Justice Department investigation in Washington.

22

The Trail: II

The week before Christmas and New Year's is perhaps the slowest time of year for a U.S. attorney's office, in

Washington and elsewhere. Judges are reluctant to impanel a jury during the holiday season, and prosecutors spend their time on catch-up work and bringing outdated files into order. The week is also a time when seemingly hopeless cases are discarded, so that they won't be around to clutter the statistics of the new year.

Sometime during the week in 1977, Donald Campbell, a lithe red-haired Scotsman who headed the Major Crimes Division in the Washington office, called in assistants Larry Barcella and Gene Propper. He tossed a meager folder onto his desk. "This is something that has been kicking around the Justice Department the better part of a year," he said, "and they don't see a prosecutable case in it. They're recommending that the investigation be terminated." Under Justice Department guidelines, dismissal of a case requires the approval of the local federal prosecutor. "Why don't you boys take a look at it and see what you make of it?" Campbell said.

The sheaf of papers—the first of what was to become a veritable roomful of documents comprising the Wilson Case—was slim. It consisted chiefly of résumés of the material volunteered by Kevin Mulcahy, John and Lou Harper on the bomb schools, and the Cubans, Rafael Quintero and the Villaverde brothers, on the assassination overture. In each instance, the initial information had been received by the CIA and turned over to the FBI.

Barcella thumbed through the pages as he walked back to his office. The name Edwin P. Wilson stood out as the key figure in the case. Wilson. Edwin P. Wilson. Barcella thought a few seconds. The former CIA man mentioned last spring in the Letelier case. That had turned out to be a bad newspaper story. But now a onetime CIA employee had said Wilson was running a terrorist training school with former American military men, and three CIA contract employees put Wilson in the middle of a murder plot.

Barcella paused, recalling what had gone through his head the previous spring when he listened to Wilson's all-too-earnest protestations that he was nothing more than a legitimate businessman. *This man is lying. He has nothing to do with Letelier, but he's into something else. Just what it is I don't know, and I may never know. But I'm putting a little tick mark by his name in my mind.*

Gene Propper, after reading the file, agreed with Barcella.

"This is the guy who 'didn't know a timer from a teapot,' remember? And here we have him conning some Cubans into trying to kill Carlos the Jackal."

Nonetheless, the Justice Department's recommendation was that no prosecution be undertaken, for its lawyers had found no indictable crime. Their analysis was that Wilson had drawn a careful line between his activities: the legal business he ran out of the Consultants International offices, and the mercenary work he did abroad. But in reviewing the Cubans' story, Propper focused on a single sentence. Wilson had called Rafael Quintero to a meeting in Washington, and he had given him expense money for the trip he and the other Cubans later made to Europe.

By happenstance, Propper had just a few years previously tried a case which established a standard by which conspiracy-to-commit-murder cases could be prosecuted in the District of Columbia. A D.C. businessman had decided to murder his wife; the man he approached to do the killing had gone to the police. With the police, Propper had devised an elaborate ruse. The supposed killer, according to the husband's plan, was to shoot the woman near the Washington Mall in the afternoon when she got off work and, as confirmatory evidence, snatch off one of her earrings and bring it to him. The killer would be paid $10,000. Told of the plot, the woman agreed to cooperate with Propper and the police. She handed over an earring, and she did not object when police had a false report of her murder broadcast on evening radio. The husband paid the "killer" $10,000, and was arrested on the spot.

Since the wife had not been killed, no murder charge could be brought. And to Propper's surprise, the D.C. statutes contained no section on conspiracy-to-murder. "For a while, it looked like my case was falling through the cracks," Propper said. "The guy was going to walk." Propper bored into lawbooks, and he found what he needed. When the District of Columbia was carved out of the states of Maryland and Virginia in 1801, the enacting legislation stated that any existing Maryland criminal statute not absorbed by or in conflict with the D.C. criminal code was to remain on the books. The Maryland code covered conspiracy to murder. Propper brought the charge, the jury convicted the husband, the appeals court upheld the conviction. The District of

Columbia now had case law permitting prosecution for solicitation to commit murder.

Barcella and Propper went back to Don Campbell and told him, "There could be a case here. Don't let Justice drop it just yet." Campbell agreed. He would let his junior prosecutors pursue Ed Wilson.

The Justice Department at this juncture made a mistake in its priorities. No sooner had Barcella and Propper decided to start inquiries on Wilson than the Letelier case came alive again. Of the two, the Letelier case was the more important—a spectacular car-bomb murder on Embassy Row versus a onetime spook who *might* have violated arms laws. Barcella and Propper could have passed the Wilson case on to someone else in the office, but they did not. They would continue to give their major attention to Letelier; Wilson would be a sidelight. As Barcella acknowledged some years later, "Both of us liked it [the Wilson case] and neither wanted to give it up. From November 1978 to February 1979, we spent 110 percent of our time preparing for the Letelier trial, then went into the trial itself, which meant several weeks of twenty-hour days."

The Cubans' story did give Propper and Barcella a reason to convene a grand jury, for now they could pursue a specific indictment. "You've got to be careful about starting a grand jury on the ground that you think somebody is a bad actor," Propper explained. "You can't use it to fish. You have to be going after evidence of a certain crime."

The "certain crime"—the murder-conspiracy charge—gave the prosecutors *carte blanche* to explore any Wilson operations they could find. Their key, and most eager, witness was Kevin Mulcahy, who seemed determined to purge his soul of his Wilson experience, and who could not understand that legal procedures dictated that Wilson at least be given a trial before he was put into jail. Larry Barcella was to deal with Mulcahy regularly for almost six years. He came to love him, to hate him, to wish that he would just go away, to prize him as a grand-jury witness who could give damning testimony about the specifics of Ed Wilson's businesses.

Mulcahy's problem was that he could not always distinguish between what he knew, what he thought and what he had been told. FBI and BATF agents who interviewed Mulcahy would not deal with him when he was obviously drunk.

"Let's try it again tomorrow, okay?" they would say. Often Mulcahy would race into Barcella's office in a rage, protesting that someone had called him an "alcoholic" whose memory of event should be either verified or dismissed.

Not only did Barcella like Mulcahy, he understood what was happening to him. And he could be paternally firm. "Kevin," Barcella would tell him, "you may be sober now, and for that accomplishment I salute you. But you must remember a hard fact: You were drunk most of the time you worked with Wilson, and you were drunk when you came in, and you have been drunk much of the time you have talked to us. The fact that you are sober now doesn't mean a thing." As friendly caretakers, Barcella and Propper drew out Mulcahy's solid information, fact by fact.

Gradually the net began to expand. Barcella and Propper got names of former Green Berets who had worked for Wilson; FBI agents tried to interview them. They met silence. BATF agents Rick Wadsworth and Dick Pederson learned that a Special Forces convention was being held in the Twin Bridges Marriott Hotel, just across the Potomac from Washington in Arlington, Virginia. The agents came to Barcella's office and got a batch of subpoenas and "went out to the convention and passed them out like door prizes," Barcella said. "They brought in a batch of people for interviews."

But the quantity of Green Beret witnesses proved more substantial than the quality, for prosecutorial purposes, of their testimony. To a man, they insisted to Barcella—and the grand jury—that they had done nothing more in Libya than teach basic military training. They laughed at the stories about terrorists and bomb-making. Since they'd drawn their pay from a Swiss corporation, they had not worked for Libya, and they had violated no American laws. At least one of the former soldiers produced a legal opinion to that effect written by lawyer Kenneth Conklin, who at the time also represented several of Ed Wilson's corporations.

What Barcella did not realize, initially, was that many of the veterans were stating the truth. Because of the two-track nature of Wilson's military contracts, the majority of the Americans were in fact not training terrorists. But what irked Barcella was the refusal of the former Green Berets to give his investigation any cooperation beyond simple direct answers, most of them "I don't know." "The loyalty wasn't so

much to Wilson as it was to their friends. They weren't going
to screw their buddies—and maybe screw themselves in the
process."

Once the Letelier case ended, Barcella turned to more
central Wilson witnesses. One obvious key player was Jerome
S. Brower, the California explosives dealer, identified by John
Harper and others as a key supplier to Wilson. Barcella,
however, had little specific evidence, documentary or other
wise. Further, Brower did not intend to help the investiga
tion. He came into the U.S. Attorney's Office in an arrogant
boastful mood; as he told Barcella, he was a leading figure in
his industry, so trusted that he served on several federal
advisory committees. In interviews with Barcella and in his
grand-jury testimony Brower talked in circular fashion, claiming
he had done nothing illegal.

Barcella and Propper tried to make plain to Brower that
on the basis of what Harper had told them, he faced serious
trouble; that cooperating was one way to help himself. But as
Barcella recognized, Brower had a double problem. If he
started talking about other persons' misdeeds, he would have
to admit his own culpability. Since at the outset of the prob
he was considered a significant target, one as important
perhaps as Wilson, the Justice Department would not consid
er granting him immunity from prosecution in return for his
testimony. "Jerry Brower was not a spear-carrier," Barcella
said. "He was a sophisticated businessman who knew the
explosives laws, and he knew exactly what Ed Wilson was
doing." A second complicating factor was that he was being
represented by attorney Edward J. Bloom, who had played a
key role in the C-4 shipments. "Thus Mr. Bloom had good
reason not to advise Brower to tell the truth, the whole truth
and nothing but the truth," Barcella said. "If Bloom told him
to bare his soul, he was saying, at the same time, 'Bury me.'"

Brower still exuded confidence as he left the grand-jury
area with attorney Bloom. As Brower entered the elevator, he
turned to Barcella. "What do you think?" he asked. "How did
I do?"

"Personally, I think you lied," Barcella snapped as the
door closed. Barcella heard fists pounding on the other side
of the door, and muffled voices, "Hey, wait, listen . . ."

Barcella smiled and walked back to his office. He would
deal with Brower on another day, when more evidence was a

hand. These were the months—the summer and early fall of 1979—when, Barcella acknowledges, "We were still dicking around, trying to get someone to break ranks."

BATF investigators Dick Pederson and Rick Wadsworth spent days at Brower's office in Pomona, California, going through records and looking for clues as to exactly what he had sold to Wilson. Brower had covered his tracks well; they found little of substance. So obviously some "live" witnesses were needed.

Pederson remembered one of the Green Berets' saying that Brower had taken "a bunch of explosives experts out to Libya" for unspecified work. Brower would not talk about them, or even supply their names.

Pederson called the Brower company and spoke with a functionary. "I'm Mike Smith of the Happy Times Travel Agency," he said, "and we've just opened an office in Pomona and would like to book your company travel." Oh, that would be impossible, the functionary said, the Brower company already used another agency. "And just who might that be?" Pederson said. "I'm new in the area, and I'm curious as to my competition."

The person gave him the name of the agency. Within days Barcella had subpoenaed records of its dealings with Brower. They included the names of persons such as John Heath and Dennis Wilson who had traveled to Libya on bomb-making missions. Slowly, the investigators were unraveling the story.

Ed Wilson kept a nervous eye on the grand jury. He learned early on that Barcella and Propper were calling in his former associates for questioning, and that they were actively seeking indictments. So Wilson switched lawyers. He retained former Justice Department attorney Seymour Glanzer, who had worked for years in the same office that was conducting the investigation. Glanzer had also been a key Watergate prosecutor while with Justice. Because of his intimate knowledge of the workings of the U.S. Attorney's Office, Glanzer could deduce with great accuracy the scope and speed of the inquiry. Indeed, Glanzer was so prescient that Barcella feared for a time that information was leaking from the grand jury. Eventually Barcella concluded that this was not true (although witnesses friendly to Wilson continued to think so,

handicapping the investigation). What was happening, Barcella
decided, was that any "Wilson" witness subpoenaed would
seek out Glanzer, who in turn referred him or her to another
lawyer, so as to avoid any conflict of interest. These lawyers
then willingly told Glanzer what the prosecutors had asked
their clients before the grand jury—information that was
quickly, and legally, channeled to Wilson. Two other "sources"
were Glanzer's knowledge of grand-jury procedures, and
items of gossip he picked up from Barcella and Propper, both
former colleagues. Properly packaged, this information was
fed to Wilson as "inside tips" about the course of the
investigation.

By late 1979, Barcella had amassed enough information
for indictments of Wilson, Terpil and Brower. He knew that
he had touched only the tip of Wilson's activities, aware that
Wilson had ordered many of his key subordinates—men such
as Alex Raffio and John Heath—to remain out of the United
States, so that they could not be summoned before the grand
jury. Barcella kept close watch on Wilson's movements: had
he come into the United States, the indictments would have
been returned immediately, and Wilson arrested.

As is customary when a person is under grand-jury
investigation, Barcella invited Wilson (via Glanzer) to come
in and testify. Thanks, but no thanks, Wilson replied. So he
and Barcella settled down for a war of attrition—adversaries
separated by thousands of miles of ocean. "I didn't want just
the indictments," Barcella said. "The important thing was to
get Ed Wilson into a courtroom."

The mere fact of the federal investigation unnerved
Wilson. He knew he was vulnerable, realizing that if prosecutors could find documentary evidence and supporting witnesses
to substantiate Kevin Mulcahy's stories, he would be indicted.
So Wilson began a discreet withdrawal to Europe. He closed
the Consultants International offices on K Street Northwest; a
lone secretary took telephone calls and answered Telex messages at the 22nd Street Northwest town house. Wilson made
brief visits to the United States in March and May 1979, but
thereafter he remained in either Europe or Africa.

But Wilson was not comfortable even in London, for if
Barcella should bring an indictment, he would be subject to
extradition from England. So Wilson increasingly sought

refuge in inhospitable Tripoli. By 1979 the Libyans had given him a more comfortable house, this one on the seashore just west of downtown. The new "villa" was actually a conventional three-storied detached house, with space for offices and storage on the ground floor. Wilson's lifeline to Europe and the United States was the Telex printer that stood at the rear of the office. He used the machine incessantly when in Tripoli, often simply to reassure himself that his London office still existed, and that the faithful Ed Coughlin would be in Geneva if needed.

For a man who claimed to be making millions of dollars, Wilson lived austerely. He would ask someone flying down from London—Heath or Bobbie Barnes—to bring him a suitcase of food items not available in Libya. The typical shopping list would be canned frankfurters, Velveeta processed cheese, peanut butter and honey. "Ed had a peasant's palate," complained Alex Raffio, a man who liked the wines and *haute cuisine* of Europe. A former Green Beret officer was astounded at Wilson's appetite for honey, which he would smear over chunks of bread. Food seemed always an afterthought. As one associate said, "You'd be working with him, and he'd forget about the time. Finally you'd have to say, 'I'm going to lunch.' Ed would look up and say, 'Oh, go ahead, I forgot.'"

Omnipresent boredom permeated the Wilson villa. Wilson read chiefly spy novels, with Robert Ludlum his favorite author. The nonfiction book he liked the most—and insisted upon employees' reading—was *Will*, the autobiography of Watergate conspirator Gordon Liddy—"my kind of guy," Wilson called him. But Wilson had trouble explaining to his paramilitaries what kinds of books he wished them to bring to Tripoli when they flew in from London or elsewhere in Europe. According to Raffio, "lots of these Green Berets were satisfied with Captain Marvel comic books. Ed would go livid at some of the stuff they offered him." And the Libyans were erratic as to what they would permit to be brought into the country. The *International Herald Tribune* and the European editions of *Time* and *Newsweek* were read carefully by customs officials; any article on Libya or Quaddafi, however innocuous, was trimmed out. Frequent travelers such as Heath learned to slip news articles in which Wilson might have an interest—stories about his indictments, for instance—

into sheafs of contracts. Wilson might curse "the goddamn Jew-dominated American media," but he was eager to know what was being written about him.

So Wilson found amusement where he could. One afternoon, he and Heath were making a minor carpentry change in the villa. Someone had acquired a stud gun for driving nails, but the color code that told of the driving power of the various cartridges had been lost. Wilson arbitrarily chose a cartridge and put the gun against an interior wall and fired. The stud tore through the wall, narrowly missing someone sleeping in the other room. Wilson apologized to the man for almost killing him, then turned to Heath. "Hey," he said, "let's go get rid of some of the cats around here. I don't like cats. I've hated the fuckers since I worked in that laundry when I was in college. The boiler room in Portland was full of them. Vermin. Let's go kill every cat in Tripoli."

"Wilson took the stud gun to the roof of the villa and tried to aim it at the cats down in the alley," Heath said. "Now, a stud gun isn't your basic military rifle, and it is not designed to shoot straight at any distance. Ed would blast away at the cats, and miss, and he would tinker with the stud gun, and try again. He spent most of the afternoon up there, and he didn't even scare a cat, much less hit one."

His own bouts of foolishness notwithstanding, Wilson was appalled by the crudities of some of his former military men. One Special Forces veteran, after too many drinks of flash, became remorseful at the lack of sexual outlet of a stray male dog that had attached itself to the villa. "I think ol' Bozo needs some action," he said, and took the dog onto the porch of the villa and began masturbating it. The other Americans looked the other way; another man's craziness is his own business. No such cultural relativity for Wilson: he ordered that the former sergeant "get the hell out of here; you are disgusting." He was sent back to the United States within days. Heath and Raffio had discovered early on that despite his sexual promiscuity, Wilson was squeamish about such things as oral sex. "It became an amusing pastime," Raffio said, "to get a conversation going about sex, and then for someone to talk about how they liked to go down on a woman. This would blow Ed's mind. He could not conceive of a sane man doing such a thing. And, of course, once we got him upset, the talk would get even grosser. Ah, but the ways you find to pass the time."

Wilson was alternately cautious and open about his own drinking. During the years of his closest ties with Libyan intelligence—1976–78—his luggage was not subjected to inspection, and bottles of forbidden Scotch came in with him. Later, as did the other Americans, he turned to flash—a drink which, as had been noted, is a rather awful libation. Wilson did keep up the fiction of abstinence when he had to meet Libyan officials. And when Wilson hosted parties, Westerners knew they must wait for Libyan guests to leave before they could drink.

As the reality of Wilson's exile became more apparent to him, he drank more and more—a quart or more of flash a day, according to John Heath, who lived in the villa during the final days in Tripoli. Heath, who knows a bit about liquor, is convinced that the sustained heavy drinking eventually affected Wilson's mind. "Flash gives you that initial jolt that tears down your defenses; every sip you take past the second or so puts you that much further around the bend. Ed had the reputation with a lot of us as a good drinker, someone who could hold it. But nobody can 'hold' flash. It knocks you off your ass and then it knocks you off your brain."

The Libyans contributed to Wilson's unease by their own strict surveillance of his villa and some murky stories about attempts on his life by outsiders. At least three times—according to what Wilson told Heath—the Libyans detected "frogmen" attempting to land on the beach near Wilson's villa; at least two of these swimmers supposedly were shot by security forces. "The Americans are trying to kidnap you and take you back to go to trial and jail," a Libyan intelligence officer told Wilson. (Prosecutor Larry Barcella laughed about the mysterious frogmen. "Where did Wilson hear these stories? From the Libyans. Who 'shot' the frogmen? The Libyans. Who had a reason to keep Ed Wilson nervous about capture? The Libyans.")

Closed-circuit television cameras aimed at the front of Wilson's villa recorded, for Libyan intelligence, all visitors. Occasionally someone would be stopped when leaving and asked to explain the purpose of his visit. From time to time, surveillance teams followed Wilson and his associates when they left the building. "They weren't surreptitious about it," John Heath said. "It was as if they were letting us know we had no real freedom." Wilson liked to run on a track at an American school (built for children of oil-company employees) and chat with other Westerners who were out for exercise. The Libyans even began to trot along after Wilson on these morning jogs. Finally he protested. The presence of the Libyan agents made the Westerners nervous, and none would talk with him. Could he please have privacy at least while running? The Libyans, after some delay, agreed.

In addition to providing lethal weaponry, Ed Wilson did some routine housekeeping chores for the Libyans. When Libyan officials complained about a shortage of cooking oil and butter, Wilson, through one source or another, managed to find a supplier. When a Wilson charter flight brought arms and munitions into Libya, Wilson would scout around Tripoli for fruits and vegetables that would fill the cargo holds on the return trip. Wilson offered an airplane-maintenance service to Western oil companies. Wilson tried to establish a recruiting office in the United States that would hire employees for the oil companies and transport their supplies to Libya. (The companies did not accept his proposals.)

Whenever a Western businessman appeared in Libya, Wilson soon sought him out. He had contacts, he would work as an "expediter," he would make his Telex and telephone facilities available, he had a full secretarial staff. Wilson presented himself to other Westerners as "the indispensable man if you are going to do business in Libya."

Despite his salesmanship and business acumen, Wilson could leave himself open for scams by shrewder dealers. In 1978 he signed a contract with the Libyan military to provide uniforms for each branch of the service. The uniforms were to be provided by a Midwestern businessman, Francis Heydt. "This was one of those Wilson deals that bounced all around the universe, with Ed taking his cut wherever he could," Heath said. Wilson did not conceal his intention; he called Heydt a "dumb farmer," and he gave both Heath and Steve Streeter the impression he intended to cheat the man. Streeter, however, saw through Heydt's folksy manner. "You are deal-

ing with a shrewd businessman who is playing country boy,"
he told Wilson. "You best be careful, or he's going to clean
your plow." Wilson laughed at Streeter.

The contract, for $4 million, called on Heydt to supply
Wilson with enough clothing to outfit the entire Libyan
military—camouflage suits for desert fighting, flight jackets
for airmen, berets for elite units. Wilson's own contracts with
the Libyan military were for $8 million, meaning he could
essentially double his money, less expenses, which would be
trivial. "Ed wasn't satisfied with fifty percent," Streeter said.
"He wanted to get off without paying the guy more than a
small share of what was due him."

Wilson claimed not to have enough money to make an
advance payment on the clothing, so Heydt agreed to post
a performance bond of about $1.5 million. Then Heydt
went behind Wilson's back. Reginald Slocombe, Wilson's
shipping expert, was unhappy about Wilson's failure to pay
him promised money, so he decided to do some conniving
with Heydt. With Slocombe's assistance, Heydt managed
to draw letters of credit against Wilson for several millions
of dollars, took them to a bank and cashed them, then
disappeared from Europe. (Slocombe, in the process, got
the money due him.) "He left us flat; he cleaned out all
of the money," Steve Streeter said. Sometime thereafter
the uniforms began arriving in Libya. "The worst part is
that most of what he shipped was *el no-goodo*," Heath
said.

The Libyans, who had specified U.S.-made uniforms,
found to their rage that the shipments were clearly marked as
being of South Korean origin. "One thing that irked the hell
out of the Libyans was the berets," Heath said. "They wanted
something in blue to go with their existing uniforms. Although no decision had been made on the exact shade, this
guy proceeds to ship the Libyans ten thousand berets in the
most awful shade of blue imaginable. And I'm talking about
ten thousand berets which the Libyans not only wouldn't use,
but *couldn't* use."

The Libyans wanted field caps with earflaps that could
be used during cold desert nights. Heydt bought thousands
of outdated billed caps in South Korea and had them shipped
to a factory in the United States. "There they stitched on this
crude earflap which looked awful. The Libyans took one look

at the things and threw them away. They wouldn't take them.
I don't blame them. I can't think of a single army that would
want to be seen wearing such crap." For field jackets, Heydt
had sat down with Heath and the Libyan procurement officials with several samples. Heath describes their method of
selection: "Once you decide which one it is going to be, you
take scissors and cut that son-of-a-gun in half; you keep your
half, he takes his half. And when the shipment comes in, they
better match. Guess what happened."

Shipments went spectacularly awry. Flight suits intended for airmen in Tripoli went to commando troops in Benghazi.
Camouflage jungle suits went to the air force. (Libyan
interservice hatreds were so intense that Heath, although
he cajoled for months, could not persuade the two services
simply to switch the shipments.) Life jackets for the airborne troops could not be inflated if worn with a parachute. "Ten thousand life jackets, down the drain," Heath
said.

The Libyans ceased payments to Wilson, who now realized he had been cheated by the "dumb farmer." His Telex
messages to London bristled with denunciations of "the
motherfucker who cheated me."

So the Libyans came to recognize Wilson's vulnerabili-
ty. Not only was he a wanted man, but his fearfulness was
keeping him in Libya, reducing his old readiness to operate
at large to the point where he could be victimized by the
likes of Francis Heydt. Using the implied threat of expulsion, they forced him to return to the business of murder—
first as a supplier of handguns, then as a recruiter of
assassins.

That dissident Libyans living in exile abroad could
criticize his government rankled the vain Colonel Quaddafi.
Since the first years of his "revolution" he had tried to have
his opponents tracked down in Europe and Africa killed.
As a revolutionary and a supporter of terrorism, Quaddafi
well realized the dangers inherent in letting political opposition fester. So he made an announcement through the
world press: During a ninety-day amnesty period, any
unhappy Libyan could return to his homeland and be
immune from prosecution or other harassment. All would
be forgiven. Once the period expired, anyone who contin-

ued to criticize Quaddafi and his regime would be subject to execution.

Few Libyans accepted Quaddafi's offer; they did not trust him. So Libyan intelligence officers gave Wilson a new order.

Part Three

THE DEATH MERCHANT

23

Guns for Murder

Given Quaddafi's contacts in international terrorism and the Soviet bloc, handguns were available by the carload. However, the Libyan intelligence corps wanted weapons of American origin, guns that could be traced directly to the United States.

In the intelligence world, a person who is told to obtain a "clean" gun knows it will be used for something other than Saturday-afternoon plinking at tin cans. A clean gun is intended for dirty work, such as killing. To hand a clean gun to someone known to be a terrorist is tantamount to being an accomplice to murder.

In two instances in 1979, persons working for Wilson were ordered to purchase and ship to Libya "clean guns," sample weapons that could eventually mean an order for 400 to 500 pistols. The persons receiving Wilson's orders were John Heath, then stationed in Belgium, and Wally Klink, a former Green Beret master sergeant who had tired of Libya and returned to work as a mechanic on Wilson's Mount Airy Farm in Virginia.

During his twenty-six years in the military, Klink had done rough duty around the world; he had not liked Libya, and he wanted a climate and terrain like those of his beloved North Carolina. Klink was in his sixties; he had the "early-morning hurts" that could be expected in an older soldier; and he was comfortable at Mount Airy. He kept the tractors running, he shared breakfast coffee and conversation with

Barbara Wilson and he did some hunting and some "light" drinking" at night. The work was manageable, the pay good, and Wally Klink kept telling himself he had found the soldier's dream, "a good deal."

One morning Ed Wilson called from Tripoli. "He said that he would like to have me purchase some handguns for him, whatever I could manage to get." Wilson wanted used .38s and .357s "just as soon as I could get them." Barbara Wilson would give Klink the necessary money.

Klink thought a moment. Not knowing any gun dealers in Virginia, he told Wilson he would "have to probably go to Fayetteville to pick them up." Wilson did not object. Klink got $1,500 cash from Barbara Wilson and left immediately for Fayetteville, North Carolina—more specifically, for the Rustic Lounge, a beer joint frequented by Green Berets, past and present, and by many other local good ol' boys.

Klink drank a few beers and talked to an old Green Beret friend, Wilford Burkett, who had spent twenty-two years in the military. Klink told Burkett he needed guns, and he had $1,000 to $1,200 to spend for them. Burkett needed no other prompting. He looked around the bar and saw Terry Wall, of the Bonnie Doone Volunteer Fire Company, an informal brigade based just outside town. When Wall heard that Burkett had cash money—Klink quietly withdrew at this point—he began calling his fireman buddies. Echoing what Burkett had told him, he said the guns were to "go overseas . . . for the personal protection of some American citizens." He found prospective sellers, so he got into his car and began making the rounds. One of the sellers, William Stuart Bryant, who had a Smith & Wesson .38-caliber revolver with a 6-inch barrel, was cautious: "I wanted to make sure . . . that it would be no trouble with the guns." Wall told him "that it might be some kind of . . . government operation overseas, but it was no detail." This explanation—plus $150 cash for a pistol that had cost him only $90—convinced Bryant. Another fireman, Steven Dale Blackburn, also asked questions, heard Wall explain "that he was purchasing them for the United States Government to be used to carry on people going overseas, and it was perfectly legal." Satisfied Blackburn sold Wall his own .38-caliber pistol as well as a .357 Magnum that was the property of his wife, Debbie.

Blackburn, a deputy sheriff in Cumberland County, North Carolina.

By late evening Wall had accumulated the desired 4 pistols, which he gave to Wally Klink in the latter's room at the downtown Heart of Fayetteville Hotel. Klink put the pistols in the back of his car the next morning and returned to Virginia. He had spent $600 for the guns, another $200-odd for his expenses. He felt good about doing the job as Wilson had asked.*

Back in Upperville, Klink turned the pistols over to Reg Slocombe, who knew exactly how to get them to Europe, surreptitiously and also illegally. Slocombe drove to the Nichols Hardware Store in Purcellville, Virginia, a few miles from his own farm, and purchased a toolbox approximately 12 inches long, 6 inches high, 6 inches wide.

"I took it home, took the handguns, wrapped them in sponge rubber, got some old tools, got some pieces of pipe, wrapped them all in sponge rubber, put some cardboard in there, put all that in the toolbox, put it in my strapping machine and put some metal straps around it."

The purpose, obviously, was to "make it look like a toolbox." Slocombe recognized that "I was taking quite a chance . . . going through a couple sets of customs." But he felt he could sneak by. "If they thought I had tools, and they shook them, they would sound like tools. They weighed a lot, they felt like tools. And if they X-rayed them, they would probably show up . . . as tools."

Slocombe flew from Dulles International Airport (where outgoing personal luggage gets only a cursory check) to London (where transit luggage is tucked into a storage area). There he called Wilson, who instructed him to proceed to Rotterdam by commuter flight and meet Peter Goulding. By car, he was then to go to Bonn and give the "package" to a Libyan intelligence officer, Ezzedine Monseur.

Goulding states that he knew nothing of the purpose of the errand other than that he was to get a rental car and meet Slocombe at the Rotterdam airport. "He had just his personal

---

*In September of 1982, Wally Klink pleaded guilty to the felony charge of unlawful interstate transport of firearms. Klink flatly denied telling any of the North Carolinians from whom he had bought the pistols that they would be used by the CIA. He said he had not known how the guns would be used, or why his employer, Ed Wilson, wanted them. He had only followed orders.

effects and a metal green toolbox," Goulding said of Slocombe. Once in the car, Slocombe opened the toolbox and stowed the guns under the back seat, "on the chance now that I might be stopped at the border and asked to open up my luggage." As they drove hurriedly toward Bonn—with only a few hours to make the 11 P.M. rendezvous with Ezzedine— Slocombe told Goulding what was under the seat. Goulding nodded without comment.

In Bonn, Slocombe hurried into the main train station, the meeting site, and found Ezzedine after some anxious moments. He told Goulding, "Take a walk," not wanting him along. Slocombe drove away after Ezzedine, on a wandering route, for perhaps fifteen minutes, until the Libyan stopped on a dark street near the Libyan Embassy. Without comment, Slocombe handed over the pistols and drove away (and spent the better part of an hour finding the train depot and Goulding, who did not know Bonn). He and Goulding went to a hotel and telephoned Wilson in Tripoli and told him, in coded phrases, that the "package has been delivered."

A year later a Libyan gunman shot and killed Omran ed-Mekdawi, who had served in the Libyan Embassy in Bonn as financial attaché and second secretary form June 1970 to May 1978, before breaking with Quaddafi. According to the German police, a "very stout citizen" overpowered the gunman, one Bashir Ehmida, and held him until officers arrived. The murder weapon was one of the Smith & Wesson revolvers that Wilson's people had supplied the Libyans. According to Slocombe, the 4 pistols smuggled were "samples" for an order that was to total some 500 handguns.

John Heath's experience with pistol-smuggling was also a tangled affair, one that he managed to execute only through devious thinking. In midsummer of 1979, Heath was working out of Rotterdam and Liège, Belgium, trying to expedite arms shipments for Wilson. "The Serte contract was hot, and I was chasing grenade launchers all over Europe," Heath stated. He spent much of his time at Wolfgang Steiniger's warehouse in Rotterdam, which had good telephone and Telex facilities. Wilson called one day. "Big Cigar has got some samples that will be delivered to you," Wilson said. "Call him and tell him where you are."

Heath understood the cryptic message. "Big Cigar" was

Armand Donnay, the Belgian arms merchant. "Samples" were illegal weapons. Just what sort of illegal weapons Heath did not know, but he called Donnay's office in Liège.

As so often, Wilson had stretched the truth. He had told Heath that cash had been paid for the "samples." A Donnay associate—"Little Cigar"—took Heath's call and told him no money had been paid for the samples.

To Heath, this performance typified a Wilson operation. "He had something going on in which it was impossible for him not to make a profit, yet he tried to cheap it—to hold up on money regardless of the problems that this caused people such as me and Bobbi who were doing the work. I was left in the ridiculous situation of trying to prove the truth of something the people on the other side of the deal knew was false."

Eventually the haggling ended with an agreement that "Little Cigar" would drive to Rotterdam and give 8—not 10—of the "samples" to Heath. It was during this telephone conversation that the specific nature of the business first became evident to Heath. Although couched in double-talk, the thrust of the message was that "silent appliances" would be delivered along with the "samples."

This revelation scared Heath. Absent from the United States since 1977, he still clung to the illusion that the CIA was somehow involved in Wilson's deals. But pistols equipped with silencers are for but one purpose: quiet assassinations. Heath was later to admit, in so many words, that he knew he was acting as the middleman in the delivery of murder weapons. Heath fought his conscience and proceeded. Wilson had co-opted him into multiple violations of the law; one more transgression was meaningless. After all, Wilson had other conduits; if Heath did not perform the job, the pistols would go to Libya some other way.

So Heath arranged a discreet meeting with "Little Cigar," who arrived in a rusted Karman Ghia with Italian diplomatic license plates, and was handed 8 9-millimeter Parabellum pistols, factory-new, with silencers.

That evening Heath moved to another hotel in an Amsterdam suburb near Schiphol Airport. He called Wilson at the London office to report that he had the "samples" and intended to catch the KLM flight to Tripoli at 8:15 A.M. the following day. Bobbi Barnes, who took the call, realized that

Heath was uneasy. "Ed says if you don't feel right about it, don't do it. Don't take a chance."

Heath awoke at 4:30 A.M. and had a cup of instant coffee. "I'm sitting there and thinking and I decided, Uh-uh, I'm not going to do it. It doesn't feel right. I'm going to get caught. I know it." Heath thought over his problem. For a self-exiled American many months in arrears in alimony and child support, with no other job visible, what might happen should Wilson fire him? In essence, he was in a hopeless situation. Either he continued with Wilson, or he returned to the United States to face whatever charges federal authorities were ready to bring against him. Drinking bitter instant coffee in the predawn hours in a foreign hotel, with 8 illegal pistols and silencers on the floor in a carry bag, Heath in essence was at the bottom of the barrel.

He knew the basic tricks to deceive the X-ray machines that European airports employ against terrorists and hijackers. Checked luggage gets less attention than carry-on, so Heath worked on the large bag. He packed the pistols and the silencers interspersed with an outsize portable radio, a tape recorder, many razors and some other items. Amateurs try to slip around the X-ray machine by putting lead or aluminum foil—the stuff you buy at the grocery store—over the items they wish to conceal. Heath, a pro, knew this tactic was worthless. "You've got this big blur on the screen, and if they're a reliable operator, they're going to say, 'Let's take a look at that.'" By cramming his bag with assorted junk Heath would avoid having the X-ray machine show "clear outlines of eight nine-millimeter Parabellums and those long cylindrical things that fit on the end"—i.e., the silencers. Heath, however, had something else in mind that would enable him to avoid the X-ray machines altogether.

Through the aviation mercenaries, he had heard of a boisterous carnival that was happening to be held that week in the hamlet of Bergen op Zoom, a few miles from the airport. Reserved much of the year, the Dutch kick up their heels and raise their glasses all night during Carnival.

Thinking about Carnival gave Heath a "white flash."

Heath checked out of the hotel and went to the bar and bought a one-shot bottle of Scotch whiskey. A bus ran from his hotel around a circle to the KLM terminal—several hundred yards at most. But Heath chose to walk, carrying a suitcase that weighed 60 pounds. He deliberately walked fast, the better to produce a sweat, and climbed over a barrier without regard to tears in his suit. He arrived at the terminal a few minutes earlier than expected, and found a dark corner where he could stand while the sweat collected on his face.

Heath opened the miniature bottle of Scotch, gulped the contents into his mouth and gargled. Some of the whiskey he spat upon the pavement, some he swallowed. But his breath was that of a man who had spent the night drinking. Heath reached up and poked at his contact lenses "until my eyes got red." He was ready for a last-minute dash to the Tripoli flight.

"I came rushing up and told the KLM people a story to the effect that I was supposed to leave last night, but I got caught in Bergen op Zoom with my friends, and what time was it? I looked for my wristwatch, which I had stowed in my pocket. 'Oh, God, I've left my watch in Bergen op Zoom. What time is it? Can I make the plane?'

"I got lovely KLM sympathy. They brought out an employee who hand-carried that suitcase with the eight pistols and went right up to the goddamn aircraft and they got another guy to go with me. We ran, and we made that plane."

Heath sank exhausted into his seat. Solicitous hostesses gave him drinks and an early breakfast, and then he sat with eyes closed, wondering what would happen when he arrived in Libya.

The arrival was anticlimactic. Libyan intelligence agents met him at the gate, walked him to their office, took the pistols and silencers, and told Heath to take the next KLM flight back to Holland.

"I walked across from Incoming to Outgoing and boarded the plane. I found the same crew that had brought me down. The steward asked, 'What happened?' and I said, 'I don't know. Those damned Arabs—I got my visa; they won't let me in the country. They deported me.' The steward said, 'Oh, what a bother. I'm not supposed to do this, but how about a drink on KLM?' I sat unobtrusively at the back of the plane for the flight back to Holland."

Wilson gushed praise at Heath for the adept smuggling job. As Heath relates, Wilson said, "You're fantastic! You did a super job. I don't know what you did to get those things through the airport, but my God, you've earned yourself a little extra."

The bonus never came. Heath didn't even bother to raise the question of extra money. Wilson had so cowed him by now that Heath was no longer his own man.

24

"Creepy"

A squat, muscular man whose face carried savage acne scars, Gene Tafoya was known around Truth or Consequences, New Mexico, as a "mean mother," a brawler who carried at least one gun in his belt and another in his truck, and who was quick to flash a sharp knife when angered. Tafoya appointed himself a sort of *ex officio* bouncer and enforcer at his favored Buckhorn Saloon. Bartender Bruce Boyer kept his distance. "He bragged about his toughness and his lack of fear of law enforcement. He talked about doing pretty much what he wanted, even if against the law." When a Buckhorn patron left the bar with a glass in his hand, Tafoya ran after him and demanded that he go back inside; carrying a drink outside a tavern violated state liquor laws. "Hell, man," the drinker said, "all I have is a glass of water—here, taste it." Instead, Tafoya went to his truck and got a pistol and marched the man back inside. "Hey, Gene,"complained Boyer, "take it easy. This is a friendly place." Tafoya snorted and left.

Tafoya's stated scorn for law officers sounded odd to residents who had known him as a youth, for Tafoya's early idol was his grandfather, a captain in the New Mexico State Police. Gene Tafoya came out of rough origins. His father was a career enlisted man in the Navy, his mother a factory worker. Tafoya remembered his father as a man who was "quite authoritative and at times quite physical in his discipline." The parents divorced when Gene was very young. He lied about his age and joined the New Mexico National Guard at age 14. He served two years and was discharged as a private first class. Tafoya apparently liked the military, for in 1953, at age 19, at the end of the Korean War, he joined the Marines. Tafoya left the Corps after a three-year hitch, worked in an aircraft factory, married and returned to New Mexico, where he worked briefly as a deputy sheriff. In 1961, he returned to the military, this time to the Army, where his physical aggressiveness and knowledge of Spanish made him a natural recruit for the Special Forces.

Tafoya now enjoyed the most satisfying years of his life. Because of his knowledge of Spanish, he drew several extended tours at the jungle-warfare training school the U.S. Army maintains in the Panama Canal Zone. The duty put strong demands on his physical strength; yet, as Tafoya told friends later, "I loved mucking around the jungle. That's one place in the world where nobody fucks with you." Tafoya also served five tours in South Vietnam, and he spent extended periods—a month or more at a clip—on clandestine missions behind Viet Cong lines. At least twice, according to his later accounts, he was on patrols that went deep into Laos in search of Communist bases and supply lines. He trained Montagnard tribesmen in the remote hills of far South Vietnam, and at one point found himself working with onetime Chinese Nationalist soldiers who had drifted to Southeast Asia after the 1949 collapse of the Chiang Kai-shek regime, yearning for a chance to overthrow the Communist government in Peking. When Tafoya retired in 1976, he had a good supply of medals, ranging from the Bronze Star to the Combat Infantryman's Badge, the silver rifle mounted on a blue enamel background that is the proudest decoration a soldier can wear, for it denotes that he has faced the enemy in battle.

Tafoya returned to New Mexico—he now had a fourth wife, Betty Jo—and proudly watched a son from an earlier marriage progress through college and enter the Army as an officer. Tafoya worked as a construction foreman; he joined the Truth or Consequences lodge of the Masons; he liked to disappear for long treks into the mountains, both on foot and in his Ford Bronco pickup (which carried, as he proudly pointed out to anyone who would listen, three extra gas tanks for added range). But Tafoya had problems, most of them stemming from whiskey. One man who saw Tafoya frequently thought him a "little off" and said he was distrusted and feared by other residents. Stories circulated about Gene Tafoya's temper. One evening he got into an argument with another drinker, chased the man's car when he drove away from the tavern and overturned his own Bronco truck at high speed. When police and other would-be rescuers scrambled down the embankment, Tafoya waved them off with a .357 Magnum. (Tafoya later claimed he was afraid someone would strike a match and start a fire with the spilled gasoline; no one credited the story.)

Tafoya eventually recognized his malaise as plain old-fashioned boredom. After fifteen years of adventure in Asia and Central America, he desired something more challenging than drinking beer in New Mexico and picking fights with the local cowboys and farmhands. Because of his heavy drinking, Tafoya had trouble holding a steady job, and his sergeant's pension, although an attractive goal while on active duty, barely covered his essential living expenses in the civilian economy.

In 1979, Tafoya fell into conversation with a man who knew the current mercenary world. The man, a computer specialist, had taught at a New Mexico college and dated Tafoya's sister (a strikingly beautiful woman who had been Miss New Mexico). The computer specialist now worked at the Navy's weapons testing and development center at China Lake, California. Through friends there, he had heard of a man named Ed Wilson who "has a bunch of projects working in Europe and North Africa and the Middle East." Tafoya got the necessary telephone number, and within weeks he was en route to Libya to meet Wilson. As he was to state later, he was hired as what he called "just a gofer, running errands." Tafoya traveled throughout Europe, delivering documents and mail to other Wilson employees. Wilson, he said, "kept kind of leading me around. He said they were going to open an office in Malta, where I was going to take charge." Such, anyway, was the story Tafoya was to tell years later. Wilson's version was that Tafoya was but one of many Green Berets brought to Libya as training noncoms, that he could not do the job, that he had angered the Libyans by his inefficiency and that he had been fired as a result.

An embellishment of Tafoya's story has it that he approached the Central Intelligence Agency in 1979 and agreed to undertake any sort of "special assignment" the Agency might have for him. In subsequent press interviews, testimony in two criminal trials and a jail-cell conversation with a Colorado detective, Tafoya was to reiterate his "CIA defense." But even when given the opportunity—and the chance of avoiding a prison sentence—Tafoya refused to name any CIA official with whom he had had contacts. If he did so, he told Sergeant Ray Martinez of the Fort Collins, Colorado, police department, he would "get my throat cut."

Tafoya was either an outright liar, or another mercenary hoodwinked by Ed Wilson. The grain of truth in Tafoya's story, a meager grain, was that he did approach CIA in 1979 and ask about prospects of joining the Agency as a contract employee. As is routine for such applications, it was sent to the CIA's Office of Security, which gave Tafoya what is called "preliminary operational approval" (or POA, in Agency talk). In itself, such "approval" is insignificant; it means only that the Office of Security has found no derogatory information about the prospective employee in either its own files or those of other police, military or intelligence agencies. The POA is the Agency's method of making an efficient initial screening of job applicants, but it is only the first of many steps for a prospective contract employee. According to a government official (not a CIA employee) who had access to CIA files on Tafoya, his "application" for a job went no further than an initial inquiry. Either he did not pursue the job, or the CIA had no interest in him.

The evidence is strong that Wilson saw in Gene Tafoya some qualities he had long sought: someone who would serve him as a personal strongman and enforcer, a thug willing to frighten, beat and even kill his enemies. According to such associates as John Heath, threats of violence were omnipresent in Wilson's conversation. "He'd decide someone had ripped him off, and he'd say, 'Go break the motherfucker's legs; give him some good shots with a crowbar,'" Heath recollected. "You learned to ignore him when he talked like this. Much of the time, I figure, he wasn't serious—he was letting off steam." But other times, Heath was not so sure just how benign Wilson's threats actually were. Heath remembers one instance when Wilson felt an Italian businessman had cheated him of his share of profits on a deal. Wilson sent a hulking former Marine to Italy "to talk it over with the guy"; he returned with the desired money and some muttered talk about having "put knots on that bastard's head."

One person who had acrimonious exchanges with Wilson over a contract was a Canadian businessman named Robert J. Manina. In the summer of 1977, Manina was vice-president of Marsland Engineering, Ltd., which had offices and an engineering facility in Waterloo, Ontario. Commencing in April 1977, Marsland and its parent company, Leigh Industries, Ltd., worked on developing a long-range military surveillance system called "Project Eye." In early August, Ed Wilson appeared at the Waterloo offices along with two potential Libyan customers. Manina has said that he had never heard of Wilson, and that he was not sure exactly how Wilson knew of Project Eye. In any case, on August 15, Marsland signed a $900,000 contract with the Libyan Department of the Interior (the chief Libyan civil intelligence and security agency) for the surveillance system.

Whatever the nature of Manina's arrangement with Wilson, it became a matter of acrimony over the next thirty months. Wilson's position was that he deserved a finder's fee for bringing the Libyans to Canada: 10 percent of the $900,000 contract. Marsland told Wilson, in effect, that the Libyan Government had expressed interest long before Wilson appeared on the scene, and nothing had been promised him. As Manina put it later, there were "substantial differences of opinion." In the early spring of 1980, Wilson sent his final angry Telex to Manina. "I wish you luck on your health," the message concluded.

On May 26, about three months later, Manina parked a rented automobile in front of his house at 221 Pandora Crescent, in Kitchener, a town adjacent to Waterloo. At about two o'clock the following morning, May 27, the car exploded and was totally consumed by flame. Kitchener police found that someone had stuffed a roll of toilet paper into the gas tank, leaving a stream of paper out the opening, and set it afire. "A rather crude way of starting a fire, but one that obviously worked quite well," stated Sergeant Joseph McDonnell. The technique suggested a "scare bombing," not an attempt to kill, to the Waterloo Regional Police Force.

Gene Tafoya stayed in a motel in the Waterloo area the night of the firebombing, and he drove a rental car. He paid for both with a Visa card issued in the name of his wife.

Several weeks later, Tafoya had a long telephone talk with his friend and mentor Jimmy Dean, another former Green Beret who worked for Wilson. The thrust of the conversation was Tafoya's plea for help in finding more work.*

"Do you know somebody that should quit breathing?" Tafoya asked. "Permanently? With some good information and no bullshit?"

Dean replied that the Iranian hostage crisis had caused cutbacks in mercenary work throughout the Middle East. "There's bad fire all over the place, particularly in the Moslem world. It's really crazy," Dean said.

Dean did mention that he had talked with "that man" —an apparent reference to Wilson. However, "that man" was unhappy with Tafoya. "He said that he had some possibilities of work, but that he believes that somehow there was B.S. in the job up North."

"That's a bunch of crap," Tafoya protested.

"Well, how can we turn that otherwise and to let him know—" Dean said.

"Okay," Tafoya interrupted, "give me a target."

"No," Dean said, "I don't mean that. I meant turn it around so that we can say it did happen and here's how. . . . I've got a copy of the *Globe Mail* newspaper from Toronto—"

"How did it read?" Tafoya interrupted, with the eagerness of an actor about to hear a review of his performance.

"Well, six days prior to six days after, not one word," Dean said.

There was a pause in the talk. Tafoya sounded puzzled when he resumed speaking. "They must have had it snuffed, because it happened."

"Well, you told me, let's see, if I'm not mistaken, that it happened at oh-two-hundred [2 A.M.] on the twenty-seventh. . . ." Dean said.

"That's exactly right."

"Well, I got the papers from the twenty-fourth through the thirtieth, and there's not one word—"

---

*Tafoya taped the telephone conversation. One of the more stupid acts of his life was to leave the cassette in a door pocket of his car, where it was seized by police raiders the following spring. As shall be seen, Tafoya was a consistent bungler when conducting clandestine missions.

Tafoya interrupted. "Because they had a ten-alarm fire. . . . and . . ." He seemed at a loss for further words. If the fire was not reported in the papers, he said, "I just don't know how in hell that you could verify that." He suggested that Dean call the Kitchener fire department, pose as an insurance investigator and ask about the fire.

Dean agreed that verification was important, because lack of any proof that Tafoya had carried out the assignment "concerned" Wilson. If he could confirm the bombing, "he would very seriously consider you for more work." Tafoya wished to "vindicate myself in his eyes, or whatever. Hell, I'd go back there on my own expenses to blow that up. . . . If I was bullshitting you, I would just completely drop out of the scene and not even try and make contact." He insisted he had done the bombing. "I laid the charge and then it fired that sucker up."

Dean and Tafoya talked at length about newspaper deadlines, and whether the fact that the arson had taken place so late at night had kept it out of print. Then they realized why Dean had not found a story: he had been monitoring Toronto's *Globe and Mail*, not the local *Waterloo-Kitchener News*. "The *Daily Globe*, hell," Tafoya exclaimed, "that's out of Toronto. . . . He lives in Kitchener. . . . This is an hour's drive from Toronto." He offered Dean a deal. "If it's not in the newspaper in Waterloo-Kitchener, I will work for you for one year. . . for free. As a matter of fact, you can have yourself a little nigger boy. All you've got to do is beat that motherfucker."

Dean agreed to try to find the local Kitchener newspaper. The talk ended without any specific offers of work; Tafoya, however, had seemingly convinced Dean that he had carried out the Manina assignment, for he was to reappear at Wilson's side within months.

Soon after the Canadian firebombing, both Tafoya and Dean became mysterious figures in the Wilson organization. As Wilson told several persons, including John Heath and Alex Raffio, Tafoya was dismissed because he could not get along with either the Libyans or other Americans at the Benghazi training base. Steve Streeter remembers Wilson announcing in Libya that Tafoya was going to be "shit-canned" (fired) because of poor performance and a general bad attitude. Dean, Wilson said, was going home because his contract had expired.

Streeter did not know what to make of these assertions, other than that he did not believe them. Wilson had deceived him once concerning Tafoya. On one of his trips to Washington, Streeter had been instructed to meet Tafoya—a man he had never heard of before—and "check him out," which Streeter took to be an instruction to see whether Tafoya was suitable for employment. "I didn't know at the time that Tafoya had already been working for Wilson for many months," Streeter said.

Streeter noted right away that Tafoya drank too much, even in the daytime, anathema to a career soldier. Tafoya asked Streeter to drive him on some unexplained errands. One was to the offices of EATSCO, which Streeter was to learn much later was the firm set up by former CIA and Pentagon officials (including Thomas Clines and some other prominent Wilson friends) to handle arms shipments to Egypt resulting from the Camp David agreements. Tafoya several times asked Streeter to stop the car at odd moments so that he could make calls from pay telephone booths. Streeter decided that Tafoya was "some sort of a loon."

But Tafoya felt confident in asking a favor of Streeter. He needed to go to Fayetteville, North Carolina, for some unspecified business with former Green Beret colleagues. He didn't want to be "hassled with a suitcase." Could Streeter come along behind him, possibly in the rental car, and bring the suitcase? Streeter had already glimpsed the interior of Tafoya's suitcase in their Thomas Circle hotel room; he saw in it identification papers in the name of someone other than Tafoya. Suspicious enough to take a closer look at the suitcase before transporting it, he found that it contained an automatic pistol, of .22 or .25 caliber (years later, Streeter could not remember the exact size), and some blasting caps. Streeter shook his head. Instead of putting the bag into the trunk of his rental car, he went to Fayetteville by Trailways bus and handed it over to Tafoya. He asked no explanation, nor was he offered one. The good soldier Streeter had been asked to carry out a bizarre chore; he needed no further instructions.

A bit later, Streeter arrived in Geneva for a prearranged meeting with Wilson. He glanced into the dining room and saw the unmistakable profile of James ("Jimmy Blue Eyes") Dean, seated at the same table as Wilson. What the hell goes here? Streeter thought; Ed said Dean went off the payroll months ago. He walked to the table and gave Wilson no choice but to acknowledge him, and to ask him to join them. Wilson kept the conversation general; he said nothing as to why Dean was suddenly around again.

After dinner, Wilson asked Dean and Streeter to accompany him to his suite. He opened a briefcase that was stuffed with hundred-dollar bills, and took out several handfuls. "Jimmy and I have some business upstairs," he said. "How about hanging around and watching TV and keeping an eye on this stuff? There's two hundred and fifty thousand, less what I have here"—indicating the bills piled in his hand. Streeter grunted and settled back to watch Swiss television, curious as to what Wilson and Dean had afoot.

Later Tafoya told Streeter that he had been in the hotel that evening, and that Dean and Wilson had given him money—"big money." What was that all about? Streeter asked. Streeter could not remember in 1983 the exact words of the reply, but their import was clear. Umar Abdullah Muhayshi, the Quaddafi supporter turned dissident who had been an assassination target since 1976, had been traced to a hospital in Kuwait. Tafoya said he and Dean had traveled there and "scouted the job," then decided, "We could knock him off, but we'd never be able to get out of the country alive." Kuwait is a one-airport nation with roads that go nowhere into the desert; the security forces are efficient, and mean. Tafoya told Streeter, in effect, We didn't want to go out there and commit suicide.

Steve Streeter's encounters with Dean and Tafoya during 1980 dashed Wilson's story that they had either quit or been fired. Other persons remember mysterious Telex cables sent by one or the other from countries throughout Europe, including some from behind the Iron Curtain. These wanderings coincided with Quaddafi's widely publicized "war of annihilation" against Libyan dissidents living abroad, in Europe and elsewhere.

Fort Collins, Colorado, is on the prairie that stretches north and east from the front slope of the Rocky Mountains, some 55 miles due north of Denver. The town is a mixture of rawness and modern. At the twenty-four-hour café on the north edge of town, the breakfast crowd wears mackinaws and stockmen's boots; they are heavy on steak and eggs, and they run the bejesus out of the waitresses who bring coffee refills. Clusters of muddy ice are welded to the underfenders of their pickup trucks, and there is enough visible armament in the rear-window rifle racks to overthrow a Central American government. But a few blocks downtown is a restaurant right out of San Francisco's Ghirardelli Square, with quiche and spinach salad on the menu. "College shit" was how one stockman described the place. The "college" is Colorado State University, the centerpiece of a mini-city of some 75,000 persons.

Fort Collins is a quiet place; as one policeman put it, "we have some dope, some head-knockings, some cowboys who go on wild drunks, but nothing much." But one disturbing element in 1980 was a small but notable colony of some 100 Libyan students at CSU, drawn there by the college's agricultural and social-studies departments. During the warm spring and summer months, the flat, dry terrain reminded many of the Libyans of their native land—one to which many of them dared not return because of Muamar Quaddafi.

Quaddafi polarized the Libyan community; although he was thousands of miles away, his presence was felt on a daily basis. Students were either pro-Quaddafi or anti-Quaddafi; those who tried to remain politically neutral were so harassed by Quaddafi supporters that they came to hate the distant ruler if for no other reason than that he indirectly made their lives miserable. Mistrust was rampant. According to intelligence informants reporting to both the local FBI office and the Fort Collins police, even the Libyans had trouble sorting through their ranks to determine who were the *agents provocateurs*. Quaddafi's demand in 1979 that expatriates return home drove a further cleavage through the community. Students who refused were spat upon by other Libyans, were cursed, sometimes even punched. The expiration of the deadline was a serious event for the anti-Quaddafi students, for thereafter they lived under a *de facto* death sentence that could be executed at any time.

Particularly anxious were Faisal and Fareida Zagallai, both in their early thirties and aspiring to careers in social service. The husband, Faisal, had become involved in anti-Quaddafi activities as an undergraduate at Tripoli University in 1973 (although he was discreet enough not to disturb his government scholarship). He held the title of lecturer at the university through his doctorate, then went to Colorado for further graduate studies in 1979. He ignored Quaddafi's order to return to take an induction physical for the military, and was unapologetic about it. "Some people did, some people didn't. If I returned, I would have been assassinated."

Faisal's wife, Fareida, was even more political, and a strong feminist in the bargain—a rarity for a Libyan woman, especially under Quaddafi's fundamentalist regime. The first member of her family to achieve more than simple literacy, Fareida had worked on the staff of Libya's delegation to the United Nations, and then served as a Libyan delegate to the World Conference of Women in Mexico City in 1977. Disgusted with the subservient role Quaddafi demanded for women, she began to speak out publicly against him. When the next women's conference was held in Copenhagen in 1979, Fareida attended, but this time not as an official Libyan representative because, as one CSU faculty friend reported, "she did not want to indicate by that position that she was a supporter of the Government of Libya." At CSU political meetings involving Libyan students, Fareida was more vocal than Faisal, who seemed content to let her play the dominant role.

Nevertheless, it was Faisal whom Quaddafi's killers marked for death. According to a Libyan student who reported regularly to the Fort Collins FBI office, Quaddafi supporters kept Faisal under constant surveillance during the spring and summer of 1980. They drew diagrams of the garden apartment complex in which he lived; they kept charts of his daily schedule, so that they knew where he was apt to be at any given time. The watchers noted that Faisal was having problems with his left arm and left knee, disabilities which one of them gloated "makes him physically unable to fight." In May 1980, FBI agents decided Faisal was being set up for an assassination attempt. They passed warning to Faisal Zagallai and Floyd Smith, the Fort Collins police chief.

Chief Smith was a Western-size man in his sixties, a combat infantryman in the Second World War and a career police professional. He took the FBI warning seriously, and when the agent asked that Smith issue Zagallai a permit to own a handgun, Smith agreed. Zagallai came in a few days later, filled out the form and purchased a .357 Magnum. He did some test firings outside town (the police evaluator adjudged him a "fair" shot), and he received the permit.

Another policeman gave Zagallai advice. "If you are attacked, don't try anything fancy. Grab the thing with both hands and aim at the guy's gut. And keep the pistol close around you all the time." Zagallai looked out of sorts as he tucked the heavy pistol into his waistband. As he left the police station, the officer thought, *He looks like a professor going off to rob a bank.*

The FBI, in both Denver and Fort Collins, received continuing reports of Libyan assassination plots through the summer of 1980. One dealt with a "mercenary broker in the Denver area" who was trying to recruit "Caucasian males... to perform terrorist acts." Another report was to the effect that a recently expelled Libyan diplomat had given a Libyan student living in Colorado a directive to "carry out actions as necessary against dissident Libyan students within this area."

Faisal Zagallai, meanwhile, had moved with his wife to a new secret apartment. He oiled his pistol weekly. When he sat in his living room in the evenings to read, he carefully stowed the Magnum under a sofa cushion. When he went to the CSU campus, he carried the pistol in his briefcase.

In June 1980, Alex Raffio flew to Tripoli to discuss business with Ed Wilson. As their meeting ended, Wilson motioned the other persons out of the room and took Raffio into his private office. "Look," he said, "I've got a guy coming here who's going to go out to Europe and do a couple of special projects for me and the Libyans, and he's going to be up in London. Whatever kinds of things he asks you for, you get it. If you need any money, you get it from Bobbi Barnes. Don't ask any questions; just give him what he wants and leave him alone. I don't want you to ask his name. He won't ask your name. He will have a telephone number where he'll get you. He'll refer to you by your code name, 'Chubby Chap.'"

The man appeared at Wilson's villa a few hours later, and he took pains to keep away from other persons there. Raffio thought him "an odd-looking fellow, bulky around the belly, white hair, balding, with a little goatee and a pockmarked face. He was a very poor dresser. I thought he looked creepy." Which was what Raffio and Diane Byrne, who ran

Wilson's London office, decided the stranger's code name would be: "Creepy." The man, as Raffio was eventually to learn, was Eugene Tafoya.

Raffio and Tafoya flew out of Tripoli together, bound for London via Switzerland. Tafoya remarked that he needed to stop in Geneva to pick up some money from Edwin Coughlin, Wilson's attorney. He didn't have a ticket through to London; could Raffio buy one for him? Raffio did, on his Diners Club card; for lack of a name, he booked Tafoya as "Joe Smith." They arrived together at Heathrow Airport and went their separate ways.

Two days later, Tafoya called Raffio and asked that they meet in the bar in the pool area of the Chelsea Holiday Inn off Sloane Street. Raffio found Tafoya sitting with an attractive, provocatively clad woman, "obviously a hooker." As Tafoya began talking, Raffio looked at him and shook his head slowly from side to side; he did not intend to discuss business in the presence of a whore. "Oh," Tafoya said. He reached into his pocket and handed the woman the room key. "Hon, why don't you go up to the room for a while? I'll be with you soon." She left, looking back at Raffio with a smile.

"What's this all about?" Raffio asked. "Are you running whores, or are you working for Ed Wilson?"

"Oh, I'm just interviewing her," Tafoya replied. "Look, do you know any good-looking, attractive women who speak French fluently and who might be willing to travel with me on a mission for Ed?"

Raffio, a single man in a swinging city, knew any number of such women, but as he told himself, Wilson's orders notwithstanding, he was making no introductions to the likes of Tafoya. So he shook his head in mock sorrow. "Gee, I'm sorry, but I don't know anybody who speaks French who's free to do any travel." Tafoya said "a lot of money" was available to the right woman, but Raffio kept saying no. Tafoya asked, "Do I really need French to travel in Tunisia?" Outside the big cities, yes, Raffio said. Tafoya gave no details of what he intended to do. Raffio wanted nothing further to do with him. "He gave me an eerie feeling."

Tafoya called a few days later; again Raffio found him in the Chelsea Holiday Inn bar with a whore. Raffio knew, from Bobbi Barnes, that he had been demanding large sums of money, which she refused to pay.

Once the woman was chased away, Tafoya had a new request. "Ed tells me you have this good doctor friend in London."

"Yes," Raffio said. "In fact, he takes care of most of the people who work for Ed in London. He's a close personal friend."

"Well, I need a serum that will put a large animal to sleep."

"What kind of animal?" Raffio asked.

Tafoya stroked his goatee. "Big dog," he said; "a very big dog."

"How big a dog?"

Tafoya thought some more. "Oh, about one eighty, one eighty-five pounds."

"That's an awfully big dog," Raffio said. This yazoo, he thought, is looking for something to put a 180-pound human being to sleep. Raffio told Tafoya his doctor friend knew he did not have a dog; besides, his friend was a physician, not a veterinarian. No matter, Tafoya said; get him to recommend a vet. "Tell him that friends of yours down in Tripoli have a big dog who's got some problems and there's no humane way of putting him to sleep and you want to send a drug down to him to do it."

Raffio figured he had better do as asked. Nor did his physician friend question the implausible story; he telephoned a veterinarian in South Kensington who sold Raffio, for £20, a 2-or-3-ounce vial containing a brownish liquid. "I gave the bottle to Creepy. He was leaving; I was glad. What he did with the drug I didn't want to know."

Tafoya also made odd requests of John Heath. At Wilson's direction, Heath obtained a Libyan visa for Tafoya at the Brussels embassy; then they retired to a bar for an afternoon of drinking and shop talk.

"I want to ask you a question," Tafoya said to Heath. "Don't bullshit me, now, because I know a little more about your background than you think I do. What do you think of mercury loads?"

The question took Heath aback. "Anybody who knows anything about this sort of thing, that tells you something immediately. Mercury load is an assassin's-type thing." (A dot of mercury is put into the slug of a pistol shell, with a multifold increase of penetration and damage.) Heath and

Tafoya talked about the merits of mercury loads for a while. ("Too much wobble," Heath said), and then Tafoya asked about buying some silencers. Heath talked around the subject; he realized he was dealing with a man whose mind was on killing.

Neither Raffio nor Heath was to see Tafoya again for several months, although they heard from associates that he had worked briefly at the Benghazi base, where he irritated both the Libyans and his American colleagues. Late in the summer of 1980, Tafoya dropped out of sight.

On October 9, 1980, Gene Tafoya was in Fort Collins. He rented a motel room at the Holiday Inn at 3836 East Mulberry Street and kept it for two nights, paying the bill with his Master Card. He drove a car rented from National Car Rental, kept it for two days and paid the $93.46 bill again with the charge card, having driven the car for 64 miles.

On October 13, in the evening, Faisal Zagallai received a telephone call from a woman who identified herself as a representative of an employment agency. Would Zagallai be interested in a position as an interpreter for a company that did work for IBM and other large corporations? The call aroused Zagallai's suspicions. He had never expressed any interest in working as an interpreter, and in the preceding days he had received numerous calls from persons purporting to be selling "coupon books" giving discounts at Fort Collins restaurants, laundries and other businesses. When he would say, "Okay, put it in the mail," the person would ask for his address. Zagallai sensed that some stranger—perhaps an enemy—had managed to obtain his unlisted telephone number, but not his address. In such instances he would hang up. But this woman somehow sounded credible, and the Zagallais did have plans to move to Vienna, Austria. Even if Faisal did not take the job, perhaps he could pass the lead to another Libyan. He gave her his address, and set an appointment for seven o'clock the following evening.

According to long-distance telephone records, a call was made from a house in North Glenn, Colorado, near Fort Collins, at 5:10 P.M. on October 13 to Zagallai's home. This was about the time Zagallai received the "employment-agency" call.

In June 1981, Fort Collins detective Ray Martinez was checking through long-distance records of phones with which Gene Tafoya had been in contact. The North Glenn number was among them, and on its records Martinez found the call to Zagallai's home. When he visited the North Glenn house, he was surprised to find there Betty Jo Tafoya, Gene's wife, talking with a woman who proved to be her cousin. The cousin—who had served ten months in federal prison for stealing money orders—denied any knowledge of the phone call to Zagallai's number. Further, she had seen neither of the Tafoyas for "several years," until Betty Jo had just happened to drop by that very day for a visit. "I swear to God," she said.

At 2:05 P.M. on October 14, Gene Tafoya rented a 1979 Chevrolet Malibu from Dollar Rent-a-Car, at 7450 East 29th Avenue, near Stapleton International Airport in Denver. He used his own Master Card and listed his local address, "Sheridan, Colorado."

At about 7 P.M. on October 14, Fareida Zagallai answered a knock on her apartment door and opened it to find a heavyset man in his late forties wearing a plaid coat, brown with yellow checks. "His face was very red; his eyes were very red. I could smell that he was drunk," Mrs. Zagallai said.

She had been distrustful of the "employment-agency" call—at her insistence, Faisal had hidden his pistol beneath the sofa seat—and the caller did little to allay her misgivings. She and her husband received him, but the man didn't say much about the job, other than that it involved "translating manuals and the like," that the pay was $12.50 an hour and that his parent company was based in Alexandria, Virginia. She offered to get the man a soda, and as she walked from the room she heard him ask her husband for a cigarette.

As soon as she had left, the man suddenly began pounding Zagallai with clenched fists. Zagallai screamed for his wife and tried to back away. The man reached inside his coat and pulled a pistol from a holster. He tried to hold it against Zagallai's head as they struggled.

The first shot tore through Zagallai's jaw. Nonetheless, he managed to hold the man in a tight grip. Next the man grabbed him by the hair and pulled his head backward.

There was another shot, which entered Zagallai's forehead. He fell to the floor unconscious.

Fareida Zagallai heard the shouts, the shots, the struggle. Fearful that the gunman would next come after her, she fled from the kitchen to a back bedroom and pounded on the window, screaming for help. Neighbors raced from adjacent apartments, and several saw a man run from the Zagallai residence, pistol still clutched in his hand. One woman chased after him for almost 100 yards across a parking lot. Then the gunman turned and stared coldly at her. As she related later, "I suddenly wondered what I was doing chasing a man with a gun. I turned and went the other way." She saw a brown late-model sedan speed away from the apartment parking lot.

The first Fort Collins officer on the scene found Zagallai lying in the doorway, conscious but in great pain. Brain matter was oozing from a wound on the right side of his scalp, and there were other wounds on his left cheek (an entry wound) and behind his left ear (an exit wound). Despite his pain, Zagallai managed to talk with an officer as an ambulance sped him to Poudre Valley Hospital.

At 9:34 P.M. on October 14, Tafoya returned his rented Chevrolet to Dollar Rent-a-Car, paying $54.46 for the daily charge and the 159 miles he had driven. That same evening, before ten o'clock, a shuttle-bus driver from an adjacent car-rental agency picked up a man wearing a plaid coat—brown with yellow checks—and drove him to the airline-terminal entrance, where he hurriedly jumped from the bus and waved the driver on.

Zagallai survived, although he lost the sight of his left eye and spent months recuperating from the brain wound. Police put tight security around his room, with coded tags required for nurses, doctors and other attendants who were permitted to enter. An officer sat inside the room, whose door was equipped with a deadbolt and a peephole.

Yet the Libyans did not desist. Numerous callers to Zagallai's office inquired, first, about his condition, then about his location. One caller with a foreign accent asked the hospital operator, "Is Zagallai dead yet?" "Who is calling?" the operator asked. "None of your goddamned business," the caller replied, and hung up. Another caller purported to be a concerned U.N. official.

Several days after the shooting, the Libyan Government boasted in a Radio Tripoli broadcast that "the shooting of the traitor Zagallai should be a lesson to all traitors and running dogs living abroad."

The next day, the United States broke diplomatic relations with Libya.

25

"Kill Her, Plain and Simple"

John Heath's favored drinking place in Liège, Belgium, was the bar of the local Holiday Inn. Heath has the old soldier's trait of finding a friendly bar or café and immediately getting on a first-name basis with the bartender, waiters and manager. In the late afternoons at the Holiday Inn bar he liked to sip Scotch while exchanging stories with the local residents and improving his French.

One evening in the late autumn of 1980, Heath had a great surprise. Eugene Tafoya, who had disappeared so abruptly several months previously, walked into the Holiday Inn bar, uncharacteristically clad in an European-cut suit, a hat and a scarf. Tafoya shook Heath's hand and joined him. He gave no indication of where he had been, or why, but after a couple of drinks, Tafoya sighed and said, "Well, I guess you heard what happened."

Heath had not, but curious as to what was on Tafoya's mind, he assumed a somber expression, said, "Yeah," and shook his head sympathetically.

"Well, it wasn't *my* fault," Tafoya said emphatically. Heath continued to draw him out. As the drinks flowed, Tafoya complained about the "unfairness" of his situation.

"Goddamn it," he told Heath, "with your experience, you know the son of a bitch ought to be dead."

"Well," Heath replied, "what did you do wrong? Your opinion. You're on the scene. We're not talking about my experience."

"Goddamn it, I shot him in the head twice."

"What did you use?"

"A .22 Magnum."

Heath cursed. "You know better than that. What did you use something like that for?"

"Well, anybody shot twice in the head with a .22 Magnum ought to be dead," Tafoya said defensively.

"I agree with you, if the shots are accurately placed. Why didn't you use a .357 with a dumdum or whatever?"

"Well, I wanted to keep the noise down," Tafoya said. Tafoya mentioned that "the wife" had been screaming during the shooting. "What did you do about her?" Heath asked. "I left her," Tafoya said. "Hey, man, I don't shoot women and kids. I may be a professional assassin, but I draw the line at women and children." Tafoya complained about the quality of the Libyans' surveillance of his target, particularly the fact that they had not known he had a pistol. "Bad deal," he said. "I could have been killed."

The two mercenaries drank and talked for more than an hour. Tafoya left with Heath knowing he had been on an assassination mission—but without the slightest idea as to the intended victim.

The next day, Tafoya introduced Heath to his wife, Betty Jo. Heath took an instant liking to the dark-haired, buxom woman, and he was pleased when Tafoya said, "You can talk around her—you don't have to worry about her. She helped me."

The Tafoyas stayed in Belgium several days; then Eugene disappeared. When he returned, he complained about a "botched surveillance job," which he could not complete because "the damned Libyans gave me a photograph that was fifteen years old." He would not discuss the matter further.

As time passed, Heath and the Tafoyas became more and more friendly, spending much of their time drinking in the Holiday Inn. Tafoya, referring to their common Masonic background, called Heath "brother" and talked with him at length about the personalities in the Libyan intelligence service. He would talk cryptically. Once he told Heath, "Goddamn, brother, I want to do something for you. I've got a job coming up. Maybe I shouldn't tell you about this, but I trust you. One million dollars. If it goes off, I'm going to give you at least a hundred thousand as a gift." Tafoya made it plain that the "job" was another assassination, but he would not say anything specific. But over the days, Tafoya did mention that the botched assassination's target had been a Libyan dissident in Colorado; and he talked about the firing of Robert Manina's automobile in Canada.

At about the beginning of 1981, the Tafoyas moved to Tripoli, where they took up residence in what the Libyans euphemistically called "Tourist City," a collection of seaside villas outside town. The most notable features of Tourist City were its isolation and the weather. The nearest grocery was a mile away, and no public transportation was available. In the summers, the temperature regularly was around 120 degrees; in the winter, the only heat came from small kerosene-fired space heaters. As Alex Raffio explained, "When the Libs put you out in Tourist City, that meant you were on ice, and they expected you to stay there."

Physical discomfort was not the only complaint for the Tafoyas. As they kept reminding Wilson, they had not been paid all the money that was due them ($50,000, according to what Tafoya told Heath). Wilson seemed indifferent. His attitude was that Tafoya had been hired for a job, and "the son of a bitch screwed up. . . . He didn't do what he was paid to do. I'm not going to keep feeding him money." The Libyans, he told Heath, had paid for Mrs. Tafoya's transportation to the country; they too wished to cut off their money because Tafoya had failed. At Wilson's insistence, Heath visited the Tafoyas several times, taking them shopping and trying to cheer them up. Wilson warned, however, "Don't get too close to them. They're not *persona non grata,* but they're not popular."

Betty Jo Tafoya eventually was in almost constant hysterics. "Please help me," she cried to Heath one evening. "Please help Gene. Can't you do something?"

Heath had a meeting with Libyan intelligence officers and Wilson, who agreed that the Tafoyas should get out of the country. But Wilson did not want Betty Jo to return to the United States. He told Heath: "Hey, this broad's paranoid.

She's going to blow everything. She's going to go back there and crack up and tell the whole story and we're all dead."

As the conversation progressed, with Wilson and the Libyan intelligence officers doing most of the talking, it was agreed that Heath would himself take Mrs. Tafoya out of Libya to Wilson's farm in southern England. Heath knew what was being asked of him. "They wanted me to kill her, plain and simple."

"If you can find the way to do it," Wilson asked him, "that Gene can't find out about and you don't endanger yourself, would you be willing to do her in?"

Heath went along with the talk (he said later he'd had no intention of killing Betty Jo Tafoya or anyone else, but he'd felt he had to give the appearance of agreeing if he wished to get out of Libya himself).

"I don't think that's a problem," Heath told Wilson.

"How are you going to do it?"

"I think the best way to do it is to get her drunk and give her an injection," Heath said. He noted that Wilson's farm had a variety of medical supplies, some of which had been acquired when Wilson was trying to arrange a deal to sell hospital materials. "Get her drunk, give her thirty milligrams of Valium intravenously; if that's not enough, it should certainly be enough to go from there."

At the airport, Wilson gave Heath $10,000 in $100 bills to pass on to Betty Jo (although her export of the money was legal, she tried to hide the cash in her bra, provoking a nasty and frightening scene with Libyan customs). Wilson's unspoken instruction was that Heath should retrieve the $10,000 after killing Betty Jo. By the time Heath and Betty Jo arrived at "The Grange"—Wilson's name for one of his English farms—both were jittery.

After dinner, they settled before the fireplace with a bottle of Scotch whiskey and began talking. "She started getting really weird—well, maybe not, considering the alcohol she'd had," Heath related. Betty Jo began telling a story: that one of the Libyans had asked her to kill Heath. "What did you tell them?" Heath asked.

"I said yes."

"Why?" Heath asked.

"Well, it wouldn't be the first time, you know. I've proved myself before."

Heath shuddered, even though he suspected that Betty Jo was reciting a booze-based fantasy. Betty Jo continued, "I don't want to kill you because I really like you. You've been very nice to us. Gene told me to do whatever I had to do to be nice to you because we need your help. He even told me that I should go to bed with you if that's what I wanted to do and that's what it took to keep you on our side."

So they went to a cold upstairs bedroom, snuggled beneath a down comforter and made love several times. A few days later, Betty Jo Tafoya flew home to the United States. Heath returned to Libya. "How'd it go?" a drunken Wilson asked. Heath gave him a story of how the circumstances hadn't allowed him to do the job, and he had had to let her go back to the States. Wilson grunted and changed the subject; he did not mention the murder plot again.

Since the October 14 shooting, the Fort Collins police investigation had ground to a virtual standstill, with many suspicions but no leads. The official FBI position was that the local police had jurisdiction over the case, and that the federal bureau's only role was to monitor events and give help where requested. Given its national resources, the Bureau had a much stronger unofficial role. At a meeting in the FBI office in Denver on October 14 with several Fort Collins officers, FBI supervisor Tom Howard made plain that any press information must come from the local police. In reviewing the evidence, Howard emphasized one lead that (although he did not know it at the time) was to prove crucial in breaking the case. He felt the car-rental shuttle-bus driver had given "legitimate" information, and that the hurried passenger who had jumped from his vehicle had appeared at the Continental Airlines ticket office at about 9:30 P.M. Continental had five flights out of Denver later that night—to Kansas City; Oklahoma City; Wichita, Kansas; Chicago and El Paso. The FBI would check passenger manifests on all these flights.

But names alone meant nothing. Fort Collins police meticulously checked the FBI lists against motel and hotel registrants for the forty-eight hours around the shooting. They turned up nothing except a few instances of motel adultery. At one point, they got so desperate that they used a hypnotist to try to reinforce the memory of several witnesses who had seen the getaway car, including a teenaged bicyclist who was almost run down.

The lead detective, Ray Martinez, had more street experience than would be suggested by his relative youth of 28 years. As a military policeman, he had conducted drug investigations in Thailand and elsewhere in Southeast Asia. After discharge, he worked as an undercover narcotics detective for the Colorado Metropolitan Enforcement Group, an elite drug unit. In 1981, Martinez was a trim man with a neat mustache and a ready smile. "You should see some of my narc-days pictures," he said. "At times, I couldn't even recognize myself, I was such a mess."

Martinez happened to "catch" the Zagallai case because he was duty detective the night of the shooting. Martinez assumed from the outset that the gunman was from out of state, for he went into the apartment without any attempt at concealing his face. The identification from the shuttle-bus driver meant that the gunman had probably left Colorado from Stapleton Airport. But the field is one of the nations's busiest, and even in the late evening, flights whisk out at a one-per-minute rate. The gunman could have been one of several thousands of passengers.

"We were so desperate for leads at one point that we had the FBI trace the manufacturer of a cheap bow tie that the gunman had lost in Zagallai's apartment. Of course, this particular tie turned out to be sold in thousands of stores, but the FBI made the rounds anyway, showing the clerks our composite drawing based on the shuttle-bus driver's description."

Martinez kept the file active—he would visit the witnesses who had seen the gunman—but the case was essentially dormant. "I knew that we were in an international terrorist situation, but how the dickens could I break this kind of case from Fort Collins, Colorado?"

In Tripoli, meanwhile, Gene Tafoya was fast wearing out what little remained of his welcome. He had discovered flash, which he consumed in awesome quantities. He complained about his lack of promised payments. He missed Betty Jo. He wanted another assignment. He did not like the isolation of Tourist City.

"Idi Amin thought it was just fine when he lived out here," Wilson said.

"Fuck you, Ed—I'm not a goddamned bush nigger," Tafoya snarled.

The Libyans' only concession was to permit him to move to a hotel.

Finally Wilson told Heath, "Listen, I've gone to the Libyans. I've asked permission to get rid of the son of a bitch. He botched the job. He's paranoid. If he goes out of here, he's going to blow the whole thing. He'll never stand up in court." The Libyans had told Wilson, in effect, "You do it; we won't." But they had insisted that he not be killed in his hotel. "Okay," Wilson told Heath, "let's get him in his villa; let's get him drunk. When he's good and drunk you hit him with an injection."

That evening, Wilson and Heath fed Tafoya drinks made of grapefruit juice generously laced with flash. They put no liquor in their own drinks. Tafoya apparently suspected that something was amiss, for he snatched up Heath's glass, took a sip and said, "There's no flash in this drink; how come?" Heath lamely explained that the phone had rung while he was mixing and he must have made a mistake. Tafoya remained on his guard; he would not get drunk. During the drive home, he alternatively praised Heath as his brother and cursed him as a bastard and betrayer; at one point, he grabbed the steering wheel as if to crash the car. But they parted with a handshake.

Wilson would have no more involvement in plots against Tafoya. He told Heath, "Get him out of here," and a few days later Heath accompanied Tafoya to Heathrow. From there they went to "The Farm" (a rural property owned by Wilson 16 miles north of Brighton, not to be confused with "The Grange"). Tafoya was so relieved to get out of Libya that he insisted on becoming a manservant to Heath, mixing his drinks and preparing his meals. Even after the two men sat up until five in the morning drinking, Tafoya was first out of bed and had a hot breakfast waiting for Heath.

Tafoya still suspected he was being set up for murder. As he told Heath, "I know the Libyans are unhappy with me, Daddy [Wilson] is unhappy with me and I don't really feel like I'm here on R-and-R. If you've been told something, I just ask you one thing. As a brother, give me an hour."

"As a brother," Heath said, "you have nothing to worry about."

Tafoya flew out of London in early February to return to his home in Truth or Consequences.

On February 8, 1981, teenagers Craig Forester and Gared Cain were walking their bikes through a drainage ditch in Fort Collins about three miles from the Zagallai apartment. Usually the ditch contained water, but that week, because of a lack of rainfall, it was dry. One of the boys kicked up a pistol. They examined it, then dropped it and ran to tell their parents.

Given Colorado's liberal gun laws, the finding of a stray pistol was not a major event to the Fort Collins police. The officers who went to the ditch to pick up the pistol wrote a routine "info report" for circulation in the department. "A hundred or so of these forms come over my desk any given week," said detective Ray Martinez. "I'll admit that most of them go unread. This one happened to catch my eye." The pistol was a High Standard Mark IV .22 Magnum, serial number S19443. "It was pretty messed up from being out in the weather all winter, but it seemed to match what our witnesses had reported [in the Zagallai shooting]. So we ran the numbers through the FBI."

The FBI found that the last owner of record of the pistol was a man then living in coastal Florida. He had purchased it from the Friendly Pawnbroker, Fayetteville, North Carolina, on April 29, 1975. Yes, the man told interviewing agents, he remembered the pistol well, but he no longer had it. He had sold it later to a former Green Beret roommate, Eugene Tafoya.

Agents obtained a photograph of Tafoya from New Mexico authorities and put it in a stack of six black-and-white photographs which they displayed to Faisal Zagallai.

When the fourth photograph was flipped up—that of Tafoya—Zagallai "had a facial expression of immediate recognition," according to Martinez. So did Fareida Zagallai when she viewed the photographs.

Martinez and FBI agent Don Lyon went through photocopies of car-rental records they had gathered early in the investigation. They quickly found one belonging to Tafoya. In separate cars, they drove from Dollar Rent-a-Car to the crime scene. The distance was 66 miles one way, or 132 round trip—close enough to the 159 miles charged to Tafoya's rental car to satisfy them. They next found that Gene Tafoya had flown out of Denver late the night of October 14 on a

Continental flight to El Paso—the nearest airport to his home in Truth or Consequences.

The morning of April 14, the FBI obtained warrants for Tafoya's arrest on a charge of unlawful flight to avoid prosecution (the catchall charge the Bureau uses to arrest persons in one state who are wanted for crimes elsewhere). Ray Martinez went along with the arrest party. They moved with some caution. "Tafoya had been a deputy sheriff down there, and Truth or Consequences is a small town. I'm not saying anything about another department, but he might have had some friends down there, and we were afraid of an accidental leak. Also, Tafoya was a Vietnam veteran, a man who knew about booby traps and explosives. We didn't want to get into a shoot-out situation in making the arrest."

By chance, the Tafoya home—a one-story frame house— was just across the street from the sheriff's department. A posse of 10 FBI agents and Ray Martinez came around to the rear of the office, and Martinez told the officer on duty they intended to make an arrest. The officer volunteered to "go ask Gene to come over for a visit," to lure him from the house and any guns he might have there. The officer did, but Tafoya gave an indefinite answer: he might be over later; again, he might not.

So the raiding party moved on the house. As agents began their timed advance from four sides, a sedan parked in front of the house and a man in a business suit strode briskly up the walk to the door. Oh, no, Martinez thought: here comes his hostage. The raiders paused briefly and talked about whether to proceed. The answer was obvious: with 11 armed men surrounding the house in full view of passersby, withdrawing would be foolish.

When Martinez rapped on the door and identified himself as a Fort Collins policeman, Tafoya turned away with an expletive. There was a minor traffic jam as 5 officers tried to go through the door at the same time, but Tafoya did not resist. (His visitor turned out to be a county tax assessor on routine business.) Martinez took Tafoya to the Sheriff's Department for questioning, as other officers searched the house.

Tafoya took the stone-wall approach. He denied ever having been in Fort Collins, or knowing anything about any Libyans. "Man, we have charge slips for airplane tickets and rental cars in your own name," Martinez exclaimed. He was now certain that they had the right man.

The search of Tafoya's house and automobile produced a rat's nest of papers and other items that only the most careless of covert agents would retain. For the Zagallai shooting, the most damning piece of evidence was a hand-drawn map of the apartment complex in which the dissident lived, with Zagallai's unit and parking space noted. There was a cassette recording of Tafoya talking on the phone with James Dean and another of Tafoya reciting procedures for making explosive devices, delivered in the cadence of someone rehearsing a classroom lecture. There were a chemical-delay timing pencil—a rather sophisticated form of detonator; three U.S. passports, all in Tafoya's name; a blasting cap and a notebook containing notations about more than a dozen Americans and foreigners, including physical descriptions, their daily habits and what personal protection they enjoyed, if any. Also an address book, thick with private phone numbers for Ed Wilson and such key persons in his organization as Roberta Barnes, his London manager, and Edward J. Coughlin, his Geneva attorney. Other listings were for fellow former Green Berets, active and retired CIA employees and persons in the defense establishment.

Agents carried enough material from the house to fill a thirteen-page typewritten inventory. Agents who studied the items paid particular attention to what they came to know as "Gene's wish list." One agent with long counterintelligence experience called it "a road map for a hit man who is out to commit murders, or set up murders." One of the names on the list was already known to American intelligence as that of a person against whom Muamar Quaddafi had sworn vengeance. Omar Yahia had been chief of Libyan intelligence in the early years of the Quaddafi regime, grown tired of its revolutionary excesses and fled to Oman and then to Egypt, where he had become a prosperous banker. Now a bitter foe of Quaddafi, Yahia was a key financial supporter of Libyan dissidents in the United States, and he had close liaison with both the FBI and the CIA. Quaddafi had recruited three Cuban mercenaries to try to kill Yahia in 1976, but they had failed. Yahia's presence on "Gene's wish list" reinforced the suspicion of American intelligence that Yahia remained an active Quaddafi target.

Another person on the list was William Pearce, who had moonlighted for Wilson's Consultants International while working at the same time for the security division of Honeywell, Inc. He and Wilson had argued, and Wilson reportedly had threatened to "break your fucking legs at the knee." Tafoya's book contained a snapshot of the man, a sketch map of the location of his house near Virginia Beach, Virginia, and a detailed physical description. A marginal note read, "HOLD RECON." In intelligence jargon, this means locate where a person is and what he is currently doing.

Tafoya was extradited to Colorado and held in high bail in the Larimer County jail, the judge agreeing with the prosecutor that given Tafoya's training as a covert operative and the severity of the charges against him, he might flee the United States. Because of the intelligence rumors that an attempt might be made on Tafoya's life, he was held in solitary confinement, with a light burning outside his cell twenty-four hours daily.

Ray Martinez dropped by Tafoya's cell for a chat a few days after his arrival in Fort Collins. He noted two things. Tafoya was reading a Robert Ludlum spy thriller, *The Bourne Identity*, and he had jotted down the name and phone number of Washington lawyer Kenneth Conklin. This lawyer, as Martinez was to learn, had been adviser to the first contingent of former Green Berets recruited by Wilson to work in Libya.

Ed Wilson's fingerprints are all over this case, Ray Martinez told himself. I wonder how I can persuade the Department to let me go to Libya to talk with him. He dismissed the notion as fanciful. But he knew the case of Gene Tafoya was far from resolved.

26

"A Grisly Damned Sight"

With the Justice Department snooping into his activities, the worst scenario Edwin Wilson could have envisioned was the sudden reemergence of his onetime associate Frank Terpil. The two renegades differed in one essential respect. Wilson posed as a legitimate businessman, a person with ties to American intelligence. Terpil presented no such facade. He was an avowed criminal and mercenary. He wanted the dollar. To Terpil, American foreign policy, as administered by the State Department, was hypocritical. American intelligence, as run by the CIA, was even worse. Lies and deceit, after all, were man's natural order. Most simply, Frank Terpil went through life unburdened with any conscience whatever.

Which perhaps is just as well, given what he did after breaking with Wilson in late 1977. Terpil became a trusted security adviser for President Idi Amin of Uganda, training his secret police and providing them with the cruel tools of their trade. Amin was one of Colonel Muamar Quaddafi's few friends among African leaders; according to one account, it was at Quaddafi's personal suggestion that Terpil started working as an adviser to the Ugandan Government. Terpil had an office in the same Kampala building that housed Amin's torture chambers. When the screams of victims got loud enough to disturb him, "I'd turn on the radio full blast," he boasted later. Indeed, Terpil seemed to relish repeating stories of Amin's savagery. Talking with undercover detectives about Amin, Terpil said: "You think you got it bad here. Try staying with [Amin]. He's paranoid about being whacked off by stuff being added to the food. Naturally, because I used to supply him with shit.

"Idi says, 'I want the most powerful.' I said, 'I'll get you the most powerful.'

"There was one that would look like a heart attack. To the day, to the day, we reckon twenty-four to forty-eight hours. Thirty-six hours later the guy had absolutely nothing wrong with him. Nothing—walked around, stuff like that. Felt the chest pains; twenty minutes later he was gone. I mean they did an autopsy on him and couldn't tell the difference."

On one occasion, Terpil claimed, he had given Amin the poison with which to kill one of his cabinet members at a formal state dinner.

"The minister got the spoon in his mouth and whoop. . . . [Amin] made a big political thing out of it. He says . . . God has punished the minister of finance because he was pulling a coup. Everybody drops their spoon.... I wish I had a film of the goddamned thing."

Laughing as he told the story to undercover officers, Terpil described the ploy the dictator had used to trick a confession from a cabinet member he suspected of plotting with the Kenyan Government for his overthrow.

"So what he did to get this information, he has the minister of defense killed. What he does, he sends to the ministers down there for a big state dinner. He said, 'I know which one of you people are working for the Kenyans.' He said, 'The minister of defense told me.' Now, nobody knows the minister of defense is gone. He said, 'One of you people is working for Kenya. If you tell me, we'll let bygones be bygones.'

"But nobody tells him, so they bring on the food... fried bananas, horrible stuff. And they bring on the meat. They bring these big trays out. They put this... fucking tray in the middle of the table. Somebody picks up the lid, one of the waiters, and there's the fucking head of the minister of defense." The suspect minister gasped at the grisly sight and arose and tried to run away from the table. "He cracked; he just went wop," Terpil said. Amin calmly took aim with his .357 Magnum and shot him dead.

Terpil was such a trusted associate—by Terpil's account—that Amin even had him help in the execution of 15 Ugandans considered unfaithful to the dictator.

"They line up these fifteen guys they're gonna shoot.... So then they decide, Okay, we'll put them under the watchtower. This is a tower actually in the town square, which is only as wide as that wall. You couldn't get the fifteen people there—but we did. We got them there anyway. And out of the fifteen people, they took twenty-one blasts to kill 'em off." On Amin's order, the bodies were thrown into the back of a truck and taken to "Paradise Island," the ironically named site of the nation's most dreaded prison camp. By Terpil's admiring account:

"Amin says, 'I want all the bodies brought out.' He didn't say 'bodies'; he said, 'I want all the people brought out....' He lines them up along the beach and he goes and lectures them and he tells them what bad people they were, but they're dead.

"He finishes his little talk to this row of corpses and then he cuts out a portion of each one's liver and eats it. Grisly damned sight, Amin hacking away with his knife. He ate just a part of it, because if you do that, the spirit cannot come back to get you."

In matter-of-fact tones Terpil described, in seeming admiration, the perverse torture techniques Amin had used on his countrymen. "The best one I saw, which you do, is, really, the rat one. You can use it very quickly. What they do is they take a rat, a real hungry rat, and put it on the guy's stomach, and strap a copper pot over it.

"They start a little fire on top of the pot. . . . And the copper starts getting hot from the top down. The rat goes crazy. . . . There's only one way out. . . . He eats right through the stomach. I've seen that done about three times. Totally effective."

Just how much of Terpil's claims is true is impossible to gauge. But that Terpil would even tell such stories reveals something about the man's character. He profited greatly from his association with Amin. Records seized in Kampala following the dictator's overthrow revealed his contracts for communications and security gear to total $3.2 million.

Terpil did not shy from personal involvement in murder. In May 1979, Bruce McKenzie, the sole white member of the Kenyan Cabinet, came to Kampala to try to negotiate an end to the constant border feuding with Uganda. Amin played the gracious host; as McKenzie left, he was presented with a stuffed Kenyan cob (a variety of antelope). It contained a bomb fashioned by Frank Terpil. Amin gave McKenzie a flowery farewell speech. As his plane approached the Nairobi airport, it exploded, killing McKenzie and the crew. Terpil would laugh when he told the story, for the plot had almost failed. "Amin's speech ran so long that I was afraid the damned thing would explode while the plane was still at Kampala airport. So I had to send a guy aboard to set the timer back another half-hour."

Terpil's partner during much of this period was Gary Korkala, proprietor of Amstech International, a New Jersey security company which manufactured relatively benign equipment such as airport metal detectors. When Terpil came calling in late 1977 or early 1978, he immediately recognized in Korkala the makings of a fellow criminal. Korkala was willing to violate government export laws in the sale of equipment that could not legally by shipped to blacklisted nations. "You're wasting your time here," Terpil told Korkala. "Come on out to the Middle East with me; we can make oodles of money."

Korkala needed little encouragement. He moved his main office to Beirut (retaining his New Jersey operation as well) and with Terpil began going after Middle Eastern business. With a file of contacts supplied by Terpil, Korkala was soon doing profitable business in half a dozen countries.

Terpil had a special affinity for the Syrians, and he spent much of his time in Damascus; he bragged that "I got about ten million out of these guys, what with one thing or another." Much of these sales apparently comprised Terpil's version of the sensitive communication equipment with which he had worked while with the Central Intelligence Agency.

Yet Korkala and Terpil would take business where they found it. During a trip to New York in the autumn of 1979, they blundered into the path of an undercover police investigation involving narcotics and stolen securities. One of the policemen happened to meet Korkala, and the talk turned to drugs.

"Sure, I can get you drugs," Korkala told the officer, "but who do you need them for? I don't want to put my neck out unless I'm sure I'm dealing with straight people."

The detective improvised a yarn that the purchasers were "Latin-American revolutionaries" who wanted to sell narcotics to raise money to buy weapons. Korkala laughed. "Oh, hell, don't bother with the drugs. If your guys have any money, we can get all the guns you want—tell me how many and what kind."

In a series of meetings that followed, a Hispanic-American policeman posed as one of the revolutionaries, and Terpil and Korkala agreed to supply as many as 10,000 light submachine guns. Most of these meetings were held in a New York hotel room—with police tape recorders whirring silently in adjoining suites. Terpil and Korkala boasted of their exploits abroad, particularly their work for Amin. To support their story of supplying poisons for the Uganda dictator, they even brought in samples they offered to sell to the officers. With high-pitched giggles, Korkala told how poisons could be selected to provide the sort of death desired.

"Maybe one guy wants a heart attack, and maybe another guy wants to see the guy scream and crawl all over the floor. [Korkala displayed a vial.] This is my favorite. That stuff will work. What the stuff does, you get a very strong tingling sensation in your fingers and your toes, the way it starts. Then your hair falls out, and . . . you can't walk. It's a metal base that's not reversible. If you really want to hurt a guy, give him this shit."

Terpil and Korkala struck a deal with the "revolutionaries." They would supply 10,000 Sten guns—British light machine guns—and 10 million rounds of ammunition for $2 million. Through an unwitting British arms dealer, Terpil arranged for one of the undercover men to inspect the weapons at a warehouse in Manchester. This was done in early December 1979. Terpil did not tell the undercover agents two important things. First, the guns did not belong to him; they were the property of Samuel Cummings' company, Interarmco, as was the warehouse. Second, Terpil had no intention of making delivery; he intended to get as much of the $2 million up front as possible, then disappear.

The night of December 22, the conspirators had their final meeting at the New York Hilton Hotel. Police burst into the room; Terpil pulled a pistol, but chose not to fire. He and Korkala had been trapped. Incredibly, a New York judge permitted them to go free on $15,000 bond each, although they faced potential prison terms of up to fifty years. Assistant District Attorney Matthew Crosson, who had masterminded the undercover operation, said as he left court, "We'll never see Frank Terpil here to stand trial."

Ed Wilson's reaction to Terpil's arrest is not a matter of record, but the consequences were direct, and serious. First, the publicity. Because of Wilson's prior links with Terpil, the press included him in accounts of how the police had broken the arms ring. British police moved swiftly after the arrest and searched Terpil's farmhouse north of London. (Larry Barcella; Carol Bruce, one of his assistants; and BATF agents Dick Pederson and Rick Wadsworth accompanied the British detectives.) Among the many items seized was a briefcase belonging to Douglas Schlachter, Wilson's longtime assistant. It contained contracts, Telex messages, financial data—a gold mine of information on Wilson's operations. Another raid, on

Korkala's Amstech warehouse in Nutley, New Jersey, produced briefcase bombs, letter bombs, grenades, a ball-point pen that could fire poison darts, and other sabotage items.

Given the new leads, Barcella and Carol Bruce intensified their efforts against both Terpil and Wilson. John Harper and his wife, Eula Mae, agreed to testify before a federal grand jury in Washington about the explosives training program. Assorted documents connected Jerome Brower to the shipping of timers and various explosives. On April 20, 1980, the grand jury returned a multicount indictment against Wilson, Terpil, and Jerome Brower, the scope of which was spelled out in an opening paragraph:

> The object of the conspiracy was to supply covertly and for a profit the government of Libya with personnel, explosives, explosive material, and other goods necessary to make explosive devices, and to teach others how to make explosive devices in a terrorist training project.

In addition to alleging violations of explosives export laws, the indictments accused Brower of perjury. Wilson and Terpil were named in other counts for trying to arrange the 1976 assassination of Libyan dissident Umar Mahayshi in Cairo.

Barcella had the indictments returned under seal—that is, in secrecy—in the hope that Wilson and Terpil could be arrested; if the indictments were made public, he feared that both men would go into hiding. An Interpol notice alerted European law officers to arrest both men; Swiss police missed grabbing Wilson (who had not been in the United States since December 1979) by a few hours. But events forced publicity. Terpil suddenly appeared at a U.S. Secret Service conference for dealers in security equipment at the Service's training school in suburban Maryland. "He was out trying to sell his wares, not knowing that we were looking for him," Barcella said. Rather than risk having Terpil slip away, Barcella ordered him arrested; he shared the view of New York prosecutor Matt Crosson that Terpil would flee the United States rather than face trial. Given Terpil's wealth, and his experience in clandestine affairs, he certainly had the capability to go into longtime hiding.

Again, despite Barcella's strenuous objections, a federal judge ordered Terpil released on a bond of less than $100,000. The day Terpil was freed, Barcella told an associate, in words reminiscent of those spoken by Matt Crosson in New York, "I'll wager everything I own that I'll never see that bastard again." Barcella did persuade Terpil to come into his office for several interviews. Terpil denied any culpability. He had never heard of the documents Mulcahy had found about the booby-trap and explosives contracts.

To Barcella's surprise, Terpil even agreed to submit handwriting samples. Terpil's assumption, a correct one, was that the Justice Department had found nothing in the files in his handwriting. What Terpil did not realize was that Barcella and BATF investigators Pederson and Wadsworth had carefully chosen some words to be included in the handwriting examination. These included "imperative," "sabotage," "simultaneously," "implementation" and "refineries."

Terpil wrote "imparitive," "sabatage," "simultaniously," "implimentation" and "refinaries"—just as he had spelled the words in the Top Secret contract Kevin Mulcahy pilfered from Edwin Wilson's files the Labor Day weekend of 1977. Pederson and Wadsworth literally danced with delight when they brought Barcella the test results. There was now strong evidence to support Mulcahy's contention that Terpil had typed the Wilson contracts.

The FBI kept Terpil under a rather difficult daily surveillance. Terpil knew the tricks of how to throw off a surveillance team. He constantly changed his appearance, one day wearing work clothes, the next a Brooks Brothers suit. He shaved off his *bandido* mustache and had his shaggy hair trimmed. The morning of September 4, Terpil and a woman friend left their $400,000 Japanese-style home on Chain Bridge Road in suburban McLean, Virginia. Terpil carried a slim attaché case; he and the girl wore casual clothing; Terpil's handicapped child, a boy of about 18 months, was with them. A few miles from the house, Terpil made a sudden U-turn on a busy street and darted away; the surveillance team could not find him.

Later that morning, Frank Terpil abandoned the child at a Catholic relief agency in Alexandria, Virginia. As the FBI later reconstructed their movements, they went to Washington National Airport, from which they flew to Chicago and thence to Canada. A week or so later they were in Beirut. The abandoned child remained in Virginia. Gary Korkola, traveling through Central America, also made his way to Beirut.

In later interviews—with CBS News, Jim Hougan of *Penthouse* and British journalist Antony Thomas—Terpil complained that he had fled because he knew that he was being "set up" for an unfair trial in New York; that the prosecutor had handpicked a judge to give him a stiff sentence, regardless of the evidence. He also claimed that one of his defense attorneys had advised him that "the FBI wants you to skip; they'll leave you alone when you run." Terpil, of course, has offered no supporting evidence for such allegations, and his broad-brush conspiracy is internally contradictory: On the one hand, unnamed authorities had rigged the New York courts to ensure a maximum sentence; on the other hand, the FBI was urging him to flee the country. By his own account, Terpil was both the victim and the beneficiary of a conspiracy.

Terpil's flight did not stop his New York trial. In early 1981, a state judge ordered him and Korkala tried *in absentia*. Both were convicted and sentenced to fifty-three years in prison. But Terpil did have the semblance of a temporary last laugh on the Federal Government. Rather than post total cash for his federal bond, he had offered (and the judge had accepted) eighty "automobile immobilizers"—the so-called Denver boot, a heavy circular metal clamp that can be locked around the wheel of a car so that it cannot be driven—valued at $24,960, and a radio transceiver valued at $19,440. But when the government moved to take possession of the physical items, the post–Idi Amin Government of Uganda objected. Terpil had stolen the radio transceiver from the Uganda Mission to the United Nations earlier in 1979, a few days after Amin was overthrown. The Ugandans prevailed: the judge ordered the radio returned to their mission.

Terpil and Korkala eventually settled in Damascus, Syria, and decided to become partners in a restaurant. For murky reasons, they were arrested by Syrian intelligence officers, held incommunicado for almost six months—during which the burly Terpil lost 65 pounds, had his hair growing to his waist and did not bathe the entire time—only to be taken to the Lebanese frontier and be dumped without explanation.

Korkala, after his release from the Syrian jail, tried to reestablish his security business. He knew that Interpol warrants were outstanding for his arrest; inexplicably, he flew to Madrid to attend an international trade show for security-equipment dealers and manufacturers. A tipster saw him there and telephoned Crosson. The information was specific; the informant even specified the booth where Korkala could be found. As Barcella recalls: "I got hold of the top American law-enforcement officer at the Madrid embassy, who happened to be a Drug Enforcement Administration agent, and he went over with the Spanish *Guardia Civil*. Gary was standing right where my man said he would be standing, wearing a card on his lapel saying, *'Buenos días, mi nombre es Gary Korkala.'*"

The Spanish cops shook their heads. Barcella had told them Korkala was a major international arms dealer, and a fugitive sought on three continents. But there he stood, wearing his name on his coat. He was brought back to New York, where his attorneys successfully appealed for him to be tried in person, rather than have the *in absentia* conviction and fifty-three-year sentence remain in effect. In June of 1984, Korkala pleaded guilty to four felony counts and was sentenced in March of 1985 to a minimum of five years and a maximum of fifteen years.

Terpil, however, remained much the fugitive—a renegade who would appear from time to time for a self-serving press interview, but who displayed no willingness to return to the United States to face the charges against him.

From a prosecutorial viewpoint, the April 1980 indictments had the desired, and expected, effect. Witnesses against Wilson began scrambling for their own self-preservation. The first person to "turn" was Jerome Brower, the California explosives merchant, who had been indicted not only in the "booby-trap case" but also for perjury. Brower actually had little choice. Barcella and BATF agents slowly but methodically had put their hands on any number of invoices and shipping waybills implicating him in the explosives deals.

Brower's first step was to disassociate himself from lawyer Edwin Bloom (who had been involved, it will be remembered, in the Houston C-4 shipment) and retain Washington trial attorney William G. Hundley. A realist who had worked both as prosecutor and as defense counsel, Hundley spent several hours with Barcella, reviewing the government's physical evidence. "Okay," Hundley said, "let's talk a plea. What do you want?"

The agreement was for a six-month prison term and a nominal fine, conditioned upon Brower's testifying against Wilson both before the grand jury and at trial.

For Barcella, Brower's decision was a turning point in the case. Theretofore the prosecution had had only scattered pieces of a very complex mosaic. No single person then cooperating with the government had a true insider's view of the entire Wilson operation. Keven Mulcahy, who thought he did, had been with Wilson for a relatively few months, and he had been drunk much of that time. As Barcella was to explain later, "We had a lot of bits and pieces, rather than the smoking pistol." Through Brower the prosecution confirmed what it suspected of the initial explosives contracts, and learned for the first time of the 20-ton C-4 shipment from Houston.

As the evidence mounted, Barcella talked occasionally with Wilson's attorney, Seymour Glanzer. (Wilson by now was on either his fourth or fifth lawyer. His natural arrogance made it impossible for him to follow professional advice. When a lawyer would not agree with his view on how to handle a problem, Wilson responded by finding yet another attorney.) Barcella said, in effect, "The evidence is piling up. If you and Wilson want to talk a plea arrangement, now is the time."

Glanzer could only relay what Wilson was telling him from Tripoli: "Go fuck yourself."

His ego undaunted, Wilson in fact had yet his grandest scheme in mind. He would give Libya a nuclear capability, and earn himself a fortune in the process.

27

An Atomic Bomb for Quaddafi

With his brief and, in the event, abortive attempt to provide Libya with nuclear weaponry, Edwin P. Wilson's greed reached its epitome. For personal profit, he would upset a nuclear balance that had kept the world from atomic warfare for more than three decades. In long talks with John Heath, he said, "We're not talking about peanuts here, four or five millions of dollars. We are talking *hundreds* of millions!"

The complicated scenario began in February or March 1981, when Wilson's Belgian arms friend Armand Donnay called with exciting information. Through a Portuguese associate, Donnay had managed to put his hands on some "fissionable material" obtained from a nuclear reactor in Germany. Donnay advised Wilson that there should be enough material to fashion a nuclear weapon. Would Wilson be interested in helping him sell it to the Libyans?

"Hey, great," Wilson exclaimed. "I think they'll love it. Make up a proposal and come on down." Wilson excitedly called in John Heath and told him to go to Belgium and work on the proposal with Donnay.

During his years as an army explosive-ordnance-disposal expert, Heath had taken several courses on nuclear weapons—a fact known to Wilson. "Part of this training was very basic physics, admittedly, but essentially, to be able to disarm a nuclear device, I had to know the fundamentals of how you build one," Heath said. "I might not be able to start from scratch and build you an A-bomb. But I can certainly look at what you are passing off as an A-bomb and tell whether it will work or not."

Heath flew to Liège and looked at the plans Donnay had drawn. "Within a few minutes, I recognized that he had absolute rubbish. His plans were very well drawn, mechanically, but they were stuff you could find in a library in most any advanced country in the world." Donnay also displayed ignorance of the principles of nuclear weaponry. The drawings contained elements of separate and incompatible firing techniques, "things so disparate that they made about as much sense as putting an Indy 500 racing-car motor in your washing machine." Heath told Donnay politely that he had about as much chance of constructing a nuclear weapon as he did of pole-vaulting to the moon. Undeterred, Donnay kept working. "If we can sell them this, we can sell them a weapon," he said.

In the late spring, Donnay and Heath took the "plans"—a sheaf of drawings and technical specifications some 4 inches thick—to Tripoli for a presentation to the Libyan officials working on nuclear development. Heath warned Donnay and Wilson in advance, "You're dealing with some sharp people here. I know these men's backgrounds. They are all nuclear physicists with Ph.D.s. They have studied in the U.S., the United Kingdom, West Germany. These are not your run-of-the-mill military officers." Donnay confidently waved his hand. "Don't worry," he said; "I can convince them." Wilson threw his arm over Heath's shoulder. "Buddy, if this comes off, we're all going to be multimillionaires."

The committee chairman asked a rather basic question at the outset. "Well, Mr. Donnay, tell us, why do you want to offer this project to Libya, of all countries?"

Donnay arose and stood with his hands clasped in front of his chest, a reverent expression on his face. "First of all," he said, "I am a Moslem. I wish to construct this device as my own contribution to the Moslem brotherhood."

Heath's face tightened as he struggled to keep himself from laughing out loud. Donnay, Heath knew, was "about as Moslem as, say, Menachem Begin." Heath glanced at Wilson. "Ed had his hand under his jaw, as if in deep thought. He had no visible reaction on his face, but I could tell he was thinking the same thing I was—that Donnay was laying out bullshit by the basket, and that the Libyans weren't buying it."

The Libyan officials did not respond to Donnay's profession of brotherhood. "What is the purity of your radioactive material?" one of them asked. "Twenty percent," Donnay replied. The Libyans shook their heads. "That's no good for us," the chairman said. "We need eighty percent. If you can't do any better than this, then we have no business."

Donnay scrambled. "Well, perhaps this very tentative initial proposal is not exactly what you need. But you must realize that I have other plans as well. I have plans for other weapons and for many, many things." Visibly dubious, the Libyans suggested that Donnay contact them when he had his papers in order.

For several days, Heath worked with Donnay in an attempt—halfhearted on the American's part—to make sense of the proposal. "He was offering them a pig in a poke," Heath said, "and not even a very fat pig. Donnay had the idea that all he had to do was tell the Libyans he was going to give them nuclear weapons to use to strike the Jews, and they would fall down handing over their money. What he finally produced for the second meeting was a child's diagram, a library-book diagram."

Heath broke the news to Wilson, who shook his head in disappointment. "Then it's just a sham?" he asked. "I'm afraid so," Heath said. Donnay made a second presentation, which the Libyans also rejected. Donnay returned to Belgium, leaving Wilson several copies of his "plans."

Facing a dead end with the Libyans, Wilson dropped the idea of making money from the scheme and switched on to another track. He telephoned Bobbi Barnes in London and told her to come to Tripoli as quickly as possible. "Ed acted very mysterious when I arrived," Barnes said. "He said he had something important to tell me, but that he didn't want to talk in the villa." They got into Wilson's car and drove into the countryside outside Tripoli. Wilson looked around to make sure that no one was eavesdropping—a theatrical gesture, given the isolation of their parking spot—and told Barnes, "The Libyans are getting the equipment and the know-how to build an atomic bomb. This is very important information and I must get it to Washington as quickly as possible." He instructed Bobbi to return to London and telephone Paul Cyr, his lobbyist friend and sometime errand-runner. Cyr, he said, should be able to come to Tripoli and pick up the documents and take them to the CIA in Washington.

Barnes did as told, but Cyr wanted no part of any trip to Libya, for any purpose—certainly not to act as a courier for nuclear plans. "This is one time I'm going to have to say no to Ed," he told Bobbi. "This is too complicated for me; besides, I don't think my health is up to such a long trip." Cyr did agree to call a lawyer friend, John Keats, who had represented Wilson on a few minor civil matters. (As a long-time friend of Cyr's, Keats had hunted on the Wilson farm in Northern Virginia; he had yet to meet Wilson in person.)

A "very distraught" Cyr called Keats and told him what was happening, and asked if he would call Bobbi Barnes in London. Keats did so. He also spoke with Wilson several times by phone in Tripoli. The mission appealed to Keats's spirit of adventure; how many times, he asked himself, does a Washington lawyer have the chance to get involved in international cloak-and-dagger work? During the phone conversations, Wilson suggested that Keats, in turning over the material to the U.S. Government, should solicit a *quid pro quo*: "favorable negotiations" to get Wilson out from under his criminal indictments.

On Wilson's instructions, Keats flew to Brussels, where he obtained a Libyan visa with Donnay's assistance, and then on to Tripoli. Keats almost lost his stomach for cloak-and-dagger work at the airport. The Libyans refused to permit him entry because his passport had not been translated into Arabic. "For a moment I thought I might be locked up," Keats said, "but Wilson showed up and managed to get me clearance. Then we went out to his villa and talked the better part of three days."

Wilson showed Keats a voluminous stack of papers, diagrams and lists of equipment, all incomprehensible to the lawyer because he could not read French, and because he knew absolutely nothing about nuclear weapons. Wilson insisted that the papers included plans for both a nuclear reactor and an atomic bomb that a Frenchman was attempting to sell the Libyans. "He was most anxious to block that," Keats said, "to get this material out, and get it to the United States to the proper authorities."

Keats was skeptical. He noted, among other things, that one of the folders contained a photocopy of Donnay's passport. Since Donnay was the arms supplier who Wilson claimed was assembling the nuclear weaponry, why was Wilson betraying him to the American authorities? Keats wanted no part in taking the papers to the United States. He told Wilson that the passport problems when he came into Libya had frightened him; what sort of chance would he be taking of being stopped again with a packet of potentially incriminating papers? "There's too much stuff in the package for me to hide it, either in my suitcase or on my person," he told Wilson. He did promise that if Wilson got the material to the United States, he would give it to "the proper authorities." Fine, Wilson said; they'll be in your office in Washington a few days after your return.

Wilson turned to another subject. He wanted Keats to talk with Larry Barcella, the prosecutor, and tell him, "I can deliver two of the Cubans you want for the Letelier murder." Wilson knew that Barcella (and, indeed, most of the Justice Department) was determined to bring the Letelier killers to trial, and that the U.S. Government was scouring the world for them. The day after Keats returned to Washington, he went to Barcella's office and asked what would be needed to start negotiations for a plea bargain, or even dismissal of all charges against Wilson.

Barcella would not even discuss the latter; Ed Wilson had too much criminal business outstanding to go totally free. And before Barcella would entertain talks about formal negotiations, he demanded a "good-faith gesture" from Wilson. Barcella correctly recognized that although Wilson was the linchpin of the Libyan conspiracy, numerous other persons were involved; if Wilson wanted special consideration, he must cooperate with prosecutors.

"How about the two Letelier-case Cubans?" Keats asked. "What if Wilson helped you find them, and arranged their arrest?"

Barcella straightened in his chair. Yes, indeed, he said, such assistance would be appreciated. (As Barcella would say years later, "Ed Wilson definitely knew what bait to dangle. To say that I *wanted* those two Cubans is an understatement.") Keats promised to get back to Barcella in a day or so; he wanted to talk to Wilson before proceeding further.

In the interim, Wilson managed to smuggle the nuclear papers out of Libya via one of his former Green Beret employees, who gave them to Bobbi Barnes in London. Barnes, in turn, shipped them to Keats, who hurried to Barcella's office to add a new dimension to the bargaining.

"Larry," Keats said, "would you be interested in some information from Ed Wilson about how an atomic bomb is about to be shipped to Libya?"

Barcella, who is not a demonstrative man, stared at Keats. Bringing the Cubans to trial on the Letelier charges would have given him great personal satisfaction. But keeping a nuclear weapon from the hands of the nefarious Quaddafi "was far more important to the world than finding two fugitive Cubans." Keats telephoned Wilson so that Barcella could hear the information directly. "The thing [bomb] is now on a railroad siding in Liège, Belgium," Wilson said. "It's going to be shipped to Libya momentarily. The man who has it has the deal all greased." If the U.S. Government did not act to keep the bomb away from Quaddafi, Wilson offered, he could use his own people to destroy it.

Barcella began thinking of some form of extralegal move himself, so acute was his reaction to Wilson's information. Yet despite Wilson's professed concern over Quaddafi's obtaining nuclear weapons, Barcella detected an odd note in the conversation. Wilson mentioned that he was paying demurrage on the freight car in which the material was stored; hence he was anxious to get the matter resolved. To Barcella, this statement indicated that Wilson was perhaps as much interested in his pocketbook as he was in national security.

The documents, Wilson had said, were the best evidence. So Keats took them to Barcella's office, and handed them over to a lawyer from the Central Intelligence Agency, whose experts would determine their legitimacy. Keats and Barcella "anxiously awaited" the CIA finding. In very short order, CIA's answer came: The papers contained "nothing of intelligence value." No bomb could be constructed from the plans. "A bunch of junk," an agency nuclear expert concluded.

Keats's initial reaction was skeptical. "I said to myself, 'Shit, they're not going to tell us if it *does* have intelligence value.'" But the more he thought about the matter, "In all candor, I have to say that it was my belief...that [I was] somewhat suspicious of whether or not this stuff had any intelligence value."

The CIA evaluation left Barcella with little faith in Wilson's credibility. Wilson had built his postgovernment career on lies and deception. Barcella decided he would not traffic in nonsense. But Wilson, through Keats, continued to insist on a face-to-face meeting. Wilson apparently remained confident that he could outtalk and outsmart the government lawyer. During this period Wilson said to Heath, "If this guy is so smart, why is he still on the government payroll? Let me get at him one on one, and I'll eat his lunch."

28

A Meeting in Rome

For the next several weeks, Keats tried to negotiate with Barcella—directly, and by phone with Wilson—to arrange a meeting on neutral ground. Barcella had other concerns. He was retrying some of the Letelier defendants whose convictions had been reversed on appeal. Keats pressed. At one point he suggested that after court recesssed on Friday afternoon, Barcella fly to Europe on the Concorde, meet with Wilson on Saturday and fly back to Washington on Sunday.

"Look, John," Barcella said, "I'm in the middle of a trial. I'm working twenty hours a day. You know what this means—I can't turn my brain off for an entire weekend and forget Letelier. Besides, Judge [Barrington] Parker is sitting on Saturdays."

"No problem, Larry," Keats said. "We'll fly you out on late Saturday, and you can still be back Sunday night."

Barcella sighed. "And just how good do you think I'd be in court on Monday morning after spending the previous forty-eight hours on an airplane, and talking with Ed Wilson? No, John, wait until the trial is over."

Although he was careful to shield it from Keats, Barcella was itching for a meeting with Wilson. Seeing his adversary in the flesh would be useful if only as a "know your enemy" encounter. Barcella expected little of a concrete nature to result. "Ed Wilson wanted to see how much he could bullshit me. Well, I've been in this business for quite some time. You can learn as much through the questions you ask as you can from the answers to your questions. And you can also give out false information through your own questions. That's the game."

Two days after the Letelier trial ended, Barcella and Keats struck an agreement for a meeting with Wilson in Rome. Barcella, in a June 5, 1981, "Dear John" letter to Keats, spoke from the high ground of authority. Barcella would listen to Wilson; he would promise nothing in advance save safe passage to the site.

> As you know, we have previously told you that the Department of Justice is not, at this time, in a position to negotiate with Mr. Wilson concerning the disposition of his pending charges and any potential charges. Since the inception of our discussions with you concerning Mr. Wilson's situation, we have emphasized the need for some show of good faith on Mr. Wilson's behalf before we would

be willing or able to enter into any negotiations with Mr. Wilson or make any promises to him about his criminal case(s). For reasons that we have already discussed, but need not reiterate here, we are unable to say that Mr. Wilson has, to date, made such a demonstration of good faith to us.

Your present proposal of a meeting with Mr. Wilson is greeted by some skepticism by us for without the precedent of a "good faith" showing by Mr. Wilson, we cannot be assured that any meeting with him is going to be even marginally productive or worthwhile.

Any meeting, Barcella continued, "may set the stage for some future negotiations and settlement of the criminal matters Mr. Wilson is implicated in." As ground rules, he put forth the following:

—The Justice Department, working through the Department of State, would arrange with the Italian Government for Wilson to come to Italy "for a period of 72 hours to meet with us." During his stay, "assuming there are no problems independent of this case, no efforts will be made to arrest, detain, deport or extradite Mr. Wilson . . . to the United States."

—"The first matter of discussion" would be the whereabouts of the two Cubans sought in the Letelier murder. "If the information concerning the above fugitives is truthful and accurate, it will constitute a demonstration of good faith on Mr. Wilson's part. However, it is understood that the United States is not obligated to promise anything in return for this information."

—Next, Wilson "will submit to a full debriefing . . . on topics of our choosing and additional topics of Mr. Wilson's choosing." Any Wilson statements would not be "used directly against him" in any criminal prosecution. But any leads developed as a result "of anything your client says to us will be fully investigated, and any evidence that is developed can and will be used against him in any criminal prosecutions if we cannot negotiate a settlement at some later date."

—Wilson must come to Italy on his U.S. passport, meet with no persons other than Barcella and his designated representatives and provide in advance a travel itinerary. If no agreement was reached, Wilson could return to Libya without arrest. Barcella got assurances from both the Italian national police and Interpol that Wilson would not be touched.

Keats knew that Barcella was looking beyond Wilson to possible prosecution targets elsewhere in the American intelligence community. A basic element of plea bargaining is that the defendant "trades upward"—that is, by giving the prosecution information about someone else a few rungs higher on the ladder, he can negotiate a better deal. Keats realized that Wilson was not about to escape without a criminal conviction, regardless of how much he offered Barcella. The Wilson case had attracted so much adverse press attention that the Justice Department must demand some jail time. As Keats told one acquaintance at the time, "Given the popular bugaboos in the press, the CIA and Libya are running neck and neck as to who is public enemy number one. Ed has the misfortune to be tied in with both."

The meeting was set for the first days of July, and Keats flew to Rome a day ahead of the American prosecutors. He feared that the active European press would learn of Wilson's trip, and that he would be besieged by *paparazzi*. "This meeting was so secret that not even the Libyans knew what was happening," Keats said. Keats checked into his hotel and returned to the airport a few hours before Wilson arrived with bodyguard John Dutcher. No reporters were visible. Keats took Wilson and Dutcher to the comfortable Cavalieri Hilton, in the hills outside crowded downtown Rome.

Before dinner that evening, Keats decided to check the dining area and make sure that the Italian police had, as promised, provided security guards. Wilson's fear was that he would be killed by an assassination squad from Mossad, the Israeli intelligence service. Keats strolled through the lobby and dining room, and when he saw no obvious security men he became nervous. "I didn't want Wilson to be out there exposed, without any protection." (None had been promised by the Justice Department.) So Keats consulted an expert.

"I went into the bar and sat next to an Italian hooker. I handed her twenty-five dollars and said, 'In your line of work, you probably know most of the cops in Rome. I wish you would walk through the lobby and see if it is heavily guarded. Come back and tell me, and I'll give you another twenty-five.'

"She nodded, and was gone, and within a couple of minutes she was back. She didn't even bother to sit down. 'Give me the twenty-five dollars,' she said, 'I must leave. The police, they are everywhere.' So Ed and I dined in the knowledge we were under guard."

In addition to Barcella, the American team included Carol Bruce, an assistant U.S. attorney (Wilson blinked when he learned that one of his prosecutorial adversaries was five months pregnant); Dick Pederson of the Bureau of Alcohol, Tobacco and Firearms, an original investigator in the case; Bill Hart of the FBI; and another FBI agent designated legal attaché in the Rome embassy.*

From the vantage point of all parties concerned, the Rome meeting was a disaster. Wilson's information on the whereabouts of the Cubans was hopelessly dated: he knew where they *might* have been six weeks earlier, but he could give no leads that might result in their arrest. The Cubans sought were José Dionisio Suárez and Virgilio Paz, both said to be affiliated with the anti-Castro group Omega Seven. Wilson's story was that he had recruited Rafael "Chi Chi" Quintero, his old CIA and TF-157 associate, to track down the men. He told Barcella that Quintero had located both Cubans in a brothel in Quito, Ecuador, but they had slipped away before they could be arrested. Wilson further alleged that Quintero had later found one of the Cubans training mercenaries in Guatemala to fight against the leftist Sandinist government of Nicaragua. What Wilson did not know at the time was that Quintero had accepted the assignment, then ignored it. Quintero is a complex man, politically and personally. Foremost in his makeup is an intense hatred of Fidel Castro and his supporters. Although he might not endorse the killing of such a Castro friend as Letelier (whose expenses in exile were partially paid by the Cuban Government), he would not involve himself in the search for the assassins. When Wilson asked Quintero to find the supposed Letelier killers he replied "¿Sí, como no?" (Sure, why not?) He did nothing.†

---

*A Jack Anderson column stated that a CIA official was also present; three persons who were there say Anderson was wrong.

†Wilson did not learn of Quintero's deception until almost two years later, when he was confined at the Metropolitan Correctional Center in New York. Many Omega Seven members were on the same jail floor. Wilson mused about "killing Chi Chi with a twenty-cent stamp"—that is, by telling the other Cubans that Quintero had helped him try to find their colleagues. Unbeknownst to Wilson, several of Quintero's associates had told Omega Seven and other elements of the Cuban exile community the true facts—that Quintero had done nothing to find Suárez and Paz. One former CIA associate of Quintero's told me, "That's the dirtiest goddamned thing anyone could do—to tell a lie about a man that could turn an entire community against him. I'm going to pray that hell is a bit hotter for Ed Wilson."

When Keats tried to steer the conversation to the terms under which Wilson might "plead out" his cases in exchange for a set prison term, Barcella replied that it was fruitless to talk of any agreement "until Wilson comes up with something in exchange." But Wilson had nothing to offer. Eventually, Barcella lost his temper. Wilson was still claiming he had ties with CIA (although when pressed for specifics, he fell silent, or pleaded "security reasons" for not responding). He could "deliver" the Cuban fugitives, if only given enough time. Furthermore, he possessed "valuable intelligence information" about the Libyan military and its equipment. Barcella grew progressively more angry as he listened to Wilson. In his view, Wilson had lied to everyone in the Federal Government for three years.

"Now Wilson was sitting there telling me even more bullshit, and expecting me to believe it. I blistered him. I told him that he was lying to me, that he thought he could continue to survive by continuing to lie. I told him, 'You are in no position to deliver the [Cuban] fugitives, and you know it. You have no information about atomic weapons that means a damned thing, and you know it. If you want to tell me the truth, okay. Otherwise, I'm not in a position to talk any further, other than to tell you to go to hell.'"

Barcella's outburst ended that day's talks. There was a breakfast meeting the next morning which moved to the hotel lounge. Barcella deliberately remained silent. He had spoken his mind; now it was Wilson's turn to think about it. Wilson tried to break Barcella's silence. "Hey, we can work this out; just give me a chance," he said. Barcella looked away.

John Keats was later to say, to several persons, that Wilson could have agreed to a plea bargain in Rome that would have called for a prison term of five years. By repetition, the "five-year plea" came to be accepted as fact. While giving no details of what might have been offered in Rome, Barcella says the five-year term "is not quite accurate." The length of the term seemed to hinge on the amount of prison time that must be served before a felon is eligible for parole.

Wilson's behavior in Rome led Keats, among others, to question whether he was fully rational. "Wilson's most overwhelming personal characteristic was monomania," Keats said. "Feeling he was smarter than any person with whom he dealt, anyone who disagreed with him was therefore stupid."

Wilson had come to Rome convinced that he could deceive Barcella—a witless assumption, given Barcella's record as a prosecutor and the resources he had behind him. But Wilson could not concede that any man was his equal in guile. As Keats put it, "He felt he was smarter than the men who had been his superiors in CIA; he felt he was smarter than the foreign officials with whom he did business, than the federal prosecutors and investigators, and especially his lawyers. The fact of the matter is that he had a very wide stupid streak, as displayed by his actions."

At the outset of the Rome meeting, an American consular official invalidated Wilson's U.S. passport. He could return to Libya, but he could no longer travel as a citizen of the land of his birth. The vise had tightened considerably. Wilson in essence had been driven to ground in Libya.

Incredibly, he continued to exude confidence that he would emerge legally unscathed. On August 25, 1981, Wilson granted an interview to ABC News in Tripoli during which he claimed that he would eventually return for trial. "I'll just wait till the heat settles down a little bit and then I'll tell my story," he said.

> Q. If you are innocent of the indictment, why aren't you back fighting, then? Defending yourself?
> A. Well, I don't, as I said before, I really don't think now is the time to go back. There's a lot of anti-Libyan feeling in the United States. These articles are—are flamboyant. I really don't believe that I could get a fair trial if I went back now. I would rather just see all the cards that are on the table; then I'll go back.
> Q. And how and when is that going to happen?
> A. Whenever I feel that—that the time is right.

Part Four

THE QUARRY

29

"These Bastards Are Dropping a Dime on Me"

His attempts to cope with the Justice Department having been rebuffed by Larry Barcella in Rome, Edwin Wilson spent the next months warning the U.S. Government—through the unwitting and often gullible media—that if it tried to bring him to trial, he would expose the secrets he had learned in two decades of covert work for CIA and naval intelligence. Wilson chose both his interviewees and the subjects he would talk about with considerable shrewdness. For instance, Philip Taubman and Jeff Gerth did the bulk of the investigative work on Wilson for *The New York Times*; both reporters repeatedly asked Wilson, via phone and cable, for interviews to hear his side of the story. Wilson would not go near them; they knew the questions he did not want to answer, and they had the background to see through brush-off responses. Harry Reasoner of the CBS News program *60 Minutes* was also rebuffed; he too was a newsman who could not be manipulated. (When Reasoner appeared in Tripoli, he alarmed several former Green Berets who encountered him in a hotel lobby. They tried to avoid Reasoner, but after being trapped in a casual café conversation, they passed themselves off as oil-company workers who had "never heard of any guy named Wilson.")

Wilson chose to talk with people whom he felt he could manipulate. A *Newsweek* stringer from Rome, for instance,

appeared at the Tripoli villa one day; Wilson sized her up
briefly, and permitted her a few questions. She was no match
for him, and her story reflected her lack of background.
Wilson depicted himself as a run-of-the-mill businessman
who knew nothing about terrorists or their training. But in
terms of getting maximum exposure for his "I'm-an-innocent-
merchant" story, Wilson enjoyed his most striking success
with *People* magazine and occasional journalist Peter Malatesta.
As *People* described him in an introductory box, "Malatesta is
no stranger to complex men. He has been an aide to Vice
President Spiro Agnew, a business partner of former Korean
lobbyist Tongsun Park and an owner of Pisces, an exclusive
private club in Georgetown." According to *People*, Wilson
"invited. . . Malatesta to spend ten days with him in Tripoli."
The resultant interview, spread over six pages of the magazine, was essentially Ed Wilson as seen by Ed Wilson—a man
who had done no wrong, whose accusers were drunks, incompetents or paranoids. Malatesta's questions and *People*'s
prefatory material did state the charges against Wilson, yet
his answers were uniformly self-serving, with no attempt
made by the reporter at follow-up. The net impression was of
a man being persecuted by a lying press and a malicious
Justice Department. As John Heath put it, "Ed brought this
guy out to Libya and talked to him about doing a book about
him. He pumped him so full of shit that it was practically
running out of his ears when he left."

Wilson suggested that he was more interested in Malatesta's
political connections than in his writing abilities. He dusted
off a set of the discredited atomic-weapon plans and asked
that they be delivered to Vice President George Bush. He
also thought that Senator Barry Goldwater of the Senate
Intelligence Committee would be interested in material he
could supply about the Libyan military, and about the Middle
East in general. Wilson felt himself deserving of clemency;
true, he might have committed technical violations of the
complex arms-export laws, but never wittingly, nor with the
intent to do violence to U.S. policy. Given his contacts, he
could be of continuing value to the United States in North
Africa and the Middle East. Wilson did not want to be forced
to trial. He had learned many secrets during his career in
American intelligence, many of them related directly to what
he had done in Libya and elsewhere. He did not want to

harm his country. But self-preservation dictated that he take care of himself. In Heath's view, "Wilson thought he had found himself a high-level messenger boy."

An even more ambitious scheme involved Wilson's stated attempt to "buy" favorable treatment in the syndicated Jack Anderson column. Let it be said immediately that Anderson denied ever hearing of any such effort. "What I wrote about Ed Wilson speaks for itself," Anderson stated. Indeed it does.

Anderson's first column, published October 22, 1980, had Wilson and Frank Terpil still together as "headmasters" of Quaddafi's "terrorist school." Wilson "is reported to be hiding out there [in Tripoli] in a hotel room down the hall from the notorious terrorist and assasin Carlos the Jackal." In fact, Wilson and Terpil had broken their partnership almost four years previously. In December 1976, Wilson had lived openly in his own villa, not a hotel; the reference to living "down the hall" from Carlos the Jackal resembles the yarn Terpil had told to Kevin Mulcahy the summer of 1976—to describe his own quarters, not those of Wilson. These errors are cited not to criticize Anderson, but to point up the difficulty the press had in reporting the early phases of what came to be known as "the Wilson case."

There were more than a dozen Anderson columns, beginning in October 1980 and continuing after Wilson's arrest. None could be considered even mildly favorable to Wilson— Anderson referred to Terpil and Wilson as "renegades" and "merchants of death" and "master terrorists" for Quaddafi, whose motive was "simple greed." One Anderson column, in fact, almost caused Wilson to be shot by the Libyan military. On September 18, 1981, Anderson wrote:

> A bizarre rendezvous occurred in Rome last July. The top U.S. intelligence official there [the CIA chief of station] met with a renegade ex-CIA agent [Wilson] to discuss the possible assassination of Libyan dictator Muamar Quaddafi. . . .
> [The] chosen instrument was a lethal poison that was to be injected into the desert dictator by means of a tiny dart disguised as one of the black flies that infest Libya.

* * *

The column had no basis in fact. The CIA station chief was not at the Rome meeting; he did not talk with Wilson at any time during his stay there, nor did any other agent. The CIA had had no plans, then or ever, to kill Quaddafi. As a retired CIA official with long experience in the planning and execution of covert operations (but never any assasinations, he adds) pointed out, CIA was still recovering from the Church Committee investigation of alleged similar plots in the past. The Senate panel had found no evidence of any CIA assassination planning that went beyond the talking stages, and now the sting of publicity made it unlikely that CIA would ever consider killing Quaddafi. Moreover, disposing of Quaddafi would not change the course of Libyan politics, and in all probability would result in the emergence of an even more fanatical leader. "Once the Libyans decide to straighten out their business," the retired spook said, "they'll do it on their own." Finally, getting close enough to Quaddafi physically to kill him with a poisoned dart was an operational improbability. "Ed Wilson himself had never met Quaddafi; how the hell was he supposed to put a dart in his belly?"

But the Libyans accepted the column as truth. Hijazzi summoned Wilson to his office and put a copy of the article—from a European newspaper—on his desk. "You must tell me, Mister Ed, just what you think you are doing." As Wilson said later, "As I read the column, I said to myself, 'Oh, my God, I'm being set up—these bastards are dropping a dime on me. They can't get me out of Libya, so they're going to have the Libyans murder me.'" Wilson realized he was arguing for his life, making his most important sales pitch ever. "It is not true," he told Hijazzi. "This is a lie that the bastard Barcella tells in the thought that you will do as he wishes and kill me. I would never do such a thing."

Hijazzi harangued Wilson for more than an hour. Quaddafi did not like the publicity that Wilson was bringing to Libya (a hollow complaint; Quaddafi hardly needed Wilson to attract world attention). Wilson protested that he could not control what the American press wrote about him. Hijazzi repeated, "The highest levels of our government do not like the constant insinuation that you are Quaddafi's intimate adviser." A shaken Wilson was finally permitted to leave, his body soaked with nervous sweat.

Wilson had the not unreasonable suspicion that either

the Justice Department or the CIA had planted the item with Anderson, with the intent of getting him either killed or expelled from Libya. Anderson gave no source for the assassination plot in the column. Barcella denied that any such plan had ever been discussed, or that any CIA representative had been at the Rome meeting. He also denied giving the misinformation to Anderson. "I didn't want Ed dead—I wanted him alive, in court, to stand trial," Barcella said.

Wilson's reaction was to attempt to recruit Anderson for his defense. Soon after the "kill-Quaddafi" column, Anderson was to write: "We began communication directly with the fugitive . . . by telephone and other, more secure means."

As Anderson told me, "Wilson called and said he was getting a raw deal, that the press was buying what the Justice Department told them, hook, line and sinker. He maintained to me that he was a legitimate businessman who happened to be working for an unpopular country. I have a policy with my column of listening to people's stories. If they claim they are being abused, I investigate, and I try to find the truth. If what they say is true, I go after the abuser. If what they say is false, well, I go after them. The main point is that if someone wants to talk to me, I'll listen, with no strings attached other than that I am free to publish what I can find."

In addition to his newspaper column, Anderson is responsible for radio and television shows, and he is also an active speaker. In the past decade, he has become more an institution than a working reporter; hence he delegates much of his actual "news-gathering" to subordinates. Some are seasoned newsmen who have worked elsewhere; some are journeymen willing to work for a pittance to earn a credit as "a former Jack Anderson associate"; some are interns from even the high school level. For the Wilson interviews, Anderson chose a controversial figure named Richard Bast.

A veteran private detective, Bast frequently works for the defense in criminal cases brought by the Federal Government. One of his prized techniques is digging up dirt on prosecution witnesses. His relationship with the Justice Department can only be described as adversarial. His clients over the years have included the Church of Scientology; Senator Harrison Williams of New Jersey, an Abscam convictee, and fixer Bobby Baker. The FBI arrested Bast in 1971 on a charge of selling illegal recording devices; to its embarrassment, the Justice Department found that he had violated no laws, and the case was dropped.

That Bast's background had made him a detested figure at the Justice Department and elsewhere did not disturb Anderson. "Dick Bast is a man who made a good deal of money on his own initiative, as a businessman, and who has the time and public spirit to devote his efforts to helping people who are in trouble," Anderson said. "Acting as an independent agent, he agreed to go to Tripoli and interview Ed Wilson for me. He passed back information that I used as the basis for my own questions when I would telephone Wilson. Bast was doing my legwork. And, of course, as I said, he was in Tripoli as an independent person."

Bast flew to Tripoli via Geneva in the fall of 1981 and spent several days talking with Wilson in his villa. Bast does not want to discuss the arrangements under which he met with Wilson; rather profanely, he told me it was none of my business, that "I waste a thousand dollars of my time every minute I talk with you." John Heath, who sat in on many of the Bast-Wilson meetings, and who heard Wilson recount the supposed substance of others, said the renegade agent had had one aim: to persuade Anderson to do a "political white-wash." Wilson told Heath that he needed $250,000 for "expenses" connected with the Anderson columns; he said he was trying to mortgage one or both of his farm properties in Britain to raise the money; whether the $250,000 was a partial or full payment, Wilson did not say. Anderson said that Wilson's claim as reported by Heath was "rubbish." Bast reacted with a profanity when Wilson's statement was read to him.

In the interviews that Heath monitored, Wilson repeated his standard claim about being a misunderstood businessman. Heath suppressed a smile when Wilson made the earnest protestation "I wouldn't know a terrorist if I met one." Several times, Wilson insisted that Heath outline for Bast his own role in the bomb-making, and how innocent the projects were. "I gave him the dog-and-pony show," Heath said, "and Ed went through his whole career. But if I were to say to you, 'My name is Ralph, I'm black and I'm a Catholic Jew,' I'd be less of a liar than Ed Wilson was on those tapes. It was all I could do to keep a straight face sometimes."

What did surprise Heath was that Wilson permitted

Bast to rummage through his files, apparently to gain information that Anderson would use as a basis for further telephone interviews and perhaps even a live interview in Tripoli. When Bast finally left, Wilson said, without amplification, "I can't get this thing going. I don't have the money up front to pay it."

Bast was to waft into and out of the Wilson case several times in the next months, generally in a capacity of attempting to find and use discrediting information about Wilson's enemies. By the time he was through, he had advanced an already unpopular reputation with the U.S. Department of Justice.

30

An Adventure in the Sudan

In retrospect, John Heath decided that Wilson's claim that he could "buy" Jack Anderson was the product of a mind increasingly demented by alcohol and the uncertainty of his future. By mid-1981, Wilson was drinking a quart or more of flash daily (a liquor, it will be remembered, that staggers most men after two or three highballs). Wilson would mix a huge tumbler of flash with orange or grapefruit juice and sip it constantly during the day, pausing often to refill the glass. Many days, Wilson was incoherent by midmorning. He would telephone Bobbi Barnes in London and speak gibberish; she learned to ignore him, for the next day, sober, he would not remember the fact of the "conversation," much less what he had said.

Wilson's mental confusion perhaps was responsible for what began as a bizarre attempt to shift his base of operations to the Sudan, and ended in a complicated double-cross that outraged both the Sudanese and the Libyans. "How we got out of that one without every one of us being marched to the wall still scares me late at night," John Heath was to remark two years later.

The sequence began with a chance meeting Ed Wilson had had in 1979 on a European flight with a Sudanese maritime captain named Elnour Zarroug. A strapping black Moslem, Elnour had been detailed by his government to try to develop the Sudanese fishing industry. The African nation with the largest land area (about one-quarter the size of the United States), the Sudan is also one of the poorest and most chronically hard-pressed to feed its population, which totals slightly more than 16 million. With Kuwaiti financial help, Elnour was seeking technical advice on how to improve primitive fishing fleets along the Sudan's 500 miles of Red Sea coast.

Wilson introduced himself to Elnour—he never passed up an opportunity to meet someone who might be of commercial interest—and the men chatted and exchanged cards. Elnour had an office in London, and he invited Wilson to drop by. "With your maritime background, perhaps we can do things for each other."

Wilson was politely noncommittal. Given his Libyan connection, he felt it unlikely he would ever do business with the Sudan, a bitter enemy of Quaddafi. Sudanese President Gaafar Mohamed Nimeiri had spent the first part of the 1970s on a tightrope between the West and Arab militants, the latter trying constantly to pressure him away from the United States. Quaddafi had targeted Nimeiri for overthrow after the Sudan accepted U.S. aid and refused to support Extreme Arabs on the obliteration of Israel. In 1976, a Quaddafi-sponsored army assaulted Khartoum, the Sudanese capital; more than 1,000 soldiers died on both sides during several days of fierce fighting before the insurgents fell back. Nimeiri had 81 rebels executed by firing squad, kicked out almost a hundred Soviet advisers whom he felt untrustworthy and aligned the Sudan even closer with the West. He was the only Moslem leader to side with President Anwar Sadat on the Camp David accords under which Egypt recognized Israel's right to exist.

Knowing this history, Wilson thought nothing more of Captain Elnour for two years, until Libya became an untenable sanctuary in 1981. Then one evening that spring, Diane

Byrne telephoned John Heath, who was in Liège enjoying an intense love affair with a Donnay employee, a beautiful Belgian woman named Michèle. The woman made him happy, especially now as an antidote to his severe dose of "Libyan fatigue."

"I hate to do this to you," Diane Byrne said, "but you're going to have to get on a plane tonight because you've got a meeting here in London tomorrow morning." All that Byrne knew of the man, she told Heath, was that "Ed thinks he's a fake, but you should meet with him anyway."

Heath flew to London and telephoned Wilson's contact—who proved to be Elnour. They arranged to meet in the lounge of the Chelsea Holiday Inn. "How will I know you?" Heath asked. Elnour chuckled. "Just ask Miss Byrne," he said. Heath questioned Diane, who said, "He's one of the ugliest creatures I've ever seen in my life. I call him Scarface."

Elnour was indeed easy to spot. An enormous man, he had three large tribal scars down each cheek. They talked in generalities, for Wilson had given Heath no guidelines as to what Elnour had in mind. The captain offered little guidance either. He said only that he had met Wilson, and hoped they could do "some business" of an unspecified nature. ("He always referred to Wilson as 'Eddie,'" Heath recalls. "He was the only person I ever heard use that name; it drove Ed crazy.") Elnour wished Heath to come to the Sudan for some meetings "with my minister." Heath just listened. "I didn't know who he was talking about. He just referred to the guy as 'the minister.' I didn't know whether it was foreign minister, prime minister or Baptist minister, although I was pretty sure it wasn't the last." Heath asked himself, What do we have to offer the Sudan? He and Elnour agreed to meet a few days later.

Heath telephoned Wilson. "I met your Sudanese captain," he said. "Just what the hell do you want me to do with him? What kind of business?"

"Goddamn it, I don't know," Wilson snapped. "Play it by ear. That's what I pay you for. Go in and listen and then react."

For their next meeting, Elnour told Heath to stand discreetly outside a London subway station. Heath complied, and shortly an eight-passenger Mercedes with diplomatic license plates pulled up. Elnour, evidently having satisfied himself that they were not under surveillance, beckoned him inside. Oh-oh, Heath thought, "we're dealing with the security boys." Knowing of the Sudan's blood feud with Quaddafi, he was nervous. The car drove to a safe house maintained by Sudanese intelligence in London, and Heath met the "minister," who proved to be Omar Mohammed el-Tayeb, the chief of intelligence and security.

Once Heath heard the title, he foresaw several business opportunities. "Possibly with our connections in Tripoli," he said, "we might even be able to help you with your diplomatic problems."

"Yes, I'd be very interested in that," el-Tayeb said. But for the moment, he wished to talk about physical security for President Nimeiri and his close aides. Heath offered to create, for the Sudan, the equivalent of the U.S. Secret Service (an organization he knew well from the days of his explosives work). After half an hour, el-Tayeb said, "Write me a proposal."

Heath's success surprised Wilson. "Was this guy real or not? Did he show you any kind of I.D.?" Heath smiled. "Ed, you're slipping. People like that don't show I.D.s." When Wilson heard that the Sudanese would pay plane fares for exploratory talks, he brightened. "Take somebody else with you. Hell, you could get run over by a car. I don't want you to be the only contact."

Heath drafted a proposal, and he suggested that Elnour spend a day at The Grange to discuss the specifics of a contract. Heath had taken up temporary residence at The Grange with Michèle, his Belgian fiancée, a woman of cool business judgment. Since Wilson was stranded in Libya, Heath wanted the support of someone he could trust.

Wilson had ordered Heath to work with John Dutcher, ostensibly to be nothing more than a bodyguard. That changed. "Dutcher began to smell big bucks in this deal," Heath said.

Dutcher came to the meeting in The Grange with his girlfriend, a law student named Daphne. Michèle sized up the situation quickly. "They're going to try to cut you out of this deal," Michèle cautioned Heath. "Be careful."

Daphne came on physically. She was wearing a loose

blouse unbuttoned many buttons down, she had neglected to
don a bra and her skirt was split, in Heath's words, "all the
way up to here." As she talked to Elnour she increasingly
leaned forward, offering her bosom to his alert eyes. Heath,
not a modest man, was surprised as "she showed me more
and more of her breasts," for he realized that for Moslems,
"that's definitely the wrong way for a woman to behave."
Elnour evidently felt the same. During a private moment
he told Michèle, "I know what Dutcher is doing. John has
nothing to worry about; I am to do the contract with
him."

The agreement eventually was that Wilson would open a
truck transportation company in the Sudan as cover for a
wide-ranging security operation intended to protect President Nimeiri and his inner circle from terrorists. A trucking
business would give Wilson's people cover for traveling anywhere in the country. Because the Sudan had only one other
truck company and one rail line (from Khartoum to the Red
Sea), a new, properly run company could turn a profit as well.
But because high Sudanese officials wanted to make a dollar
for themselves, Wilson would have to invest approximately
$500,000 in the cover company, in staggered payments. This
money would go to the Sudanese. Wilson would recoup the
sum several times over through the covert security contract.

To celebrate, the party went to a restaurant in the
English countryside. The sight of Elnour, with his flaring
tribal scars, caused a flutter among diners for whom such an
imposing black man was a rarity. Elnour looked around the
room, smiled broadly and waved; the gesture charmed the
British, and people smiled back at him. When the waiter took
his order, Elnour said he wished steak. "The outside," he
said, "must be black, like my arm. The inside I wish pink,
like the inside of my mouth," and he opened his lips wide.
The waiter did a local equivalent of a guffaw, and the day
ended a success.

For everyone save Dutcher. Elnour had decided he was
"no good" and shortly made it clear that he could not come to
the Sudan. Whereupon Dutcher wrote a letter to the Sudanese
Embassy in London charging that Heath was a Libyan intelligence agent who had made the contact with Elnour as part of
a plot to kill President Nimeiri. Dutcher signed the letter

with his own name. Fortunately for Heath, he had by then
become so close to Elnour that the Sudanese put no credence
in Dutcher's charge.

When Heath told him of the letter, Wilson snorted, "I'll
fix that son of a bitch, and in a way that is going to cause his
ass some pain." Wilson happened to know details of a gun-
smuggling plot in which Dutcher hoped to help some mercenaries overthrow the Government of Haiti and establish a
"free-trade zone" as a haven for gambling casinos and tax-
avoidance schemes. Wilson, in one of his more ironically
inspired moves, telephoned Jack Anderson, who wrote a
column that sent Dutcher diving for shelter; many months
passed before he dared travel on his own passport without
fear of arrest.

Heath went to Khartoum with another sometime Wilson
associate, Carl Mount. They received red-carpet treatment,
and Heath noted with pleasure that the Sudanese winked at
Moslemic strictures on alcohol. "There isn't any air conditioning
in the entire country, only lazy overhead fans. Beer did taste
good." The business discussions were with Captain Gossam
Ahmed Gossam, el-Tayeb's deputy. Gossam wanted an expanded security plan. He gave Heath and Mount detailed
intelligence information on the Libyan training camps for
terrorist operations against the Sudan, as well as names and
addresses of Sudanese opposition leaders in London and
Tripoli. The implication was that Wilson should find a way to
kill or otherwise neutralize these enemies. Wilson's connection with Libyan intelligence apparently posed no problem
for the Sudanese. And Gossam had some tempting bait: Since
the Sudan enjoyed favored status with the U.S. Government
for an African-Arabic nation, if Wilson would do the same
things for the Sudan as he had done for Libya, "they would
intercede for him" in Washington. Such an offer, Heath knew,
was exactly what would appeal to Wilson.

But some of the requests made by the Sudanese were
overly ambitious. They wanted an electronic surveillance
system along their border with Libya, to detect guerrilla
invaders. A glance at the map told Heath that this was
impossible. He explained, "You've got too much border. It
would cost you hundreds of millions of dollars." Heath finally
pinned down the primary Sudanese concern: control of three
bridges at the convergence of the Blue Nile and the White

Nile in the center of Khartoum. As the Sudanese had learned during the 1976 Libyan-backed attack on their capital, control of these bridges was essential. Other sensitive positions to be protected were the presidential palace, some military barracks, a sugar mill and three dams, the last-named important to the economy. Heath wrote a revised security plan; for a fee of £1,000, Wilson would send down a "survey team" to work out the final details. The "team" would consist of Heath, for physical security, and Alex Raffio, for the electronics portion.

When Heath returned to Libya, he was dismayed to find that Raffio had chosen this exact time to make his final of many exits from the Wilson organization. Ed Wilson had not paid him money due on contracts; his former wife had him under a criminal contempt-of-court citation for nonpayment of child support; the FBI was harassing his parents with calls. Raffio had disappeared. Heath made a halfhearted attempt to find him. ("Go to his house [in London] and kick in the fucking door" was Wilson's order, which Heath ignored.)

Heath's report excited Wilson. Perhaps he had found a way to get out of Libya. Heath scurried between Tripoli, London and Geneva, reactivating a company named Gerex that Wilson had formed some time before, meeting with lawyers and moneylenders, and briefing the Sudanese. The final arrangement, a deliberate corporate snarl, specified as prime contractor an offshore company based on the Isle of Jersey; this company, in turn, would be controlled by a Liberian corporation. "That way," Heath said, "you could pretty well funnel off everything."

Heath's negotiations pleased Wilson, who saw endless economic opportunities in the Sudan. Drillers were beginning to find significant deposits of oil, which meant a source of revenue, but the Sudan's economic infrastructure was a mess. The country needed roads, a new airport, bridges, housing development. Wilson saw, fleetingly, a chance to achieve what he had sought to do in Libya: to transform a nation's economy and earn himself a fortune. This time, he told Bobbi Barnes, he would not be sidetracked by grubby assassination plots and covert arms deals.

Wilson asked Barnes to go to the Sudan as his emissary, to finish the contracts that Heath had drafted. Although Barnes has not said so, the circumstantial evidence is that Wilson suspected Heath might cut him out. He knew that

Heath was unhappy at the forced stay in Tripoli, and that
Heath had so tight a personal relationship with Elnour that
he could likely take away the contract himself.

So Bobbi Barnes went to Khartoum to talk bribes. There
would be "administrative expenses" involved in setting up
the contracts; thus Wilson would post hundreds of thousands of dollars to compensate the Sudanese for the use of
their "valuable time." Beneath this charade was the knowledge that the money would go from Wilson's Swiss bank account directly to the Swiss bank accounts of the Sudanese.

Barnes had come to Khartoum hoping it would provide
a final and comfortable refuge for herself and Wilson. But
after several days in the Sudan, she was not eager to stay.
"Khartoum was far nicer than Tripoli, with green palm
trees and serenity you did not find in Libya. Go outside
town a few miles, though, and YICH! I told Ed that he
might live down there, but that *no way* was I leaving
London to set up house in the jungle."

Heath made a second visit, during which the Sudanese—
especially Captain Gossam—made it plain that they "knew"
Ed Wilson worked for the Central Intelligence Agency. Here
is a mystery. "Of course, Ed tried to give this impression to
everyone," Heath said; but Minister Omar el-Tayeb, the
person making the decision on the contracts, never met
Wilson personally. However the Sudanese gained their
"knowledge," Heath seized the opportunity. With his own
survival at stake—knowing he faced criminal prosecution if
forced to return to the United States—he worked hard for
Wilson. "The best job I ever did of selling anything was
selling Ed Wilson to Omar," Heath said. "I had him so
convinced he said, 'You know, I never met Wilson, but I
like him and I know you and if he's anything like you
personally, I know I will like him. We're going to do
everything we can to help him out.'"

Now commenced the most delicate phase of the talks.
Minister el-Tayeb told Heath that the Sudan could make
serious overtures in Wilson's behalf to Vice President George
Bush and Secretary of State Alexander Haig. "I need to know
more first," ed-Tayeb told Heath. "Ask Ed to write out the
details of his legal problems." As Heath outlined Wilson's
expectation:

"It basically was going to be set up like this. If Ed came there and was not involved in any more hanky-panky sneaky nefarious deals, and he kept his nose clean for, let's say, a period of two years, maybe the States would decide to drop some of the charges. Ed would like to be able to come to the States once again with a guarantee of safety to visit his children and his farm. He guaranteed he would do so unobtrusively and not cause the United States Government any embarrassment. Of course, he wanted to try to get the charges against him dropped."

Heath outlined these wishes to el-Tayeb, who was infuriatingly noncommittal. There was a barrier of "a rather nice hunk of cash." Through Captain Gossam, el-Tayeb let it be known that he expected half a million dollars, to be paid in increments through foreign accounts. Wilson lacked ready cash. He already had The Grange on the market; now he pushed Ed Coughlin, his Geneva lawyer, to hurry along any deal that materialized. The Grange did not attract a buyer. Wilson became desperate. To get into the Sudan, he needed a sum that a year earlier he could have found in petty cash. So he tried to trim the Sudan contract. He studied Heath's plan for a trucking company that would be the cover organization for the planned security operation. "What do you need so many trucks for?" Wilson asked. "Can't you get by on just one truck?"

Wilson's logic staggered Heath. "Goddamn it, Ed, we're talking a big country, where eight hundred companies are standing in line for a license to run a trucking company. You go to the head of the line, and you run one piddly truck, and you're so obvious you might as well put a light on your head." Heath did agree to reexamine the figures. Captain Elnour, his original contact, a man with shipping experience, was dismayed. "This is where we began to lose the Sudanese," Heath said. Wilson would go for more than one truck, but the others must be "reconditioned vehicles."

Heath sensed that the entire deal was going sour, that Wilson was retrenching for reasons that he was not stating, even to Heath.

Heath's intuition was correct. In the fall of 1981, President Anwar Sadat of Egypt was killed. Within two days,

Wilson was on the phone to Heath in Khartoum.* Talking in pidgin code phrases ("that guy" . . . "the guy up North"), he said the Libyans were interested in supporting a coup in which el-Tayeb would depose Nimeiri, who was in Cairo for Sadat's funeral. "They'd like to talk with him about working together and solving some of the mutual problems between the two countries and maybe he would step in," Wilson put it. "He's acceptable to them and there's no strings attached."

Heath spent several days on the telephone, cautiously sounding out trusted Sudanese as to whether they would support an el-Tayeb coup if it meant rapprochement between Libya and the Sudan. Through Captain Gossam, el-Tayeb expressed an interest, although in an altruistic manner—"for the good of both countries." Gossam was enthusiastic. He told Heath, "I will use all my influence and pressure, because he [el-Tayeb] is the only man who can control the North and the South [the ethnically diverse parts of the Sudan] and the military as well." Other Arab nations also thought well of el-Tayeb.

In an attempt to give himself yet another option in the Sudan, Wilson sought to involve the Soviet Union in his scheme. Concurrent with his work on the Sudan, Wilson was negotiating with a veteran international spook named Ernest

---

*The Sadat assassination may not have come as a total surprise to Ed Wilson, given certain guests he entertained at his villa in the late summer of 1981—a group of Arabs who asked keen questions about a project in which Wilson had had fleeting involvement four years earlier.

In the late 1970s, Retired Brigadier General J. J. Cappucci, a former ranking officer at Air Force intelligence, had worked with Wilson to obtain a contract for the personal security of Sadat. What the Egyptians needed—and Cappucci provided—was routine protective measures.

The Arabs who talked with Wilson in 1981 asked for details of Sadat's security screen. It is doubtful that Wilson had anything to tell them, for while he knew about the Cappucci contract, he was ignorant of its details. The Arabs thanked Wilson, and left.

Since this occurred at a time when Wilson was trying to mend his fences with the U.S. Government—offering such "intelligence" as the bogus atomic-bomb plot in an illusory effort to pave the way for a deal and a possible return to the United States—his failure to report the Arabs' visit is at best puzzling, at worst ominous. Two classes of persons would have had an interest in the security of the Egyptian President: those bent upon protecting him, and those intending to kill him. Given the anti-Egyptian climate that permeated Libya, Wilson must have known that he had talked with the latter.

Two weeks later Moslem fanatics gunned down President Sadat during a military review. Colonel Muamar Quaddafi hailed his death as "a victory for the Moslem revolution."

Keiser on a supposed agreement that would bring him back into the fold of American intelligence, in charge of certain operations in Central America (a negotiation detailed in Chapter 34). According to Keiser, "When I met Ed in Tripoli, he asked me to make contact with a KGB representative in London. This KGB man handled liaison with the PLO and other Arabic groups. Ed wanted to bring the Russians into the Sudan as part of his deal if necessary." Wilson went so far as to schedule a time and place for Keiser to meet the KGB agent in London. Keiser refused. "I wanted nothing to do with the KGB, and especially not for Ed Wilson," he stated.

Wilson's instigation of a plot to overthrow Nimeiri was more than casual mercenary mischief. It would have undone years of careful diplomatic work in one of the world's most sensitive areas. Nimeiri had broken with the Arab block with considerable personal bravery, for his alignment with the West made him a target in every terrorist gunsight in the Middle East.

Fortunately, the plot stalled because of indecision on the part of el-Tayeb. Heath heard a succession of excuses from Gossam and other Sudanese officers. The minister did not think the time opportune; he wanted to "marshal his forces"; he could not "just jump up and do it now."

When the Libyans learned of el-Tayeb's reluctance to move, they set into motion an elaborate plot that they thought would force him to assassinate President Nimeiri to save his own life. The Libyans moved with skill and guile. First, they persuaded Heath to have el-Tayeb write a letter to a Colonel Karubi, of Libyan intelligence, asking him to a meeting at el-Tayeb's private residence in London. The ostensible purpose was to talk about rapprochement between the two countries.

Actually, the Libyans had no intention of carrying out any such meeting. Such was made plain to Heath when he carried el-Tayeb's invitation to Tripoli. He told the Libyans that el-Tayeb expected an answer within forty-eight hours. Nothing happened for a week. Finally, Wilson enlightened Heath as to the cross-treachery afoot.

"I've given the Libyans a full memorandum about all our dealings in the Sudan, and the *baksheesh* [bribes] we were paying for the deals," Wilson said. "I'm using this whole thing as leverage to get my $4.7 million [a contract claim] out of the Libyans. If this deal goes off, I get it." Wilson said he had included in the memorandum the statement that el-Tayeb was "not going to take this risk and pull a coup and take over the government for free. He's from a poor country and the Libyans have all the oil money. He'll do it for a half a million."

Heath was stunned. "What are you talking about? I've heard nothing from el-Tayeb about any half a million dollars. He tells me he would do this [the coup] for the good of the Sudan. He never mentioned money." Heath felt as if he'd been stabbed in the back.

The Libyans sent an emissary to tell el-Tayeb the new terms. They no longer wanted a coup; they now demanded that he kill President Nimeiri. If he did not do so, they intended to release to the world press an array of documents that would display him as a traitor: Wilson's reports of his back-door dealings with Heath in behalf of a coup; the invitation to meet a Libyan intelligence officer in London; papers telling of the half-million-dollar payment. With Wilson's active assistance, the Libyans had concocted a classic blackmail scheme. But the unpredictable term in the equation proved to be el-Tayeb.

"Somehow he survived," Heath was to marvel later. "His government got the whole package of documents; he talked his way through it; he managed to save his skin." Several weeks later el-Tayeb sent word to Heath that he wished to resume discussions of the original deal—to provide security for the Sudanese capital—and asked that he meet Captain Elnour in London.

Given Wilson's role in the double-cross—one that could have cost el-Tayeb his life—Heath did long and hard thinking before meeting Elnour again, even on the relatively safe ground of London. He concluded that Elnour and el-Tayeb had no reason to distrust him personally. Besides, the Sudanese had offered to issue both him and Wilson diplomatic passports to facilitate their travel through Europe, Africa and the Middle East. For Wilson, who had just lost his American passport, the Sudanese document was vital.

But Heath was due a final jolt. When he got to Elnour's office, the Sudanese shook his head sadly and pushed a thick folder of papers across his desk. Heath skimmed through the documents. They were intelligence reports Wilson had written to the Libyans, relating in great detail Heath's observations about the inner secrets of the Sudanese security system.* Heath had elicited this information when writing his proposal on how to provide better security for such places as the presidential palace and the chief government office buildings. Nausea swept over Heath as he read the papers. "What Ed had done was tell the Libyans the best way to go about killing the president of a country friendly to the United States," he said. "If Nimeiri had been killed by a Libyan hit team, Wilson would have been as guilty as if he had pulled the trigger himself. Having worked with the Secret Service around the White House, I knew this was the most sensitive sort of information that a government could have—and especially when Quaddafi had already tried to kill Nimeiri in the past."

Tears were welling in Elnour's eyes when Heath dared look up at him. "Why did you do this to me?" the Sudanese cried. "Why did Eddie do this to me? We're friends. We're doing nothing but trying to help him to cure his problem, to make business for him, to help me, to help you. Why have you done this to me?"

Heath did not answer. "I could not answer."

"I am now *persona non grata* in my own country," Elnour continued. "I cannot go back to my country. Eddie has cut all our throats."

When the painful encounter ended, Heath knew he had lost more than a business deal; he had lost the trust of a friend. He flew back to Tripoli and told Wilson of the denouement of the Sudan affair.

"Don't worry," Wilson said; "no problem. I've got a lot of things going. Hey, how about fixing us a big orange, old buddy?" Wilson reached for the bottle of flash.

---

*Heath never established to his full satisfaction how the reports got from Wilson's files to the Sudanese. All Elnour would say was that they had been given to the Sudanese Ambassador in Washington. Two outsiders had access to Wilson's files in Tripoli shortly after the time the reports were written: Richard Bast, the private investigator, and Ernest Keiser, a businessman/spook of whom more shall be said. Either man could have passed them to officials in Washington for transmission to the Sudanese.

31

A PLO Flirtation

The Federal indictments in April 1980 had caused Edwin Wilson problems in Libya. For four years he had posed in Tripoli as an American insider who could obtain what was needed from the United States. Now, for the first time, the Libyans made a calculated appraisal of what Wilson had promised, and what he had delivered. The balance was not in Wilson's favor. The Libyans began to see Wilson as more of an embarrassment than an asset. "They told him, in effect, that he had outlived his usefulness," Alex Raffio said.

Wilson quietly began putting out feelers for a new base of operations, and a client to replace Quaddafi. Hence, Wilson's Sudanese adventure. And hence, too, his receptivity when directed, unwittingly at first, toward the Palestine Liberation Organization (PLO).

Despite their common interest in obliterating Israel and restoring the Palestinians to their historic homeland, relations between the PLO and the Libyan Government had been politely formal, even cool. The PLO balked at Quaddafi's attempts to impose policy controls and dictate their strategic course. Although he had offered the PLO arms and money, they refused to become financially dependent upon Libya. Weaker Arab nations—Kuwait, the United Arab Emirates, Oman—willingly give their oil money to the PLO with no strings attached. Nonetheless, the PLO maintained a covert presence in Libya. And unbeknownst to Ed Wilson, one of the key PLO operatives in Tripoli was a nondescript man who worked in his own office—"Zak" Zacharias. Fluent in several languages including English, well versed in the byways of

Libyan laws and bureaucratic procedures, effusively gregarious, Zacharias was an essential expediter for the Wilson organization. It was Zak who could get an incoming Green Beret through the Tripoli airport, or find a repairman to fix the electricity in the villa, or obtain an appointment with a procurement functionary.

Such was Zak's overt life. His secret purpose in Tripoli was to penetrate the Libyan military and intelligence hierarchy in the guise of an expatriate Palestinian who "might be of service." Such Wilson associates as Alex Raffio (who learned of Zak's role belatedly) doubt that the Libyans were aware of Zak's dual role. "Ed Wilson certainly didn't know," Raffio says.

In March 1980, Wilson asked Zak an open-ended question. Zak knew the Middle East, and its politics. Could he suggest a new country where Wilson might live and continue to make international business deals?

As Wilson reconstructed the scenario later in long talks with Raffio, Zak decided to recommend to his superiors that Wilson be taken under PLO protection. Zak felt that Wilson could use his connections to help the PLO in its own operations—that the same explosives, electronic gear and armament that Wilson sold to the Libyans could just as well go to the PLO.

Another matter of concern to Wilson was his safety should the Quaddafi regime be toppled by a coup. Although Quaddafi ran a tight police state, with security forces trained and augmented by East German "advisers," the remnants of the Libyan middle and upper classes opposed his government vehemently. As John Heath put it, "We were a little worried about what would happen to us, whether we would be considered as neutrals or as the guys who were supplying Quaddafi with guns and other things." Any deal with the PLO must guarantee Wilson and his men protection.

In any event, a few days after his approach to Zacharias, Wilson was taken to a meeting in a PLO safe house in a slum apartment in the middle of downtown Tripoli. With ten flats spread over several floors and many entrances to the congested streets on either side, the building seemed to have been built with discreet meetings in mind. At this first meeting, Wilson was offered a deal: If he would go to work for the PLO, the PLO would guarantee him sanctuary in a country of its choice, probably Lebanon or Malta. Wilson's expertise and equipment would give the PLO a degree of independence from the Soviet bloc for its supplies (Wilson was not foolish enough to think that the PLO was renouncing Communist support; it simply desired a "second force" with which to whipsaw its other friends).

Wilson called Raffio into his office soon after the meeting, closed the door and said in a low, firm voice, "Listen, I'm going to tell you something now which involves the most precious thing to me in the world: my life. I am having more and more problems, as you know, in the United States. Zak has introduced me to a group of people who can help me. I'm going to introduce you to them as part of the *quid pro quo*, where you can help them because they're helping me. If you breathe a word of this to Bobbi, to Heath, to anyone in this organization, you're a dead man."

"What is the 'group of people'?" Raffio asked.

"The PLO," Wilson replied.

"Oh, hell, I'm really elated, Ed; that's the best news I've heard in years," Raffio exclaimed. "You must be out of your goddamned mind!" He told Wilson he would not raise a hand to help the PLO. "But Ed wasn't taking any 'no's' that day," Raffio said. "He told me to shut up, that he wanted me to go to another meeting with these people."

The next day, Raffio went with Wilson to a "noisy smelly fourth-floor apartment where these PLO guys had their headquarters." The PLO spokesman—obviously Zak's superior—was a thickly bearded man in a rumpled suit. He seemed content to let Wilson do the talking.

"Mister Alex here is my electronics and electro-optics expert," Wilson said. "He is internationally recognized as one of the best men in his field, anywhere. Since you are offering a favor to me, I offer you Mister Alex's services in return." (Under his breath, Raffio murmured, "Like hell you do.")

Wilson told Raffio to detail some of the projects he had carried out for the Libyans. Raffio responded in as cryptic a fashion as possible. He had no intention of going to work for the PLO, fearing that if Libyan intelligence heard of the meetings and disclosures of his secret work, he was likely to be shot. Wilson, desperate for sanctuary, didn't consider any

such fears. He proceeded to outline the entire course of
Raffio's work, adding fictitious details from time to time to
enhance the story.

The meeting ended with the PLO people making no
commitments; obviously, they had to talk to their superiors.
"I think we have ourselves a deal under way," Wilson told
Raffio as they drove back to Wilson's villa. Speak for yourself,
Ed, Raffio thought. I'm cutting out as soon as I reach London
and get the money you owe me.

Wilson did have the sense to realize that the PLO
stratagem would leave him a prisoner of persons he could not
control. Thus he took some precautionary actions. He had his
Geneva lawyer, Edward J. Coughlin, open accounts in a
Luxembourg bank and transfer all his money there. (The
Swiss never moved against Wilson; eventually, his money was
returned to the Swiss banks.)

When Interpol arrest warrants followed the U.S. indictments, Wilson was trapped within Libya; if he went to
Europe, he could be seized and returned to the United
States. "This was devastating to Ed," Raffio said. "He had to
be able to get out, to make phone calls, to do things not
under Libyan surveillance, to have meetings with people who
wouldn't come to Libya."

So Wilson tried to get a false passport. Through a source
that he kept to himself, he learned of a British ring that could
obtain perhaps half a dozen genuine United Kingdom passports a year. (One reputed earlier client of this ring had been
Ronald Briggs, a principal in the 1963 "Great Train Robbery"
that netted $7 million cash; Briggs managed to escape to
Australia, then South America.) The documents were produced to order by a confederate within the government
passport office, and have been described by John Heath as
"absolutely perfect . . . with government seals. They [the ring]
demand a great deal of detail about the person who's going to
get one, so that the description matches and there is good
family history. It's not a cemetery scam."

Wilson first asked Bobbi Barnes to pick up the passport
for him. She refused. "I don't want anything to do with that,"
she told Wilson. So then Heath drew the assignment. He
met the contact, a sometime aircraft flight engineer, and they
drove from Heathrow Airport in the direction of Windsor

Castle. "These people are very careful," the engineer explained
to Heath. "We will stop at one of these roadside rest places
and telephone. They'll have spotted us with a minimum of
two cars. We'll never see the cars, but they want to make
sure we're not followed." When they stopped, the engineer
let Heath listen to the telephone conversation. The engineer
described their location and added, "You can pick us up
anytime coming on in."

The voice on the other end said, "We've already got you.
Your passenger has gray hair and he smokes Marlboros."
Heath shook his head in admiration: someone had been close
enough to spot his brand of cigarette.

The engineer drove to the parking lot of a roadside
restaurant, vacant save for one car. A man sat behind the
wheel with a road map, as if trying to find directions. The
engineer got out with a map of his own and went over and
talked to the man. The maps changed hands. When the
engineer returned, he dropped the map on the seat beside
Heath. It contained a brand-new United Kingdom passport
with Wilson's photograph and false identification data. "We'll
take it," Heath said. The engineer returned to the other car
and passed £2,000 to the driver, concealed in a newspaper.

As they drove back to Heathrow, the engineer told
Heath, "You know, I went through a lot of risk on this deal. I
think I need some more money." Heath called Wilson. "Ed
told him to go suck a bone or something—he refused to pay. I
said, 'Well, Ed, it's a pretty good piece of paper, and Lord
knows but you need it.' He wouldn't listen. He couldn't stand
to be taken, even when he was desperate."

In the early summer of 1980, the PLO representative in
Tripoli told Wilson that he could travel to Malta—some 400
miles distant from Libya—with impunity. He claimed that
the PLO had so much influence in Malta that Wilson would
not be arrested, and that the PLO and the Maltese Government, working together, would "put you under our wing."
Zak also promised Wilson protection in the event the Quaddafi
government was overthrown. According to Heath, Zak told
Wilson, "There is no problem. If anything happens, you will
be taken out of here [Libya] immediately. My people will
provide you with everything you need." To Heath, who heard
this promise in the company of Wilson, Zak's statement was
"a very firm commitment."

Wilson flew to Malta perhaps half a dozen times in the summer of 1980, all without incident. Bobbi Barnes met him on several occasions; they inspected villas, and Wilson purchased a particularly attractive place that had a large swimming pool. Bobbi liked Malta; it was cleaner than Libya, more sophisticated than the Sudan, and it lacked the political paranoia endemic in a revolutionary Moslem society. For several happy weeks, Wilson seemed to come alive again. He could do business from Malta, which had modern Telex and telephone service, and business associates could fly there easily from Europe. Wilson made a halfhearted attempt to conceal these trips from many of the persons who worked for him. "I'm going up to Benghazi for a few days," he would say. He fooled no one.

One frequent visitor to Wilson's Malta villa was the Washington lawyer Kenneth E. Conklin, who had represented various Wilson corporations and business ventures since the mid-1970s. According to Bobbi Barnes, who was present at the meeting, Conklin talked about the procedures to follow to get a U.S. passport under a false name. Conklin, Barnes said, suggested getting the birth certificate of someone who was dead and using it "as appearing that the man was still alive." Conklin told Wilson the expenses and fee would be around $25,000. (Conklin later said that although Wilson had asked him about a false passport, he had never offered to help him obtain one.) But the chief reason for this three visits to Malta in mid-1980, Conklin maintains, was to advise Wilson as to "what countries had extradition treaties with the United States." By keeping away from these countries, Wilson could avoid arrest and extradition.

Larry Barcella, meanwhile, continued to put former Wilson employees before the grand jury in Washington, seeking additional details for the prosecution. His knowledge of the inner workings of the Wilson organization was by now so deep that he knew which men were visiting his adversary regularly. One of these persons said to Barcella in an interview before testifying, "You know, Wilson's not around Libya much anymore."

"Oh?" Barcella said.

"Yeah, he spends a lot of his time running back and forth to Malta. He even says he likes it so much he might start living there."

Within the hour, Barcella had an arrest order en route to Malta. Authorities there arrested Wilson on August 18, 1980. But then, examining his wallet, they found a piece of paper covered with Arabic script. In translation, it read as follows:

Mr. Ed Wilson

The above-named is of American nationality and works under the authority of the Ministry of Military Intelligence. Please render him any assistance possible within the limits of the law.

Mohammed Abdullah Hijazzi
17 Rashan 1318 AH
31 August 1977

"This obviously made the Maltese authorities nervous," Raffio said. "Libya is a lot closer and potentially a more hostile neighbor than the United States could ever be. They read this note in Wilson's wallet and realized that with a permit signed by Abdullah Hijazzi, Wilson was fairly important in Libya, if not an actual agent of Libyan intelligence. They saw that they might have committed a grave *faux pas* diplomatically vis-à-vis their relations with Libya."

For almost twenty-four hours after his arrest, no one in Wilson's organization knew his whereabouts. When he did not make an expected telephone call to London, Bobbi Barnes Telexed Libya, asking whether Wilson had been heard form. Barnes busied herself on the telephone; she soon found that Wilson was in a jail cell, and she sent a coded Telex to Tripoli telling of the arrest.

Wilson had long prepared for such an eventuality. His plan was to keep the news of any arrest from the Libyans, lest they cancel his remaining contracts. Wilson had given Steve Streeter a letter delegating him as *de facto* head of the Tripoli office, empowered to sign checks and make necessary decisions.

Streeter quietly summoned Wilson's Americans to the villa office and told them that despite Wilson's absence—he did not give the reason—business would continue as usual. There was shock, but no panic; everyone knew that Wilson had been squirming to avoid arrest; many persons sensed he had been caught. There was a brief rebellion by Bob Hitchman, head of the aviation program. "No one is giving orders to my pilots," he said. "That is my operation."

"I am not in charge of pilots," Streeter replied. "I am in charge of Mr. Wilson's business until he returns." No further clashes developed.

The great fear was that Wilson would be detained indefinitely. Streeter did not want to inherit the business by default. He still had problems about many phases of it, and as long as Wilson was present, Streeter had a buffer between him and the Libyans' dirty work; with Wilson gone, Streeter knew he would be the man ordered to arrange murders and manufacture bombs. Streeter decided to stay in Libya a few weeks and see what happened. Enough money was on hand to meet the payroll and other continuing expenses. But when the till began to run low after a week, Streeter (at Bobbi Barnes's direction) lied to Fadal of the defense ministry: "I honestly don't know where Mister Ed is." Fadal was shown Wilson's letter delegating authority to Streeter and replied, "Don't worry, your payments will continue." In anxious Telexes from London, Bobbi stressed the importance of the Americans' maintaining occupancy of the villas; lose it, she said, and the Wilson organization would no longer have a base in Libya.

Although the U.S. Embassy pressured Malta to extradite Wilson, Maltese officials stalled. They required more documentation from Washington. Their own legal procedures must be followed. Wilson fretted in jail for ten days. At least one sizable package of money—$29,000 is the amount mentioned by Barnes—was smuggled to him. One of the persons who assembled the package and got it into Malta told me, "My feeling is that he bought his way out; but Ed always said later the Maltese got chicken; they were scared of the Libyans, so they turned him loose. I don't know. The money disappeared, anyway." Around midnight on August 28, Wilson was suddenly removed from his cell and put aboard a flight to London. As a gesture toward the Americans, Maltese officials did cable British immigration that their quarry was en route—something Raffio feels was meaningless. "He's arriving in the middle of the night. The Telex goes into a bin with dozens of pieces of paper that some immigration bureaucrat is going to get around to reading after his second cup of tea in the morning."

Wilson got through customs and immigration with a ruse

that he and his associates used scores of times in their years of operation. On his landing card, he wrote "In Transit" and listed a flight to another European city that would be departing a few hours after his arrival from Malta. A passenger who makes such a declaration does not go through immigration, although a watch book at the customs desk should contain his name. Raffio, no stranger to the ruse, explains, "It's optional whether the British civil servant has to check his book. Wilson is wearing a business suit; he looks okay. So he is lucky, and the Brit doesn't check the book. I used to do the same thing continually. I would enter London two or three times a month for six years. Two or three times out of ten trips, the guy would check the book. It gives you an idea of the Russian roulette game you're playing."*

Wilson walked on through the airport; if he had any luggage, he did not bother to retrieve it. Technically, someone should have challenged him when he walked out of the transit lounge. But as Raffio explains, "By putting down 'in transit,' you just tell the guy you're going over to Terminal Two for a couple of hours to kill time. That doesn't bother him because Heathrow is so scattered. You can do that—it's permissible."

Wilson walked out onto the sidewalk, hailed a cab and rode to Piccadilly Circus. He telephoned Bobbi Barnes and told her, "Go over to the Portman Hotel and get the largest and most expensive suite they have. I'll join you once you're checked in." Wilson figured that the police would be unlikely to look for a fugitive in one of London's most lavish hotels, and he was right. He stayed there the next ten days while making arrangements to sneak back to Libya.

---

*Raffio routinely committed to memory numbers of flights that left Heathrow for the Continent at various times of day: "If you put down that you're proceeding on to Holland on KLM flight so-and-so, you're less likely to be checked. The best time to get away with this scam is in the middle of the morning when Heathrow is operating at 120 percent of capacity and people are lined up to go through their immigration booth maybe twenty, thirty in a row. When Wilson came in, there were probably only two or three other flights flying in. Wilson was just lucky."

Facing arrest himself in New York for nonpayment of child support, Raffio devised his own means of sneaking into the United States. He would fly from Europe to Toronto, then scout the car-rental agencies until he found one with an auto with New York State license plates. Raffio would drive across the American border in the guise of a short-term tourist or business traveler, waving his New York driver's license to an uninterested agent for identification.

Shielding his identity as much as possible, Wilson through intermediaries chartered a small plane for the flight back to Libya—by way of Sardinia, for refueling. The pilot, Mike Lucker, had flown for Wilson in the past; Raffio considered him "flaky, but competent." By now Barcella and the Justice Department knew Wilson was in Britain and were pressing the police to find and arrest him, so Wilson had to avoid immigration controls, even in the private plane. As a ruse, Lucker listed him on his flight plan as "flight engineer," and Wilson slipped onto the craft as it sat on the tarmac at Gatwick Airport.

All week Wilson had stressed the urgency of the flight. "We can't have any slip-ups," he told Lucker. "If we do, buddy, I go to jail—but I'm going to kick your ass first." Lucker assured him the aircraft was in good condition.

To Wilson's horror, Lucker could not get the engine started. "The starter motor seems busted," he said.

"Well, get the hell out and *fix it!*" Wilson screamed. He knew that the longer the plane sat on the tarmac, the greater the risk that airport authorities would become suspicious about the deliberately inconspicuous "flight engineer." After a long wait, the engine rumbled to life, and Lucker managed a weak smile at the glowering Wilson. They left the United Kingdom without further incident.

But, incredibly, another problem arose in Sardinia. Lucker had neglected to get the proper insurance on the plane, and Sardinian authorities refused to let the plane depart without it. Because this was on a weekend, Lucker had no place to turn to in Sardinia to buy the required policy. The resourceful Wilson telephoned London and in couched phrases told one of the office employees the problem. Within an hour, the Telex machine in the airport clicked out a message, supposedly from an insurance broker, giving the number and effective dates of a "policy" for the aircraft. The message was bogus, a creation of the Wilson employee in London. But it satisfied the Sardinians, and Wilson continued on his flight.

Word that Wilson was free and en route to Tripoli reached the Americans there in the form of a terse, coded Telex: "Red Ball Express." There was a burst of elation, and everyone prepared for a gala welcoming party. "You would have thought Ed was King Tut, the way he was greeted," said

Gloria Streeter. "Everyone showed up." Even the Libyans came around to pay their respects, briefly. Once they left, Wilson broke out the flash, and the Americans settled down to an evening of raucous drinking. Around two in the morning, the diehard guests left and the Streeters went off to bed, leaving Wilson—"smashed out of his mind"—with the pilot, Lucker, who was babbling incoherently.

An hour or so later, Wilson came into the Streeters' bedroom and woke them. He was wobbly drunk. "Get up," he said; "I have a problem. I hit Lucker. I may have killed him. Check him out. See if he's dead."

Lucker was on the floor, "the side of his face bashed in," Streeter said. "Blood was everywhere. He was breathing, but barely." The Streeters could do little for him in the middle of the night other than ensure that the blood did not clog his nasal passages. They wiped up what blood they could, and put Lucker on a rug in a back bedroom. "He was so drunk I couldn't rouse him," Streeter said, "so I decided the best thing to do was let him sleep it off, worry about it in the morning."

Streeter then turned to Wilson. "What the hell happened?" he said. "You came near to killing this man."

Wilson explained that he had gotten Lucker drunk to see what kind of fee he could bargain for the charter flight from London. Lucker had asked for $100,000 to $250,000, which Wilson considered extortion. Wilson felt that Lucker was threatening to report him to British authorities if he did not pay the demanded amount, which could have led to British confiscation of the aircraft. By Wilson's account, the drunken Lucker suddenly fell to the floor and began licking Wilson's feet and murmuring how much he admired him.

"A goddamned foot fetish!" Wilson said. "He was trying to get his rocks off by licking my goddamned feet. I pulled him up and hit him as hard as I ever hit a man in my life. Bastard! What a creep!" Wilson ordered Streeter to "get him out of the country first thing in the morning."

Streeter managed to get Lucker awake around 6 A.M. The man's eyes were blackened, his nose and jaw broken, his cheekbone shattered so severly it left a depression in his face. He professed to have no memory of how he had been injured. "What happened to me?" he asked Streeter again and again. "Ed and I were sitting there drinking, and I suddenly wake up like this." Streeter related what Wilson had told him about the foot-licking. Lucker shook his head. "I just don't remember," he said. "I was drunk out of my mind."

The Libyans were at first reluctant to let someone leave their country in such battered condition, but Streeter insisted that Lucker needed medical attention he could receive only in London. So Lucker left, nursing his battered face. "As he went up the ramp, the last thing he said was 'What the hell happened?'"

Instead of the demanded fee of $100,000 to $250,000, Lucker got $2,000—about enough to cover his medical bills. Bobbi Barnes met Lucker at the London airport, paid him off and took him to a doctor. She called Wilson and demanded angrily that he give Lucker extra money; he was "dangerous" because he knew many details of how Wilson had managed to evade law enforcement officers. Wilson shrugged off her protests, and Lucker got no more money.

32

"Ed, Get Me Out of Here"

By the end of 1980, Bobbi Barnes's love for Ed Wilson had soured, although not quite to the point where she wished him out of her life. Many problems tormented Barnes. Although she had tried to keep her distance from Wilson's criminal activities, she had done several things that she knew put her at risk of criminal indictment. Federal investigators from the United States had made repeated attempts to interrogate her; she had always refused, and many days she kept away from the Wilson offices so that she would not have to confront U.S. agents directly. "Bobbi got into the bottle quite heavily," recollected Alex Raffio. "She would come into the office in the morning with a whiskey breath that would make you turn your face away. She looked awful." Her secret involvement in Wilson's escape from Malta through England made her wary of troubles with British authorities. Bobbi's overriding fear was that should she be arrested, she would lose custody of her son. And when she needed Wilson the most, for psychic support, his fear of arrest kept him from being at her side, other than during her hurried, unsatisfactory trips to Tripoli.

Her role as Wilson's *woman*, rather than Wilson's *wife*, grated on Bobbi. She tried to ignore the leering winks when she would come to Tripoli for a few days and Wilson ordered everyone to move out of the villa for the duration. A couple of times she told Wilson, "I'll work for you, but nothing else," and kept Wilson from her bed. But the breaks did not last more than a few days, and "then we'd be back together again."

Since 1979, Wilson and Bobbi had talked frequently about marriage. "Ed cared for me; I cared for Ed, deeply. He was a man you could hate, but he was also a man you could really love. He was strong, he was smart and when he wasn't drinking he could be fun to be around. I admired what he had done in life."

But each time Bobbi brought up specific marriage plans, Wilson would toss his head angrily and complain about "that bitch Barbara." He would talk about his tangled financial affairs, and how his wife Barbara was co-owner of all his property. "To get away from her would be very difficult," he told Bobbi. His chief concern was to retain ownership of the Upperville estate, which symbolized his life's achievement—the dirt farmer become lord of the manse. Barbara's price for a divorce, according to what Wilson told Bobbi, was a cash settlement, a "firm" lump sum of $4 million. This amount, Wilson claimed, he did not have at hand, and to raise it he would be forced to sell his farm. So he stood stalemated: He wanted out of the marriage so that he could marry Bobbi (at least, so he convinced her), but getting a divorce was financially impossible.

Such was the story Wilson told Bobbi Barnes repeatedly

through 1979, 1980 and well into 1981.* If I can get rid of this woman, he would say, we'll be man and wife. Bobbi believed him—most of the time, at any rate. Part of Bobbi wanted Wilson out of the mercenary business, for him to take what cash he could and return to the States. Even if Wilson had to serve a brief prison term, his life would be better in the long run. Yet another part of Bobbi Barnes realized Wilson would never be "a country gentleman sitting on some farm out in Virginia, counting his cows and watching his horses eat grass. Ed Wilson wasn't that kind of man. He had to be active."

Although Wilson could be good company—and, Barnes hints somewhat coyly, satisfying in bed—he was by no means the perfect companion. Sober, Wilson was a gentleman and a door-holder, quick to compliment her or to buy a pretty and unexpected present. But several inches deep into a bottle of Scotch, a different Ed Wilson appeared: a bully, a foul-mouthed tyrant, who said awful things about his employees, about people with whom he did business and on occasion even about her. And Wilson did not know how to relax, even on vacation. Whatever self-imposed goals drove him would not permit him to rest. Bobbi's photo albums contain many pictures of the "vacationing" Wilson—on a beautiful Parisian street, in a Scandinavian garden, at the foot of soaring Alps. In each photo, there is a sadness to Wilson's face; his body faces the camera, but his eyes are blank, his jaw is sagging. He seems a man whose mind is elsewhere.

Because she wrote Wilson's checks, Barnes realized the financial drain of the Virginia properties. Monthly he paid out between \$60,000 and \$120,000 in mortgage installments and expenses. Wilson had bought many of his properties with a low down payment, the intention being to pay off the notes with revenues. In the instance of the Upperville farm, the income was to come from the cattle operation. But two bad drought years in Northern Virginia in the late 1970s caused

---

*Barbara Wilson filed a divorce petition against Edwin Wilson on June 17, 1981, in Fauquier County Court, Virginia. Her suit stated that they had decided in May 1979 "to discontinue permanently the marital cohabitation and to live separate and apart thereafter permanently." Service to Wilson was made via a post-office box in Tripoli, Libya; he did not respond. Mrs. Wilson was granted the divorce on December 5, 1981. Her testimony, and that of the Mount Airy Farm secretary, Joanne Cole, was that the Wilsons had not been together since May 1979. The division of the Wilson property remained before the Virginia courts in February 1984.

the farm to operate at a loss that siphoned off much of the profits Wilson was earning in Libya. Nor had the constant rise of the real estate market helped. Wilson's net worth—as measured on paper—had increased astronomically; the most informed outside estimate, that of federal tax agents, put the rise from $2 million in 1976 to about $20 million by 1980. Yet because Wilson (by his own claim) was so cash-poor, he could not buy his way out of an unhappy marriage and wed the woman he claimed to love.

Bobbi Barnes never deceived herself into believing that Ed Wilson was a faithful lover. Stories of his various affairs with Western women who worked for oil companies in Libya constantly reached her ears. One woman who lived on and off in Wilson's villa in Tripoli deliberately left personal items in Wilson's bedroom when she knew Bobbi was coming to visit. Alex Raffio, among others, doubted that Wilson had it in him to be sexually faithful to one woman. "Wilson doted on prostitutes," Raffio said. "Even when Bobbi or another woman was available, Wilson preferred to buy sex. He liked to come into London and not let Bobbi know he was in town, then spend several days at the West End hotel where the whores congregated."

Raffio managed to get involved in one complicated weekend in Geneva during which Wilson juggled three women at once. The scenario, unbelievable if presented as French bedroom farce, ran roughly as follows. After a series of deceitful cables to Bobbi Barnes concerning his travel plans, Wilson brought a sometime paramour from Britain to Geneva for a weekend of sexual relaxation. Raffio happened to be in Geneva on business at the time, and he and Wilson sat in a hotel room and laughed about the stunt. At that moment the phone rang. Bobbi Barnes, her curiosity aroused by the cables, was coming to Geneva herself that weekend.

Wilson stumbled through the conversation. "I'm tied up with Alex," he said. "He's not leaving until eight o'clock. Why don't you come around the hotel then?" Raffio actually was leaving Geneva at six o'clock; he laughed and went along with the ruse. "I need two hours' leeway," Wilson told Raffio. "Bobbi suspects I'm here with this other dame."

"Well, Ed, you *are* here with this other dame," Raffio said.

"Yeah, but that's Bobbi's problem," Wilson said.

Wilson had an early dinner with the British woman, and

was beginning to think about a way to persuade her to retire early and unattended when the maître d' approached him and said, very quietly, "There is a woman in the lobby who claims to be your wife, and who would like to have a private word with you." Wilson excused himself. Sure enough, Barbara Wilson awaited him outside the dining room. She had been visiting friends in Italy, heard Wilson was in Geneva and decided to stop by to discuss their divorce settlement. Raffio does not know what Wilson said to her, but whatever it is, Barbara went away silently.

Several days later in London, Wilson gloated to Raffio how he had managed to keep the three women in separate Geneva hotels throughout the weekend without public embarrassment. Barbara learned of the British woman's presence, but apparently by this time she did not care. As for Bobbi, Wilson claimed to have kept her unaware that his wife and a current paramour were sharing the weekend with her. But Bobbi knew. As she eventually told me, she too had swallowed her pride and remained silent.

For another year, Wilson kept Bobbi Barnes hooked. "He would constantly say, 'Do this one more thing for me.' I would rationalize that I really should; that we were—or had been—so close that I could not walk away from him." But she finally did, in December 1981. No longer could she see the man she loved on any regular basis. Her son, Mark, was growing more remote by the day, and her former husband was threatening to challenge her custody rights. Both American and British law-enforcement officials were checking her movements. Much of that autumn Barnes had spent in an uncertain haze of pills and alcohol; her good friend Diane Byrne saw her through the ordeal, but also had the sense to raise the basic question "Is he worth what he is doing to you?" Originally Barnes had fallen in love with an affectionate, prosperous man who gave her dazzling exposure to the glamour of international business and finance. Now she found herself making furtive journeys to a stinking North African country to visit a balding fugitive with bad breath, alcoholic tremors and arrest warrants outstanding.

In early December, Bobbi put her son aboard a plane for Texas; she followed several days later, intending to spend the Christmas holidays with her parents and other family members in the Austin area, then to return to London and pack her belongings and leave Wilson for good. She moved cautiously, knowing that U.S. investigators wished to question her about Wilson. Although she was uncertain whether she was subject to arrest, she took no chances. Before leaving Heathrow Airport outside London, she carefully counted her cash: forty-nine hundred-dollar bills, and £23 in British currency. By her calculation, this amount was just under the $5,000 limit of cash that one can bring into the United States without filing a customs declaration. "I knew I was on every possible kind of 'watch list,'" Bobbi said, "and I was trying to be very careful to obey the letter of the law."

Despite her caution, when she came through the immigration area of Dallas–Fort Worth Airport the night of December 22, her passport number "made all sorts of gray stuff jump up on the computer."

"Ma'am, would you mind stepping back to this office for a minute?" an agent asked. There the customs people recounted Barnes's money; by their tally, she had fifty hundred-dollar bills, not forty-nine; given the British pounds, she was over the $5,000 limit. "We are going to have to hold you for not declaring this money," the agent said. (Eighteen months later, Barnes remained adamant that "someone" had slipped an extra bill into the stack so that the federal agents would have a pretext for detaining her. "I counted and recounted that money a dozen times before leaving Heathrow," she said. The point soon became moot.)

Barnes protested loudly—and, she thought for a few minutes, successfully. The watch list, however, carried the notation that in the event Barnes was detected entering the United States, guidance should be sought from E. Lawrence Barcella, assistant U.S. attorney for the District of Columbia.

The call reached Barcella at his home in Northwest Washington in early evening. "Forget the customs stuff," he said. "I'm sending down a warrant to hold her as a material witness for the grand jury."

As Barnes sat and fretted in the customs detention area, the federal bureaucracy went into motion. At 11 P.M., two FBI agents arrived with an arrest warrant. "Come with us, lady," one of them told Bobbi; "we're going to jail."

The Justice Department had two choices as to where to hold Barnes before taking her to Washington for her grand-jury appearance: the Dallas County Jail, a relatively modern and comfortable facility constructed during the early 1970s, and the Tarrant County Jail in Fort Worth, a rougher place whose overseers consider themselves more jailers than *hôteliers*. In terms of psychological impact, spending several days in the Tarrant County jail would be much more jarring than Dallas. So when the FBI car left the airport, it turned not east toward Dallas but west to Fort Worth.

If indeed agents intended to "shake Bobbi right down to her fancy panties," as one later joshed, they succeeded. "The first night, I was so hysterical, they had to put me in a medical ward, I was that shaken," Barnes said. "I mean, I had flown into the United States first class, and now here I was being dragged off to this absolute hole of a jail." Her immediate thought was to secure a lawyer, and the only name that came to mind was that of John Keats, of Washington, whom she had met during Wilson's abortive nuclear-weapons hoax. "Sit tight," Keats told Barnes by telephone; "I'll have a lawyer with you in the morning."

But Bobbi Barnes sat in the Texas jail for three days. After the first night, she was taken from the medical ward to a solitary-confinement cell. She sat and cried all the day. Ed, somebody, get me out of here, she said to herself, time and again.

Finally the lawyer came. "The Federals want half a million dollars for bail," he said. "They think that you'll skip off to Libya and never be seen again." Bobbi cried again. "I'm not going anywhere," she said. "All I want is to get out of this jail." As she sobbed incoherently, the lawyer sought out the chief jailer. "Look," he said, "this woman is about at the edge. I think you'd better get her back in the medical ward before she goes over." The jailer obliged.

Around noon on Christmas Day, federal magistrate Alex McGlinchey held a special court session and reduced the bail from $500,000 to $200,000. The money was secured by Bobbi's father, a retired Air Force lieutenant colonel, and her brother-in-law, an Austin attorney. Deeply shaken, Barnes went off to a somber Christmas dinner with her son and other relatives.

During her anguished hours in jail, Bobbi had received several phone calls. A high school classmate who had seen her photograph in the Texas newspapers asked if she could be of any help. The family gave what cheering calls it could. But although the arrest was the subject of press accounts world-wide—she being the first person in Wilson's employ actually to go to jail, even if temporarily—one desired voice of support never came: that of Ed Wilson.

"He didn't call me for weeks. But, damn him anyway, that was typical of Ed Wilson. He cared for no one but himself. When I finally did speak with him, weeks later, he said, 'I knew you could take care of yourself.'"

In coming months, despite her resolve in London and all she had been through, Bobbi Barnes would resume her role as Wilson's lover, adviser, faithful worker. She couldn't help loving him again, although now it was without the same deep and trusting intensity that had marked their past relationship. She had come to accept the fact that Wilson lived by his own moral code and standards of personal loyalty, and under this code, Ed Wilson came first. But for her, supposedly his intended wife, to be allowed to sit alone in jail for three days because of her association with him, and for him not to convey a single word of solace, remained primary among the factors that were, eventually, to drive the final wedge between Bobbi Barnes and Ed Wilson.

In mid-January 1982, Bobbi flew from Austin to Washington. Richard Bast, the private investigator, met her at the airport and took her to the 16th Street office of columnist Jack Anderson. The next day, when Barnes arrived at Lawrence Barcella's office for an interview before her grand-jury testimony, she was accompanied by Bast and attorney Robert Flynn of Washington.

Barcella refused to permit Bast to sit in on the interview. He told him bluntly, "You have no standing in this case, and I'm not talking with Mrs. Barnes while you are here." (Thrown out of Barcella's office, Bast spent several days "roaming the courthouse, bad-mouthing me to any reporter he could find," Barcella said.) Barcella also made pointed comments to Bobbi about her representation by Flynn. Did he have her best interests at heart? Or was he bent on shielding Wilson? Or, yet again, was he there to help Jack Anderson get stories? In time Barnes was to return to John Keats for representation; for now, however, she said she was satisfied with Flynn. Over the next weeks, Barcella and Flynn worked out an agreement guaranteeing Barnes immunity from prosecution provided she cooperated with the federal investigation.

Despite her lingering, tortured affection for Wilson (and her nigh hatred of Barcella for her anguish in the Fort Worth jail), Bobbi after several weeks began to talk freely of the business of her employer/lover. In fact, Wilson, still convinced he could make a deal with the government (and actually believing he was working on one, as will be seen), encouraged her to do so. "Look," he told her by telephone, "they've got you; tell them what you have to say to get out of there. I understand." It is doubtful that he understood how *much* she had to say.

So beginning in March, Bobbi Barnes spent six or more hours every day with Barcella and Carol Bruce; FBI agent Bill Hart; Dick Pederson and Rick Wadsworth of the Bureau of Alcohol, Tobacco and Firearms, and the Central Intelligence Agency. Barnes's memory proved phenomenal. She recollected dates and places of meetings, and what participants had said. She knew the paper maze Wilson had contrived to conceal his businesses from scrutiny. She recited the details of Wilson's contracts with the Libyans.

Bobbi Barnes came to respect Barcella, if not to like him. (Several times I was present when one party was talking to the other on the telephone; their body language and facial gestures indicated continuing reluctance by each party to advance beyond a politely adversarial position.)

After several months, Barnes once again traveled to Libya to spend time with Ed Wilson. She could reintegrate him into her life, if not into her full confidence.

For Barcella, the turning of Bobbi Barnes was the key point in the Wilson prosecution. He now had a witness who knew the intricacies of Wilson's business life—and one who did not lie.

With increasing intensity, the tide of events now began to flow against Ed Wilson and the enterprises with which he had been associated. The mere presence of a Wilson associate, present or past, in an arms-related business was enough to prompt the curiosity of federal investigators. One such firm to fall under suspicion was the Egyptian-American Transport and Service Company, or EATSCO, which had been created to ship arms to Egypt as an aftermath of the 1979 Camp David talks.

With former Egyptian intelligence official Hussein Salem

as its president in partnership with Tom Clines, the CIA retiree and Wilson friend, EATSCO had shipped more than $1 billion worth of arms to Egypt through two Baltimore transport companies, R. G. Hobelmann & Company and a subsidiary, Air Freight International (AFI). Once Clines was linked to Wilson in press accounts—chiefly as a "friend and former CIA associate"—Pentagon auditors began to take a closer look at EATSCO records. Almost immediately they turned up evidence of massive corruption.

Using established procedures, the Baltimore companies would ship equipment to Egypt and forward bills for their service to EATSCO, which in turn passed them on to the Defense Security Assistance Agency, a Pentagon branch. Between November 1979 and February 1982, EATSCO made thirty-eight such shipments through the Baltimore firms. Bills for thirty-four of these shipments were padded, and by gross amounts. According to court pleadings by assistant U.S. attorney Theodore Greenberg, Salem, Clines and AFI president Rolf Graage "did enter into an unlawful agreement . . . to file false invoices with the United States." The overcharges amounted to some $8 million over the period. In some instances the conspirators nearly doubled the actual cost. For example, on September 11, 1981, EATSCO billed the government $1.34 million for shipments aboard the M.V. *Paul Bunyan*; the actual cost was $623,060, for an overrun of $716,940. Two months later, on November 12, 1981, EATSCO collected $1,209,334 for a shipment aboard the S.S. *Lash Atlantico*, when in fact the cost was $779,034.*

To Bobbi Barnes, the EATSCO matter had an ironic outcome. "Ed loaned Tom Clines half a million to get the whole thing started, and trusted him so much he didn't bother to put the deal on paper. By the time EATSCO started operating, Ed was in trouble elsewhere, and Clines in effect told him to go whistle, that he was not going to pay the money and what did Ed intend to do about it? Ed never got a dime for the EATSCO profits. But Clines did get cold feet about the half-million for he eventually paid Ed back."

*When the investigative detail work was finished in 1983, Salem pleaded guilty to charges of submitting inflated invoices. He paid a personal fine of $40,000 and handed the U.S. District Court in Alexandria, Virginia, a $3.02-million cashier's check in partial reimbursement of the false claims.

In 1981, the denouement of EATSCO remained two years away. But there were many other problems confronting a suddenly besieged Ed Wilson.

33

"The Dumbest Man on Earth"

By September 1981, Gene Tafoya had sat alone in a Fort Collins, Colorado, jail cell for more than four months. He was frustrated. Denver lawyers Walter Gerash and Scott Robinson were representing him. Both are tough in the courtroom; they specialize in personal-injury suits for the plaintiff and are known around Colorado courts as "guys who will give you a helluva lawsuit." Nonetheless, community feeling in Fort Collins ran so high about the attempted murder of Faisal Zagallai that the lawyers had not been able to get Tafoya's bail reduced to an amount he could afford. (Gerash, in an angry court outburst, likened the sentiment against Quaddafi and Libya to that of the "yellow journalism...jingoism...and propaganda" that preceded the 1898 war with Spain.)

Hired by Tafoya's grandfather, a retired New Mexico State Police officer, Gerash and Robinson were unaware that some of the money for Tafoya's defense came from Ed Wilson, via James ("Jimmy Blue Eyes") Dean. At Wilson's order, Dean had flown to the United States in the spring of 1981 and given Betty Jo Tafoya at least $5,000 cash. (Several days later, Mrs. Tafoya visited her husband in jail. A matron insisted on searching her, and found twenty-five hundred-dollar bills in each cup of her bra. Jailers kept the $5,000 until she finished her visit. Security tightened after this episode, jailers fearing that Tafoya intended to try to buy his way to freedom.)

Tafoya was visibly restless on September 29 during one of his many pretrial hearings. As the session ended, Tafoya arose and told the judge he wanted to testify before the Senate subcommittee on terriorism. The judge gaveled him into silence and recessed the court.

Curious, Fort Collins detective Ray Martinez asked Tafoya's lawyer Scott Robinson what he meant. Robinson did not know. Tafoya called to Martinez, "Come over here, Ray; I'll tell you." Martinez sat at the counsel table and Tafoya said that a subcommittee headed by Senator Jeremiah Denton, an Alabama Republican, had been holding hearings on international terrorists. "I could be helpful, Ray, if I could only testify." Tafoya paused, then continued: "Testifying is better than sitting in jail. . . . Hell, I'm guilty, guilty as hell." Robinson intervened at this point and told Tafoya to shut up.

When Martinez returned to the Fort Collins police offices, he found a message: "Tafoya is extremely anxious to speak with you." Martinez checked with a lawyer in the district attorney's office, who said it would be permissible for him to see Tafoya alone provided he gave him the proper "rights" warning before they talked.

For the first time, Tafoya gave his version of how he had come to Colorado to shoot Zagallai--an act he freely admitted. A year or so before the shooting, he said, a CIA agent had talked with him in Toronto and asked whether he would be available for occasional special assignments. Tafoya had said he would.

In the summer of 1980, Tafoya told Martinez, a CIA contact had talked with him in London and said that a dissident Libyan in Colorado had been making speeches attacking the Quaddafi Government. The U.S. Government was trying to better relations with Libya, the CIA man supposedly said, and the dissident must be silenced. He had ordered Tafoya to go to Colorado and "rough him up some." Afterward, someone from CIA would call Zagallai and "warn him to stop making statements against the Libyan Government, specifically on Quaddafi." (Zagallai had made no public speeches.)

"Things got out of hand," Tafoya told Martinez. He had brought along a pistol himself "just in case," and was surprised when Zagallai fought back. He claimed that Zagallai had actually grabbed the pistol from his (Tafoya's) holster. Tafoya had tried to snatch back the gun during the struggle, and the pistol had discharged twice, both shots hitting Zagallai in the head. How about the cut on the back of Zagallai's head? Martinez asked. Tafoya paused, then said, "Well, he must have fell on the table or something."

Tafoya emphasized that he had worked for CIA on the mission, and that this had not been his first assignment for the Agency. But Martinez could coax no details from him on any other such jobs. When Martinez asked about the $8,623 he had deposited in his Truth or Consequences bank in February 1981, Tafoya claimed the funds had been given him by "a CIA agent in London." (John Heath, who disavows any CIA connection, had given Tafoya $10,000 when he left London for the United States the same month.)

Martinez then turned the talk to Edwin Wilson. "Sure, I know him; I worked for him," Tafoya said. "You cannot help but know Ed Wilson when you go to Libya." He was also acquainted with Frank Terpil. Martinez got tougher. As Martinez stated later:

"Tafoya would not come out and admit that Edwin Wilson hired him in this shooting, but would not deny it either. He also stated that he never contacted the CIA about doing special assignments, but that they had always contacted him. He would not reveal the names of his CIA contacts because 'It wouldn't do me any good.'

"[Tafoya] further expressed that if I was to reveal this conversation as to what he had to say about the CIA, he would 'get his throat cut'—demonstrating with his hand. Tafoya further stated that he did not want to elaborate on Edwin P. Wilson because of Wilson's ability to seek revenge."

To Martinez' surprise, the stoic Tafoya began at this point to cry. He was deeply disappointed that the U.S. Government had not come to his aid. Instead, federal agents had played a major role in putting him in jail. He had tried to call his "CIA contact" several times, he lamented to Martinez. "They act like they don't know me."

"How are you so sure this is a CIA-sanctioned plot?" Martinez asked.

"I know my contacts," Tafoya insisted. "I know what I am talking about. This is a setup. They're letting me hold the bag."

Tafoya was indeed "holding the bag." But the question remained, who owned the bag—the CIA, or Edwin P. Wilson? There is strong but nonprovable evidence that Wilson had lied so credibly to Tafoya that he had in fact convinced the former Green Beret he was on a CIA mission. No one who knows Gene Tafoya has ever mistaken him for a smart man. He is a *macho* blusterer who desperately wished to be a civilian soldier-of-fortune. Given Wilson's background and his persuasive skills, convincing the gullible Tafoya that he was working deep-cover CIA would have been child's play.

Supportive evidence for Tafoya's *belief* that he had been hired by CIA came in a roundabout fashion. Some months before Tafoya's arrest, a former CIA agent named Frank Snepp received a frantic phone call at his Arlington, Virginia, apartment. Snepp had been prominent in the news because of CIA attempts to seize royalties from his book *Decent Interval*, which detailed Agency shortcomings during the frantic final days of the Vietnam War. Snepp had served two tours in Vietnam; he was convinced that CIA misread the war, then callously abandoned Vietnamese who had worked for the CIA station in Saigon. Snepp did not submit his manuscript for CIA review, although he had signed an agreement not to divulge Agency secrets. The government ultimately won the resulting suit in court and confiscated more than $100,000 of Snepp's royalties. But the woman who called was not interested in Snepp's case; she had a problem of her own.

"She was Bonnie Tafoya, Gene Tafoya's sister," Snepp stated. "She called out of the blue to say that her brother was on the CIA's payroll, and he was in trouble, and he needed help. She sounded crazy, but I listened to her. All I knew was that I had a hysterical woman on the telephone who needed legal answers for her brother, who she said had been working for the Agency and did a shooting. 'What should I do?' she asked."

Snepp suggested that she not go to the press; that her brother's greatest weapon was the *threat* of exposure. (For this advice, Snepp said, prosecutors accused him of "masterminding Tafoya's defense.")

To Snepp, the significance of Bonnie Tafoya's statement was that "she volunteered the information. She absolutely believed it. She heard it from her brother, who absolutely believed it. She was pristine, because she hadn't been talking with the lawyers." Snepp, who handled any number of agents during his year in CIA, "put great credence" in Tafoya's account.

Tafoya tenaciously clung to the story through two criminal trials—for the Zagallai shooting, and later on income-tax charges (for not reporting the funds he received from Wilson). Tafoya would rant in his cellblock about his "betrayal" by the U.S. Government. What he apparently did not realize, even by late 1983, was that the betrayal had been committed by his supposed friend Edwin P. Wilson.

By then, Tafoya was serving two prison terms—two years for simple assault and conspiracy to commit simple assault in the Colorado case (the jury acquitted· him on the greater felony charge of assault with intent to commit murder), and six years for violating income-tax laws." And he still faced extradition to Canada on charges that he had firebombed the automobile of Robert Manina.

During his income-tax trial, Tafoya told a reporter for the *San Antonio Express-News*, "I'm afraid I was used—terribly used. Right now I feel like the dumbest man on earth."

34

Keiser

When a defendant flees the United States to avoid trial, or refuses to return to appear in court, he becomes a legal outlaw, a person subject to capture by any ruse the government can contrive. Constitutional niceties do not protect the fugitive. In simplified form, the rule is "Finders keepers, losers weepers." As the Supreme Court stated in a 1952 case, "There is nothing in the Constitution that requires a guilty person rightfully convicted to escape justice because he was brought to trial against his will."*

---

*Frisbee v. Collins, 342 U.S. 519 (1952).

The United States, through an Interpol warrant, had secured Edwin Wilson's arrest in Malta in 1980, only to have him slip away to safety through the United Kingdom. The United States, through prosecutor Larry Barcella, had tried to negotiate Wilson's voluntary return at the Rome meeting in 1981. He refused, and returned to Libya to boast that he would face justice at a time of his own choosing, if ever. So for the time being, Wilson was a man beyond justice.

Larry Barcella heard—and rejected—many schemes for extricating Wilson. John Dutcher, Wilson's onetime employee and now a bitter enemy, offered to storm Wilson's villa from the sea and carry him away bodily. No way, Barcella said. There was even talk of the United States' giving Libya desperately needed parts for its C-130 cargo aircraft in exchange for the fugitive. A group of retired CIA agents, sick of having their former agency's name blackened by Wilson's notoriety, put together an *ad hoc* committee which discussed ways Wilson might be lured into Britain again, and grabbed. Some were for disposing of him outright "by putting cement on his shoes and giving him a swim in the North Sea," according to a participant. Others, a minority, would "dump him on the runway at Dulles and call the FBI."

However broad the law on fugitive capture, the Justice Department was having a hard time finding a way to get its hands on Ed Wilson and return him to the United States to stand trial. Finally its solution came, in the form of a sometime spook who seemingly stepped almost literally out of the shadows and volunteered for the mission.

Ernest Keiser was 63 years old early in 1981, when he began his serious quest for Ed Wilson. A slender, hawk-featured man with thinning blond hair, Keiser walked with a confident stride. A strong Germanic accent overlies his fluent English, especially when he is excited. Keiser does not volunteer much personal information. As a professional intelligence officer, he prefers to cast as small a shadow as possible. Only once in recent years has he been forced to put what he called "verifiable information" onto paper. This came when he visited Edwin Wilson in Libya, and suspicious Libyan intelligence officers forced him to write a biographical summary. They got little, but enough to satisfy them that he was not *then* with the CIA. Keiser was born November 27, 1918, in New York City, the son of German immigrant parents who moved to Blumenau, Brazil—known as the "little Germany" of South America—in 1921. Keiser was educated at elementary and secondary schools in Brazil, then attended a university in Santiago, Chile, receiving degrees in law and journalism in 1942.

Thereafter the details become somewhat vague. Keiser told the Libyans only that he had been a "free-lance correspondent" for NBC News in Egypt and elsewhere during the 1950s, and thereafter a private businessman. Actually, he was an intelligence officer, first with the G-2 section of the old War Department, then as a contract employee of CIA when the Agency was formed in 1947. Over the next decades Keiser (by his count) was to work for more than 20 Western intelligence agencies, always as a contract employee, and usually with a cover job. Much of this time he lived in the Middle East, ostensibly a correspondent for the Hearst newspaper organization, then with NBC News. In Beirut he was a neighbor, sometime drinking crony and journalistic competitor of H. A. R. "Kim" Philby, the Soviet mole who rose to the top of British intelligence before being exposed. (Philby then worked for *The Economist*.) Keiser also met and befriended President Gamal Abdel Nasser of Egypt—a coup that got him on what he called "the inside track" both in the Middle East and at NBC. In 1958 he married a Lebanese woman, Bahira Demashkish, whose father had been his country's ambassador to Egypt, Great Britain and the United States.

But Keiser's chief occupation was intelligence, with assignments that took him worldwide—even behind the Iron Curtain and into the Soviet Union. "I helped a lot of people come out of Communist countries. In other words, to sneak people out, yes, on many occasions. I'm talking of refugees, political prisoners." Through a peripheral role in the Bay of Pigs invasion he met Edwin P. Wilson, then assigned briefly as a paymaster for persons supporting the Cubans.

During the 1960s and 1970s, Keiser began dabbling in real estate and investment ventures on an international scale. He had a brief association with Robert Vesco, the financier-turned-swindler. He worked with Jimmy Hoffa, the deposed Teamster president, in "an oddball scheme to get the Vietnam prisoners released in return for Hoffa's pardon. Crazy—too many con men; it fell without trace." There were times when persons dealing with Keiser thought he did business by the laws of the jungle, not the marketplace. By early 1981 he was living in suburban New York, pursuing what he called "real estate investments," with options on lands in Florida and North Carolina. One day he received a visit.

The person was a U.S.-based covert agent of Mossad, the Israeli intelligence agency. "The man asked what I knew about Edwin P. Wilson. 'Only what I've read in the papers,' I said. He told me. 'Well, we want you to go find him, and to kill him, either in Libya or wherever you have to do it.'" Mossad knew that Keiser had lived in the Middle East, and that he had the professional expertise for the mission. Keiser turned down Mossad. Strictly from operational considerations, he did not think anyone could assassinate Wilson in Libya and survive.

But the fact that Wilson was running a renegade operation repelled Keiser. "I made some phone calls to intelligence agencies in Washington and inquired whether he was as bad as pictured in the press, and whether anything was being done to get him back." The answers, in order, were yes and no.

Would there be any objection if Keiser tried to get Wilson back to face justice? No, there would not.

At this point the sequence becomes murky. Keiser states that in the late spring of 1981 he read two long articles about Wilson by Seymour Hersh in *The New York Times Magazine*, for which Kevin Mulcahy was the primary source. Keiser had known Mulcahy's father, Donald, at the CIA station in Cairo years earlier. In due course, Keiser was talking to Kevin Mulcahy about "helping to get Mr. Wilson back to the United States."

Keiser flew to Washington and met Mulcahy and Hersh in the latter's office. Hersh, who detested Wilson, stepped beyond the reporter's role. If Keiser would "assist the government," he would "make an immediate contact with the National Security Council." "Fine," Keiser replied. Two hours later he, Hersh, Mulcahy and lawyer Robert Schwartz of New York were at the White House. There they met with Richard V. Allen, then President Reagan's national security adviser, and Fred Fielding, counsel to the President. Keiser wanted an assurance that Wilson was "a hundred percent wrong" and not a deep-cover U.S. intelligence agent who had been cut adrift. If he could be satisfied that Wilson indeed was a crook, he would help "bring him back." Allen said he would check with Rear Admiral Bobby Ray Inman, who a few months earlier had become deputy director of Central Intelligence (and who as head of the Office of Naval Intelligence had fired Wilson from Task Force 157 in 1976).

At this point, Allen, Inman, Hersh and Mulcahy vanish from Keiser's account. The intelligence-community figures who dealt with Keiser thereafter will not talk, under any ground rules whatever, about the origins of or the twists of the plot. But intuition and circumstantial evidence permit the construction of a scenario far more likely than the shaky story told by Keiser. The scenario runs something like this:

Wilson's continuing freedom, and his claims of being a betrayed CIA agent, were a source of ongoing embarrassment to CIA and the American intelligence community as a whole. The change of command in early 1981, with veteran spook William J. Casey becoming director of Central Intelligence, gave new impetus to efforts to nab Wilson, one way or another. Keiser was an outstanding choice to be the bait, for he had backgrounds in both intelligence and international business. Because his financial record contained some shadows— not criminal ones, understand—Keiser would be especially appealing to a corner-cutter such as Wilson.

Involving Mulcahy and Hersh as unwitting participants in the early stages of the scheme served to mask its true origins. Mulcahy certainly wished Wilson to be caught; he could talk of little else. In wilder moments he even suggested that the First Marine Division invade Tripoli and seize Wilson. As one acquaintance recalls, "Kevin had maps of Tripoli, and he would talk about how a fast strike force of helicopters could land on top of Wilson's villa during the night and kidnap him. When I told him, 'Things just aren't done that way, Kevin,' he raged about the United States Government being chicken."

So a simple nudge would have been enough to send Mulcahy in Keiser's direction. That Mulcahy would then use the respected Hersh as his pipeline to the National Security Council was an added bonus. Thus was created the legend that Keiser materialized out of the blue to help the government catch Wilson. (Eyebrows did rise when Keiser retained as his lawyer Eugene M. Propper, one of Wilson's original prosecutors, by now in private practice.)

Whatever Keiser's provenance, his next contact was with Larry Barcella and Carol Bruce of the U.S. Attorney's Office, in July 1981. Keiser had no specific plan in mind, although he told the prosecutors that he intended to pose as a "representative" of the National Security Council. Such a guise appealed to Barcella, who loves a good conspiracy. "The audacity of Ernie Keiser was that he aimed high; had he claimed to be CIA or FBI, Wilson conceivably could have gotten behind his cover. But the National Security Council—how do you go about checking out something like that?" Barcella did take the precaution of doing his own background check of Keiser's credentials. He avoided normal channels, for he did not want word to circulate that Keiser would be working for him on an undercover mission. That Keiser's business background had some dark corners did not deter Barcella. "I felt this was just the sort of guy who was needed to deal with Wilson."

Keiser planned his operation with considerable cunning, and he acted largely on his own. When he first discussed visiting Wilson in person, "the government was very much against it." Keiser disagreed. "I was convinced that the only way for me to do anything was for me to go to Libya. I sometimes shocked people in the government, [as well as] my own attorney, doing things that I had to explain afterwards .... I am my own man. I was not led by anyone, including my attorney [Propper]."

Keiser at the outset had no specific plan in mind. As he was to tell Wilson's lawyer later in a court hearing:

"You are talking about the trade again. I have no answer. I can't answer that. It is not that I do not want to answer; I just can't answer. There are things, I believe, which you put together in your mind. You approach a problem, talking about something like this, you play it by ear. You have to feel a situation. There was [*sic*] no directions given to me, nor did I have any direction. I knew I had to do a job and somehow I would do it."

Keiser spoke repeatedly by phone with Wilson during the summer of 1981, as did one of his real estate employees, Dan Drake. Keiser was vague. He told Wilson only that he wanted to "talk some business with you that might help you settle your problems with the government." He mentioned that he was a consultant to the NSC, and that he knew many people in the intelligence community. Drake made two introductory visits to Tripoli, in July and October 1981, chiefly to check the mechanics of travel and to gain his own impressions of Wilson. The second trip, he took along a sealed envelope which he handed to Wilson. Just what the envelope contained, Keiser would not disclose; apparently it convinced Wilson that Keiser was in fact with the NSC.

One person not deceived by Keiser's scam was Wilson's then-attorney John Keats. A trial lawyer, Keats makes a comfortable living because of his ability to sense when someone is attempting to peddle nonsense. When Keiser and Dan Drake appeared in his law offices in downtown Washington, Keats folded his hands behind his head and listened with mounting skepticism. Keiser identified himself as a "consultant" to the NSC who had known Wilson in the past. The NSC "wants Wilson to do a job." If he did so, "we can work out a situation" whereby he would be free of any criminal charges.

Keats thought the proposition outlandish. Although he had no intelligence background, he had been around Washington long enough to realize that the NSC "just doesn't work that way."

"You say you have the NSC's authority to make such an offer?" he asked.

"Yes," Keiser replied.

"Good," Keats said, rising from his chair and reaching for his coat. "Let's go downstairs to the street, hail a cab and ride over to the NSC offices. You introduce me to the person responsible for this offer, and I guarantee that you'll be in Libya, talking with Wilson, within two days." Keiser backed away hurriedly. No, no, he said, an introduction would be impossible because of "security considerations." They talked a bit longer, but Keats had heard enough. "I suspected something phony was under way, an entrapment." He sensed that Keiser was a "bounty hunter." Such was the message that he gave by phone to Wilson in Tripoli. Keep away from Keiser and Drake, he told Wilson; they're trying to lure you into a trap.

Wilson, however, was not one to follow advice if it ran counter to his own wishful readings. Since Keats had previously told him things he did not wish to hear, he shoved the lawyer aside. "Wilson even called Larry Barcella and told him not to deal with me anymore, that Keiser was now his 'representative,' whatever the hell that means. Barcella told him to go to hell; that as long as John Keats was his attorney of record, he intended to deal with him [Wilson] through me."

Keats warned Wilson once more. Wilson replied, "John, there are a lot of things you don't know about."

Keats responded, "Ed, it's a trap—stay out of it." Wilson ignored him.

In December 1981, Wilson directed John Heath to go from Belgium to London and assist Keiser in getting a visa for Libya. "He's with the NSC," Wilson said, "and he's working on a deal to get me out of here." Heath distrusted Keiser from the outset. "He was just too nervous and upset," he said. Over a long breakfast in the Park Lane Hilton, Keiser gulped down ten to twelve cups of coffee and lit one cigarette after another. Keiser also talked a bit more than Heath thought appropriate about his background in CIA and his work for the NSC. "I just thought, Hey, he's not a door-to-door salesman. Why is he working so hard to convince me? He's got to convince Ed Wilson." Heath noted some other inconsistencies. Keiser first claimed to be a nondrinker, but that evening, when Diane Byrne joined them for dinner, Keiser insisted on ordering two bottles of champagne, from which he imbibed frequently.

During his days of talks with Heath, and later Diane Byrne, Keiser said he could find a "sanctuary" for Wilson in either South America or a Caribbean nation, possibly the Dominican Republic. But Keiser would need Wilson's passport to obtain the proper visa. Byrne and Heath gave him not one but three passports; Wilson's old American passport, which had been stamped "cancelled" by the U.S. consul in Rome during the July 1981 meeting; an Irish passport in the name of "Phillip McCormack"* and a Maltese passport in the name of "Giovanni Zammit."

---

*Wilson bought the Irish passport through an Irish citizen living in Libya who supplemented his oil-company income through selling flash. Heath said the Libyans knew of his bootlegging, but let him continue because he did minor spying for them. The bootlegger's brother obtained the passport through his contacts in the Irish Republican Army. The passport contained a visa for travel to the United States, issued by the American Embassy in London on December 22, 1981. Heath got the visa by going to the embassy and posing as "McCormack." To conceal his obvious physical difference from Wilson's photograph in the document, Heath crammed a hat low on his head. Diane Byrne stood alongside him and chatted nonsense to distract the clerk. They left with the visa.

Keiser seemed disappointed to learn from Heath that there was no assurance the Libyans would let Wilson leave Tripoli; that he was being held under virtual house arrest. They discussed means of getting him out of Libya illegally. "Well, he's got a plane down there," Keiser suggested. "How about we just go out to the airfield and take off?"

"First of all," Heath said, "you'll never get to the plane. Secondly, if you did get to the plane and take off, which is highly improbable, you'd be shot down or forced down."

They talked over several other ideas. Heath told Keiser, "I'm here on behalf of Ed Wilson. I have to relay not only what you say to me, by my personal recommendation. My personal recommendation right now is November Foxtrot Whiskey." (Former sergeant Heath used the military alphabet for the letters N, F and W—to mean, in this context, "No fucking way.")

Diane Byrne was even more emphatic. "I don't believe you," she told Keiser. "I think you're a crook."

The protesting Keiser could sway neither Heath nor Byrne. Heath passed along his fears by telephone to Wilson, who this time seemed agreeable to being advised on Keiser. "Goddamn right," he said; "I'm not leaving this place without a written letter, a guarantee from the NSC."

But when Keiser finally reached Tripoli in person, in early January 1982, Wilson was gullible once again. All Keiser brought with him was a vague promise that the NSC letter would be forthcoming. The NSC wanted to bring Wilson back into the legitimate intelligence community, Keiser assured him; it would set him up as overseer of a vast spy network based in the Dominican Republic and responsible for all of Central America. Once he was "rehabilitated" by this service, all criminal charges would be dropped.

The prospect of clearing himself obviously thrilled Wilson. During the five days Keiser was in Tripoli, Wilson drafted a nine-page report outlining plans for a "Project X" that would be the cover name for his Central American intelligence operation. As he had done with CIA and Task Force 157, Wilson would shield the intelligence work behind a series of cover companies, whose parent firm would be based in Washington. Financing would come through "grants" and contracts with the Department of Defense. The home office would handle recruiting (with lie-detector tests for prospective employees) and liaison with CIA and military intelligence. Branch offices of an "export-import firm"—the project's cover—would be located in Guatemala, Honduras, Costa Rica, Belize and "other nations as might prove appropriate." The fiction of the cover company would enable CIA to funnel arms and security advice to Latin nations covertly, without visible government involvement.

Wilson wrote this document with the intention that it be given to William C. Clark, who a few months earlier had replaced Richard V. Allen as President Reagan's national security adviser. In an attempt to burnish his reputation, Wilson also contrived three other "reports" to show his continuing assistance to U.S. intelligence. One, concerning the "nuclear-weapons plot," had been sent to Washington the previous summer only to be immediately discredited as worthless by CIA experts. Another report claimed that Wilson had dissuaded the Libyans from carrying out an assassination plot against President Reagan the previous autumn. As Wilson boasted, "It was quite evident there was planned actions against President Reagan, including the possibility of his assassination by Libyan Hit Squads. I sincerely believe that as a result of my positive influence in this matter, the Libyans were content to relax their hostility." American intelligence was to dismiss this claim as a pipe dream. John Heath, who was in almost daily contact with Wilson during the "plot period," never heard such an affair mentioned. "If Ed had had a role, he would have bragged about it," Heath said.

In yet another report, Wilson described his venture in the Sudan as an attempt to better relations between that nation and Libya. Wilson wrote, "I believe that I have dampened down a potentially explosive situation where the two countries were moving toward a confrontation." (In fact, as we have seen, Wilson's initial interest in the Sudan had been to find a refuge and make money; this involvement had evolved into complicity to murder President Nimeiri of the Sudan and install a government subservient to Quaddafi).

In a cover letter to Clark, the White House security adviser, Wilson repeated his assertion that he had enjoyed "long ties" with the intelligence community, even after leaving government. He did concede that he had lost his "main channel" of communication upon the retirement of Theodore

G. Shackley in 1979. But on this basis of his record, he hoped that "any consideration you might give my case would be deeply appreciated if it would benefit the United States."

Keiser brought the Clark letter and the "reports" to Barcella, who circulated them to the FBI and CIA. The verdict: a "worthless pile of self-serving paper, so misleading as to be laughable." CIA did not even bother to send the papers to Clark.

Not a word of this rejection was passed back to Wilson, however. As far as he knew, Keiser had channeled the reports directly to the NSC.

35

"Senor Wilson, Please Step This Way"

In February 1982, Larry Barcella was in a meeting at the Justice Department when John Keats called. According to what Wilson had just told him, Keats said, Frank Terpil had commissioned the PLO to kill Barcella, his wife and their child.

"I had strong reservations about the truth of this information," Barcella said. "Terpil was obviously 'missing,' although I knew Syrians had him in jail in Damascus because of some passing irritation with him. Further, I wasn't deep into Terpil at that point; I was going after Ed Wilson."

And the noose was tightening on Wilson. On November 30, 1981, Douglas Schlachter had voluntarily returned from Burundi and become a witness against Wilson. Bobbi Barnes had been arrested in December; she was testifying regularly before the grand jury. "Ed Wilson feels the pressure; he's desperate," Barcella said. He dismissed Keats's "tip" as an attempt by Wilson to divert the prosecution's attention, and to cause problems for his former associate. Wilson apparently thought Barcella would be so outraged by the "threat" that he would make Terpil his primary target.

But the Justice Department nonetheless insisted that Barcella and his family be protected. Howard Safir, director of the U.S. Marshals Service, quietly told him, "Larry, you know the drill; you've seen it many times on the other side [when federal witnesses were threatened]." Barcella protested that the threat was "Ed Wilson's hot air." Nonetheless, over the next two months marshals guarded Barcella and his family around the clock. And as subsequent events established, Barcella's intuition was correct: Ed Wilson, not Frank Terpil, was the person who wanted him murdered.

At this juncture, Larry Barcella became nervous about continued use of the NSC ruse, and for reasons other than legality. Wilson had attempted to justify his Libyan activities by claiming he was funneling information to American intelligence. Trapping Wilson through a subterfuge involving intelligence would only lend a false credence to those earlier claims. "Get the NSC out of it," Barcella told Keiser. "I want this one clean, with no complications."

Keiser protested: "This whole deal is built on the NSC." Forget it, Barcella said; come up with another idea. Keiser groused about the change of plans, but said he would comply.

In fact, he simply ignored Barcella. Keiser sent his associate Dan Drake to a printer in Northern Virginia with a story that the National Security Council intended to have its stationery printed thereafter by a private company. Would the printer run off some sample sheets so that he could bid on a contract which might run into the tens of thousands of dollars? The printer happily obliged (apparently oblivious of the fact that the Government Printing Office supplies all such items for federal agencies). Keiser now had a supply of letterhead on which he would write Wilson any assurances he demanded.

In return for his months of dealing with Wilson, all that Keiser received from the Federal Government was expenses, a relatively modest $15,000 to $17,000. But Keiser profited handsomely—from Wilson's pocket. During his talks with Wilson, Keiser mentioned that he had options to develop several properties, including one near Walt Disney World, in Florida. "Hey, I'd like a piece of that," Wilson exclaimed. So Keiser offered him a 5-percent share, in return for a five-year low-interest loan from which he eventually pocketed about $300,000. Wilson was to claim later that he gave Keiser these sums as "front money" to establish companies for the Central American intelligence operations. Keiser laughed about the loans. "Ed Wilson will be pleased to know," he said, "that I am putting his money to good use, and that his five-percent share of the project is being well protected." Repayment is due in 1987.

Unaware that Barcella was orchestrating the Keiser contacts, Wilson continued to talk with the prosecutor—directly and through attorney Keats—about arranging another neutral-site meeting. Circumstances suggest that Wilson was scheming to humiliate Barcella: that he would go through the motions of setting up the meeting, then suddenly produce the "NSC agreement" that negated all his legal problems. Barcella had no objection to two-tier negotiations. He was willing to meet again, but again he wanted some advance show of good faith, evidence that Wilson was ready to cooperate. He demanded, and Wilson supplied, numerous business records, which Diane Byrne obtained from lawyer Edward Coughlin in Geneva and brought to Washington. Informally, Barcella then talked to more than half a dozen Western European governments about acting as neutral-site host for a meeting. Given Wilson's notoriety, and Libya's standing in the world community, no nation was willing to cooperate. At one point, Turkey seemed amenable, with Wilson to be given safe passage for the meeting only, but as Barcella made clear in an April 26 letter to John Keats, no travel was to take place until the exact terms were confirmed in writing.

At this point Wilson began to blend, in his own mind, the Keiser project and the prospect of another meeting with Barcella. Apparently he remained confident that he could talk his way through his problems. During one telephone conversation with Keiser, he even suggested bringing Yasir Arafat and other PLO leaders to the Turkey meeting, so that they could talk face to face with Americans. As Keiser recounted, "The intention obviously was . . . that the parties would understand each other and try to finally create a dialogue again and it would help Mr. Wilson tremendously."

Wilson's idea was embarrassingly naive. The problems between the U.S. Government and the PLO are far beyond the purview of an assistant U.S. attorney; nor was it realistic to expect that Turkey would permit Arafat or anyone else connected with the PLO to cross its borders.

Then, in June, Keiser told Wilson that the Turkey meeting was off—the Turkish Government would not allow Wilson into the country. He suggested that instead, the two of them travel to the Dominican Republic, where the NSC would guarantee him sanctuary. They agreed to meet in Zurich, Switzerland, and then fly together to Santo Domingo. At Wilson's request, Keiser bought airline tickets for Wilson under the name "Phillp McCormack," from Zurich through Madrid to the Dominican Republic.

When Wilson relayed this news to John Keats, the lawyer rose from his chair and screamed over the long-distance telephone: "You've been suckered! You have no letter that means anything; you have no guarantee." This time Keats thought he convinced Wilson. "He said, 'All right, I won't go.'" Relieved, Keats put the matter out of his mind. Keats was wrong. Wilson had fallen.

John Heath also had his doubts. He and Wilson began drinking flash the day before he was to leave. Heath repeated his doubts about Keiser's *bona fides*. "There's something fishy about that guy," he told Wilson. Why, for instance, was it imperative for Keiser and Wilson to pretend that they had known each other for years and had worked together? Wilson insisted that such a lie was necessary for the NSC to accept the scheme. Heath found this reasoning incredible. But Wilson would not listen. He and Heath drank flash nonstop for twenty-six hours, and Wilson staggered as he walked toward the plane that would take him to Zurich. He turned and waved his hand, as if saying farewell to all of Libya. "I'd rather spend two *years* in a federal prison than two more *days* in this goddamned place," he muttered back to Heath.

Earlier that week, in Washington, Larry Barcella casually asked Bobbie Barnes, "Do you intend to go down to Libya this weekend to see Ed?" Bobbi thought through the question and replied with an honest, "No." She did plan to see Wilson, but in Zurich, not Libya. She had no inkling of the Keiser scam, a closely held secret within the Justice Department. Bobbi met Diane Byrne in London and was told as much as the Wilson people knew of what was going on, and together they flew on to Zurich.

Wilson was drunk when he arrived at the Zurich airport in late afternoon, and he kept a glass in his hand throughout most of his stay there—almost twenty-four hours. Keiser came with a traveling partner he identified as "Phil Tucker, a business associate of mine." In fact, Tucker was a U.S. marshal. They were joined by Diane Byrne and Bobbi Barnes.

"Let's go talk business; let's get us a quiet place," Wilson said. He escorted everyone to a table in the rear of the transit lounge, and once drinks were ordered he asked Keiser about final details of their deal.

"Where's the NSC letter?" Wilson demanded. "I know you read it to me over the phone, but I want to see it myself."

The demand momentarily flustered Keiser. "I burned it, of course. I wouldn't carry something such as that on an international flight." But he assured Wilson that there was no problem. "I can call the NSC and have another copy of it flown out by courier plane tonight. It will be here tomorrow." Wilson grunted assent.

He and Keiser talked about their real estate venture. Earlier Coughlin had put a plastic bag stuffed with cash on the table. Rather than count it publicly, Keiser put the bag on the floor next to his foot. Wilson reached down and scooped out a double handful of bills. "I need some travel money," he said. "I'll make it up later." Keiser pulled the bag closer. Bobbi Barnes returned from an errand. "I need some cash," she said, and she too dipped into the bag. Keiser put the bag *under* his feet. "Two grabs," he said, "and maybe $90,000 is gone."

Wilson and Bobbi Barnes spent the night together on cots in the nursery area of the transit lounge. Wilson's lawyers later were to complain that he had been "locked in" the lounge on the demand of the U.S. Government. Actually, Swiss authorities routinely lock off the area at 11 P.M. so that sleepers will not be disturbed. In the words of one federal official, "The privacy meant that Ed Wilson could enjoy the last piece of ass he'd get during his lifetime. What's he complaining about?" More formally, a government brief stated, "This hardly sounds like ... torturous treatment. . . ."

Keiser, meanwhile, found a typewriter in an unoccupied airport office, pulled out a sheet of his bogus NSC stationery and wrote Wilson the desired letter. No copy exists, but as Wilson was to assert through attorney Herald Price Fahringer, "This letter in essence provided that the NSC agreed to meet with Mr. Wilson in the Dominican Republic for certain discussions and that it was agreed that Mr. Wilson would not be deported, arrested or extradited while in the Dominican Republic. The letter also stated that the NSC agreed to furnish Mr. Wilson with a U.S. passport valid for one year." The letter bore the signature "Thomas Henderson"—a name that Keiser pulled from the air.

When the party reassembled in the lounge the next morning, June 14, Keiser handed the letter to Wilson, who read it slowly, saying, "That's great, that's wonderful, that is just what we need." Wilson put the letter on the table in front of him and covered it with his forearms as he continued talking.

Keiser interrupted. He asked that Wilson give back the letter. Wilson frowned. "No, I'm the one who needs it. Don't you think I had better take it with me?"

Keiser reached into this jacket pocket and pulled out an envelope containing airline tickets and Wilson's false passport. "No," he said, "let me handle everything. It is better that I carry it all." So Wilson gave back the letter, without even making notes on its content.

Bobbi Barnes felt a flicker of suspicion. Since Keiser and Wilson would be traveling together, what difference would it make if Wilson carried the letter? She thought Keiser seemed overly insistent on retrieving it. Then other inconsistencies came to mind. Although all parties had supposedly come to Zurich in deepest confidence, Bobbi the day before had noticed Keiser talking animatedly to a man on the far side of the airport concourse. Just who is that? Barnes had wondered, but had said nothing. And there was a discrepancy in what Keiser expected of Wilson. Before the meeting, Keiser had told Wilson that in return for immunity and forgiveness he would have to serve the government "for at least one year." But at Zurich, he said, "That might run a bit more."

Bobbi said nothing of her suspicions, for "I wanted it to work; I wanted Ed to be free again."

Barnes and Diane Byrne left Zurich for London at six in

the evening. Wilson's plane was not to leave until 8 P.M. "Ed was drunk as a lord when Di and I left," Bobbi was to recall later. "Two hours more and I'll bet they had to pour him on the plane."

During the first leg of the flight to Madrid, Wilson talked angrily to Keiser about Larry Barcella. "That dago bastard," he said. "He put Bobbi in a fucking Texas jail just to scare her. He's behind most of this whole rotten business. I'm going to kill that son of a bitch if he's seventy-one and I'm a hundred and one." Wilson had a plan in mind. He would set up a law firm and secretly control it; through that firm he would offer Barcella a salary sufficient to lure him from his job as a federal prosecutor. Once Barcella was no longer protected by the U.S. Government, "I'll have the bastard killed." Wilson asserted that Barcella "is jealous of me. He knows I left the government as a GS-15. He's been a government lawyer for a dozen years; he's only a GS-12. I spend more in tips than Barcella earns a year."*

Philip Tucker, the undercover U.S. marshal, was sitting just behind Wilson and had no trouble overhearing the comments, for Keiser was sitting across the aisle and had to lean over to talk to him. Wilson drank Chivas Regal Scotch steadily throughout the flight. When Wilson finally subsided and dozed, Tucker slipped away to the lavatory and made notes. Tucker now had no doubt as to the source of the death threats against Barcella the previous February.

Wilson was drowsy and hung over when Iberia Airlines flight 945 arrived in Santo Domingo at 5 o'clock the morning of June 15. A Dominican official met Keiser and Wilson when they came into the international lounge and approached the customs desk. The official took Wilson's passport, glanced at it and said, "Come with me; there is something wrong with your papers." Wilson looked around. A man in a business suit, an American by his appearance, stood a few feet away. Ernie Keiser had vanished into the night. "Shit," Wilson said softly. He was led to a small office within the airport complex and was effectively held under arrest until a few minutes before 9 A.M.

Several Dominican officials came into the office. "Your

---

*As an assistant U.S. attorney, Barcella did not have a GS rating. His salary was the maximum for a federal employee—slightly more than $62,000 per year.

papers are not in order," one of them said. "You are being put on the next plane to New York, which is leaving within a few minutes. You are to come with us."

Wilson protested. "Hell, no," he said, "I'm not going to New York. I don't want to go to New York. Here, look, I have a visa. Look in my passport: a visa for the Dominican Republic."

"Ah, yes," the ranking official said. "Your passport. That is the paper that is not in order, Mr. Wilson. You are to come with us immediately, please." He was escorted to Dominicana Airlines flight 902. (Because Wilson was never admitted into the Dominican Republic, no extradition proceeding was needed to ship him out of the country.)

Wilson spent part of the flight frantically going through papers in his briefcase. One sheet he crumpled and put into an airsickness bag and left on his meal tray. Phil Tucker retrieved the paper from the trash. It was a net-worth statement showing some of the wealth Wilson had accumulated during his career. The bulk of Wilson's holdings was in real estate—properties valued at $15,209,500, encumbered by mortgages totaling $2,512,134. He listed them as follows:

Mount Airy Farms, Upperville, Virginia, 2,338 acres	$8,183,000
Vienna, Virginia, 21 acres	399,500
Rental property, Vienna, Virginia	86,000
Rental property, Washington, D.C., town house	500,000
Beach property, Loveladies, New Jersey	92,000
5.9 acres, Sterling, Virginia	300,000
Property, North Carolina	94,000
39.5 acres, Sterling, Virginia	580,000
1,000 acres, Marshall, Virginia	2,500,000
Morgan Lowers Farm, Middleburg, Virginia	225,000
West Virginia property	350,000
Mexican property	350,000
Lebanese property	50,000
Maltese property	1,500,000

Wilson's liquid assets, according to the balance sheet, were relatively small: $100,000 "cash on hand and in banks." He valued his various corporate holdings at $200,000 "fair market value," and cattle and machinery on Mount Airy Farm at $300,000. He listed his three airplanes at $450,000 and "operating capital" of $750,000. In addition to the $2.5 million in real estate mortgages, he listed his liabilities as $1,000 in household accounts and $10,000 estimated federal and state income taxes.

As a true picture of Wilson's wealth, the balance sheet was grossly misleading. It made no mention of the lucrative supply contracts he then held with the Libyan Government, which brought him profits of more than $2 million a year. It ignored his two English farm properties. And to investigators familiar with Wilson's business dealings, the $100,000 "cash on hand and in banks" seemed suspiciously low. But even taken at face value, the account showed a dramatic rise in Wilson's wealth—from $2 million when he left Task Force 157 in the spring of 1976 to a shade more than $14 million—in six years' time.

Whatever thoughts Edwin P. Wilson had of enjoying his fortune evaporated when he walked off the airliner at Kennedy International Airport in New York. Two federal agents awaited him, and one of them held a pair of handcuffs. "Mr. Wilson, you are to come with us," he said. He read an arrest warrant, warned Wilson of his right to remain silent and slipped the cuffs over his wrists. The fugitive was now in the hands of the Department of Justice.

A few hours later, a dour Wilson glowered at Larry Barcella at a bond hearing before U.S. Magistrate A. Simon Chrein in the Federal Building in Brooklyn. At least once, his lips silently formed the words "You bastard." Chrein set bail at $20 million. Just before he was led away, Wilson called, "Larry, I've got to see you about something. Something is going on you don't know about."

"Keats isn't here," Barcella replied. "We're going to have a lot of time to talk. A lot of time."

"No, no," Wilson insisted. "I've got to see you now. Something is going down you don't know about." Barcella agreed to come to Wilson's cell once Keats arrived.

One part of Barcella's deal with Keiser was that the former spook's role in the arrest not be revealed. The cover story contrived by the U.S. Attorney's Office and the U.S. Marshals Service was to the effect that an alert visa clerk in the London embassy had recognized Wilson's photograph on the "Phillip McCormack" passport, leading to a worldwide watch for anyone attempting to travel with the document. Keiser would disappear; Wilson would never know how he had been tricked.

The cover story survived only a few hours. Attorney General William French Smith personally announced the arrest at a new conference. He simply praised the marshals for "a job well done," but his aides could not resist leaking bits and pieces of the true story to the press; within hours, Justice Department reporters knew that someone described as "a trusted associate" had lured Wilson from his sanctuary. Within two days, Keiser's name was in the papers, to the chagrin of everyone directly involved in the operation. Eugene M. Propper, Keiser's attorney, called the leak "incredibly damned dumb; and Ernie suffered for it."

John Keats heard news of the arrest in a radio report. "I was pissed," Keats said, probably as a considerable understatement. He hurried to New York to aid his client. Wilson insisted that he talk to Barcella. "Keats and I went down to the cellblock," Barcella recounted. "Ed gave me what sounded like a wild story about coming out of Libya on an 'NSC mission.' He claimed that Keiser had shown him a letter on NSC stationery. Since I had told Ernie to get off the NSC track, I thought that Wilson was either lying or mistaken." But when Bobbi Barnes returned to Washington several days later, she told the same story.

Barcella confronted Keiser, who smiled. "You told me it was no legal problem, only appearances," said Keiser. "I was hoping you would not find out." Barcella was sore for a few weeks, but finally conceded that had Keiser put forth the NSC ruse as the only possible means of trapping Wilson, he would "probably" have approved.

When John Keats began discussing tactics with Wilson, he found his client surprisingly unconcerned. "Keiser will get me out of this thing," Wilson said confidently. "Things are in motion."

Keats tried to telephone Keiser. If the NSC assurances

were true, as Wilson still insisted they were, Keiser should be able to walk Wilson out of jail. Keats was able to reach only Keiser's wife, who would tell him nothing of her husband's whereabouts. Finally Keiser called Keats. "Stop telephoning here—you are bothering me and my wife," he said, and hung up. Keats never talked to him again.

"It took three or four days in jail to make Ed Wilson realize Keiser had fucked him," Keats said.

36

Victims

The realization that he had in fact been caught by Barcella staggered what was left of Edwin Wilson's mental stability. Even in talks with his lawyers—people who knew the truth—he continued to insist that he had done nothing wrong, that eventually "my high-placed friends" in the intelligence community and the Defense Department would see to his freedom. The kernel of truth in his insistence was that Wilson had indeed continued contacts with such persons as Theodore Shackley and Thomas Clines of CIA and Major General Richard Secord of Pentagon procurement long after he came under official investigation. One person who talked with Wilson in the days immediately after his arrest stated, "Ed felt that the very fact that he had associated with these people would cause them to come forward in his behalf. He had told the lie about his 'intelligence involvement' so many times that I think he had convinced himself."

Wilson refused to accept any responsibility for his arrest. Somehow attorney John Keats was to blame—despite Keats's having warned Wilson from the very beginning to avoid any contact with Ernest Keiser—and so Wilson once again began lawyer-shopping. Someone recommended Herald Price

Fahringer, a New York criminal and personal-injury lawyer who had recently gained publicity for handling the appeal of Jean Harris in the "Scarsdale Diet Doctor" murder case. A man of imposing confidence and florid speech, Fahringer immediately began telling the press that Wilson, if he was forced to trial, "would shake the Central Intelligence Agency to its core." Keats, who had counseled a more conventional defense, remained on Wilson's legal team, but answerable to Fahringer. As the summer wore on, new indictments came down against Wilson: the C-4 case in Houston; the pistol and M-16 smuggling charge in Alexandria, Virginia.

Wilson's announced "I-did-it-for-the-CIA" defense never materialized, even though he and his lawyers had several opportunities to invoke it. Wilson, by happenstance, was the first former intelligence officer brought to trial since passage in 1980 of the Classified Information Procedures Act—the so-called "graymail law." Several times in the 1970s the government had been hampered in attempts to try persons with former intelligence connections because of their threats to disclose classified information in their defense. (In one case, the government chose to abandon several prosecutions arising from CIA's involvement with ITT in attempts to overthrow the Allende Government in Chile.)

The graymail law, Congress' solution to the problem, spelled out specific pretrial procedures to be followed by a defendant intending to use classified information. Foremost was submitting proof that the secret material was relevant to the case at hand. The judge was to review such material in a closed court hearing and make the determination. But Fahringer, having announced his "intelligence defense," showed little enthusiasm for following the procedural dictates of the act; a succession of federal judges had to enter orders to bring him into compliance (once to obtain the necessary security clearances, again to file with the court a description of the material he intended to use).

In all, five federal judges heard Wilson's lawyers argue the intelligence defense—two in Alexandria, one in Houston, and one in Washington, one in New York. In each forum Wilson's attorneys outlined three areas in which Wilson had "helped" the CIA while working in Libya: procurement of samples of Soviet military equipment which he had passed along to the United States; the sabotage of the Libyan attempt to purchase an atomic bomb from Armand Donnay, the Belgian arms dealer; and his attempt to find the fugitives wanted in the Letelier murders. In each instance, the government presented compelling rebuttal testimony that Wilson's claims were hollow. And in each instance the judge ruled against Wilson.

The flaw in Wilson's case was that although challenged frequently to do so, he could not name a single official of CIA to whom he had reported, formally or informally, after his official contacts with Ted Shackley ended in 1977. Had he identified one such contact, the government would have been compelled to produce the person.

Of course the reason Ed Wilson did not name such a contact was that none existed. Wilson now found himself in a situation in which bluff and lies did not count—only the verifiable truth.

Aside from the perfunctory court appearances in the cities where he faced indictments, Wilson spent his days restlessly pacing the corridor of Floor 9 South of the Metropolitan Correctional Center, at 150 Park Row in lower Manhattan, adjacent to the U.S. District Court House on Foley Square. As jails go, the MCC is a tolerably attractive place—from the outside, and on the ground floor, at any rate. Its facade of rough-surfaced beige stone is slit by tall, deep windows. Save for a discreet bronze sign announcing it as a facility of the Federal Bureau of Prisons, the MCC could pass for a brokerage house or an insurance headquarters. A holding center for persons awaiting trial in the Southern District of New York who cannot make bail, and considered the epitome of modern penal technology, the MCC is known as a "secure jail." Prisoners can be held there by varying degrees of control form run-of-the-ward to maximum-security isolation. One discreet function of the MCC is to house "hot prisoners"—men whose informing activities lead in other institutions to their being maimed or murdered by fellow inmates.

In prison, the most detested of all inmates is the informer, a person who tells on his fellows in the hope of better treatment or release. Wayne Trimmer was one such MCC inmate. Trimmer wanted out of jail, desperately so. He went to sleep at night dreaming of freedom; he awoke to the same thought. Trimmer had been 22 years old in 1966 when he and two other men mugged a drunk behind a bar in Buffalo, New York. Although Trimmer protested that he had no part in "stomping and kicking" the victim to death, he went to prison in 1968 for murder under a term that meant he would not be up for parole until 1989. Griping about "injustice," Trimmer did hard time. At the notorious Attica prison he carried the yard name "The Beast," and there he aligned himself with the *mafiosi* who controlled prison rackets. In 1971, Trimmer told an inquiring reporter who visited the prison that Attica was "about to blow." When the prison did "blow" a few weeks later, Trimmer was cast in the media as a "riot leader"—a designation he did not warrant. (Frank "Big Black" Smith, a black gang leader in Attica, told me, "Trimmer was a pussy. He walked with a swagger not because he was tough, but because he had tough friends.") Guards beat Trimmer black-and-blue, and he was transferred to Greenhaven, another Upstate prison. In 1979 he put on a smuggled new suit and, mingling with visitors, walked out of the Greenhaven front gate—then ran pell-mell to Florida.

During eighteen precious months of freedom, Trimmer smuggled drugs. He made fifteen, perhaps twenty flights from Colombia to Florida and Georgia. He learned to fly a plane with no formal training: He watched another pilot, and afterward "it was monkey-see, monkey-do"—even for solo hops across the Gulf of Mexico. He made little money, but he breathed free air. And when Florida police finally arrested him as an escapee in May 1981, he was willing to do anything to get out of jail again.

So Trimmer became an informer. He told New York officials about corruption among Greenhaven prison guards. As a reward, he received a relatively meager 1½-to-3-year additional term for escape. When the sentencing judge inadvertently blurted out that Trimmer had informed, New York authorities arranged for Trimmer to be housed in the Metropolitan Correctional Center for his own protection. His guise was that of a suspected drug smuggler whose case was about to be thrown out on a legal technicality.

This was May 1982—a month before Edwin Wilson was arrested and jailed at MCC. Trimmer had a standing arrangement. When he heard information he thought of interest, he would contact Benedict Serrano, an investigator for the U.S.

Marshals Service who worked out of the U.S. Attorney's Office in Manhattan. Trimmer, by his own account, was a "passive informant"; he would listen, but not initiate conversations about criminality.

The arrival of Edwin P. Wilson, former CIA officer and accused international arms dealer, created a minor stir on 9 South. The nature of Wilson's charge, his CIA background, his imposing physical appearance, his reputed wealth all made him a conspicuous figure. Trimmer knew nothing of Wilson's background, but in casual exploratory conversations he was told that "I'm former CIA," and "They've got me in here on a bunch of trumped-up shit." Trimmer, for his part, identified himself as "a convicted murderer who busted out of jail once" who now was being held on a drug-smuggling charge. "But they ain't got nothing," he said. "I'm going to be out of here in a bit. They gotta run me through the court Upstate, but I'll be on the street before the snow is there."

Soon Trimmer and Wilson were spending many hours together daily, either sitting in the 9 South dayroom or on the bunks in one of their respective cells. Prisoners can move as they wish on 9 South from 7 A.M. until 11 P.M. (although in the segregation wing, inmates are in their cells all but five hours weekly.)

Trimmer apparently impressed Wilson as a can-do sort of thug: a convicted murderer who had survived Attica, had escaped and made money running drugs from Latin America. With his inventive imagination, Trimmer had no problem satisfying Wilson's curiosity, blending a yarn that was partial truth (based on his Florida experiences) and outright lies (the big-time details he felt Wilson wished to hear).

The talk turned to a partnership in drugs. "Ed had a couple of airplanes, and I said I had some drug connections in South America," Trimmer related. "I told him I had a friend on the street who was running the drug business for me while I was still in jail."

Trimmer reported the conversations to investigator Benny Serrano, who on November 2 outfitted Trimmer with a concealed tape recorder and sent him back to 9 South to continue talking with Wilson.

Trimmer at the outset found Wilson preoccupied with one subject: Kevin Mulcahy, the onetime CIA technician who had worked for him, then broken with him, then pursued him with ferret tenacity; then had been found dead under mysterious circumstances outside a $50-a-week motel cabin in the Shenandoah Valley of Virginia.

Perhaps appropriately, Kevin Mulcahy's last days were tortuous. As other former Wilson employees returned to the United States to testify before grand juries and to give interviews to prosecutors and FBI agents, he had seen his status slip from "key figure" in the Wilson investigation to one-witness-among-many. Mulcahy did not take kindly to his fall from prominence, but he continued to feed tips to the media on the Wilson probe, receiving in some instances liberal "expenses" that were tantamount to payments for news. He struck up a close friendship with Dale Van Atta, an aggressive young reporter on the Jack Anderson staff, and during two days of interviews provided the meat for several strong columns. (Mulcahy did not receive any money from Anderson—only a couple of meals at the Trio Restaurant, which Van Atta rightly described as "one of Washington's less fashionable eateries.")

To the disgust of many reporters, Mulcahy learned to play one organization against another. He would give one newspaper or network a lead on a Wilson story, then nudge a competitor in the same direction. According to Van Atta, a team of *New York Times* reporters acting independently of Mulcahy found the Wilson farm in south England where Eugene Tafoya had stayed after trying to kill the Libyan dissident in Colorado. "Mulcahy cheated them [*Times* reporters] out of a scoop by tipping off *CBS Evening News* and, for a fee, being interviewed outside the house the same day the *Times* found it. . . . The *Times* reporters were furious at being robbed by Mulcahy, who, in effect, had gone to the highest bidder."

Mulcahy also wore his welcome thin with the Justice Department. At one point, to Larry Barcella's considerable annoyance, Mulcahy took it upon himself to negotiate the return of Douglas Schlachter to the United States. Barcella told him, in essence, to go to hell: if Schlachter wished to discuss a deal, he or his lawyer should call the Justice Department. Mulcahy had no standing in the case, and Barcella would not deal with him.

The rebuff angered Mulcahy. The next Barcella heard

from him was a late-afternoon phone call. Mulcahy announced, "Dan Rather is on the other line. In five minutes CBS News is going on the air with the story that you are refusing to make a deal to get Schlachter's testimony because you are afraid of him. Schlachter knows too much. You are hushing up a major scandal." He demanded that Barcella talk with Rather. Barcella dropped the phone receiver onto the hook and began a mental count. Mulcahy's call back would begin with his dialing the area code, 202 . . . then 633 . . . Barcella said the ten digits of his phone number, and the phone rang. He picked it up and said, "Hello, Kevin. You and Dan Rather say what you want to say," and hung up again. CBS did no story.

In the fall of 1982, as Wilson's first trial approached, Mulcahy began drinking heavily again, this time cheap wines and domestic champagne. He had little money. He talked with several writers about doing a book on Wilson. But there were obstacles. One journalist said, "Keeping Kevin sober and on course long enough to do a book would have made Job's lot look like a picnic." Because of Mulcahy's past employment with the CIA, and the Snepp court decision, any manuscript would require Agency clearance.

So Mulcahy began roaming. He put suitcases, his box of precious "Wilson files" and half a dozen or so bottles of wine into his ramshackle 1968 pickup truck and drove to friends' homes to talk long into the night. To at least one person he spoke of suicide. "I'm going to drink until I don't wake up," he said. The friend did not take him seriously. "Try shooting," he said; "it's easier." "No, I don't have the stomach for that," Mulcahy replied.

On October 20, 1982, Mulcahy rented a $50-a-week cabin at the Mountain View Motel Court in Edinburg, Virginia, a Shenandoah Valley hamlet about 90 miles west of Washington. He told the owner, David M. Stocker, Jr., that he was a journalist working on a story about migrant-labor conditions. The next days Mulcahy for the most part stayed in his cabin, emerging occasionally to buy more wine. Two friends came by one evening and found him incoherent. On Monday afternoon, October 25, he inexplicably fired a 12-gauge shotgun out the window. Stocker told him he must leave.

At dusk, Mulcahy put five suitcases, a quilt, a carton of Camel cigarettes and his shotgun into the cab of his truck; there was also an unopened bottle of wine wrapped in a windbreaker. Another resident saw him staggering around the parking lot in the early hours of the evening. Several times he got into the truck and honked the horn and called out the manager's name. His behavior had been so erratic in the past that no one took any notice of him.

The overnight temperature was in the low 40s, and a light rain fell sporadically. The next morning, October 26, a woman who lived in an adjacent cabin was walking her son to the school bus when she noticed Mulcahy slumped against the door of his cottage. His slacks were around his knees, and only a light sports jacket covered his upper body. As the woman told the reporters later, "He was in a hunched-up position with his arms crossed. I didn't touch him or nothing. I just screamed." Kevin Mulcahy's body was rigid and cold.

The door to Mulcahy's cabin was locked. Inside, on the bed, were the keys to his truck. Also in the cabin was a cardboard box containing a dozen empty fifth-size Gallo Rhine wine bottles.

The death touched off a media frenzy: Had Ed Wilson— or the CIA itself—reached out to kill Mulcahy to keep him from testifying at the forthcoming trial? The previous March, someone recollected, Rafael Villaverde, one of the Cubans whom Wilson and Frank Terpil had tried to recruit for the Cairo murder of a Libyan dissident, had died when his boat exploded and burned off Florida. That death—seemingly accidental at the time—suddenly became a "mystery death." And now reporters swarmed over the remote Virginia hamlet of Edinburg. To their dismay, the local sheriff, Marshall Robinson, would not share in the excitement. In his rural county, Robinson said, "the biggest problems we have is dead cows."

Then the FBI flooded Edinburg with agents, for the Wilson case had been marked throughout by bizarre twists.

Several days later, a Virginia state medical examiner put the "mystery" to rest. Kevin Mulcahy, already suffering from bronchial pneumonia and emphysema, had died of natural causes, aggravated by exposure to the cold and rain.

The man whom Dale Van Atta had called the "supersource" for the Wilson probe was buried from a funeral home in Northern Virginia. He was 40 years old.

In somewhat less dramatic fashion, linkage to Edwin Wilson ended the career of Major General Richard V. Secord, the Air force foreign-sales executive. In a CBS News interview in November 1981, former Wilson associate Douglas Schlachter, then under indictment, charged that Secord had helped Wilson sell military equipment to Iran in the early 1970s and shared in the profits. Secord in 1981 was deputy assistant secretary of defense for the Near East, Africa and South Asia. Because of the sensitivity of his position, and the gravity of the charges, the Justice Department initiated an investigation. In January 1982, Secord was offered promotion to three-star rank only to have the Defense Department retract the offer and put him on indefinite leave as a result of the probe. Four months later, the Defense Department determined that Schlachter's allegations were "without merit," and Secord was reinstated to his previous position.

Nonetheless, in the highly competitive military world, even the unfounded charges permanently blighted Secord's career. He had been on a track that would have put him into the directorship of the Defense Security Assistance Agency, which handles all foreign military sales. Given his relative youth (Secord was 50 years of age in 1982), he could conceivably have become air chief of staff. But as Francis J. West, assistant secretary of defense for international security affairs, was to testify in later court proceedings, further high promotions "would not be possible because of Schlachter's allegations."

Secord sued Schlachter for libel and slander. Schlachter, living under a new identity in the Federal Witness Protection Program, did not respond to the suit. In April 1983, Judge June L. Green of the U.S. District Court in Washington gave Secord a default judgment of some $1 million. But the court victory was hollow: in his new life, Schlachter had effectively disappeared from the face of the earth. The Justice Department would forward court papers to him, but would make no effort to help Secord collect the money. Schlachter had no visible assets. As one of Secord's lawyers said, "It's like suing a cloud—you reach out your hand and nothing's there."

The embittered Secord took early retirement from the Air Force, his professional life at a premature end. "He's as much a victim of Ed Wilson as if Wilson had shot him," his lawyer stated.

* * *

Another person caught in the investigative net was Waldo Dubberstein, the Defense Intelligence Agency expert on the Middle East who had passed information to Wilson—and thence to the Libyans—beginning in 1977. The case against Dubberstein was tight: Bobbi Barnes admitted paying him the initial $1,000 for travel expenses to Libya, and Douglas Schlachter testified to a grand jury that he acted as a conduit for documents Dubberstein passed to Wilson. Schlachter also produced a selection of these documents which counterintelligence experts easily traced to Dubberstein; some even bore the fingerprints of Dubberstein's German-born girlfriend. To the grand jury, the old man insisted that he was innocent. Any work he had done for Wilson was in the role of "private consultant," and no classified material had left his hands. But since entire paragraphs in these documents had been lifted verbatim from Secret and Top Secret DIA papers, Dubberstein's defense rang hollow. Nor was he convincing when he argued that he had acted for Wilson "on Agency business." If innocent, why had Dubberstein not reported his foreign travel and outside contacts to Defense Department superiors, as required by security regulations? Dubberstein could supply no answers.

By late April 1983, Dubberstein—now 75 years of age, and distraught—knew he was to be indicted. The weekend of April 24–25, he went to a sporting-goods store in suburban Annandale, Virginia, and bought a 12-gauge shotgun and a box of shells. On April 28, a federal grand jury in Alexandria returned a seven-count indictment charging Dubberstein with conspiracy, unauthorized disclosure of classified information and bribery. That afternoon, Dubberstein met with his lawyers, Howard Bushman and Louis Koutoulakos, to discuss plans for his surrender and arraignment the following day. Dubberstein was agitated: after four decades in intelligence, he was to be branded publicly as a man who had broken the rules, and to the benefit of a hostile nation.

Regardless of the outcome of any trial, "Doobie" Dubberstein knew his life was over. But to his lawyers, who tried to lend a sympathetic ear, Dubberstein continued to insist that he was innocent. All he had done, he protested, was help his old friend Ed Wilson "in a special mission involving Libya for the CIA." He said much the same thing that evening when he dined with his estranged wife. He then went off to spend the night with his girlfriend.

Dubberstein did not appear in court at 9 A.M. on April 29, as he had promised. Judge Albert V. Bryan, Jr., waited an hour, then issued a bench warrant for his arrest, and FBI agents began a search. At about two in the afternoon, an Arlington citizen called the local police and suggested they "check on the welfare" of a man in the storage area of River Place, the apartment building where Dubberstein had lived with his young girlfriend.

A policeman opened the door to the small basement room and turned away, bile rising in his throat. The old spook had put the 12-gauge shotgun in his mouth and blown away most of his head. Three notes—one each to his lawyers, his wife and his girlfriend—repeated his claim "I am not guilty."

Later that day, Herald Price Fahringer called Howard Bushman and said he wished to pass on a direct quotation from Ed Wilson: "Waldo was a good American patriot who never did anything wrong." Thinking of Dubberstein's family, Bushman asked Fahringer if Wilson would make such a statement public. As a convicted felon, Wilson carried little public credibility, but Bushman felt that any gesture at all would ease the pain of Dubberstein's wife and son.

No, Fahringer replied, Wilson would not make any public statement, for he had his own appeals to consider.

Bushman, who had come to loathe Ed Wilson during the weeks he represented Waldo Dubberstein, stated bitterly, "In Ed Wilson, the government created a monster."

And, finally, Edwin Wilson's criminality touched the upper echelons of the Central Intelligence Agency. As noted, Wilson had lent $500,000 to Thomas G. Clines, formerly a high official in CIA's Operations Directorate, the clandestine arm. Clines invested the sum in a company he created (Systems Services International) to handle shipments of arms sold to Egypt under the 1979 Camp David agreements. During an intricate investigation that lasted more than two years, assistant U.S. attorney Theodore Greenberg documented that during a twenty-month period, the shippers by means of inflated invoices, had cheated the Defense Department out of more than $8 million. On behalf of SSI, Clines entered a guilty plea, and the firm agreed to repay the government $100,000 (of its profit of $2.5 million from the inflated bills). SSI also paid the maximum $10,000 fine.

The nature of the pleas was such that Clines did not personally receive the felony conviction. But SSI was his company, and he was the person who stood before a federal judge to admit its guilt. Further, he agreed to tell a grand jury how the Pentagon had come to award the contracts in the first place—which meant that this particular offshoot of the Wilson cases would be around the courts for months to come. (The other guilty pleas came from the Egyptian-American Transport and Services Corporation, or EATSCO, and its president, Hussein Salem, each fined $20,000, and Air Freight International of Baltimore, fined $10,000. Additionally, EATSCO repaid the government $3 million and AFT $100,000.)

There was one outstanding piece of Wilson business remaining to be resolved in Europe.

In 1980, when Wilson was maneuvering to shift his base of operations from Libya to another country, he still had some of the 20-ton shipment of C-4 explosives he had smuggled into Libya in 1977 with the help of dealer Jerome Brower. Wilson recognized that if he abandoned Libya, he abandoned the explosives as well, so he made a deal with Libyan intelligence. He shipped the C-4 to the Rotterdam warehouse of Westship, the shipping agency controlled by Wolfgang Steiniger, the German-born entrepreneur whose services had often been used by the Wilson organization. The agreement was that Steiniger would hold the explosives on a "shipment on call" basis, and make them available to Libyan intelligence agents based in Europe as directed by Wilson.

The presence of the explosives prompted an immediate dispute between Steiniger and Wilson which continued over the next few years. By Steiniger's claim, Wilson owed—and refused to pay—$45,000 in storage charges for the explosives. And then, after a few weeks in the warehouse, the 5-gallon containers of C-4 began to "sweat"—that is, beads of liquid condensed on the outside of the cans. Alex Raffio, working at the time on a non-Wilson electronics contract with Steiniger, agreed to take the complaints to Libya. "Steiniger didn't tell me he had C-4 in his warehouse," Raffio said; "he said only to advise Ed that 'the soap was leaking.'" In Tripoli, Raffio offered to repackage "the chemicals" and arrange to move them to satisfy Steiniger.

Wilson cursed. "Chemicals, hell," he told Raffio; "what

Steiniger is bitching about is C-4. Keep your hands off it—that's the most dangerous explosive in the world." Raffio wished to hear no more.

At Wilson's order, John Heath went to the Westship warehouse and spent a laborious day removing the compressed C-4 from Brower's original containers and repacking it into more secure tins.

"Ed told me he wanted to send part of this stuff to London, but how I got it there was my concern," Heath said. So he put several pounds of the C-4 into a paint container, filled the can to the brim with a heavy paint and sealed it. "I put the can in the trunk of a car and rode the ferry to England. I went through customs without a ripple." Following Wilson's directions, Heath went to a juice bar and waited until he was approached by a young Arabic man. "We got into our cars and did some riding around, and eventually he stopped and I handed over the C-4. Who he was, and where he took it, I don't know. But I understood that he was with the Libyan Embassy."

Wilson and Steiniger, meanwhile, continued to haggle over the storage charges. At one point Wilson sent the German $10,000 in cash, refusing to pay the remaining $35,000. After Wilson's arrest, Raffio urged that Steiniger "dump the stuff into the ocean," but Steiniger refused; he was still owed $35,000, and he would sell the C-4 where he could.

"You're out of your goddamned mind," Raffio stormed at Steiniger when he heard this over the phone. "The only people who would buy this stuff now is the PLO—and you know what they're going to do with it."

Steiniger laughed at Raffio. He mentioned that a CBS reporter had been coming around his warehouse, asking about his involvement with Wilson. The reporter knew nothing of the C-4. "If you don't like the deal," Steiniger said, "there's always CBS. Maybe they would listen to me."

Raffio put down the phone in a rage. Although Wilson was in jail, his murderous crimes threatened to continue after him. If nothing else, Raffio thought, he had to keep the C-4 from getting to the PLO. He was living in London now, and the PLO was bombing people in London. He had a responsibility to do something about this.

Raffio did not like the CBS reporter, but he did know a

Washington reporter for rival NBC—James Polk, a next-door
neighbor in Arlington, Virginia, of a Raffio classmate from
Fordham. On December 10, 1982, Raffio telephoned the
United States. He was coming home, and he wished to talk to
both NBC and the FBI.

Acting on Raffio's information, Dutch police raided
Steiniger's warehouse in the final days of 1982 and seized the
last of Wilson's C-4. "I felt that I had finally purged myself of
Ed Wilson and all he represented," Raffio said.

37

The Hit-List Case

But as the human debris of his onetime associates swirled
around him, Edwin Wilson could think of only two things: his
own freedom, and revenge upon the persons who had put
him in jail. The first day informant Wayne Trimmer went into
Wilson's New York jail cell with a concealed tape recorder, he
heard much talk about Kevin Mulcahy. Wilson shed no false
tears for his colleague-turned-adversary. "I'd have loved to
knock the guy off, but I didn't do it," Wilson said, as
Trimmer's recorder spun silently. Wilson's sole concern was
Mulcahy's impact on his own case.

"The problem is that this guy getting killed hurt
me ... because it brought a lot more publicity down on
me.... I couldn't have picked a worse time.... Except they
would have used him to testify about some of this bullshit
testimony, you know.... [I]t probably helped a little bit.... I
think I'll beat the fucking thing."

The talk then turned to their narcotics plot, and how
they might stay in contact in the event that either was
released from jail, or transferred. Wilson mentioned a New
York law firm where "They don't talk; they don't squeal."

TRIMMER: Here's what I am going to need from you, I think. When I first get out I'm going to go down and set that thing up with those people in... South America.

WILSON: Yeah.

TRIMMER: The first thing I'm going to take is the coke deal.

WILSON: YEAH.

TRIMMER: I might even take... that guy [unintelligible] talking about you can move that in that pouch routine, you're talking about maybe three hundred pounds.

WILSON: Yeah.... They can meet and introduce you to the person who will set the whole thing up. They got the connections... they represent South American countries and people down there... but more important, they can do the pouch thing... a buyer and a seller.

There was talk about the need for a "no-problem" American passport, and the mechanics of maintaining contact, with both Herald Fahringer and Diane Byrne mentioned by Wilson as conduits.* Wilson admitted to a cash-flow problem. He had sold Broxmead Grange at a loss, realizing only $130,000 for a property for which he had paid $300,000, and he had disposed of other properties at fire-sale prices: a Beechcraft plane, purchased for $175,000, had gone for $66,000. Wilson desperately needed money for lawyers; but then he claimed that he held a $10-million clothing contract which would soon bring him $200,000 to $300,000 monthly, for a total of $1.5 million. This money, he told Trimmer, "keeps me active until I can get out of here and get shit going on the street again." The only problem he foresaw was timing.

WILSON: It depends on how much you'd need. If you need a couple hundred thousand bucks, that shouldn't be a problem, in fact, but by March or April if you need five hundred grand that shouldn't be that much of a problem.

TRIMMER: Okay. 'Cause you know I can't afford to finance that deal myself.

WILSON: No. What would it take to finance it?

TRIMMER: It wouldn't take that much—not five hundred thousand.

WILSON: Two hundred and fifty grand?

TRIMMER: [Unintelligible]

---

*Neither of these persons was shown to have any knowledge of Wilson's drug plot.

WILSON: We could do that.

Wilson then mentioned his pending trials in Washington, Houston and Virginia. He expected that "it's going to be like [the] Lindbergh trial . . . a thousand fucking reporters from all over the world there." He continued:

"Oh, they want my ass bad. This fucking prosecutor [Barcella] wants me bad. . . . But he's going to have to take a lot of people down to get me, you know, because . . . I did my job and all that bullshit. I'm not trying to justify it, but I'm just not going to do the fucking time when all these other assholes hung around there and after I put them . . . in business for five hundred thousand and they made . . . fucking millions of dollars.

"They beat me out. I barely got my five hundred grand back and I should sit back now and say, 'Oh, well, fine. I don't want to bother you,' and do a Lebanon-type martyr bullshit. . . .

"Fuck them. They all agreed to testify now. The general, the former number two guy in CIA [unintelligible] . . . have agreed. They will get on the stand and say I was working for U.S. intelligence to hand them information.

"I think they got to get smart somewhere along the line and say, 'Listen, we just can't stand all this fucking talk, all this publicity, let's go over there and talk to this guy [Barcella] and make a fair deal for everybody.' I can't see them not wanting to do that. Unless they are really getting stupid here."

Wilson was indulging himself in wishful thinking in this attempt to convince Trimmer that he was a betrayed man who would be free once his friends came to his aid. The context makes plain that he referred to Major General Richard Secord, the Pentagon procurement official, and Theodore Shackley, the retired CIA executive. Through either guile or ignorance, Wilson slid around the fact that both men had already told Wilson's lawyers they would not testify for him.

Trimmer reported the talk about narcotics smuggling to Benny Serrano, who consulted with superiors in the U.S. Attorney's Office and found that the government was not interested in pursuing any such investigation. As one agent told Trimmer, "Look, forget this guy; he's got so many problems already that we don't want to waste any more time on him. He's not in any position to make a drug deal anyway."

The agent's point was real. The federal case against Wilson was strengthening daily, and the government did not wish to spend any more time and money on new probes. Furthermore, Trimmer might unwittingly draw Wilson into talks about his defense plans for his pending trial. Courts had held repeatedly that such an intrusion, even if unwitting, can jeopardize a conviction, and the Justice Department had expended far too much effort to bring Wilson to trial to risk losing the case on an inadvertent breach of his constitutional rights.

Trimmer groused at his rejection. "Fuckers," he said. "I bring you a guy who is just dying to become a big drug dealer, and you tell me to go home and sit down."

But Trimmer and Wilson continued talking—the two men by now had the semblance of a jailhouse friendship, chiefly because they considered themselves a cut above the other inmates—and later in November the subject matter changed abruptly.

Wilson raised the subject of murder. As Trimmer was to recount later, "He had a bunch of people who were going to testify. If he could get rid of these people, he had a pretty good chance of keeping out of jail." Wilson asked Trimmer if he could be of any help. "I have a partner on the street," Trimmer said. Actually, he did not, but he had decided to string Wilson along. Beginning in early November, Wilson and Trimmer talked about assassinations daily. The first person named by Wilson was Ernest Keiser.

"How much do you want?" Wilson asked.

"Fifty thousand," Trimmer replied. "Half up front, half on completion."

Wilson was taken to Alexandria in mid-November for a hearing. When he returned, he began pushing Trimmer to contact his partner and get the plot under way. "I was stalling," says Trimmer. "I didn't have no partner out there." But Trimmer began to concoct the background of a totally fictitious partner based roughly on the career of a onetime fellow inmate of Attica. Trimmer told Wilson his friend was "connected with organized crime" and intended to pay a judge $50,000 to get him out of jail on a legal technicality. "I made it up," Trimmer said. "I told Wilson that this friend would go to work for him, carrying out the killings."

Wilson told Trimmer he had "people in Europe" but did not want to use them for the murders, because if caught they could be connected directly to him. But if Trimmer and his partner had other future murders, they were welcome to their services.

In the next days, Wilson gave Trimmer names and specific descriptions and locations of the persons he wished killed, as well as bitter summaries of how they had betrayed him. The priority Wilson put on each intended victim, and the sequence in which he wished them murdered, varied even daily, but his basic list comprised Ernest Keiser; Francis Heydt, the clothing manufacturer he claimed had cheated him on the uniform contract; Reginald Slocombe, his onetime shipper, whom Wilson suspected of conniving with Heydt; Rafael "Chi Chi" Quintero, his former CIA friend and business associate, a key witness in the Cairo murder plot; Edward J. Coughlin, his lawyer and money-handler in Geneva; John Heath; Jerome S. Brower, the California explosives magnate involved in the C-4 smuggling, and, first as a seeming afterthought, but then as serious targets, prosecutors Larry Barcella and Carol Bruce, his chief antagonists in the Justice Department. Of Barcella and Bruce, Wilson said, according to Trimmer, "These were the two people solely responsible for all his problems. The United States Government was not anxious to prosecute. They were trying to make a name for themselves at the expense of his reputation." Wilson did not include Alexandria prosecutor Theodore Greenberg on his hit list, although he referred to him as a "Jew bastard" and a "fucking asshole."

Wilson insisted on providing a scenario for each of the murders. His ideas ranged from feasible to outright bizarre. In his nuttiest scheme, he would have Trimmer and friend buy a camper, drive to Oklahoma or Kansas and kidnap Francis Heydt; they would then force Heydt to contact Reginald Slocombe in Virginia and have him come to a meeting, whereupon Trimmer and friend would shoot Slocombe "in the head" to show Heydt they meant serious business. Heydt supposedly would be so frightened he would contact one of his sons, who worked in his business, and have $3.5

million transferred to a bank account in Europe. The scheme suffered from a certain fuzziness of detail; it bore virtually no resemblance to a professional murder plot. Trimmer did not argue or point out the many junctures at which such a plan could go awry. "It was Mr. Wilson's idea," he said.

The Ed Coughlin plan seemed more realistic. Wilson was pushing Coughlin to sell his airplanes. Trimmer would be sent to Europe as a prospective buyer. Once they met, Trimmer (or the hit man) would "put a quart of whiskey down his throat and throw him off the seventeenth-floor balcony" of his penthouse apartment. "Then we'd torch his apartment. Wilson wanted all his records burned." If this failed, Trimmer and the hit man would drive Coughlin to a wooded area near the Geneva airport and shoot him.

To cover Brower's murder, he should be killed during a bogus robbery attempt. "If not possible, shoot him outright," Wilson said.

To shield their conversations, Wilson referred to intended victims by code names. Coughlin was "C" or "Europe." Brower was "West Coast"; Heydt, "Middle West"; Quintero, "South" or "Chi Chi." Wilson's son Erik, when he became involved, was called "Junior."

Although the original talk was about half-payment in advance on each $50,000 murder, Wilson convinced Trimmer that because of temporary trouble in raising cash he should have the first killing done for $10,000 of "front money," with the $40,000 balance to be paid later into an Austrian bank account. Wilson said Diane Byrne, in Wales, would arrange to open the account, and he gave Trimmer her phone and Telex numbers, as well as her address.

In giving information to Trimmer, Wilson resorted to spook tradecraft. He would come to Trimmer's cell with notes on victims—descriptions, how to find them, how to kill them—and either dictate them to Trimmer or have him copy them. "Ed said it would look bad if something in his handwriting was found in my possession," Trimmer said. After the copying, Wilson would tear up his notes and flush them down the toilet.

In mid-December, Wilson's plight darkened drastically. Judge Ross Sterling, after a hearing in Houston, held that Wilson's arrest through the Keiser scam was legal. Wilson returned to the Metropolitan Correctional Center in a frantic mood. "I'm running out of time," he told Trimmer. "Can't you get your friend off his ass and get him into motion?" Trimmer said the friend was "wrapping up some business; he wants to spend the [Christmas] holidays with his family. He'll be up right after the first of the year." Wilson confided that he had tried to find some hit men on his own while in Houston, and failed. He paid two men "from the Midwest" $10,000 on a $20,000 contract to kill Brower. Nothing happened, Wilson said, and he felt cheated. One of the men said Brower was not at his California home or office; the other that Brower was guarded by a U.S. marshal. Whatever the truth, Brower was not killed, and Wilson lost his $10,000.

Perhaps out of carelessness, Wilson broke his own security rules when giving Trimmer detailed information on Heydt. He handed Trimmer four pages torn from a legal pad with copious notes, in his own hand, about Heydt's home and business, his physical description ("6-2, 200 pounds, thick glasses, almost blind, former football player gone fat, devious, dominated his sons"). Trimmer could offer no explanation as to why Wilson let him keep these pages.

During December, Wilson also tossed out names of other people he wished dead. He spoke of Thomas Clines, his old colleague from the Central Intelligence Agency. Clines, Wilson said, "owes me two hundred thousand dollars. You collect the money, you kill him, you give me one hundred thousand and keep the rest for yourself."*

Wilson did raise some cautionary points. Because of the notoriety of his case, the deaths of the witnesses and prosecutors could bring repercussions. Under Coughlin's name, address and description, for instance, Wilson wrote, "lots of publicity; pressure would be on; accident; possible guard." Wilson directed that in each of the murders, if it was possible, Trimmer or his hit man was to "make it look like an accident."

Wilson seemed dubious about Trimmer at one point,

---

*The government did not include Clines in the list of intended victims cited in the indictment against Wilson. One prosecutor stated that Wilson's threat was "a onetime casual remark" which he had never pursued; hence chances were slight that "a real case could be made." Another explanation, perhaps a more valid one, was that including Clines would open up testimony about Wilson's involvement with former CIA officials, an area which the government wished to avoid during trial.

saying he had had "a nightmare about you being another Ernie Keiser." Trimmer a few hours later went to Wilson's cell and told him, "I'm not too happy about that dream."

Wilson laughed. "I didn't have any fucking dream. I was looking for your reaction. Another guy in the block has been telling me you're an informer, that sometimes you go out on a court call when your name doesn't appear on a court-call list. That's all."

With the money agreed upon, Trimmer next promised Wilson he would provide the hit man. John Martin, the U.S. attorney for the Southern District, by now had assigned an assistant, Eugene Kaplan, to oversee the case. Kaplan and Martin met on January 13, 1983, with Benny Serrano and Kenneth Walton, assistant head of the FBI office in New York. "We need a *mafioso*," Kaplan said. The chosen actor was Lynn DeVecchio, an FBI agent with seventeen years' experience, who can pose as a Milanese banker one day and a sausage peddler the next. DeVecchio in an instant can lapse into the quasi-sentence, garbled-syntax talk that makes him sound like a tough but illiterate Mafia hood. He would be "Tony DeAngelo."

Through Trimmer, Wilson said that his son Erik, aged 20, would be the intermediary to pass along the $10,000 down payment for the murder of Jerome Brower. Wilson never said anything to Trimmer that would indicate Erik Wilson knew why he was being paid the money.

To ensure that Erik could recognize DeAngelo, Trimmer and Wilson arranged that both would come to the MCC as visitors the afternoon of January 5. DeAngelo would be visiting Trimmer; he would not attempt to talk with Wilson because he knew Wilson could not have visitors other than the persons on his approved list.

On arriving at the MCC visitors' room, DeAngelo saw Wilson talking with his son, a stocky, blond-haired youth with a neat mustache. He and Erik did not speak, but they did exchange long unblinking glances; when they met again, they would recognize each other.

At this meeting Trimmer handed DeAngelo the hit list that Wilson had given him the previous evening. The murder sequence now was to be Coughlin, Quintero, Slocombe and Brower.

"We on?" Wilson asked Trimmer once the visitors had left.

"Yeah, we are," Trimmer replied. "But we're going to need the ten thousand dollars front money." Wilson said he would arrange for the $10,000 to go to his son, who in turn would give it to DeAngelo. Once the down payment was received, DeAngelo should go to California and kill Brower.

Obtaining the $10,000 took somewhat longer than Wilson had anticipated. Fortunately for his purpose, Bobbi Barnes had left London soon after his arrest and settled into a Northern Virginia town house Wilson had bought her just outside Washington. Bobbi remained torn about Ed Wilson: some days she hated him; other days she was pulling for him, keeping alive the hope that somehow he could shed himself of his troubles, even if it meant a short jail sentence, and they could still have a life together; most often, however, she was confused. No longer could she love Wilson wholeheartedly, but neither could she abandon him. So she continued doing his chores and his odd jobs, but now with the inescapable realization that she was doing them for a criminal.

On January 6, Wilson telephoned Bobbi Barnes and told her to have Diane Byrne withdraw $10,000 from one of his London accounts and transfer it to Barnes in Washington. Wilson told Barnes he needed the money "very quickly" to pay legal fees owed to Fahringer and Marian Rosen (his Houston lawyer). Barnes noticed that Wilson suggested a slightly different route than normal to acquire the money. Usually, he would ask that funds for his legal expenses be transferred into the "EPW Special Account" at the Riggs National Bank in Washington. But this time he asked that the money come to Barnes directly, and that she give it to Erik personally.

Barnes had no reason to believe that the money was for any purpose other than lawyer fees. But she did a bit of maneuvering herself. Realizing that the transfer of $10,000 or more triggers a bank notice to the Internal Revenue Service, she asked that Diane Byrne send her only $9,000. She took $1,000 from her own account to make up the balance. If the $10,000 should be reported to the IRS, she explained, "I did not want to be held accountable." She also had Erik sign a receipt: "Received from Bobbi Barnes, $10,000 for legal fees for Edwin Wilson."

That Wilson was so cash-short that he had trouble rummaging up the $10,000 down payment on a murder contract (which would eventually total $1.25 million) casts doubt on his ability to finance the complex scenario he discussed with Trimmer. Wilson's associates excited themselves in 1983 with talk about "hidden Swiss bank accounts" and caches in faraway countries. Had such secret cash been available, Wilson surely would have used it, rather than have the murder contracts abort for lack of money. Given Wilson's past record, my surmise is that he would have dribbled out what funds he had, a few thousand dollars at a time, to have his "hit man" kill as many enemies as possible before abandoning the project for lack of payment.

As directed by his father, Erik flew to New York and booked a room at the Sheraton Inn near La Guardia Airport. Using his father's answering service as a message center, he arranged a meeting with DeAngelo for that evening. Erik handed over an envelope containing $9,800 in hundred-dollar bills (explaining that he was keeping $200 for his travel expenses) and left, refusing to be drawn into any conversation.

The next morning, January 11, Wilson told Trimmer that the money had been passed—DeAngelo had the down payment for the murder. "He's en route to California now to do the job," Trimmer replied. Trimmer also told Wilson, "I'm getting out of here [the MCC] today; I'm going up to Buffalo to post bail on this bond application." (Trimmer had told Wilson he was in the MCC on a drug charge, and that a corrupt judge was taking a bribe to release him from jail.) Once he was released on bail, which he expected would happen within a few days, "I'll come back down here and contact you." (Trimmer's "release," in fact, had been staged; authorities simply shifted him to another jail.)

The afternoon of January 14, Trimmer called Wilson's answering service and left a message (using the name "Gene Adams," as agreed in advance).* When they made direct

<hr/>

*MCC prisoners awaiting trial could use a telephone-answering service to receive messages and to make long-distance telephone calls. For the latter, the prisoner put up a deposit. He would call the answering service from a pay phone, and the service would "patch through" his call. During the first weeks of his confinement, Wilson telephoned John Heath in Libya as many as four times daily. Libyan intelligence officials could not understand how a man in jail was permitted such access to a telephone.

contact, at 8:30 P.M., Trimmer reported that DeAngelo wa
returning from the West Coast, that something "fairly impor
tant" had arisen. Wilson was irritated. Because of changes i
the trial schedules, Trimmer and DeAngelo could forge
about the "real Far South guy [Quintero] till, probably
mid-February." This meant priority for Brower, whom h
called "the real crux of the whole goddamned thing." Whe
Trimmer mentioned that he wished to "start making som
bucks," Wilson told him, "Man, you just head for the Mid
west, anytime you're ready" (meaning: carry out the Heydt
Slocombe contract).

The next day, January 15, Trimmer led Wilson eve
deeper into incriminating telephone conversations, again o
tape. Trimmer said that DeAngelo had returned and reporte
that someone was guarding Brower. (DeAngelo, of course
had never left New York.) DeAngelo had taken photograph
of the person; he wanted Wilson to look at them to se
whether he was known to him.

"Well, you know who I told you it might be," Wilso
said. Earlier, Wilson had warned that a U.S. marshal migh
be guarding Brower.

"Yeah, that's what I'm concerned with," Trimmer said.

"Yeah. Well, that's, that's probably the fact. I don't thin
we need waste any time. That's probably the facts of life, an
that's probably what they're doing," Wilson continued.

"Well, if that's the case," Trimmer said, "and you're sur
of that, uh, you know what that means. That consists of one (
those long-range deals." (In earlier talks in the MCC, Trim
mer and Wilson had agreed that "long-range" meant a killin
with a rifle.)

"Yeah, let's do it," Wilson said.

"You don't want to, uh. . . ." Trimmer said.

"I'm desperate," Wilson insisted.

Trimmer again asked if Wilson wished to see the phot
graphs. "Ah, no, I think it would be a waste of time. Be
very big waste of time," he said. When Trimmer repeate
"He could be a fuckin' government agent," Wilson replie
"Yeah, I'm sure he is. I'm almost sure now that he is."

"And you want this guy taken care of too?"

"Well, any way we can do it. Any way," Wilson sai
"Ideally, you know, just the way we talked about it."

"All right," Trimmer said, "Uh, it's a different ball game

"I know. Whatever it takes."

"It's gonna. . . . Your bill will be increased," Trimmer
aid. "You know that."

"That's fine. No problem. No problem," Wilson said.

Wilson changed the subject to the sequence of future
its. Since "the southern deal is put off until February . . . the
ther guy overseas is a real big problem," he told Trimmer.

"You talking about 'C'?" Trimmer asked (meaning Ed
Coughlin in Geneva).

"Yeah, uh-huh," Wilson said. But he emphasized, "The
ey one is out there [Brower on the West Coast], and
vhatever it takes."

Four hours later, Wilson and Trimmer spoke by phone
gain, with the tape recorder on. Trimmer and "Tony" had
alked over the situation on the West Coast; they intended to
eturn that evening.

TRIMMER: Ahhh, if this guy turns out to be what we think
e is—an agent—

WILSON: Yah.

TRIMMER: That's gonna cost.

WILSON: Whatever.

TRIMMER: That's gonna be double.

WILSON: Okay, whatever.

Trimmer pressed Wilson to come up with more money
or expenses, saying that the original $10,000 had vanished.
Vilson pleaded for time. He would talk with his son Erik,
ut raising more money could take days. Then Trimmer also
varned that Wilson could expect a backlash from the murders.

TRIMMER: You know what's gonna happen with this, don't
ou?

WILSON: Yeah.

TRIMMER: You realize the fuckin' you're gonna be swamped
n.

WILSON: Yeah, I understand.

Vilson continued that "this first one" might "limit my, ah
ommunications, so I may have to have my son come out and
nake some calls for me. So, y'know, give me a week or so and
rust me."

If the Brower murder delayed the Houston trial, Trim-
ner and DeAngelo should go ahead with the murders of
Ieydt and Slocombe, and obtain the $3.5 million being held
y Heydt, rather than going after Coughlin. The money they

got from Heydt "would be useful to all of us," Wilson sa
(Circumstances suggest that putting his hands on Heyd
$3.5 million was Wilson's only hope of paying for the murd
contracts he had set into motion.)

On January 18, federal marshals flew Wilson to Houst
under heavy guard for the C-4 smuggling trials. Persons
the periphery of the trial—such as Alex Raffio and Jo
Heath, and Heath's lawyer, Peter Lamb—though that secu
ty was extraordinarily tight. Marshals kept the witnes
sequestered on a single floor of a hotel, and even roo
service waiters were screened carefully. When some witnes
insisted on watching the Super Bowl football game—t
Washington Redskins were playing Miami—marshals clear
patrons from a room of a downstairs lounge. Heath,
stranger to security from his days with the Secret Servi
thought, Something is going on here they aren't telling
about. The witnesses were taken to the courthouse in u
marked cars which followed roundabout routes and enter
the basement parking garage in a final burst of speed. Wils
was kept in an isolated cell in a Houston jail; he wore leg a
wrist manacles when brought to court.

What worried marshals was the possibility that Wils
might have set a second murder plot into motion, one oth
than the Trimmer-DeAngelo operation which the Feder
Government was stage-managing. They had in mind Wilso
boast to Trimmer that during an earlier appearance in Houst
when pretrial motions were argued, he had managed
contact two "Midwestern hit men" whom he paid $10,000
murder Brower. The marshals feared that this might ha
happened, and that the persons contacted might still inte
to carry out their assignment.

Nothing impeded the trial. Brower gave the most dam
ing testimony. He told of procuring the C-4 for Wilson, a
arranging its shipment to Libya disguised as "drilling mud
Slocombe told of getting the C-4 through the Houston a
port. Lawyer Edward Bloom, angry at both Wilson and h
former friend Brower, testified how he had arranged for t
transfer of money from Switzerland to the C-4 suppliers, h
drafted the sales contract, leased the cargo plane and accom
panied the C-4 from Houston to Tripoli. The surprise appea
ance of Heath stunned Wilson ("I watched the hair rise on h
neck when I entered court"). Heath told of seeing the C-4

a Libyan arms warehouse. This testimony was crucial, for it completed the chain that put the C-4 in Quaddafi's hands. The jury needed only several hours to return a guilty verdict.

After one of the Houston proceedings, Wilson was flown back to the East Coast on a Justice Department aircraft. Larry Barcella sat with Justice investigators and lawyers in the rear of the plane, relaxing and enjoying beer and sandwiches. Wilson was at the front, his handcuffs connected by a chain to shackles around his ankles.

Wilson tried to drink a cup of coffee, but because of the restraints he had to hoist his feet off the floor in order to raise his hands high enough to put the cup to his mouth. Barcella thought, You son of a bitch, if you had just played straight with me in Rome, you wouldn't be sitting there in such a situation.

As the trial progressed, what came to be known to federal investigators as the "hit-list case" also continued. The same day that Wilson was transferred to Houston (January 18), DeAngelo telephoned Erik Wilson.

"Listen, uh, we just, uh, Wayne and I just finished our work out in California," DeAngelo said.

"Mmmm uh," Erik replied.

DeAngelo continued that he and Trimmer intended to go to Europe "as soon as possible. . . . Your dad asked if we could do that other business quickly." But, DeAngelo went on to say, neither he nor Trimmer could locate Wilson, and they needed money. "We're looking to get a few more dollars before we go over there. We're a little, uh, it's getting a little tight, right now."

"What are you looking at?" Erik asked.

"Well, we'd like to get, uh, somewhere between five and ten, right now. I understand we can get, uh, who was it, Di over in Europe?"

"Yeah," Erik said.

"Who had access to the extra money?" DeAngelo asked.

"Uh, it's gonna take me a little while to figure this out," Erik said.

They finally agreed that DeAngelo would call late in the afternoon. "All right," DeAngelo said. Then, as a seeming afterthought, he added, "Oh, were you, were you aware of this work that we did out there? I mean, did your father brief you on that, uh?"

"No, he didn't," Erik replied.

When Erik and DeAngelo spoke again that day, at 6:45 P.M., Erik still had not managed to contact his father. All he could determine was that Wilson had been transferred from the MCC. Before moving any money, he must speak with either his father or his father's lawyer.

"Well, yeah," DeAngelo said, "but we're in, ah.... You know, we're in a position that he wants the business taken care of in Europe, on this, ah, I think is a Mister C [Coughlin]."

"Mmm-hmmm," Erik said in an affirmative tone.

The next morning, January 20, Erik called Herald Price Fahringer's office in New York, and learned that his father had been moved to Houston. He then called Diane Byrne in England, who told him no funds were readily available to the Wilsons in Europe. Then Erik called DeAngelo. Although he knew his father wanted to "expedite this and all," he could not arrange to transfer any funds until he had spoken with him.

A few hours later, Erik Wilson heard a knock on the door of the 22nd Street Northwest town house in Washington that he had occupied the past months. An FBI official asked that he identify himself. Then he handed Erik a subpoena directing him to appear before a grand jury in New York the next day.

Soon after his arrest, Erik talked with Bobbi Barnes, who had become both close friend and surrogate mother. Bobbi would not tell me exactly what Erik confided in her, but whatever his story, it was enough to convince her that Ed Wilson had made his own son an unwitting accomplice in a murder plot. To Bobbi Barnes, this act was "unforgivable." As she told me in the spring of 1983, some months after the grand jury indicted both Wilsons, father and son: "Here he walked off the end of the rope, as far as I am concerned. That did it. Nothing he can ever say to me could cause me to forgive him. What I had felt, what I had sensed, all along was now very clear to me. Ed Wilson cares about Ed Wilson.... To involve his very own son, a boy in his early twenties, in something such as this is so low I wouldn't even call it despicable."

Both Wilsons were indicted on February 16—Edwin on

seventeen counts, Erik on fifteen, all involving conspiracy for contract murders. Erik, penniless, remained in jail for two months, unable to raise bail money. According to Bobbi Barnes, when Erik turned to his mother, Barbara Wilson, for help, she replied, "You got yourself into this mess; you get yourself out of it." On April 14, Barnes managed to scrape together enough cash to get Erik out of jail. A month later, when we talked about the episode, tears welled in her eyes. "Ed Wilson," she said: "I hate the name, the man."

Doggerel was pinned to the inside door of Barcella's office. It was a quotation from the outlaw Dick the Butcher in Shakespeare's *Henry VI, Part II*: "The first thing we do, let's kill all the lawyers." Someone had drawn a line through Shakespeare's name at the bottom of the quotation and written in, "Edwin P. Wilson."

Later that spring, several former Wilson associates—Bobbi Barnes and John Heath, among others—discussed sending a joint letter to the Justice Department asking that the charges against Erik be dropped. A draft of the letter stated that the youth was an unwitting "victim of his own father"; that even if he had committed a criminal act, he had done so from a sense of loyalty, and not with any real intent to have anyone killed. They knew that Barcella at one time had shown sympathy for Erik. When his mother had thrown Erik off Mount Airy Farm in 1980, he had come to Tripoli briefly and worked for his father, doing general office chores. Barcella, occasionally speaking with Wilson by long-distance phone during this period, had warned Wilson, "I don't want that kid to get involved, but if he does, he's as liable as anyone else." Both Alex Raffio and John Heath had urged strongly that Erik return to the United States and enter college; he eventually did.

The thought of the former Wilson associates was that the joint letter would give the Justice Department a chance to back away from an unnecessary prosecution, and at the same time give Wilson an incentive to break his silence and provide information on conspirators who had thus far escaped justice. Barcella dissuaded them from sending the letter. "Ed's driven so far into the corner that he's not going to listen to anyone," he said. Besides, Barcella continued, he found "unconvincing" the argument that Erik had been an unwitting participant in the conspiracy.

38

"Take Her Off and Break Her Neck"

What came to be called the "hit-list indictments" had been returned by a grand jury on February 16, 1983. Two days later, at a sentencing hearing in Houston on the C-4 smuggling conviction, Judge Ross Sterling gave Wilson the maximum sentence of seventeen years in prison, to begin after he finished the fifteen-year term he had received in Alexandria in December for arms smuggling. Justice Department lawyers, citing the new indictments, asked that Judge Sterling declare Wilson a "special dangerous offender" and add eight years more to the sentence, as allowed under law. Sterling refused. But he did assess Wilson a fine of $145,000. (Wilson looked at one of his lawyers and grinned: "Fat chance they'll ever see *that!*")

A month later, Wilson broke his losing streak in the courtroom. The trial, held in Washington, involved the three Cubans he and Frank Terpil had tried to recruit for a murder mission in Egypt in 1976. Rafael Quintero and Raul Villaverde recounted in detail how Wilson and Frank Terpil had brought them to Geneva in 1976, ostensibly to talk about killing the terrorist Carlos the Jackal, but actually to murder a Libyan dissident in Cairo. But defense lawyer Patrick Wall got an admission from Quintero that he had continued his business dealings with Wilson long after the abortive plot, and in fact had lent him substantial amounts of money. Attorney Kenneth

Conklin, testifying for Wilson, told of an ambiguous account Quintero had given of the affair—in essence, that he was uncertain as to whether Wilson or Terpil had been the prime mover. The predominantly black jury acquitted Wilson. A Washington lawyer who closely monitors D.C. jury trials stated, "Black juries in Washington have a thing for cases involving Latins. They don't believe them. Had the Cubans been Caucasian, Wilson wouldn't have walked." Another factor was Quintero's testimony that he had worked with Wilson in both the CIA and naval intelligence. As one juror stated later, "This seemed like some kind of spook deal when all dudes were lying on one another. We get to the jury room, I say, 'Shit, let them folks work out their own goddamned business. They ought to go make some of them James Bond movies.'"

After the Washington trial, Wilson was transported to one of the more remote federal prisons in the Eastern United States—the Federal Correctional Institution in Otisville, in Upstate New York. Wilson's inclusion of prosecutors Larry Barcella and Carol Bruce on his assassination list touched a sensitive nerve in the Justice Department. Several years earlier, a man facing a narcotics trial in San Antonio had hired a gunman to shoot the federal judge who was to hear the case. One of Bruce and Barcella's Washington colleagues had been hit by an intended assassin's bullet outside the Federal Court House. Although prosecutors pride themselves upon professional impersonality, Wilson had put himself beyond the pale. Given his long background in intelligence, and his friendship with renowned thugs of the mercenary world, Wilson might well choose a more reliable accomplice if he tried to reactivate the murder contracts.

Wilson arrived in Otisville in mid-March 1983 under the name of "Worthington" and was placed in a solitary-confinement cell, measuring perhaps 10 by 5 feet. A standing order directed, in the words of a prison official, that "no one was to talk to Mr. Wilson, about anything." Wilson was taken from his cell, under heavy guard, for five hours weekly, for "exercise" and a shower. Food was passed through a 5-by-18-inch slot in the steel door of his cell. There was a peephole on the door, but no one other than a guard was supposed to open it.

Otisville officials had their orders: the Justice Department did not wish Ed Wilson to have the chance to concoct any further murder schemes.

But, incredibly, Wilson proceeded to do just that. The "accomplices" with whom Wilson made contact this time were a pair of career jailbirds who were such inept bunglers that prosecutors came to call them, with ill-concealed humor, "The Blues Brothers."

The major figure was David Ray Vogel, a ne'er-do-right bank robber and dope addict who had been in jail most of the time since 1970. Thirty-six years old in 1983, slovenly, overweight, unconcerned that his clothes bore an aromatic coating of spilled food, Vogel was an orderly in the disciplinary unit. He padded down the halls, a stocking cap over his unkempt greasy locks (for reasons unclear to other prisoners, he occasionally tied a filthy T-shirt atop the cap). Vogel wanted two things: first, his freedom, and until that happy day, as much ersatz dope as he could scrounge. He would knock out a tooth to get painkillers from the prison dentist (he did not seem to realize that his mouth did not contain enough teeth to support his habit indefinitely); he would save sinus pills until he had fifteen or so, which taken in a gulp would put him into euphoria. Such was the character whom Edwin Wilson chose to make his confidant when he arrived at Otisville.

The rules about not talking with Wilson did not disturb Vogel; he ignored them, and when the guards caught him, they ignored Vogel. When Wilson told him his true name, and that he had been a CIA agent, fantasy rushed through Vogel's pudgy body with the impact of a good heroin hit. ("I'd always wanted to be a CIA agent," he was to testify at Wilson's last trial, and at least one former CIA officer in the court leaned forward and covered a pained face with his hands.) Wilson talked tales of intrigue: about the Congo, Libya, the Bay of Pigs, the Kennedy assassination (concerning which, he hinted darkly, he knew untold secrets), Idi Amin of Uganda, letter bombs. The jailhouse geek and the jailed spook: one sitting on a mail crate in the corridor, leaning forward so that he could listen through the food slot; the other sitting on the commode just inside the cell door, spinning war stories into the night. Other convicts called the graying Wilson "Pops." To Vogel, he was "The Agent."

Vogel told his own stories in return, of the competing gangs that lived in vicious coexistence in the American prisons, divided on racial grounds. The white band was the Aryan Brotherhood, or "AB." Vogel never made AB membership, but he had a buddy—a cellmate—who did: John "Little John" Randolph, another Californian and inept bank robber who had been hidden in Otisville after testifying against AB members in a Western prison murder. Soon Randolph was talking with Wilson about the AB, and how members on the outside would murder for money. Randolph claimed AB membership.

Talk about the Aryan Brotherhood stirred Wilson's interest. "I wish I had known you guys sooner," he said. Wilson confessed that he had been hoodwinked by "a rat named Trimmer at the MCC," who had offered to kill witnesses, then betrayed him. Wilson leaned closer toward the slot and told Vogel, "I got something pretty serious for you. How would you and John like to make enough money to be set for the rest of your life?"

Given the context to the talk, Vogel knew what Wilson meant. "Man, I don't know—I've got a pretty big drug habit," he said.

"I want these witnesses eliminated," Wilson continued. "As you guys say around here, 'taken off the calendar.'"

"You mean murder?"

"Yeah," Wilson said. He complained that the Houston and Virginia trials had cost him $250,000 each in lawyer fees, and "no telling what it's going to cost me down in New York." (He was referring to the "hit-list trial," on the MCC indictments, then scheduled for September 1983.) Wilson allowed that he would just as soon spend the money to murder the witnesses. "The lawyers are going to get that [much] anyway and I'm going to be convicted." He briefly described the witnesses, then offered Vogel $250,000 to "take out" Jerry Brower, and "the same goes for Slocombe."

"Ed, you're talking big figures," Vogel said.

Wilson avowed he was good for the money. He mentioned Trimmer. "I'm really going to make that one worthwhile," he said. "I'll pay you a hundred and fifty thousand to murder Trimmer."

Easier planned than done, Vogel replied. By now Trimmer certainly was in the Federal Witness Protection Pro-

gram, which meant a changed identity and heavy guards.
Even finding Trimmer, not to mention getting close enough
to kill him, would be impossible.

Wilson thought over the problem. "They [the hit men]
got to take him in the courtroom," he said. "If that's what it
comes to, take him out in the courtroom."

"That's pretty heavy shit, Ed," Vogel said.

"Dave, do you have cancer?" Wilson asked.

"What the hell are you talking about?"

"I mean, if the guy who did the hit had terminal cancer,
and would live only six months or so more anyway, he could
take the job and even if he was killed doing it, his family
would be fixed for life," Wilson said.

"Ed, I really don't know any hit men with cancer, and I
think the chances of finding one are pretty damned slim,"
Vogel said.

They discussed finding a convict who would connive to
become an informant, so that he would himself be put into
the witness-protection program, and have the opportunity to
find and kill Trimmer. "Ed," Vogel said earnestly, "I don't
know any informers."

"I want that fucking rat dead," Wilson said. "He's no
good."

Killing Larry Barcella and Carol Bruce, Wilson said,
would "represent power" on his part, and make other prosecutors fearful of continuing the cases. Barcella had "caused all
my problems."

Wilson came to consider Randolph the more responsive
of the two men, and was soon going into detail about how to
do the murders. Randolph suggested using two persons as
the hit men: a man named "Bobby" who had been prominent
in the Aryan Brotherhood, and one of his own relatives, who
had just been released from a Western prison.

By this time, Randolph and Vogel were telling prison
authorities of their conversations with Wilson. After getting
sworn assurances that Wilson had initiated the talks about
murder contracts, prison officials and the FBI decided to
permit Vogel and Randolph to continue talking with him.

Because Wilson lacked ready cash, he asked Vogel and
Randolph to accept property as payment. In a semblance of
formality, he produced a photostatic copy of the net-worth
statement that had been seized during his arrest the previous

June. Wilson told the two jailbirds to "pick any two properties totaling five hundred thousand" as payment for the murders. Vogel signed with his initials. Randolph wrote the letters "AB" (for Aryan Brotherhood) and the numerals "666"—some AB mumbo jumbo; beneath them he drew a three-leafed clover, another AB symbol, and his initials "L.J.," for "Little John," his prison name. Wilson said they should not worry about money. Internal Revenue Service liens of $23 million "are going to be lifted." He expected other income from the sale of his life story; he had contacted a publisher, and a ghostwriter was to begin work soon. The Libyan Government, through a Washington attorney, was about to pay him $2.5 million of the $5 million owed him by that country.

No one, Wilson emphasized, had any reason to fear a double-cross on money. "I'm putting my life up," he said. He explained that he expected to serve his time in the federal prison in Marion, Illinois, where the Aryan Brotherhood was strong. If he did not pay, he knew he would die. He wanted a long-term relationship with Vogel and Randolph—their own version of a "Murder, International." Wilson told of seeing a "computer printout of a hit list" in Libya that showed prices of $20,000 up to $1 million for specific murders. "We're going to start a whole new organization," Wilson said.

Almost as an afterthought, Wilson suggested another murder, one that made even the tough-stomached Randolph feel fleetingly ill. Wilson's former wife, Barbara, was suing him for her share of their property, and she wanted $7 million. "I'm not going to give her seven million dollars," Wilson told Randolph. "I want her to go on a long, long trip. Can you guys put Brower aside right now?"

Wilson wanted Randolph's "outside man" to find Barbara. He had a contact in a prison in San Diego—a man who had previously been confined at the MCC in New York—who was holding some of his money; if approached by an intermediary, this man would turn over $5,000 for expenses. Wilson gave Randolph copies of the liens the IRS had filed on him, some $23 million in all. "IRS will get about ten cents on the dollar," Wilson said. "I got ten times that much. Now you see why Barbara's gotta go."

Wilson became boastful. "Barbara is scared of me. She's

seen some murders that happened in Europe."* While abroad
in the late 1970s, Wilson continued, he had raised cash by
mortgaging some of his properties to Arabs whom he did not
identify further. He told Randolph he had telephoned Barbara
and said, "If you try to sell any of these properties, they will
come over here and kill you."

Owing to the "urgency" of getting rid of Barbara, Wilson
suggested that Randolph use the president of the Aryan
Brotherhood—let us call him "D.B."—for the murder. Wilson
wrote out some notes to guide D.B. to his former wife, under
the cover heading "To Buy Property, See:"

The instructions described Mrs. Wilson: "54, 5-9, gray
hair, thin, 120." Wilson added, "She cracked up when she
was forty-eight. She shouldn't be any problem." Wilson listed
a series of possible locations where D.B. could seek out
Barbara. The first was a Wilson beach house just north of
Atlantic City, New Jersey. A pretext telephone call was
suggested to determine whether Barbara was there: "Ask to
rent a house—is Mrs. Wilson there?" Wilson told Randolph.
"First thing off the bat, call that number." He drew a sketch
map showing the location of the house. If Barbara could not
be found at the beach house, the next stop should be Mount
Airy Farm. The instructions listed the farm's exact location,
and the phone number of the woman who acted as farm
secretary. Next was the address and phone number of Mrs.
Wilson's lawyer, in central Virginia, a contact Wilson called a
"last resort." If she could not be found at the farm or the
beach house, the hit man should kidnap the lawyer, "take
him somewhere and squeeze him."

Another route to Barbara could be a Middleburg, Virginia, real estate firm that was handling sales of certain of the
Wilson properties. D.B. would "have to dress real nice and
have cards showing he represented an investment firm from
California." But Wilson cautioned that D.B. should not surrender the card. "Tell them it's his only one," Wilson said.
He joked that he had used "one single damned card" during
two years he had worked on domestic affairs for the CIA.
D.B. should focus on a property in Tysons Corner, Virginia,
and insist on seeing exact boundary markers. He should

---

*This statement smacks of Wilson fancy. Barbara Wilson would not be interviewed
for this book.

demand that the realtor "produce Barbara Wilson" so that she could give her personal assurance that the property titles and abstract were accurate. After the formal business meeting, D.B. should invite Barbara to lunch or dinner.

Then, Wilson said of his former wife, "Take her off somewhere and break her neck."

Randolph asked Wilson, in effect, "How can you justify Barbara's death to your sons?"

"That's just one of the things they're going to have to learn to face," Wilson replied. "It's to their good eventually."

A day or so later, Wilson changed his plan. If D.B. broke Barbara's neck and staged a car wreck to make the death appear accidental, her estate would be liable to "death taxes" (Randolph's words). As Wilson said, "Between that and the IRS, I wouldn't be better off. Let her disappear. Otherwise, IRS is going to come in and have a fire sale of the properties."

Wilson had a final instruction for whoever would kill Barbara: she should be stripped of all her jewelry—her necklace, her bracelets and especially her largest diamond ring. The killer could do what he wished with everything except the diamond ring. Wilson wanted this returned to him, for the diamond was a "good-luck piece."

An old story followed. Several decades earlier, Wilson told Randolph, as a merchant seaman he had helped a Chinese family escape from Singapore to Hong Kong. On later visits he had found that the family had become prosperous merchants. Out of gratitude, the husband gave Wilson two teak tables ("They were worth ten thousand dollars each") and an attractive diamond. Wilson did not care for rings on men: "They look faggy." So he had had the diamond mounted into a setting for Barbara. He had given it to her, during a happier phase of their marriage, and she had worn it proudly.

With Barbara due to "disappear" forever, Wilson saw no reason for the ring to go to waste. "It's my good-luck piece; I want it back," he told Randolph.

What would be the price for killing Barbara? "She's worth two hundred and fifty thousand," Wilson said.

The Justice Department, of course, brought new indictments against Wilson for the Otisville talks. Essentially, the new charges concerned already-covered ground—Wilson's hopes of killing two prosecutors and seven witnesses; the main addition was Barbara Wilson as an intended victim. Once again, Wilson was represented by new defense lawyers. For reasons he would not discuss, Herald Price Fahringer had resigned himself to handling the appeals on the Houston conviction, and the active defense evolved to a three-man team of Michael G. Dowd, David Lewis and William Mogulescu. Scrappers all, the new lawyers had attracted attention earlier in 1983 by winning acquittal for persons accused of smuggling guns to the Irish Republican Army. Dowd, the lead counsel, said only, "We got a phone call, and Ed Wilson was suddenly our client, six weeks before trial. Whew."

Given Wilson's propensity for writing out lists of his intended victims and their whereabouts in his own distinctive hand, and his indiscriminate use of the telephone, his lawyers fought an uphill battle when he went to trial in early October 1983 before Judge Edward Weinfeld. Dowd took the only conceivable course. He called Wilson's accusers "three despicable men" who "would do anything to get out of jail." The scenario they described was a "completely harebrained scheme." He found it incredible that Wilson, a "man of great stealth, cunning and shrewdness," would turn to a "bungling murderer like Wayne Trimmer... who concocts a scheme that couldn't be sold to a situation comedy."

For all his adult life, Wilson had "pretended to be something and somebody he was not, in the name of the United States Government and the people of the United States itself." Wilson had nothing to gain by killing witnesses, for if anyone associated with him died, under any circumstances, "the whole world comes down on him." (In a sense, Dowd was right: when the hapless Waldo Dubberstein blew off his head with a shotgun in early 1983, there was a gabble in the press about the "third mysterious Wilson death"—the other two being Rafael Villaverde and Kevin Mulcahy.)

An informer had much to gain by smearing Wilson: "He was a CIA man, which is like a cop. If you frame a cop, who cares in prison?"

Wilson's lawyers signaled their defense the week before the trial via a leaked article to John Cummings of *Newsday*, a reporter consistently cynical about the CIA.

"I consider myself a patriot," Wilson said in a statement

given Cummings by his lawyers. "I have never done anything to hurt my country, and I intend to talk freely about everything I know and have done." Wilson repeated the long-discredited story that he had tried to help the government find two Cuban exiles wanted in the killing of Chilan dissident Orlando Letelier in Washington in 1976. Wilson called himself a "sacrificial lamb" and declared his determination to testify. *Newsday* ran the Wilson story the week before the trial under a large headline: "Ex-CIA Agent 'Intends to Talk.'" One government lawyer called it "a pitch to the jury" (the jury panel included persons who lived on Long Island, *Newsday*'s circulation area). Michael Dowd laughed in response. "Barcella has been laying out crap on Wilson for four years—now *he* complains about leaks?"

For the fourth time in as many trials, government objections prevented Wilson and his lawyers from evoking any "CIA defense." And in closed-door pretrial hearings, Wilson could offer no evidence that he had worked for American intelligence after leaving Task Force 157 in 1976. Judge Weinfeld refused to permit as testimony Wilson's claims to have passed "components of a nuclear bomb" to the United States to prevent Libya from acquiring a nuclear capability. Whenever Wilson's lawyers attempted a question concerning intelligence activities, Judge Weinfeld shut them off, saying, "We're not trying the CIA." Nor did Wilson follow through on his statement that he would take the stand in his own defense and detail his career as an intelligence agent.

So all that Dowd, Lewis and Mogulescu could do on cross-examination was try to poke holes in the stories of informers Trimmer, Vogel and Randolph. They found any number of minor inconsistencies; they brought out ambiguities in the tapes that existed, and scored the government for not having recordings of the more important jail-cell conversations. They also raised questions as to whether Wilson could benefit, in any way, from the murders he was said to have planned. Marian Rosen, one of his lawyers in the Houston case, stated through stipulation that she had talked with Wilson about the "preservation" of evidence once a witness has testified and been cross-examined. If the conviction is overturned, and the witness for any reason is not available,

his or her previous testimony can be used, Ms. Rosen said
she had told Wilson. As Dowd argued, murdering the witnesses
after they had already testified made no sense.

Dowd did gain one tactical victory: He persuaded Judge
Weinfeld to strike the count of the indictment accusing
Wilson of plotting his former wife's murder. Since Mrs
Wilson was not listed as a witness in any pending trial at the
time he had supposedly planned her murder, Wilson could
not be accused of a "conspiracy to obstruct justice." The jury
was instructed to disregard what they heard of the plot
against Mrs. Wilson, and conceivably they made a good-faith
attempt to do so. But as an old courtroom adage holds, "You
can tell a skunk to get out of the jury box, but the smell
remains."

Prosecutor Eugene N. Kaplan argued persuasively that
the jury should heed the core message of ten days of
testimony: "This is a case about assassination, about hired
murder, about arrogance and greed and retaliation and
revenge, a case about obstruction of justice." The jury
received the case shortly after five o'clock on October 20;
four hours later, it convicted Wilson on all counts save that
of conspiracy.*

So now Edwin P. Wilson faced the prospect of spending
the rest of his life behind bars.

On November 8, Judge Weinfeld sentenced Wilson to
twenty-five years' imprisonment, saying that the defendant
had "utter disrespect" for law and "ruthless indifference to
human life." Attorney Michael Dowd repeated his argument
that Wilson was a "product" of many years of government
service. "Mr. Wilson lived in a nightmarish world," Dowd
said. "There has to be some recognition for his past life and
service."

"The case did not involve CIA activities here or abroad,"
Judge Weinfeld replied. The sentence was solely for the
crimes charged, and did not concern "whether the defendant
is a patriot or a traitor."

Wilson heard his sentence shortly after 10 A.M. Marshals
immediately took him to a waiting Justice Department aircraft, and he was flown midway across the continent to the

---

*The collapse of the conspiracy charge meant that Erik Wilson avoided trial. He
accepted a year of "deferred prosecution"—a federal procedure that meant his
record would be expunged after one year of good conduct.

ederal prison at Marion, Illinois, toughest and most secure of
ll penitentiaries in the United States—"the modern Alcatraz,"
enologists call it. Wilson arrived at his Marion cell in time
or the 2 P.M. head count. Because of his convictions in the
murder plots—plans conceived while he was in custody—
Wilson was told he could expect to spend many, many
months in "segregation"—penal terminology for solitary confinement. Under guidelines prevailing in late 1983, he will
not be eligible for parole until the year 2000, when he will be
3 years of age.

Bobbi Barnes came out of it all with clear title to a
200,000 brick town house several blocks from the Potomac
waterfront in Alexandria, Virginia. Well into 1983, she was
receiving many letters from Wilson. They professed his undy-
ng love; they told of his plans to get into "prison reform"
nce he was out of jail. Bobbi realized, eventually, that she
was reading Wilson's letters with academic interest only. She
had become a surrogate mother to Wilson's son Erik, indicted
long with his father in the "hit-list case." She had guaran-
eed Erik's bail so that he could get out of jail.

She had come to detest Wilson, and finally she told him
o in a letter. She would not let me read it. But she did tell
me about it.

"I blistered him. I told him that he had ruined lives, and
e thought about no one other than himself. I told him to get
ut of my life." She had not heard from Wilson since. "Good
iddance," she said.

We were having lunch one late-spring noon in a water-
ront restaurant in Alexandria. (Wilson had "ordered" her not
o talk with me.) She had lost weight and changed her
airstyle—reddish brown locks that used to be drawn back
ver her ears now hung freely, to her advantage.

Barnes, despite what she said, had not entirely slipped
he emotional bonds Wilson had put upon her. She could still
emember, with obvious pleasure, the good days when a
netime bookkeeper had entered a glamorous international
ircuit. But she could also bring herself back to the reality of
he present.

We talked about punishment. I gave Bobbi Barnes baiting
uestions. Wilson and I are a lot alike physically, I said; we
re both men used to the outdoors, and the joys that the

open air brings. Wilson spent many years in U.S. intel
gence. Isn't it inhumane to confine a man of such restle
energy, to keep him in prison for what will surely be the re
of his life?

Barnes flared. "So he's active, and a man of the outdoor
a man who loves his goddamned farm. I don't feel sorry
him. Punishment? He's getting just the sort of punishme
he deserves."

Barnes sipped at her glass of soda, her knuckles white.
hope they give him more time," Bobbi Barnes said; "mo
time to think about the people he's hurt, the people h
ruined, the people he's killed. There aren't enough years
that."

Appendix A

Where They Are Now

ROBERTA J. "BOBBI" BARNES lives in Northern Virginia with her teenaged son. She is taking college courses (in French and economics) and trying to reenter the business world.

JEROME S. BROWER remains in the explosives business in Pomona, California, although federal licenses for his companies are now held by his sons.

DIANE BYRNE lives in Wales with her two small children, and continues to operate her business-service company, Brilhurst.

THOMAS CLINES operates several international business ventures from his Washington base; acquaintances say that "the Wilson case" caused him severe financial problems, particularly in legal fees.

EDWARD J. COUGHLIN was declared *persona non grata* overnight by several Swiss banks as a result of Wilson publicity. But he managed to shift client accounts elsewhere, and he survives.

PAUL CYR pleaded guilty to the charge of accepting a gratuity. His probated sentence required community service at an alcoholic treatment center. He conquered his drinking problem. He has retired from Federal service.

ARMAND DONNAY was arrested by Belgian authorities for arms deals arising from his association with Wilson; the cases remained in court without disposition in late 1983.

PETER GOULDING is a "field engineer" for a defense-oriented company in California; with his security clearance restored, he is active in the Army reserves.

JOHN HEATH does security work in Southern California. He is working with a screenwriter on a movie about his career in bomb work.

FRANCIS HEYDT remains in the clothing-brokerage business in Oklahoma.

ERNEST KEISER is dealing in real estate in Northern Virginia, quite profitably.

RAFAEL "CHI CHI" QUINTERO lives in Mexico City, and he remains spookier than a Halloween parade.

ALEXANDER RAFFIO is in the Federal Witness Protection Program, under a new identity.

DOUGLAS SCHLACHTER, after serving a federal prison term, also went into the witness-protection program. He lives with a woman he met through Ed Wilson, and they have two children.

THEODORE SHACKLEY is in the import-export business around Washington; he is sometimes seen at old spook meetings.

REGINALD SLOCOMBE lives on a farm near the Potomac River in Northern Virginia. His job interviews often end with the question "By the way, are you the Reg Slocombe who . . . ?" He replies, "But I was never charged. . . ."

WOLFGANG STEINIGER was convicted on an explosives charge by a Dutch court in January 1984 in a case arising from Wilson's C-4. He received a six-month prison sentence.

STEVE STREETER lives in the Pacific Northwest, where he operates a "snack boat" that sells food to fishermen. His wife, Gloria, manages a small retail business.

EUGENE TAFOYA is in federal prison on an income-tax conviction; he faces extradition to Canada for trial in the Manina car bombing.

FRANK TERPIL has no listed address, although reports have put him in Lebanon and Rumania. He faces a fifty-two year prison term if returned to the United States. Marilyn Terpil left him.

BARBARA WILSON maintains such a low profile that not even the FBI could locate her to testify at her husband's October 1983 trial in New York for conspiracy to commit murder. Many persons with whom she was friendly in the past insist, "She dropped off the face of the earth." She was said to remain frightened of her former husband.

ERIK WILSON lives in a Washington town house that his father formerly used for an office; with the support of Bobbi Barnes, he has tried to put his life back on track.

EDWIN P. WILSON is an inmate at the U.S. Penitentiary, Marion, Illinois 62959. There was testimony at his New York trial that Wilson had hired a ghostwriter to do his memoirs. I asked a CIA lawyer in the courtroom what the Agency would do when he submitted a manuscript for security clearance, as the law requires of former agents. She sighed. "The law covers real operations," she said, "but it doesn't permit us to deal with outright lies."

Appendix B

Code of Conduct, Central Intelligence Agency

The Wilson-Terpil affair prompted the Central Intelligence Agency to remind its officers and employees of the "standards of conduct they are expected to meet both during and after their Agency service." The text of the CIA's "Code of Conduct," issued in 1977, reads as follows:

1. Current and former CIA personnel are expected to maintain high standards of conduct consistent with the Agency's mission. There has long been a tradition of discipline and loyalty to the Agency that has guided the conduct of Agency personnel in the performance of their official duties and in their private lives. The Agency continues to rely heavily on this discipline and loyalty, not only during the period of employment but, of equal importance, after employment.

2. Certain types of activities are specifically prohibited by law and regulation. These various prohibitions and other standards of conduct which employees are required to observe are set forth in Agency regulations. This bulletin summarizes information contained in regulations and with which employees must be familiar and are required to review annually. Additional standards of ethical conduct are imposed on Agency employees by Executive Order 11222. This order, among other things, restricts the receipt of gifts, limits the

use of insider information, bars the use of public office for
private gain, and directs employees to avoid situations which
might result in or create an "appearance of impropriety."
Given the special position of trust in which employees are
placed by virtue of their Agency service, employees are
expected to honor this trust through their own integrity and
conduct in all official actions. Because of this special position
of trust, certain obligations also are contained in each employee's contract agreement to protect from unauthorized
disclosure information that is classified, information concerning intelligence sources or methods, and other sensitive
information the disclosure of which may adversely affect CIA
or national security equities. The obligation to protect such
information from unauthorized disclosure applies during an
individual's employment or other service with the CIA and at
all times thereafter. On occasion former employees and others
may try to exploit their prior and current relationships with
Agency personnel. The conferring of any preference or privilege upon former employees as a result of past or present
relationships should be avoided, and Agency personnel
constantly must be on guard to ensure that such relationships
are not being misused. Once an employee has terminated his
or her service, that person is not entitled to be treated any
differently than other individuals conducting business with
the Agency.

3. Besides the continuing obligations contained in a
former employee's contract agreement, the Agency expects,
and indeed depends on, continued adherence by former
employees to the same high standards of conduct which
governed them during their employment. This continuing
duty is implicit in their seeking and accepting Agency employment. Certain postemployment activities are restricted
by explicit provision of law (18 U.S.C., Section 207). Beyond
these requirements provided by law and contract, former
CIA personnel also are expected to avoid any personal or
professional activity which could harm or embarrass the
Agency or the United States. In this regard, former Agency
personnel may draw upon their prior training and experience
in pursuing second careers or opportunities outside the Agency. An employee's former Agency status should not be traded
upon to obtain preferential treatment for the employee or his
or her private employer, or to otherwise create any appear-

The Death Merchant

ance of sponsorship, endorsement, or approval by the Agency of such activities or transactions. This does a disservice not only to the individual involved but also to the Agency and its present employees.

4. Former Agency personnel also should avoid entering into financial transactions in reliance upon information, contacts, or relationships developed through and available only as a result of Agency employment. The use of such "insider information" for personal profit is an abuse of the position of trust which employees occupy, which abuse adversely affects the confidence of the public in the integrity of the Agency and its mission, brings discredit to the individual involved, and may involve a possible violation of law. Former employees also should carefully consider any proposed involvement with or provision of services to a foreign government, particularly any military, intelligence, or security service of such government. In this regard, various provisions of law apply to such business transactions and should be reviewed by the individual before engaging in the proposed activity. When former personnel have questions as to whether a proposed activity may fall within the Agency's concern, the Agency is prepared to provide guidance upon request. Former employees who are rehired by the Agency are subject to the above standards of conduct and are expected to fully comply with and familiarize themselves with this Code of Conduct.

Sources and Acknowledgments

The subject matter of *The Death Merchant* makes obvious the impossibility of formal source notes. Many persons who spoke with me are still involved in covert intelligence work; others continue to worry about criminal prosecution. But some persons and sources who were helpful can be acknowledged, and thanked.

Alexander W. Raffio, who worked on and off for Edwin P. Wilson for six years in both Europe and North Africa, and who knew him for years before their formal association, was valuable for two reasons. First, Raffio's involvement gave him an insider's view into how Wilson did business. Because he was not financially beholden to Wilson for many of the years they worked together, Raffio enjoyed a certain independence of action. Further, Wilson gave him rare and candid opportunities to share his private life. Second, Raffio knew the people who had worked for Wilson—and, even more important, where to find them. At the height of the federal investigations of Wilson in the late 1970s, persons associated with him scattered to the winds, to avoid both publicity and (in many instances) prosecution. Raffio's address book brimmed with telephone numbers and addresses, and eventually I found and talked with most of the persons I sought. Because Edwin Wilson wore many faces and told many stories, this multiplicity of interviews enabled me to hear the same story from several viewpoints—and, as I found, the versions often differed. The transcripts of my formal interviews with Raffio total far more than a thousand pages.

John H. Heath was my second-most-important primary source. Heath spoke from the valuable vantage point of someone who had worked with Wilson from 1977, commencing as a relatively low-level functionary and in time becoming one of the two persons closest to him. Heath had an intimate involvement in many of Wilson's largest deals; at the end, he shared the loneliness of a Tripoli villa with Wilson when both men were in exile in Libya, unable to return to the United States. Heath is one person whom Wilson eventually stopped trying to deceive, for he knew too much to listen to lies. Heath and I spoke many times, over a six-week period, into a tape recorder; he also shared with me certain documents concerning Wilson.

Other persons who had worked for Wilson who spoke with me, to varying degrees, include Roberta J. Barnes, Reginald Slocombe, Peter Goulding and Steve Streeter. Alex Raffio, in his role as collaborator, interviewed numerous persons in Europe who cannot be named. Several other persons I interviewed in the United States must also remain nameless.

Ernest R. Keiser detailed for me, to a certain extent, his role in the deception and capture of Edwin Wilson, but I am not convinced that he is ever going to tell the full story of how the scam came about. I accept that what Keiser told me was the truth—but not the *whole* truth, by any means. Lelae von Meister of Arlington, Virginia, helped arrange the Keiser interview.

Specific details of the four prosecutions of Wilson come from court testimony and other documents: the smuggling of handguns and an M-16 rifle, in Alexandria, Virginia; the smuggling of 20 tons of C-4 explosive, in Houston, Texas; the attempt to hire assassins to kill the Libyan dissident in Cario, in Washington, D.C.; and the so-called "hit-list" case, in New York. All were tried in U.S. District Court. E. Lawrence Barcella, the assistant U.S. attorney with overall responsibility for the prosecution, gave me invaluable guidance on the congeries of incidents that came to be known as "the Wilson case." Barcella made plain the guidelines for our many informal interviews: He would talk about what was in the official court record and his own actions during certain phases of the pursuit, capture and prosecution of Wilson. However, he was scrupulous about other material, particularly classified information entrusted to him by the Central Intelligence Agency and other intelligence bodies. Countless times he broke off a line of questioning with the remark "I can't talk about that." Theodore Greenberg, the assistant U.S. attorney who handled other phases of the investigation, was also helpful—and also careful to stick to the record. I had less luck with Wilson's many defense lawyers. Herald Price Fahringer, his chief counsel for much of the post-1982 period, declined even to return phone calls. John Keats, who represented Wilson at an early stage, detailed the negotiations that almost resulted in Wilson's receiving a minimal jail term; he also represented Bobbi Barnes for a period. Michael G. Dowd and David L. Lewis were informative concerning Wilson's defense in the hit-list trial. Assistant U.S. attorney Eugene Kaplan, who prosecuted this case, provided copies of numerous court exhibits. Other lawyers who were helpful in diverse ways include John Kotelly, counsel for Alex Raffio, and Peter Lamb, who represented John Heath.

For the investigation of Eugene Tafoya in his attempted murder of a Libyan dissident, I am indebted to Sergeant Ray Martinez of the Fort Collins, Colorado, Police Department, and to that department's late chief, Ralph Smith, who died in early 1984. Martinez made available to me the thousands of pages of files he accumulated during his probe of what seemed at first to be a local shooting, then turned into an international murder scheme.

To my regret, two law-enforcement agencies refused to permit interviews of their personnel who had worked on the Wilson case: the Federal Bureau of Investigation, and the Bureau of Alcohol, Tobacco and Firearms. For that reason, some good officers who worked hard to bring Wilson to justice are denied proper recognition.

The Central Intelligence Agency also declined any formal cooperation. Fortunately, I have been around the intelligence community long enough that I eventually found the people I needed, including some who had worked with Wilson, and some who helped bring him down. I am satisfied that what I was told is true, and that Edwin Wilson's connection with American intelligence post-1976 is just as depicted in this book—which is to say, nonexistent. One person who did speak for the record about Wilson, and at length, was my fellow Texan Admiral Bobby Ray Inman, who served as deputy director of Central Intelligence (the agency's number two position) when he retired from government in 1982.

Inman had first encountered Wilson when both worked for naval intelligence. Other than Inman, my guides and the persons to whom they pointed me cannot be identified.

Newspaper reporters from whose ongoing coverage I benefited from time to time include Philip Smith of *The Washington Post* and Philip Taubman and Jeff Gerth of *The New York Times*. Some details of Frank Terpil's early career are from *Frank Terpil: Confessions of a Dangerous Man*, telecast January 11, 1982, by the Public Broadcasting System and copyright by the WGBH Educational Foundation of Boston. Background on Kevin Mulcahy's exploitation of the media (and vice versa) came in part from "Life and Death of a Supersource" by Dale Van Atta, *The Washingtonian* magazine, March 1983. The evolution of the Libyan Revolution and the rise and turbulent times of Colonel Muamar Quaddafi are perhaps best recounted in *Libyan Sandstorm* by John Cooley, published by Holt, Rinehart & Winston. Quaddafi's revolutionary philosophy is stated in his *Green Book*, published in English by Martin Brian & O'Keeffe of London (two volumes, unintelligible, but mercifully slim).

Special thanks must be paid to James Polk of NBC News, an old friend who was kind enough to introduce me to Alex Raffio and start the chain of events which produced this book. Both Jim and his wife, Cara Saylor Polk, gave continuing support, a large part of which involved the care and keeping of Alex Raffio. Good research assistance came from Vicky Leonhart of Washington, D.C.; Murray Waas of Huntingdon Valley, Pennsylvania; Gordon H. Montgomery of San Antonio, Texas, and Charles Covert of Portland, Oregon. For typing I am once again indebted to two of the surest and fastest typewriters in the East, Christine Herdell of Stony Man, Virginia, and Lucille Cohen of Washington. My appreciation also to Karen, Patti and Smitty of Spee-Dee-Que Duplication, of Washington.

One person *not* interviewed for this book was Edwin P. Wilson. I tried. I sent him many messages via his lawyers and other conduits. He refused any contact with me. Further, he forbade his son Erik and his longtime friend and associate Bobbi Barnes to talk with me. (Barnes by this time did not take any orders from Ed Wilson; her input into this book was considerable.) In the end I concluded that I missed little by not talking with Wilson—or more accurately, by not *listening* to Wilson. Wilson's story is what he *did*, not what he claimed. I have learned nothing to convince me that Wilson ever intends to say—or to accept—the truth about himself.

JOSEPH C. GOULDEN
Washington, D.C.
February 1984

Index

423

ABOUT THE AUTHORS

JOSEPH C. GOULDEN has published 14 books of nonfiction. They include *The Superlawyers*, on Washington attorneys, a national best seller; *The Best Years*, on America between 1945 and 1950, a main selection of the Book-of-the-Month Club; and *Korea: The Untold Story of the War*. A native of Marshall, Texas, Mr. Goulden lives in Washington with his wife, Leslie C. Smith. He has two sons, Trey and Jim Craig Goulden.

ALEXANDER W. RAFFIO, an electronics expert with business connections throughout Europe and the Middle East, cooperated closely with Mr. Goulden to provide leads and extensive information out of his own association with Edwin Wilson and the Wilson Organization. Having cooperated fully with U.S. law-enforcement agencies, Mr. Raffio is now in the Federal Witness Protection Program under a new identity.

QUANTITY PURCHASES

"The most authoritative book on the Battle of the Bulge is now available. . . . MacDonald writes as only a person with firsthand experience could tell the story. And few with combat experience have the writing ability of MacDonald."

—The Checkerboard
Official Publication, 99th Infantry

A TIME FOR TRUMPETS:
The Untold Story of the Battle of the Bulge
by Charles B. MacDonald

Adolf Hitler set in motion the greatest German attack in the West since the campaign that had defeated the Netherlands, Belgium, Luxembourg and France. Involving more than a million men, he precipitated an unparalleled crisis for the Allied armies. Despite one of the most shocking failures in the history of American battlefield intelligence, the Bulge became the greatest battle ever fought by the United States Army.

"A master historian, marvelous storyteller and participant, Charles B. MacDonald has written a story of an epic battle from the unusual perspective of the soldiers who fought it."

—General William E. De Puy
U. S. Army, Retired

A TIME FOR TRUMPETS

On Sale December 1985

TEN YEARS LATER, THEIR LEGACY LIVES ON

This is the story of that special breed of warrior, the
fighter pilot; the story of the valiant men who flew
the F-105 "Thud" Bomber over the heart of North
Vietnam.

THUD RIDGE

By Colonel Jack Broughton
With an Introduction by Hanson W. Baldwin
Special Illustrated Edition

From the briefing rooms to the bombing runs, this is
the incredible true story of wing commander Colonel
Jack Broughton who recounts with terrifying detail
and accuracy the high-speed, low-level fights over
the war-torn landscape of North Vietnam. THUD
RIDGE is a graphic memorial to the courage of these
valiant men who braved the barrage of SAM missiles
and the heat-seeking rockets of the enemy MIG's.
They fought, flew and died in the blazing war for
the sky.

Available October 10, wherever Bantam Books are
sold.

We Deliver!
And So Do These Bestsellers.

The Fighting Elite ™

AMERICA'S GREAT MILITARY UNITS

by Ian Padden

Here is the magnificent new series that brings you into the world of America's most courageous and spectacular combat forces—the Fighting Elite. Each book is an exciting account of a particular military unit—its origins and training programs, its weaponry and deployment—and lets you re-live its most famous battles in tales of war and valor that will live forever. All the books include a special 8-page photo insert.

- ☐ *U.S. AIR COMMANDO* (25059 • $2.95)
- ☐ *U.S. RANGERS* (24703 • $2.95)
- ☐ *U.S. MARINES* (24702 • $2.95)
- ☐ *U.S. NAVY SEALS* (24954 • $2.95)

Don't miss any of these exciting histories, available wherever Bantam Books are sold, or use this handy coupon for ordering: